The Mammoth Book of

INSULTS

Also available

The Mammoth Book of 20th Century Science Fiction
The Mammoth Book of 20th Century Science Fiction
The Mammoth Book of Best New Erotica
The Mammoth Book of Best New Horror
The Mammoth Book of Best New Manga
The Mammoth Book of Best New SF
The Mammoth Book of Celtic Myths and Legends
The Mammoth Book of Chess
The Mammoth Book of Comic Fantasy
The Mammoth Book of Comic Quotes
The Mammoth Book of CSI
The Mammoth Book of the Deep
The Mammoth Book of Dirty, Sick X-Rated & Politically Incorrect Jokes
The Mammoth Book of the Edge
The Mammoth Book of Egyptian Whodunnits
The Mammoth Book of Erotic Photography
The Mammoth Book of Erotic Women
The Mammoth Book of Extreme SF
The Mammoth Book of Famous Trials
The Mammoth Book of Great Detective Stories
The Mammoth Book of Great Inventions
The Mammoth Book of Haunted House Stories
The Mammoth Book of Historical Whodunnits
The Mammoth Book of Illustrated True Crime
The Mammoth Book of International Erotica
The Mammoth Book of IQ Puzzles
The Mammoth Book of Jokes
The Mammoth Book of King Arthur
The Mammoth Book of Lesbian Erotica
The Mammoth Book of Modern Ghost Stories
The Mammoth Book of Mountain Disasters
The Mammoth Book of New Terror
The Mammoth Book of New Jules Verne Adventures
The Mammoth Book of On the Road
The Mammoth Book of Perfect Crimes and Impossible Mysteries
The Mammoth Book of Pirates
The Mammoth Book of Polar Journeys
The Mammoth Book of Roaring Twenties Whodunnits
The Mammoth Book of Roman Whodunnits
The Mammoth Book of Secret Code Puzzles
The Mammoth Book of Seriously Comic Fantasy
The Mammoth Book of Sex, Drugs & Rock 'n' Roll
The Mammoth Book of Sorcerers' Tales
The Mammoth Book of Sudoku
The Mammoth Book of Space Exploration and Disasters
The Mammoth Book of SAS & Special Forces
The Mammoth Book of Short Erotic Novels
The Mammoth Book of Special Ops
The Mammoth Book of Sudoku
The Mammoth Book of Travel in Dangerous Places
The Mammoth Book of True Crime
The Mammoth Book of True War Stories
The Mammoth Book of Unsolved Crimes
The Mammoth Book of Vampires
The Mammoth Book of Vintage Whodunnits
The Mammoth Book of Wild Journeys
The Mammoth Book of Women Who Kill
The Mammoth Book of the World's Funniest Car
The Mammoth Book of the World's Greatest Che

The Mammoth Book of

INSULTS

Edited by
GEOFF TIBBALLS

ROBINSON
London

Constable & Robinson Ltd
3 The Lanchesters
162 Fulham Palace Road
London W6 9ER
www.constablerobinson.com

First published in the UK by Robinson,
an imprint of Constable & Robinson Ltd, 2007

A copy of the British Library Cataloguing in
Publication Data is available from the British Library.

ISBN 978 1 84529 633 9

Printed and bound in the EU

3 5 7 9 10 8 6 4 2

CONTENTS

INSULTS ABOUT THE FAMOUS

CONTENTS

INTRODUCTION

There are few things more irritating or frustrating in life than being stuck for a witty, barbed response after someone has insulted you. It's not enough just to swear back in a Neanderthal manner – you're really looking for an intelligent comment that will cut your adversary to the quick, preferably causing long-term psychological damage. Usually you can think of the perfect riposte three hours later but now, thanks to this book, you can absorb thousands of insults for use anytime, anywhere . . . although it might be advisable to go easy on them for the father of the bride speech. Rather like a good belch, you should never underestimate the satisfaction derived from delivering a clever insult. As Alice Roosevelt Longworth said, 'If you haven't got anything nice to say about anyone, come and sit by me.'

This, the biggest, most comprehensive collection of put-downs ever published, contains words of vitriol ancient and modern, from such seasoned practitioners as Dorothy Parker, Winston Churchill, George Bernard Shaw, Edmund Blackadder, Clive James, John Simon, and P. J. O'Rourke. These people really know how to wound. Nobody is safe from their barbs. Vacuous celebrities, dissembling politicians, ham actors, overrated artists, under-achieving sportsmen, pompous royals, dreary authors and tuneless musicians all come under fire. In addition to these named targets, the book features hundreds of random insults aimed at nobody in particular, relating to appearance, age, intelligence (or lack of it), promiscuity and personality. If subtlety is not your forte, these are supported by a wide array of the tasteless but popular Yo Mama snaps. For anyone not familiar with the genre, they are not exactly the sort of remarks you find in the standard Mother's Day card. And with quick-fire comebacks, street talk, a selection of foreign swear words, curses, gender bashing, and national insults, the result is a venomous volume of pithy put-downs guaranteed to make even Anne Robinson blush.

As always, thanks are due to Nick Robinson (no relation to Anne) and Pete Duncan at Robinson Publishing for their continued support and expertise, and to my wife Carol for not heading for the divorce courts when I tried out some of the material on her.

Geoff Tibballs
April 2007

INSULTS ABOUT THE FAMOUS

ARCHITECTURE

In my experience, if you have to keep the lavatory door shut by extending your left leg, it's modern architecture. – Nancy Banks-Smith

Architect: one who drafts a plan of your house, and plans a draft of your money. – Ambrose Bierce, *The Devil's Dictionary*

(New York's) Solomon R. Guggenheim Museum is a war between architecture and painting in which both come out badly maimed. – John Canaday

(of Eurodisney, Paris) A horror of cardboard, plastic and appalling colours. – Jean Cau

A monstrous carbuncle on the face of a much-loved and elegant friend. – Prince Charles, on a proposed new wing at London's National Gallery

You have to give this much to the Luftwaffe – when it knocked down our buildings it did not replace them with anything more offensive than rubble. We did that. – Prince Charles

All architecture is great architecture – after sunset. – G. K. Chesterton

(of Paris Opera House) A stranger would take it for a railway station and, once inside, would mistake it for a Turkish bath. – Claude Debussy

The architectural style of Dublin's O'Connell Street is neon-classical. – Terry Eagleton

The architectural profession gave the public fifty years of modern architecture and the public's response has been ten years of the greatest wave of historical preservation in the history of man. – George E. Hartman

Large buildings in London and elsewhere today are too often designed in the lift going down to lunch. – William Holford

(of the John F. Kennedy Centre for the Performing Arts at Washington, DC) The building is a national tragedy – a cross between a concrete candy box and a marble sarcophagus in which the art of architecture lies buried. – Ada Louise Huxtable

(of Sydney Opera House) It looks like a typewriter full of oyster shells; like a broken Pyrex casserole dish in a brown cardboard box. – Clive James

Architecture is the art of how to waste space. – Philip Johnson

I think all modern architects should be pulled down and redeveloped as car parks. – Spike Milligan

(of Manhattan's municipal asphalt plant) The most hideous waterfront structure ever inflicted on a city by a combination of architectural conceit and official bad taste; the Cathedral of Asphalt. – Robert Moses

(of the Empire State Plaza, New York) Half a cantaloupe sliced on the bias, a croquet wicket with avoirdupois, an upside-down orange half from a Kraft salad, and four little towers and a high tower resembling forms of cubistic coition. – *Progressive Architecture*

ART

(to the diminutive Reginald Birch) If you were half a man . . . and you are. – Franklin P. Adams

(of Tracey Emin) Junk masquerading as art. – Anon

Walt Whitman is as unacquainted with art as a hog with mathematics. – Anon

Paul Klee's pictures seem to resemble, not pictures, but a sample book of patterns of linoleum. – Cyril Asquith

The only major influence on (Francis) Bacon has been his own surname. – Julian Barnes

Of course we all know that (William) Morris was a wonderful all-round man, but the act of walking round him has always tired me. – Max Beerbohm

Brian Sewell is a fool. For some years he seemed to have it in for me and (David) Hockney and (Ronald) Kitaj. Even if he wasn't writing about us, he'd always find a way of bringing us in. He'd say, "so and so was a bad artist but not as bad as Hockney, Kitaj or Blake". – Peter Blake

To my eye (Peter Paul) Rubens's colouring is most contemptible. His shadows are of a filthy brown, somewhat the colour of excrement. – William Blake

J. W. M. Turner himself would have no hope of winning the Turner Prize nowadays, unless, of course, he consented to turn his paintings into "installations", generating storms at sea with hair dryers and paddling pools, and fiery sunsets with a couple of one hundred and fifty-watt light bulbs, a bit of corrugated iron and some brightly coloured tissue paper. – Craig Brown (of Paul Gauguin) Many of his figures are distorted, and all of them have a smutty look, as if they had been rubbed with lampblack or coal dust. When the Parisian becomes a degnerate, he is the worst degenerate of all, a refined, perfumed degenerate. − John Burroughs

Most of those who call themselves artists are in reality picture dealers, only they make the pictures themselves. − Samuel Butler

(of Paul Gauguin) I'd like to wring the fellow's neck. − Paul Cézanne

(on the portrait of him by Graham Sutherland) It makes me look as if I were straining a stool. − Winston Churchill

(Edgar) Degas is nothing but a peeping Tom, behind the *coulisses*, and among the dressing-rooms of the ballet dancers, noting only travesties of fallen debased womanhood. − *The Churchman*

A single picture by (Hans) Memling is delightful, but a collection of several monotonous. − Martin Conway

The real meaning of this Cubist movement is nothing else than the total destruction of the art of painting. − Kenyon Cox

(of Damien Hirst) For 1,000 years art has been one of our great civilizing forces. Today, pickled sheep and soiled beds threaten to make barbarians of us all. − *Daily Mail*

(of Paul Cézanne) A catastrophe of awkwardness − a painter of decrepit structures of the past − Salvador Dali

(of Claude Monet) A skilful but short-lived decorator. − Edgar Degas

Dada's art is just turpentine intoxication. − Marcel Duchamp

What I can't bear (with a painting) is the word "untitled". Give me a title. I don't want to guess what it is, I want to know what the artist thought it was all about. − Jenny Eclair

To my mind the old masters are not art; their value is in their scarcity. − Thomas Edison

(of John Opie) The fellow can paint nothing but thieves and murderers, and when he paints thieves and murderers he looks in the glass. − Henry Fuesli (of art critics) These gentlemen flutter about the world like bats which flap their wings in the twilight and whose dark mass appears to you in every direction; animals disquieted by their fate, their too heavy bodies preventing them from rising. Throw them a handkerchief full of sand and they will stupidly make a rush at it. – Paul Gauguin

A critic is someone who meddles with something that is none of his own business. – Paul Gauguin

Sister Wendy is to art what Saint Teresa was to sex education. – A. A. Gill

His work is what you'd expect – dull, mechanical, lifeless – making the sculpture look as though (Jacob) Epstein had gnawed it with his teeth. – Eric Gill

If landscape can be satisfactorily painted without either drawing or colour, (Charles) Daubigny is the man to do it. – P. G. Hamerton

(of a painting by Benjamin Haydon) Why did you paint it so large? A small canvas might have concealed your faults. – William Hazlitt

(of Charles Saatchi) He only recognizes art with his wallet. – Damien Hirst

Anyone who sees and paints a sky green and pastures blue ought to be sterilized. – Adolf Hitler, on modern art

(of Antonio Corregio) The properties of his figures are sometimes such as might be corrected by a common sign-painter. – William Hogarth

(of modern art) Cold, mechanical, conceptual bullshit. – Kim Howells

(of Jeff Koon) The last bit of methane left in the intestine of the dead cow that is post-modernism. – Robert Hughes

One reassuring thing about modern art is that things can't be as bad as they're painted. – M. Walthall Jackson

(Pablo) Picasso kept finding new ways of avoiding maturity. – Clive James, *Flying Visits*

The goitrous, torpid and squinting husks provided by (Henri) Matisse in his sculpture are worthless except as tactful decorations for a mental home. – Percy Wyndham Lewis

The biggest disadvantage of a modern art party is having to look at the art. – Laurence Llewelyn-Bowen

Who among us has not gazed thoughtfully and patiently at a painting of Jackson Pollock and thought, "What a piece of crap?" – Rob Long

Conceptual art is . . . pretentious, self-indulgent, craftless tat. – Ivan Massow

(to plummy-voiced English art critic Brian Sewell) You make the Queen sound rough. – Paul Merton

(of Henry Moore's sculptures in Hyde Park, London) They look as if something's fallen off a Jumbo Jet. – Laura Milligan

To me, the "Mona Lisa" looks like she's chewing a toffee. – Justin Moorhouse

Many painters and writers have made beautiful works out of repulsive objects; Picasso enjoys making repulsive works out of beautiful objects. – Raymond Mortimer

If I met Picasso in the street I would kick him in the pants. – Alfred Munnings

French painters know as little of nature as a hackney-coach horse knows of pasture. – James Northcote

Why is it that modern art should make you feel so clumsy for not understanding it? It's a curious feeling of inadequacy to stand and look at a roomful of carefully hung, expensively lit objects, which someone considers paying nearly a thousand pounds for, and to find them as meaningful as a tin of anchovies. – Michael Palin, *Diaries 1969–1979*

They ought to put out the eyes of painters as they do goldfinches in order that they can sing better. – Pablo Picasso

English painting is entirely derivative: it is what study and imitation of the French have made it. – G. J. Renier

(of Vincent van Gogh) The visualized ravings of an adult maniac. If this is art it must be ostracized, as the poets were banished from Plato's republic. – Robert Ross

(Edouard) Manet must be the greatest and most uncritical ass who ever lived. – Dante Gabriel Rossetti

(of James Whistler's "The Falling Rocket") I have seen and heard much of Cockney impudence before now; but never expected to hear a coxcomb ask two hundred guineas for flinging a pot of paint in the public's face. – John Ruskin

The Turner Prize suffered an almost mortal damage when it was awarded to Martin Creed for automatically switching the Tate Gallery's lights off and on for intervals of five seconds and calling this a work of art. – Brian Sewell

(of Tracey Emin) Ignorant, inarticulate, talentless, loutish. – Brian Sewell

(of Damien Hirst's pickled sheep) It is no more interesting than a stuffed pike over a pub door. Indeed there may well be more art in a stuffed pike than a dead sheep. – Brian Sewell

(of Anthony Williams' portrait of Queen Elizabeth II for her seventieth birthday) She deserves better than to be perpetuated as an old age pensioner about to lose her bungalow. – Brian Sewell

Cézanne was fated, as his passion was immense, to be immensely neglected, immensely misunderstood, and now I think, immensely overrated. – Walter Sickert

I have always disliked van Gogh's execution most cordially. I execrate his treatment of the instrument I love, those strips of metallic paint that catch the light like so many dyed straws; and when those strips make convolutions that follow the form of ploughed furrows in a field my teeth are set on edge. – Walter Sickert

Mr (Percy Wyndham) Lewis's pictures appeared to have been painted by a mailed fist in a cotton glove. – Edith Sitwell

The nastiest smear of paint I had ever seen. – Leo Stein, on a painting by Henri Matisse

Art needs (John) Ruskin like a moving train needs one of the passengers to shove it. – Tom Stoppard

Skill without imagination is craftsmanship and gives us many useful objects such as wickerwork picnic baskets. Imagination without skill gives us modern art. – Tom Stoppard

(of J. M. W. Turner's painting "The Slave Ship") It resembles a tortoiseshell cat having a fit in a platter of tomatoes. – Mark Twain

(of a Jacob Epstein sculpture) It only looks to me like a child's first attempt with plasticine, the sort of unfortunate child who later gets looked at by a doctor and sent home. – *Universe*

If Botticelli were alive today, he'd be working for *Vogue*. – Peter Ustinov

(of Andy Warhol) The only genius with an IQ of sixty. – Gore Vidal

(Dante Gabriel) Rossetti is not a painter. Rossetti is a ladies' maid. – James Whistler

There are moments when art attains almost to the dignity of manual labour. – Oscar Wilde

(of Aubrey Beardsley) A monstrous orchid. – Oscar Wilde

With our James (Whistler) vulgarity begins at home, and should be allowed to stay there. – Oscar Wilde

(of James Whistler) The only thoroughly original ideas I have ever heard him express have had reference to his own superiority as a painter over painters greater than himself. – Oscar Wilde

(of James Whistler) For that he is indeed one of the very greatest masters of painting, is my opinion. And I may add that in this opinion Mr Whistler himself entirely concurs. – Oscar Wilde

Mr Whistler always spells art, and we believe still spells it, with a capital "I". – Oscar Wilde

Last night, Mr Whistler made his first public appearance as a lecturer on art, and spoke for more than an hour with really marvellous eloquence on the absolute uselessness of all lectures of the kind. – Oscar Wilde

Just explain to Monsieur Renoir that the torso of a woman is not a mass of decomposing flesh, its green and violet spots indicating the state of complete putrefaction of a corpse. – Albert Wolff

Dorothy Todd is like a slug with a bleeding gash for a mouth. – Virginia Woolf

To convince Cézanne of anything is like teaching the towers of Nôtre Dame to dance. – Emile Zola

CELEBRITY

Paris Hilton's feet are size eleven – almost as large as her mouth. – Cindy Adams

The reason why Jamie Oliver is so alive in people's consciousness is the same reason why Geri Halliwell is alive in people's consciousness, why Ronan Keating is alive in people's consciousness, why Lulu can make a comeback. They're all vacuous two-dimensional nonentities. We get the government we deserve and the celebrities we deserve. – Keith Allen

I don't hate Victoria Beckham, I just think she gives a bad image to young children. No one should be that skinny. I don't care how much she says that's her natural weight. That's just bullshit. – Lily Allen

Peaches Geldof did this documentary about Islam and it was really awful. I watched her on *Richard and Judy*. She was like, "You know, I just really think that, like, kids in this country just, like, don't know enough about Islam." What do you know about Islam, you useless oaf? – Lily Allen

Loyd Grossman suffers from irritable vowel syndrome. – Anon

When David Gest dies, he could donate his body to the local Tupperware factory – after all, that's probably where the raw material came from in the first place. – Anon

The difference between Jade Goody and a cattle grid is you slow down for a cattle grid. – Anon

Anne Robinson called us (Baddiel and Skinner) fat. I think she's entitled to her gaunt, ugly, menopausal opinion. – David Baddiel

(of Anna Nicole Smith) America's worst nightmare: white trash with money. – Roseanne Barr

Paris Hilton is jealous of anyone her age who is more successful. – Mischa Barton

(on the wedding of Donald Trump to Martha Marples) There wasn't a wet eye in the place. – Julie Baumgold

(to Jordan) Who let the dogs out? Woof, woof. – Victoria Beckham

Arianna Stassinopoulos is so boring you fall asleep halfway through her name. – Alan Bennett (of model Erin O'Connor) Walking in clothes represents the limit of her proficiency. – David Bennum

Richard Gere and Cindy Crawford – he's elastic and she's plastic. – Sandra Bernhard

(of Paris Hilton) This is one Hilton that should be closed for renovation. – Mr Blackwell

Anna Nicole Smith looks like a rag doll trapped in a wind machine. – Mr Blackwell

Paris Hilton is just famous for being infamous. – Jon Bon Jovi

It look as though the plastic surgery has left (David) Gest closely resembling the halfway point in a horror movie transformation sequence . . . If he didn't wear sunglasses all the time it'd be hard to know whether his face was on the right way up. – Charlie Brooker, *The Guardian*

(of Gillian McKeith singing on TV's *X Factor: Battle of the Stars*) I won't get over that in a hurry: my least favourite atrophied Hazel McWitch lookalike in the world singing "I just want to make love to you", right there on primetime telly. She has to be the only person on Earth who can take a lyric like that and make it seem like a blood-curdling threat without changing any of the words. – Charlie Brooker, *The Guardian*

(of Jerry Hall) She has snaggle teeth, size nine feet, and the face of a Grand National winner. – Tina Brown

(of David Beckham and Princess Diana) They have a cookery "O" Level between them yet their antics have dominated the media for twenty years and counting. They were made for each other, but sudden death prevented them from ever getting it together. – Will Buckley

Z-list personalities such as Vanessa Feltz come out with astoundingly self-pitying statements about how fame has ruined their lives, as if she hadn't pursued it with all the dignity and restraint of a rat up a drainpipe. – Julie Burchill

Posh has said to David Beckham that if she doesn't become a star in America in six months, she's going to try for another baby. I think they may as well start thinking of names. – Greg Burns

Liam Gallagher's going around the clubs saying he's going to rearrange David Gest's face. I think somebody's already done that. – Greg Burns

Was Jade Goody guilty of racial prejudice? No. She's responsible for facial prejudice – I can't stand looking at her. – Garry Bushell

(of Victoria Beckham) I'm never going to be as skinny as Posh. And I hope people don't think I sing like her either. That would be a bit worrying. – Charlotte Church

(of Rebecca Loos) I hate the woman. She needs to get a job, put her tits away because they're horrible and get a nose job. – Charlotte Church

David Blaine isn't glamorous, he's scruffy. He can't be bothered to get dressed up. He's wearing what a bum on the street would wear. I don't think he puts anything into magic at all – I think he was a street performer who did half a dozen tricks very well. – Paul Daniels

Pope John Paul II has the posture of a jumbo shrimp. – Nick DiPaolo

Nicole Richie is not a model, she is a wannabe. She has starved herself and clearly has a problem. – Petra Ecclestone

You can cheat your way through with *Vogue* if you have absolutely no feeling for style. You simply buy the outfits you see there. It works pretty well, as you can see with Victoria Beckham. – Tamara Ecclestone

(of Coleen McLoughlin) It doesn't matter how gym-toned the girl might be, there is still something about her that looks like she was designed to bring in the washing. – Jenny Eclair

I don't want to catch anything. That thing has been passed around more often than Paris Hilton. – Theo Epstein, baseball general manager, refusing to handle the World Series trophy.

I don't know what Anne Robinson spends on injecting her face with deadly poison, but it's not enough. – Bruce Forsyth on Anne Robinson's surgical makeover, *Have I Got News For You*

The only way Hugh Hefner can get stiff now is through rigor mortis. – Gilbert Gottfried

(of Jerry Hall) Try interviewing her sometime. It's like talking to a window. – Bryant Gumbel

Her husband says that Jackie Onassis suffers from chronic affluenza. – Joyce Haber

Why did God create the Paris Hilton sex videotape? – So retarded people would have something to masturbate to. – Neil Hamburger

(of Tara Palmer-Tomkinson) She was born with quite a lot going for her and she's screwed up quite a lot along the way and I think people find that irritating. She's a bit of a flibbertigibbet. – Christine Hamilton

I feel for Victoria (Beckham). She's always in the Press and wears child sizes even though she's a grown woman. It's sick. Have some food. – Sarah Harding

We're all basing this on what Stephen Hawking said, and the fact is, he's subject to interference from minicabs. – Jeremy Hardy

(of David Gest) He's got the kind of face that looks like he's sat next to a fire for too long. – *heat* magazine

We don't airbrush to that extent. – Hugh Hefner, dismissing Kelly Osbourne's hopes of becoming a *Playboy* pin-up

Victoria Beckham looks like a Pepperoni with two big boobies stuck on it. She's even the same colour. – Ian Hyland

Dear Heather Mills McCartney. My, what a terrible mess. You must be kicking yourself! – *I'm Sorry, I Haven't a Clue*

Mocking Hugh Hefner is easy to do, and in my mind should be made easier. – Clive James

Alan Sugar's usual expression is of someone who's just had a brick thrown through his front window . . . Seeing him smile was like finding the Mona Lisa had a toothy grin. – Ian Johns

(of Nancy Dell'Olio) She is deluded with a capital D. She's off her trolley. She's like a pantomime horse. – Ulrika Jonsson

(of Elizabeth Hurley) They can have all the money in the world but they've got no class. – Jordan

(of Jodie Marsh) She'll never be as big as me – look at her nose and her boobs, she's ugly. – Jordan

Richard Gere and Cindy Crawford – his body's by Nautilus and her mind's by Mattel. – Sam Kinison

Jordan said Gareth Gates was very inexperienced and didn't know where to put his hands. If anyone is in that position again: round her throat and squeeze till her eyes pop. – Mark Lamarr, *Never Mind The Buzzcocks*

(to U.S. celebrity chef Mario Batali) You look like Kiefer Sutherland after he was stung by bees. – Artie Lange

Paris Hilton has filed a lawsuit demanding the closure of a website where visitors can pay money to view naked photos of her. Which is pretty amazing . . . that there are still people out there who haven't seen Paris Hilton naked. – Jay Leno

This Paula Jones woman is unbelievable. She says yes to posing nude in *Playboy*. She says yes to boxing Tonya Harding. The only thing too sleazy for her is President Clinton. – Jay Leno

Apparently action star Vin Diesel has a crush on Anna Nicole Smith, which makes sense. A guy named Diesel attracted to a woman as big as a truck. – Jay Leno

(Fidel) Castro took over in 1959. He's the longest-reigning dictator in power currently, if you don't count Martha Stewart. – Jay Leno

Martha Stewart published her recipe for disaster – mix one part arrogance with two parts incompetence, simmer in the juices and then serve hot in the can. – Jay Leno

It's so cold in New York City today, Donald Trump's hair went into hibernation. – Jay Leno

As you know, Tom Cruise and Katie Holmes had a baby girl. It weighs seven pounds seven ounces and is twenty inches long . . . wait, that's Tom. – David Letterman

(of Victoria Beckham) A determined young woman who has never let lack of talent stand in the way of her career. – Victor Lewis-Smith

(of Jade Goody) A woman devoid of talent, education, intelligence or achievements, whose sole claim to fame was that you could shine a torch into one ear and see the beam emerge from the other side undimmed. – Victor Lewis-Smith

I reckon it's only a matter of time before Jamie Oliver's transatlantic capers nosedive, especially if the fat bastard takes up my invitation to compete in the javelin event at the 2012 Olympics (not as a thrower but as a catcher). – Victor Lewis-Smith

(of Piers Morgan) As talentless and unattractive as Jade Goody. – Rod Liddle

He was once hired by the BBC to make Anne Robinson look funny but her plastic surgeon beat him to it. – Trevor McDonald, *Have I Got News For You*

(to Debbie McGee) What first attracted you to the millionaire Paul Daniels? – Mrs Merton

Bill Gates is just a white Persian cat and a monocle away from being a villain in a Bond movie. – Dennis Miller

Why are O.J. Simpson and Heidi Fleiss bad golfers? Because he's a slicer and she's a hooker. – Robert Mitchum

The news is that Victoria Beckham has the second most desired body shape for our country's women. I am quite prepared to believe women want her husband's body, but hers? Really? There isn't enough to go round. – Suzanne Moore

Feeling too exhausted for work, like Lindsay Lohan? You may need rehab. A little anti-Semitic outburst like Mel Gibson? Get thee to rehab immediately. A member of the Osbourne family? Well, you might as well check in at birth. – Suzanne Moore

(of Naomi Campbell) She just appeared to be the pure personification of celebrity evil: a hard-faced, arrogant creature who seemed to revel in treating everyone she dated, met or worked with, like dirt. The tales of her appalling behaviour were endless. She was always late, always unrepentant, always scowling, always blaming the media for her own self-induced problems. – Piers Morgan

Paris Hilton: the very epitome of global talentless celebrity. – Piers Morgan

The greatest privacy bleater in showbusiness is Liz Hurley. Not a week goes by without this poor little lamb moaning about the appalling media intrusion into the pampered multi-millionaire lifestyle she has built on the back of a magnificently impressive lack of discernible talent. – Piers Morgan

(of Heather Mills) The woman is a ludicrous, hypocritical, shameless, grasping creature of such splendid, unrelenting awfulness that her very existence now brings daily joy to my life. – Piers Morgan

Kate Moss is an unpleasant, foul-mouthed, egotistical little madam. A stroppy, pinch-faced little coke-snorter from Croydon. – Piers Morgan

(Carol Vorderman) looks increasingly like Olive Oyl's older, less attractive sister. – Piers Morgan

The live feed of *Celebrity Big Brother* operates on a fifteen-minute delay, which caused confusion when Jimmy Savile entered the house, as he operates on a thirty-year delay. – Dara O'Briain, *Mock the Week*

According to Britney Spears' pre-nup agreement, after she divorces Kevin Federline she'll have to pay him thirty thousand dollars a month. When you add that to Kevin Federline's other sources of income, he'll be making a total of thirty thousand dollars a month. – Conan O'Brien

According to a new international survey, people in the US believe in evolution less than any other industrial country. When asked why they don't believe in evolution, Americans said, "Kevin Federline." – Conan O'Brien

Paris Hilton is reportedly upset because her private diaries have been stolen. Police say the suspect must have had access to her bedroom. So it could be anyone. – Conan O'Brien

It was reported last week that Paris Hilton doesn't pay for her drinks when she goes out. Don't worry, she's still getting plenty of fluids. – Conan O'Brien

Mary-Kate Olsen admitted she hates Paris Hilton because Paris slept with her ex-boyfriend. After hearing this, Paris said, "She's going to have to be a lot more specific." – Conan O'Brien

Paris Hilton said she turned down plans for a life-size Paris Hilton doll even though they would have sold for fifty thousand dollars each. Paris questioned why you would pay fifty thousand dollars for a look-a-like if you could have the real thing for three drinks. – Conan O'Brien

Paris Hilton's birthday was earlier this week. She threw herself a birthday party and she brought two dates, which explains why Paris told her guests, "No cake for me, I had a sandwich in the car." – Conan O'Brien

It has been reported that Spain is the number one consumer of cocaine in the world. Apparently, Spain narrowly beat Kate Moss. – Conan O'Brien

It's been reported that Kate Moss recently warned Lindsay Lohan about the danger of drugs. Moss's exact words were, "Stay away from my drugs!" – Conan O'Brien

Magician David Blaine is going to crawl into a block of ice and stay there for two days. Apparently, Blaine has been preparing for the stunt by having an affair with Martha Stewart. — Conan O'Brien

Ashlee Simpson has announced that she's interested in being an interior designer. She says she wants to prove to everyone that there are other things she's not good at. – Conan O'Brien

Donald Trump has agreed to endorse a line of premium vodkas. Trump's vodka doesn't give you a hangover, but it does give you a combover. – Conan O'Brien

(of Naomi Campbell) I won't use her. We have a no-assholes clause. – Todd Oldham, designer

Who hasn't, it's no big deal? I mean, it's no secret that Kate's not the most timid girl ever. – Jack Osbourne after kissing Kate Moss

(of Paris Hilton) I don't associate with people like that. She is very false. – Kelly Osbourne

(of Heather Mills) Like the Queen, only grander. – Allison Pearson

Heather Mills says she will never marry again. Three hundred million men can now uncross their legs and breathe a sigh of relief. – Allison Pearson

(of Nicole Richie) This pelt-wearing party girl is all animal skin and bones. She's an incredible shrinking woman with the heart to match. – PETA, animal rights group

My first reaction on hearing that David Beckham may have been playing away with his former PA, Rebecca Loos, was who could blame the poor soul? – Amanda Platell

Victoria Beckham is to women about as real as Tanya in *Footballers' Wives*. But more calculating. The only real thing about her is her ambition. – Amanda Platell

Jade Goody's the only woman I can think of who always makes the rest of us feel slim, fit and talented. – Amanda Platell

This week, Donald Trump introduced a new twelve-inch doll of himself that speaks seventeen different phrases, which is amazing, as that's five more than the real Donald Trump. – Amy Poehler

I couldn't give a fuck what that jumped-up little French twat thinks. The only reason he's in Britain is because he failed in France. When I heard Maison Blanc had gone tits up, it added two inches to my cock! – Gordon Ramsay on fellow chef Raymond Blanc

Anton Mosimann – more famous for his bow ties than his cooking. – Gordon Ramsay

(of Fearne Cotton) Anyone who claims, as she has, that her heroine is Davina McCall, can never be accused of being overly highbrow. – Mary Riddell

Paris Hilton is doing a new reality show, *I'm a Celebrity, Get Him Out Of Me*. – Joan Rivers

(of Donatella Versace) That's the kind of face you hang on your door in Africa. – Joan Rivers

(of David Blaine) Are we so starved of entertainment that we are entertained by a trickless magician sitting in a box for forty-four days with no food? – Chris Rock

(of Eric Morley) Was there a star in the East when this self-worshipping little man was born? – Jean Rook

Liz Hurley longs for the day when people stop pointing cameras at her. Speaking as someone who has seen all her films, I couldn't agree more. – Jonathan Ross

Heather Mills is a liar. I wouldn't be surprised if we found out she's actually got two legs. – Jonathan Ross

Poor old Kate Moss. Looks like she's reached the end of the line. Luckily she's got another seven chopped out already. – Jonathan Ross

Abi Titmuss? She's been tied to more bedposts than David Blunkett's dog. – Jonathan Ross

Christine Hamilton is a drama-seeking missile in slingbacks. – Justin Ryan

The worst thing a little acid could do to Tricia Nixon is to turn her into a merely delightful person instead of a grinning robot. – Grace Slick

I heard that Jessica Simpson is running her mouth again about not wanting to be compared to me. Well I've got news for you, honey – the feeling is mutual. – Anna Nicole Smith

People say, "Ooh, doesn't Lionel Blair look good for his age?" Well, no, not really. Not unless he's about five hundred. Otherwise he looks like nothing more than an elaborately coiffured scrotum. – Linda Smith

Who would you rather sleep with – Andrew Lloyd Webber or David Gest? You have to admit, it's a hard one . . . With Gest, I would be worried that even just kissing him might make his face fall apart. – Jaci Stephen

(of Jade Goody's mother, Jackiey) This ignorant, rude, embarrassing halfwit whose only claim to fame is giving birth to a daughter only marginally less stupid than herself. – Jaci Stephen

Vanessa Feltz is as indestructible as a jumbo cockroach. – David Thomas

Did you watch *House of Wax* again? You know that Hilton girl gives you nightmares. – *Veronica Mars*, taking a swipe at Paris Hilton

(of TV fashion guru Susannah Constantine) A carthorse in a badly fitting bin liner. – Carol Vorderman

(of TV fashion guru Trinny Woodall) An anorexic transvestite. – Carol Vorderman

(of Antony Worrall Thompson) The squashed Bee Gee. – Marco Pierre White

COMEDY

Jack Benny's so cheap he wouldn't give you the parsley off his fish. – Fred Allen

Milton Berle has done everybody's act. He's a parrot with skin on. – Fred Allen

Stephen Fry: What's the commonest material in the world?
Clive Anderson: Jim Davidson's. – *QI*

(of Russell Brand) Ghastly, hugely overpraised, the man is everywhere. Why?
– Nigel Andrew

Lucille Ball was to comedy what Vanessa Feltz is to hang-gliding. – Anon

(of Jim Carrey) A man whose comedic talent is limited to pulling faces. –
Anon

(of Jim Davidson) Laugh? I nearly started. – Anon

Do I worry that I'll always be known as Roseanne's ex-husband? Yeah, I do.
But it's sure better than being known as her current husband. – Tom Arnold

I'm only upset that I'm not a widow. – Roseanne Barr, following her divorce
from Tom Arnold

(of Ray Richmond) I approached reading his review the way some people
anticipate anal warts. – Roseanne Barr

(of Bob Hope) A venerated, self-satisfied boob. – Charles Bickford

(of Lucille Ball) I hated working with that bitch. She was the biggest bitch
in the business. Thank God I'll never have to work with her again. – Tom
Bosley

(of Matt Lucas) I found him prissy, a niggly diva. – Boy George

Remember, tonight isn't all about comedy. Here's Ben Elton! – Frankie Boyle,
Mock the Week

Bob Hope is like a junkie, an applause junkie. Instead of growing old
gracefully or doing something with his money, all he does is have an
anniversary with the President looking on. He's a pathetic guy. – Marlon
Brando

When Jack Benny has a party, you not only bring your own scotch, you bring
your own rocks. – George Burns

British scientists will be allowed to create part-human, part-animal embryos
for research. They got the idea from Jo Brand who is eighty per cent Friesian.
– Garry Bushell

Bobby Davro's career is now so far off course he doesn't need an agent, he needs a St Bernard. – Garry Bushell

I've seen Don (Rickles) entertain fifty times and I've always enjoyed his joke. – Johnny Carson

Good riddance to him, the freeloading bastard! I hope he fries. – John Cleese's joke speech at Graham Chapman's memorial service

(of Bob Hope) Occasionally funny, usually superficial, always pompous. – Bobby Darin

I'm Patrick Kielty – I'm Irish, I've got spikey hair, so in theory I should be as loveable and funny as Graham Norton. So much for theories. – *Dead Ringers*

I don't really find any silent comedians funny. I don't identify with it. I've never had to wallpaper a room while delivering a piano upstairs. – Angus Deayton

(to Roseanne Barr) Tell me, is there anything you wish you hadn't eaten? – Dame Edna Everage

Steve Martin has basically one joke and he's it. – Dave Felton

Groucho Marx is a male chauvinistic piglet. – Betty Friedan

Robin Williams's technique is to say 500 things with a joke rhythm, and at least two of them might be funny. – Libby Gelman-Waxner

Jennifer Saunders is a one-trick horse; Dawn French is a one-trick carthorse. – A. A. Gill

Sandra Bernard is as much fun as barbed wire. – Tom Hutchinson

Joan Rivers's face hasn't just had a lift, it's taken the elevator all the way to the top floor without stopping. – Clive James

Bob Hope is a funny guy, but if he was drowning he couldn't ad lib "Help!" – Hal Kanter

Joan Rivers has a face like a Siamese cat in a wind tunnel. – Kit and the Widow

(of Richard Blackwood) A man who can list on his CV rapper, comedian, presenter, actor, writer – all after the word "failed". – Mark Lamarr, *Never Mind The Buzzcocks*

"Hi Ho Silver Lining" has ruined more wedding receptions than Phill (Jupitus) being first in line at the buffet. – Mark Lamarr, *Never Mind The Buzzcocks*

(of Faith Brown) I think she's rather a sad lady, who can't accept her career is over. – Jan Leeming

(of Phyllis Diller) I treasure every moment that I do not see her. – Oscar Levant

I am not thrilled by comparisons to Jim Carrey. – Jerry Lewis

Arthur Smith is about as funny as an outbreak of rabies in a Guide Dogs for the Blind home. – Victor Lewis-Smith

Bob Hope is a barely funny, very selfish reactionary and user. He used patriotism and the troops overseas for publicity. – Myrna Loy

Jimmy Tarbuck doesn't tell gags – he just refreshes your memory. – Bernard Manning

Milton Berle is an inspiration to every young person that wants to get into show business. Hard work, perseverance, and discipline: all the things you need when you have no talent. – Dean Martin

Jerry Lewis takes criticism much too personally. He explodes, then he stews, then he explodes again. It's as if to criticize him is treason. – Dean Martin

(Bob) Hope is not a comedian. He just translates what others write for him. – Groucho Marx

Jimmy Tarbuck is now older than his jokes. – Derek McGovern

(to Bernard Manning) So, Bernard, apart from Adolf Hitler, who else do you admire? – Mrs Merton

(of Jay Leno) Those ties look like they were made in summer camp, like fabric ashtrays he's wearing around his neck. – Dennis Miller

Over the past fifty years Bob Hope employed eighty-eight joke writers who supplied him with more than one million gags. And he still couldn't make me laugh. – Eddie Murphy

Ellen DeGeneres and Anne Heche are talking about having a baby. They're worried, though, because if the baby is anything like Ellen, it's going to take much longer than nine months to come out. – Conan O'Brien

When Joan Rivers has her makeup confiscated by airport security, even the terrorists will realize that they have made a huge mistake. – Conan O'Brien

(of Groucho Marx) The man was a major comedian, which is to say that he had the compassion of an icicle, the effrontery of a carnival shrill, and the generosity of a pawnbroker. – S. J. Perelman

(of Russell Brand) The drugs, the women, the lifestyle . . . the country knows everything about him, apart from when his show is on. – Jonathan Ross

(of Frank Skinner) The amount of money he's earned for not making me laugh is staggering. – Will Self

Lisa Simpson: Only one person in a million would find that funny.
Professor John Frink: Yes, we call that the 'Dennis Miller Ratio'. – *The Simpsons*

I like Don Rickles. But that's because I have no taste. – Frank Sinatra

I would have sex with sand before I'd have sex with Roseanne (Barr). – Howard Stern

Phyllis Diller's so ancient she's just a carcass with a mouth. – Ruby Wax

Most comedians aren't funny in real life. Take Jennifer (Saunders) – she's so boring if you meet her. Her natural state is flatlining. – Ruby Wax

Of all Russell Brand's addictions, only one remains – himself. – Simon Wilson

Ben Elton. Do you know this guy? He started out as an "alternative" comedian, railing against Thatcherism and the like, and now earns a fortune writing the librettos for truly awful West End musicals. I mean, his name has become a byword for shameless hackery. He's the biggest sell-out of his generation. – Toby Young

LITERATURE

(of an unnamed author) He writes so well he makes me feel like putting the quill back in the goose. – Fred Allen

(to Jeffrey Archer) Is there no beginning to your talents? – Clive Anderson (of Samuel Taylor Coleridge) A huge pendulum attached to a small clock. – Anon

(of Algernon Charles Swinburne) A man standing up to his neck in a cesspool, and adding to its contents. – Anon

I don't think Robert Browning was very good in bed. His wife probably didn't care for him very much. He snored and had fantasies about twelve-year-old girls. – W. H. Auden

(of Edgar Allan Poe) An unmanly sort of man whose love life seems to have been largely confined to crying in laps and playing mouse. – W.H. Auden

(of Alfred, Lord Tennyson) There was little about melancholy that he didn't know; there was little else that he did. – W. H. Auden

(of Honoré de Balzac) A fat little flabby person, with the face of a baker, the clothes of a cobbler, the size of a barrel maker, the manners of a stocking salesman, and the dress of an innkeeper. – Victor de Balabin

(of Richard Adams's *Watership Down*) Frankly I would prefer to read a novel about civil servants written by a rabbit. – Craig Brown

Thank you for sending me a copy of your book. I'll waste no time reading it. – Anon

(after a lengthy debate with Ambrose Bierce) I have only been mildly bored. – Gertrude Atherton

(of M. M. Kaye's *The Far Pavilions*) This is one of those big, fat paperbacks, intended to while away a monsoon or two, which, if thrown with a good over-arm action, will bring a water buffalo to its knees. – Nancy Banks-Smith

(to George Bernard Shaw) You ought to be roasted alive: though even then, you would not be to my taste. – J. M. Barrie

(to an unnamed poet) I've read some of your modern free verse and wonder who set it free. – John Barrymore

(of George Sand) She is stupid, heavy and garrulous. She has good reasons to wish to abolish Hell. – Charles Baudelaire

Byron! He would be all forgotten today if he had lived to be a florid old gentleman with iron-grey whiskers writing very long, very able letters to the *Times* about the repeal of the Corn Laws. – Max Beerbohm

George Bernard Shaw uses the English language like a truncheon. – Max Beerbohm

The covers of this book are too far apart. – Ambrose Bierce

I had thought that there could be only two worse writers than Stephen Crane, namely two Stephen Cranes. – Ambrose Bierce

(of Oscar Wilde) The sovereign of insufferables. He had nothing to say and he said it. – Ambrose Bierce

(of Marie de Sevigne) You can gain nothing by reading her. It is like eating snowballs, with which one can surfeit one's self without satisfying the stomach. – Napoleon Bonaparte

(Edward) Gibbon is an ugly, affected, disgusting fellow and poisons our literary club for me. I class him among infidel wasps and venomous insects. – James Boswell

(of Aldous Huxley) The stupid person's idea of a clever person. – Elizabeth Bowen

Henry Miller is not really a writer but a non-stop talker to whom someone has given a typewriter. – Gerald Brenan

(Henry Wadsworth) Longfellow is to poetry what the barrel-organ is to music. – Van Wyck Brooks

Balzac was so conceited that he raised his hat every time he spoke of himself. – Robert Broughton

(of Dorothy Parker) To those she did not like, she was a stiletto made of sugar. – John Mason Brown

Barbara Cartland: Baby Jane crossed with Liberace. – Julie Burchill

(of Camille Paglia) The "g" is silent – the only thing about her that is. – Julie Burchill

It was very good of God to let (Thomas) Carlyle and Mrs Carlyle marry one another and so make only two people miserable instead of four. – Samuel Butler

(of Dylan Thomas) That insolent little ruffian, that crapulous lout. When he quitted a sofa, he left behind him a smear. – Norman Cameron

I knew William Faulkner well. He was a great friend of mine. Well, much as you could be a friend of his, unless you were a fourteen-year-old nymphet. – Truman Capote

Jacqueline Susann looks like a truck driver in drag. – Truman Capote

I guess Gore (Vidal) left the country because he felt he was under-appreciated here. I have news for him: people who actually read his books will under-appreciate him everywhere. – Truman Capote

(of Samuel Taylor Coleridge) Never did I see such apparatus got ready for thinking, and never so little thought. He mounts scaffolding, pulleys, and tackles, gathers all the tools in the neighbourhood with labour, with noise, demonstration, precept, and sets – three bricks. – Thomas Carlyle

(of Ralph Waldo Emerson) A hoary-headed and toothless baboon. – Thomas Carlyle

Poor (Percy Bysshe) Shelley always was, and is, a kind of ghastly object; colourless, pallid, tuneless, without health or warmth or vigour. – Thomas Carlyle

(of Percy Bysshe Shelley) He has said or done nothing worth a serious man taking the trouble of remembering. – Thomas Carlyle

(of Algernon Charles Swinburne) Sitting in a sewer and adding to it. – Thomas Carlyle

(George Bernard) Shaw's brain is a half-inch layer of champagne poured over a bucket of Methodist near-beer. – Benjamin de Cassères

(of Alfred, Lord Tennyson) A dirty man with opium-glazed eyes and rat-taily hair. – Lady Frederick Cavendish

(of James M. Cain) Everything he touches smells like a billygoat. He is every kind of a writer I detest, a faux naïf, a Proust in greasy overalls. – Raymond Chandler

(of Eugene O'Neill) He is the sort of man who could spend a year in flophouses, researching flophouses, and write a play about flophouses that would be no more real than a play by a man who had never been in a flophouse, but had only read about them. – Raymond Chandler

(of William Faulkner) He uses a lot of big words, and his sentences are from here to the airport. – Carolyn Chute

(of James Boswell) Silly, snobbish, lecherous, tipsy, given to high-flown sentiments and more than a little humbug . . . he needed Johnson as ivy needs an oak. – Cyril Connolly

(of George Orwell) He would not blow his nose without moralizing on the conditions in the handkerchief industry. – Cyril Connolly

(of Vita Sackville-West) She looked like Lady Chatterley above the waist and the gamekeeper below. – Cyril Connolly

The world is rid of Lord Byron, but the deadly slime of his touch still remains. – John Constable

(of a friend's first short story) Frankly, I should bury it in a drawer and put a lily on it. – Noël Coward

(of Edith Sitwell) I am fairly unrepentant about her poetry. I really think that three-quarters of it is gibberish. However, I must crush down these thoughts, otherwise the dove of peace will shit on me. – Noël Coward

(of Oscar Wilde) What a tiresome, effected sod. – Noël Coward

(of George Bernard Shaw) The simplest clues to life escape him, as he scales impossible pinnacles of unnecessary thought, only to slip down the other side. – Edward Gordon Craig

(of Oscar Wilde) He festooned the dung heap on which he had placed himself with sonnets as people grow honeysuckle around outdoor privies. – Quentin Crisp

Jeffrey Archer is proof of the proposition that in each of us lurks a bad novel. – Julian Critchley

(of Ezra Pound) He was humane but not human. – e e cummings

I have tried lately to read Shakespeare, and found it so intolerably dull that it nauseated me. – Charles Darwin

Your Majesty, do not hang George Wither lest it be said that I am the worst poet in the kingdom. – John Denham

If it were thought that anything I wrote was influenced by Robert Frost, I would take that particular piece of mine, shred it, and flush it down the toilet, hoping not to clog the pipes. – James Dickey (of Edward Bulwer-Lytton) He never wrote an invitation to dinner without an eye to posterity. – Benjamin Disraeli

(of Ford Madox Ford) An animated adenoid. – Norman Douglas

Robert Benchley has a style that is weak and lies down frequently to rest. – Max Eastman

(of Charlotte Brontë) I wish her characters would talk a little less like the heroes and heroines of police reports. – George Eliot

Of Byron one can say, as of no other English poet of his eminence, that he added nothing to the language, that he discovered nothing in the sounds, and developed nothing in the meaning of individual words. – T. S. Eliot

Henry James had a mind so fine that no idea could violate it. – T. S. Eliot

(Alfred Lord) Tennyson is a beautiful half of a poet. – Ralph Waldo Emerson

(of Walt Whitman) Half song thrush, half alligator. – Ralph Waldo Emerson

(of William Wordsworth) A bell with a wooden tongue. – Ralph Waldo Emerson

Even those who call Mr (William) Faulkner our greatest literary sadist do not fully appreciate him, for it is not merely his characters who have to run the gauntlet but also his readers. – Clifton Fadiman

Gertrude Stein was a master at making nothing happen very slowly. – Clifton Fadiman

Ernest Hemingway has never been known to use a word that might send the reader to a dictionary. – William Faulkner

(of Henry James) One of the nicest old ladies I ever met. – William Faulkner

(of Mark Twain) A hack writer who would have been considered fourth rate in Europe, who tried out a few of the old proven "sure-fire" literary skeletons with sufficient local colour to intrigue the superficial and the lazy. – William Faulkner

Mrs (Elizabeth Barrrett) Browning's death is rather a relief to me, I must say. No more Aurora Leighs, thank God! A woman of real genius, I know; but what is the upshot of it all? She and her sex had better mind the kitchen and the children; and perhaps the poor. Except in such things as little novels, they only devote themselves to what men do much better, leaving that which men do worse or not at all. – Edward Fitzgerald

(of Ernest Hemingway) Always willing to lend a helping hand to the one above him. – F. Scott Fitzgerald

(of Gertrude Stein) What an old covered wagon she is. – F. Scott Fitzgerald

(of George Sand) A great cow full of ink. – Gustave Flaubert

Lord Byron writes with the thoughts of a city clerk in metropolitan clerical vernacular. – Ford Madox Ford

(Joseph) Conrad spent a day finding the *mot juste*; then killed it. – Ford Madox Ford

Listening to Alexander Woollcott is like being hit with a cream puff; you are uninjured but rather sickened. – Robert Forsythe

An editor should have a pimp for a brother so he'd have someone to look up to. – Gene Fowler

(of Alice B. Toklas) She was incredibly ugly, uglier than almost anyone I had ever met. A thin, withered creature, she sat hunched in her chair, in her heavy tweed suit and her thick lisle stockings, impregnable and indifferent. She had a huge nose, a dark moustache, and her dark-dyed hair was combed into absurd bangs over her forehead. – Otto Friedrich

(of D. H. Lawrence) Obsessed with self. Dead eyes and a red beard, long narrow face. A strange bird. – John Galsworthy

(of Ernest Hemingway) A man must be a very great genius to make up for being such a loathsome human being. – Martha Gellhorn

Welcome To My World reads as if Coleen (McLoughlin) has been forced into the basement of her publishers at gunpoint and ordered to dictate eighty thousand random words into a Dictaphone. – Tanya Gold

There is no arguing with (Samuel) Johnson; for when his pistol misses fire, he knocks you down with the butt end of it. – Oliver Goldsmith

(of Ernest Hemingway) He's got hold of the red meat of the English language and turned it into hamburgers. – Richard Gordon

That's Kingsley Amis and there's no known cure. – Robert Graves

(of Robert Benchley) An enchanting toad of a man. – Helen Hayes

(of Charles Lamb) His sayings are generally like women's letters; all the pith is in the postscript. – William Hazlitt

To me, (Ezra) Pound remains the exquisite showman minus the show. – Ben Hecht

(Johann Ludwig) Uhland's poetry is like the famous war horse, Bayard; it possesses all possible virtues and only one fault – it is dead. – Heinrich Heine

Poor (William) Faulkner. Does he really think emotions come from big words? – Ernest Hemingway

(of Algernon Charles Swinburne) A perpetual functioning of genius without truth, feeling, or any adequate matter to be functioning on. – Gerard Manley Hopkins

(of critics) His trade is one which requires, that it may be practised in perfection, two qualifications only: ignorance of language and abstinence from thought. – A. E. Housman

Nature, not content with denying him the ability to think, has endowed him with the ability to write. – A.E. Housman

George Eliot: a fungus of pendulous shape. – Alice James

Barbara Cartland's eyes were twin miracles of mascara and looked like two small crows that had crashed into a chalk cliff. – Clive James

(of Judith Krantz's *Princess Daisy*) As a work of art it has the same status as a long conversation between two not very bright drunks. – Clive James

(of Rudyard Kipling) I doubt that the infant monster has any more to give. – Henry James

(of Plato) Take from him his sophisms, futilities, and incomprehensibilities and what remains? His foggy mind. – Thomas Jefferson

(of the Earl of Chesterfield) This man, I thought, had been a lord among wits; but, I find, he is only a wit among Lords! – Samuel Johnson

The misfortune of (Oliver) Goldsmith in conversation is this: he goes on without knowing how he is to get off. – Samuel Johnson

It is amazing how little Goldsmith knows. He seldom comes where he is not more ignorant than anyone else. – Samuel Johnson

(of Thomas Gray) He was dull in company, dull in his closet, dull everywhere. He was dull in a new way and that made people think him great. – Samuel Johnson

(of John Milton's *Paradise Lost*) One of the books which the reader admires and lays down, but forgets to take up again. Its perusal is a duty rather than pleasure. – Samuel Johnson

(of Thomas Sheridan) Sherry is dull, naturally dull; but it must have taken him a great deal of pains to become what we now see him. Such an excess of stupidity is not in nature. – Samuel Johnson

(George Bernard) Shaw, most poisonous of all the poisonous haters of England; despiser, distorter and denier of the plain truths whereby men live; topsy-turvy perverter of all human relationships; a menace to ordered social thought and ordered social life; irresponsible braggart, blaring self-trumpeter. – Henry A. Jones

(to W. B. Yeats) We have met too late. You are too old for me to have any effect on you. – James Joyce

(of Gertrude Stein) An immense priestess of nonsense expounding her text in nonsense syllables. – Alfred Kazin

(William) Wordsworth has left a bad impression wherever he visited in town by his egotism, vanity and bigotry. – John Keats

(of G. K. Chesterton) He grew up from manhood into boyhood. – R. A. Knox

(of William Faulkner) For my part, I can rarely tell whether his characters are making love or playing tennis. – Joseph Kraft

Mr (David) Baddiel, I've got all of your novels. I ticked the wrong box on my book club form. Should I read them? – *The Kumars At No. 42*

(of Lord Byron) Mad, bad, and dangerous to know. – Lady Caroline Lamb (of William Wordsworth) Dank, limber verses, stuft with lakeside sedges And propt with rotten stakes from rotten hedges. – Walter Savage Landor

(of James Joyce) Nothing but old fags and cabbage-stumps of quotations from the Bible and the rest, stewed in the juice of deliberate, journalistic dirty-mindedness. – D. H. Lawrence

This awful (Walt) Whitman. This post-mortem poet. This poet with the private soul leaking out of him all the time. All his privacy leaking out in a sort of dribble, oozing into the universe. – D. H. Lawrence

The trouble with Ian (Fleming) is that he gets off with women because he can't get on with them. – Rosamond Lehmann

Reading Joseph Conrad is like gargling with broken glass. – Hugh Leonard

(of Arnold Bennett) The Hitler of the book racket. – Percy Wyndham Lewis

(of Ford Madox Ford) A flabby lemon and pink giant, who hung his mouth open as though he were an animal at the zoo inviting buns – especially when the ladies were present. – Percy Wyndham Lewis

Gertrude Stein's prose is a cold, black suet-pudding. We can represent it as a cold suet-roll of fabulously reptilian length. Cut it at any point, it is the same heavy, sticky, opaque mass all through, and all along. – Percy Wyndham Lewis

I denounce Mr Bernard De Voto as a fool and a tedious and egotistical fool, as a liar and a pompous and boresome liar. – Sinclair Lewis

People who like this sort of thing will find this the sort of thing they like. – Abraham Lincoln, reviewing a book

(H. L.) Mencken's prose sounds like large stones being thrown into a dumpcart. – Robert Littell

(of John Keats) It is a better thing to be a starved apothecary than a starved poet. So back to the shop, Mr John. Back to plaster, pills and ointment boxes. – J. G. Lockhart

(of Emily Bronte's *Wuthering Heights*) All the faults of *Jane Eyre* are magnified thousandfold and the only consolation which we have in reflecting upon it, is that it will never be generally read. – James Lorimer

Jeffrey Archer has issued a strenuous denial – as good as a signed confession, really! – Des Lynam

It was a book to kill time for those who liked it better dead. – Rose Macaulay

(of John Dryden) His imagination resembles the wings of an ostrich. – Thomas Babington Macaulay

The more I read Socrates, the less I wonder they poisoned him. – Thomas Babington Macaulay

(of J. D. Salinger) The greatest mind ever to stay in prep school. – Norman Mailer

(of Gore Vidal) I've had to smell your works from time to time, and that has helped me to become an expert on intellectual pollution. – Norman Mailer

(reading a long novel by Thomas Wolfe is like) making love to a three-hundred-pound woman. Once she gets on top, it's all over. Fall in love or be asphyxiated. – Norman Mailer

(of James Thurber) A tall, thin, spectacled man with the face of a harassed rat. – Russell Maloney

E. M. Forster never gets any further than warming the teapot. He's a rare fine hand at that. Feel this teapot. Is it not beautifully warm? Yes, but there ain't going to be no tea. – Katherine Mansfield

(of Barbara Cartland) The white and creamy look of an animated meringue. – Arthur Marshall

(of a book by S. J. Perelman) From the moment I picked up your book until I laid it down I was convulsed with laughter. Someday I intend reading it. – Groucho Marx

Alexander Woollcott looked like something that had gotten loose from Macy's Thanksgiving Day Parade. – Harpo Marx

Henry James had turned his back on one of the great events in the world's history, the rise of the United States, in order to report tittle-tattle at tea parties in English country houses. – W. Somerset Maugham

To hear W. B.Yeats read his own verses was as excruciating a torture as anyone could be exposed to. – W. Somerset Maugham

(of Lillian Hellman) Every word she writes is a lie, including "and" and "the".
– Mary McCarthy

Life to (George Bernard) Shaw is not a poem, but a series of police regulations. – H. L. Mencken

George Eliot had the heart of Sappho; but the face, with the long proboscis, the protruding teeth of the Apocalyptic horse, betrayed animality. – George Meredith

Some call (Alexander) Pope "little nightingale" – all sound and no sense. – Mary Wortley Montagu

Cicero's style bores me. When I have spent an hour reading him and try to recollect what I have extracted, I usually find it nothing but wind. – Michel de Montaigne

What is (Joseph Conrad) but the wreck of Stevenson floating about in the slipslop of Henry James? – George Moore

(of Thomas Hardy) An abortion of George Sand. – George Moore

Probably (James) Joyce thinks that because he prints all the dirty little words he is a great hero. – George Moore

I think of Mr (Robert Louis) Stevenson as a consumptive youth weaving garlands of sad flowers with pale, weak hands. – George Moore

Oscar Wilde's talent seems to me to be essentially rootless, something growing in glass on a little water. – George Moore

(of W. B. Yeats) Looking himself in his old cloak like a huge umbrella left behind by some picnic party. – George Moore

Coleridge was a muddle-headed metaphysician who by some strange streak of fortune turned out a few poems amongst the dreary flood of inanity that was his wont. – William Morris

A bad review is even less important than whether it is raining in Patagonia. – Iris Murdoch

I cannot abide (Joseph) Conrad's souvenir shop style and bottled ships and shell necklaces of romanticist clichés. – Vladimir Nabokov

(of J. M. Barrie) The triumph of sugar over diabetes. – George Jean Nathan (of George Bernard Shaw) He writes his plays for the ages – the ages between five and twelve. – George Jean Nathan

(of Dante Alighieri) A hyena that wrote poetry in tombs. – Friedrich Nietzsche

(Ralph Waldo) Emerson is one who lives instinctively on ambrosia – and leaves everything indigestible on his plate. – Friedrich Nietzsche

(of C. P. Snow) A man who so much resembled a Baked Alaska – sweet, warm and gungy on the outside, hard and cold within. – Joseph O'Connor

(of W. H. Auden) A sort of gutless Kipling. – George Orwell

In places, this book is a little over-written because Mr (Edmund) Blunden is no more able to resist a quotation than some people are to refuse a drink. – George Orwell

(Rudyard) Kipling is a jingo imperialist, he is morally insensitive and aesthetically disgusting. – George Orwell

(of George Bernard Shaw) He writes like a Pakistani who had learned English when he was twelve years old in order to become a chartered accountant. – John Osborne

The affair between Margot Asquith and Margot Asquith will live as one of the prettiest love stories in all literature. – Dorothy Parker

This is not a novel to be tossed aside lightly. It should be thrown with great force. – Dorothy Parker

Mr (T. S.) Eliot is at times an excellent poet and has arrived at the supreme eminence among English critics largely through disguising himself as a corpse. – Ezra Pound

Mr (William) Wordsworth, a stupid man, with a decided gift for portraying nature in vignettes, never ruined anyone's morals, unless, perhaps, he has driven some susceptible persons to crime in a very fury of boredom. – Ezra Pound

(of George Bernard Shaw) I remember coming across him at the Grand Canyon and finding him peevish, refusing to admire it or even look at it properly. He was jealous of it. – J. B. Priestley

(of William Hazlitt) An overgrown pimple, sore to the touch. – *Quarterly Review*

(Wilfred) Owen's tiny corpus is perhaps the most overrated poetry in the twentieth century. – Craig Raine

To say (Agatha) Christie's characters are cardboard cut-outs is an insult to cardboard. – Ruth Rendell

(of Robert Frost) A nice, acrid, savage, pathetic old chap. – I. A. Richards

(of a fellow writer's two-line poem) Very nice, though there are dull stretches. – Antoine de Rivarol

(of Henry James) A little emasculated mass of inanity. – Theodore Roosevelt

(William Makepeace) Thackeray settled like a meat-fly on whatever one had got for dinner, and made one sick of it. – John Ruskin

Waldo (Ralph Waldo Emerson) is one of those people who would be enormously improved by death. – Saki

Jane Austen's novels, which strangely retain their hold on the public taste, are tedious to those who dare to think for themselves. – Kate Sanborn

(of Charles Dickens) He has never played any significant part in any movement more significant than that of a fly on a wheel. – *Saturday Review*

Concerning no subject would (George Bernard) Shaw be deterred by the minor accident of total ignorance from penning a definitive opinion. – Roger Scruton

With the single exception of Homer, there is no eminent writer, not even Sir Walter Scott, whom I can despise so entirely as I despise Shakespeare when I measure my mind against his. It would positively be a relief for me to dig him up and throw stones at him. – George Bernard Shaw

As a bankrupt thief turns thief-taker, so an unsuccessful author turns critic. – Percy Bysshe Shelley

(of Louisa May Alcott) Living almost always among intellectuals, she preserved to the age of fifty-six that contempt for ideas which is normal among boys and girls of fifteen. – Odell Shepherd

(Norman) Mailer wallows in self-pity, pride, and a world-historical egomania, thereby providing an accurate portrait of the mental state of most writers most of the time. – Judith Shulevitz

(of his biographer, Kitty Kelley) I hope the next time she crosses a street four blind guys come along driving cars. – Frank Sinatra

(D. H.) Lawrence looked like a plaster gnome on a stone toadstool in some suburban garden. – Edith Sitwell

Virginia Woolf's writing is no more than glamorous knitting. I believe she must have a pattern. – Edith Sitwell

(of Thomas Gray) He walked as if he had fouled his small clothes and looks as if he smelt it. – Christopher Smart

(of Noah Webster) In conversation he is even duller than in writing, if that is possible. – Juliana Smith

(of a work by Henry Peter Brougham) It is long, yet vigorous, like the penis of a jackass. – Sydney Smith

Thomas Carlyle has occasional flashes of silence that make his conversation perfectly delightful. – Sydney Smith

(of Thomas Babington Macaulay) He not only overflowed with learning, but stood in the slop. – Sydney Smith

(of James Joyce's *Ulysses*) It is written by a man with a diseased mind and soul so black that he would even obscure the darkness of hell. – Senator Reed Smoot

(of Jeffrey Archer) That guy would bottle your pee and sell it for a fiver. – Ringo Starr

(of D. H. Lawrence) He's impossible. He's pathetic and preposterous. He writes like a sick man. – Gertrude Stein

(of Ezra Pound) A village explainer. Excellent if you were a village, but if you were not, not. – Gertrude Stein

Valley of the Dolls – for the reader who has put away comic books but isn't ready for editorials in the *Daily News*. – Gloria Steinem, reviewing Jacqueline Susann's novel

(of Walt Whitman) A large shaggy dog, just unchained, scouring the beaches of the world and baying at the moon. – Robert Louis Stevenson

(of Max Beerbohm) He has the most remarkable and seductive genius – and I should say about the smallest in the world. – Lytton Strachey (of Alexander Pope) The verses, when they were written, resembled nothing so much as spoonfuls of boiling oil, ladled out by a fiendish monkey at an upstairs window upon such of the passers-by whom the wretch had a grudge against. – Lytton Strachey

Then Edith Sitwell appeared, her nose longer than an anteater's, and read some of her absurd stuff. – Lytton Strachey

(Richard) Steele might become a reasonably good writer if he would pay a little attention to grammar, learn something about the propriety and disposition of words and, incidentally, get some information on the subject he intends to handle. – Jonathan Swift

Fine words. I wonder where you stole them. – Jonathan Swift

(of Ralph Waldo Emerson) A gap-toothed and hoary ape, who now in his dotage spits and chatters from a dirtier perch of his own finding, and fouling. – Algernon Charles Swinburne

(of Robert Browning) He has plenty of music in him, but he cannot get it out. – Alfred, Lord Tennyson

(Thomas) Carlyle is a poet to whom nature has denied the faculty of verse. – Alfred, Lord Tennyson

(of critic Churton Collins) A louse in the locks of literature. – Alfred, Lord Tennyson

(of Ben Jonson) Reading him is like wading through glue. – Alfred, Lord Tennyson

(of Jonathan Swift) A monster gibbering shrieks and gnashing imprecations against mankind – tearing down all shreds of modesty, past all sense of manliness and shame; filthy in word, filthy in thought, furious, raging, obscene. – William Makepeace Thackeray

(of Richard Church) A cliché-ridden humbug and pie-fingering hack. – Dylan Thomas

(of Edith Sitwell) Isn't she a poisonous thing of a woman, lying, concealing, flipping, plagiarizing, misquoting, and being as clever a crooked literary publicist as ever? – Dylan Thomas

Walt Whitman was not only eager to talk about himself but reluctant to have the conversation stray from the subject for too long. – Henry D. Thoreau

(to Maxim Gorky) You talk about yourself a great deal. That's why there are no distinctive characters in your writing. Your characters are all alike. You probably don't understand women; you've never depicted one successfully. — Leo Tolstoy

Of (Charles) Dickens's style it is impossible to speak in praise. It is jerky, ungrammatical and created by himself in defiance of rules. — Anthony Trollope

To me Edgar Allan Poe's prose is unreadable — like Jane Austen's. No, there's a difference. I could read his prose on a salary, but not Jane's. — Mark Twain

Jane Austen's books, too, are absent from this library. Just that one omission alone would make a fairly good library out of a library that hadn't a book in it. — Mark Twain

(of Bret Harte) If he were to write about an Orphan Princess who lost a peanut, he would feel obliged to try to make somebody snuffle over it. — Mark Twain

(of Henry James) Once you've put one of his books down, you simply can't pick it up again. — Mark Twain

George Bernard Shaw: the spinster aunt of English literature. — Kenneth Tynan

Writing criticism is to writing fiction and poetry as hugging the shore is to sailing in the open sea. — John Updike

Critics are like pigs at the pastry cart. — John Updike

Critics search for ages for the wrong word, which, to give them credit, they eventually find. — Peter Ustinov

(Truman) Capote's gift for publicity is the most glittering star in his diadem. — Gore Vidal

(of Truman Capote) He's a full-fledged housewife from Kansas with all the prejudices. — Gore Vidal

It is inhuman to attack Capote. You are attacking an elf. — Gore Vidal

(of Truman Capote's death) It was a good career move. — Gore Vidal

What other culture could have produced someone like (Ernest) Hemingway and *not* seen the joke? – Gore Vidal

(of Norman Mailer) No one reads him, they hear of him. – Gore Vidal

Norman Mailer is now what he wanted to be: the patron saint of bad journalism. – Gore Vidal

An hour with a dentist without Novocaine was like a minute with Carson McCullers. – Gore Vidal

What a nightmare, to wake up in the morning and realize that you are John Simon. – Gore Vidal

(of Gertrude Stein) In her last days, she resembled a spoiled pear. – Gore Vidal

This is not all bad, except as prose. – Gore Vidal, reviewing *The Winds of War* by Herman Wouk

(of Harold Robbins) He is able to turn an unplotted, unworkable manuscript into an unplotted and unworkable manuscript with a lot of sex. – Tom Volpe

Like eating haggis, reading Dick Francis is something that must be done once but never again. – Guy Walters

Do they keep throwing the book at Jeffrey Archer as an act of revenge for his lousy novels? – Keith Waterhouse

(of Hillaire Belloc) He is conscious of being decrepit and forgetful, but not of being a bore. – Evelyn Waugh

(of Beverly Nicholls) A mercenary, hypochondriacal flibbertigibbet who doesn't take in one of the six words addressed to him. – Evelyn Waugh

To see him (Stephen Spender) fumbling with our rich and delicate English is like seeing a Sèvres vase in the hands of a chimpanzee. – Evelyn Waugh

Oscar Wilde was over-dressed, pompous, snobbish, sentimental and vain. – Evelyn Waugh

(of Henry James) Bare verbs he rarely tolerates. He splits infinitives and fills them up with adverbial stuffing. He presses the passing colloquialism into his service. His vast paragraphs sweat and struggle. – H. G. Wells (of George Bernard Shaw) The more I think you over the more it comes home to me what an unmitigated Middle Victorian ass you were! — H. G. Wells

(of the Earl of Chesterfield) If he is rewarded according to his desert his name will stink to all generations. — John Wesley

Hiring someone to write your autobiography is like paying someone to take a bath for you. — Mae West

(of H. G. Wells) He is the old maid among novelists. — Rebecca West

It is terribly hard not to dislike Evelyn Waugh. — Antonia White

(of H. L. Mencken) With a pig's eyes that never look up, with a pig's snout that loves muck, with a pig's brain that knows only the sty, and with a pig's squeal that cries only when he is hurt, he sometimes opens his pig's mouth, tusked and ugly, and lets out the voice of God, railing at the whitewash that covers the manure about his habitat. — William A. White

Tell me, when you're alone with Max (Beerbohm), does he take off his face and reveal his mask? — Oscar Wilde

Mr Hall Caine writes at the top of his voice. He is so loud that one cannot hear what he says. — Oscar Wilde

(of Charles Dickens) One must have a heart of stone to read the death of little Nell without laughing. — Oscar Wilde

(of George Meredith) As a writer he has mastered everything except language; as a novelist he can do everything except tell a story; as an artist he is everything except articulate. — Oscar Wilde

George Meredith is a prose (Robert) Browning — and so is Browning. — Oscar Wilde

(of George Moore) He leads his readers to the latrine and locks them in. — Oscar Wilde

George Moore wrote excellent English until he discovered grammar. — Oscar Wilde

(of James Payn) He hunts down the obvious with the enthusiasm of a short-sighted detective. — Oscar Wilde

There are two ways of disliking poetry; one way is to dislike it, the other is to read (Alexander) Pope. — Oscar Wilde (of George Bernard Shaw) He hasn't an enemy in the world, and none of his friends like him. – Oscar Wilde

(William) Wordsworth went to the lakes, but he never was a lake poet. He found in stones the sermons he had already hidden there. – Oscar Wilde

(of W. B. Yeats) Books of poetry by young writers are usually promissory notes that are never met. – Oscar Wilde

Monsieur (Émile) Zola is determined to show that if he has not genius he can at least be dull. – Oscar Wilde

I always said little Truman (Capote) had a voice so high it could only be detected by bats. – Tennessee Williams

(of Evelyn Waugh) His style has the desperate jauntiness of an orchestra fiddling away for dear life on a sinking ship. – Edmund Wilson

Don't you loathe the critics? Their mere existence seems to me an impertinence. – P. G. Wodehouse

(of Elizabeth Barrett Browning) Fate has not been kind to Mrs Browning. Nobody reads her, nobody discusses her, nobody troubles to put her in her place. – Virginia Woolf

Pale, marmoreal (T. S.) Eliot was there last week, like a chapped office boy on a high stool, with a cold in his head. – Virginia Woolf

(of E. M. Forster) He is limp and damp and milder than the breath of a cow. – Virginia Woolf

No one has written worse English than Mr (Thomas) Hardy in some of his novels – cumbrous, stilted, ugly and inexpressive. – Virginia Woolf

I am reading Henry James . . . and feel myself as one entombed in a block of smooth amber. – Virginia Woolf

(of James Joyce's *Ulysses*) The work of a queasy undergraduate squeezing his pimples. – Virginia Woolf

(of Katherine Mansfield) Her mind is a very thin soil, laid an inch or two upon very barren rock. – Virginia Woolf

I don't care for Osbert (Sitwell)'s prose; the rhododendrons grow to such a height in it. – Virginia Woolf

In the throes of composition George S. Kaufman seems to crawl up the walls of the apartment in the manner of the late Count Dracula. – Alexander Woollcott

Reading Proust is like bathing in someone else's dirty water. – Alexander Woollcott

I have just read a long novel by Henry James. Much of it made me think of the priest condemned for a long space to confess nuns. – W. B. Yeats

(of George Moore) A man carved from a turnip looking out from astonished eyes. – W. B. Yeats

The way Bernard Shaw believes in himself is very refreshing in these atheistic days when so many people believe in no God at all. – Israel Zangwill

MEDIA

Newspapers and Magazines

(Piers) Morgan shows himself to be an ill-mannered, thin-skinned, easily flattered, narcissistic ignoramus, given to stupid jokes, banal observations, casual rudeness and hypocritical pieties. – David Aaronovitch

Howard Cosell was gonna be a boxer when he was a kid, only they couldn't find a mouthpiece big enough. – Muhammad Ali

They should give gossip columnist Joyce Haber open-heart surgery – and go in through her feet. – Julie Andrews

Nigel Dempster thinks he has the might of a duke and the gravitas of a senior politician. He believes that if Britain's 200 top men were profiled, he would be among them. – Anon

Take one black widow spider, cross it with a scorpion, wean their poisonous offspring on a mixture of prussic acid and treacle, and you'll get the honeyed sting of Hedda Hopper. – Anon

Self-worship was Hedda Hopper's approach. Her living room had a shrine centred on a magazine cover of Hedda, framed in real gold, she said. The cover was blown up to worship-size, and there were even votive candles flanking the holy likeness of St Hedda, whose favourite pastimes were her cocktail bar, going to the races, and trying to crucify anyone who crossed her or she didn't like. – Lew Ayres

People used to throw Christians to the lions. Now they just throw them to the Press. – Tammy Faye Bakker

The four pillars of wisdom that support journalistic endeavours are: lies, stupidity, money-grubbing, and ethical irresponsibility. – Marlon Brando

By the year 2015 all newspaper articles will be delivered to your cerebral cortex via wireless connection the moment they're written. Apart from Richard Littlejohn's columns, because he won't be writing them any more. Instead he'll scrape a living masturbating for pennies in abandoned shop doorways. I hope. – Charlie Brooker, *The Guardian*

Journalism could be described as turning one's enemies into money. – Craig Brown

The food is excellent. The beer is cold. The sun nearly always shines. There is coffee on every corner. Rupert Murdoch no longer lives there. Life doesn't get much better than this. – Bill Bryson, on the joys of Australia

Drew Pearson can find scandal in Snow White's relations with the Seven Dwarfs. – William F. Buckley Jr.

There's Adam Clymer, a major league asshole from the *New York Times*. – George W. Bush to a colleague during the 2000 Presidential campaign. Bush was unaware that his microphone had been switched on and that his confidential aside would be heard by millions.

(of the *Daily Mail*) Vile, the worst of British values posing as the best. – Alastair Campbell

Gossip columnist Rona Barrett doesn't need a steak knife. She cuts her food with her tongue. – Johnny Carson

Journalism is popular, but it is popular mainly as fiction. Life is one world, and life seen in the newspapers another. – G.K. Chesterton

(of Howard Cosell) If you split this guy open, demons and poison would spill all over the floor. He's one of the least attractive human beings I've ever been associated with. – Bob Costas

Julie Burchill is just the Glenda Slag of modern pop-writing. – Elvis Costello

My loathing of critics and gossip columnists isn't buried deep. It's right on the surface. – Joseph Cotten

Every building you come out of, there is a parasite there exercising his constitutional right to make money out of being a parasite, trying to take your photo. – Russell Crowe on the paparazzi

Archibald Forbes rarely waited for the end of a battle to report it and sometimes did not even wait for the beginning. – R. J. Cruickshank

What's the difference between a three-week-old puppy and a sportswriter? In six weeks, the puppy stops whining. – Mike Ditka

(of Clare Boothe Luce) No woman of our time has gone further with less mental equipment. – Clifton Fadiman

Many people would no more think of entering journalism than the sewage business – which at least does us all some good. – Stephen Fry

I believe in equality for everyone, except reporters and photographers. – Mahatma Gandhi

Hedda Hopper was a mental defective. She wore corrective hats. – Stewart Granger

(of James Gordon Bennett) A low-mouthed, blatant, witless, brutal scoundrel. – Horace Greeley

If you can't get a job as a pianist in a brothel you become a royal reporter. – Max Hastings.

Personal columnists are jackals and no jackal has been known to live on grass once he had learned about meat – no matter who killed the meat for him. – Ernest Hemingway

Jack Anderson is the lowest form of human being to walk the earth. He's a muckraker who lies, steals and let me tell you this . . . he'll go lower than dog shit for a story. – J. Edgar Hoover

Mocking (Hugh) Hefner is easy to do, and in my view should be made even easier. – Clive James

Rude, vile pigs. That's what all of you are. – Elton John to paparazzi

The fact that a man is a newspaper reporter is evidence of some flaw of character. – Lyndon B. Johnson

Louella Parsons' writings stand out like an asthmatic's gasp. – Nunnally Johnson

Nobody beats a bunch of journalists for inflating their rather mundane, straightforward chores with a lot more melodrama and self-importance than the job should be asked to contain. – Larry King

Those of us forced to read the London papers sometimes speculate about which is greater: the average British hack's sloth, mendacity, ignorance, obsequiousness, capacity for drink, or aversion to paying for that drink. Smart money tends to split between the latter two. – Larry King

Never trust a smiling reporter. – Ed Koch

Journalist: a person without any ideas but with an ability to express them. – Karl Kraus

More than illness or death, the American journalist fears standing alone against the whim of his owners or the prejudices of his audience. Deprive William Safire of the insignia of the *New York Times*, and he would have a hard time selling his truths to a weekly broadsheet in suburban Duluth. – Lewis H. Lapham

The invasion of photographers in a lot of people's lives is too much. If you took away their cameras they would be stalkers and freaks. Most of them are anyway, or at least they look like it. – Jude Law

Sean Penn has published a four-thousand-word essay in Friday's *New York Times* defending his visit to Iraq and his position on the war. That's pretty amazing, a writer for the *New York Times* who actually visited the places he's writing about. – Jay Leno

Did you see what made this week's *New York Times* bestseller list for fiction? It was the *New York Times*! – David Letterman

The basic difference between a sportswriter and a sports talker is that one wishes he could write the Great American Novel and the other wishes he could read it. – Bernie Lincicome

What a squalid and irresponsible little profession it (journalism) is. Nothing prepares you for how bad Fleet Street really is until it craps on you from a great height. – Ken Livingstone

If I blow my nose, the *Daily Mail* would say I'm trying to spread germ warfare. – Ken Livingstone

I don't read the tabloids much. I've even trained my family not to call me and tell me what the garbage is, because unless they're saying you're killing dogs in the stairway for some religious ritual, it's better not to know. – Jennifer Lopez

What's the penalty for killing a photographer – one stroke or two? – Davis Love III, professional golfer

Every journalist has a novel in him, which is an excellent place for it. – J. Russell Lynes

If a person is not talented enough to be a novelist, not smart enough to be a lawyer, and his hands are too shaky to perform operations, he becomes a journalist. – Norman Mailer

One reporter asked me if my arms had always been this long. I told him that, no, they had grown, just like the rest of me. – Kevin McHale, basketball player

Every time Conrad Black's in the paper, he's aged ten years. He looks like Gollum now. – Rick Mercer

Oh, how I love to be interviewed! How I look forward to answering certain questions which have, since they've been asked so often, become like old friends, family even. – Bette Midler

Hedda Hopper was venomous, vicious, a pathological liar, and quite stupid. – Ray Milland

(of Peter Arnett) How am I supposed to trust the honesty of a reporter that has that bad a combover on top of his head? He's got four hairs left and he's swirling them around . . . This guy is dangerously close to pulling hair over from another guy's head. Hey, guess what Pete? We know you're bald, OK? The outside of your skull is as empty as the inside. – Dennis Miller

(of Ian Hislop) A minuscule balding lump of cynical lard. – Piers Morgan

Sure I know where the Press room is. I just look for where they throw the dog meat. – Martina Navratilova

I wish I could sue the *New York Post* but it's awfully hard to sue a garbage can. – Paul Newman

(Richard) Littlejohn, who in the farmyard of humanity would surely occupy a sty. – Matthew Norman

Now that Martha Stewart is out of jail, she's going to go back to writing a monthly column for her magazine. This month's column explains how to hot-glue seashells to your electronic ankle bracelet. – Conan O'Brien

(of Louella Parsons) A very old tadpole. – Lilli Palmer

(of movie critic Pauline Kael) A demented bag lady. – Alan Parker

(on hearing that Clare Boothe Luce is supposedly kind to her inferiors) Wherever does she find them? – Dorothy Parker

This is a newspaper, isn't it? It just has to be true until tomorrow. – Terry Pratchett, *The Truth*

In the next issue of *Cosmopolitan*, Howard Cosell will be the centrefold with his vital organ covered – his mouth. – Burt Reynolds

Hello! Magazine is to serious issues what the World Wrestling Federation sticker album is to children's literature. – Mary Riddell

No self-respecting fish would want to be wrapped in a (Rupert) Murdoch newspaper. – George Royko

Rona Barrett has all the warmth of a self-service station at 2 a.m. – Tom Shales

Hedda Hopper is as timid as a buzzsaw. – Casey Shawhan

(It's) Piers Morgan, who used to be editor of *The Mirror*. He's got a whole new career now, as the bloke who used to be editor of *The Mirror*. – Linda Smith

The *New York Times* list is a bunch of crap. They ought to call it the editor's choice. It sure isn't based on sales. – Howard Stern

In one year I travelled four hundred and fifty thousand miles by air. That's eighteen and a half times around the world or once around Howard Cosell's head. – Jackie Stewart

Where journalists are concerned there is no word so derogatively stinking that it sums up the congested stink of their constipation. – Caitlin Thomas

Journalists are like whores; as high as their ideals may be, they still have to resort to tricks to make money. – Pierce Thorne

The only qualities for real success in journalism are ratlike cunning, a plausible manner and a little literary ability. – Nicholas Tomalin

(of Drew Pearson) There is one columnist in Washington who wouldn't have room on his breast if he got a ribbon for every time he's been called a liar. – Harry S. Truman

How often we recall with regret that Naopleon once shot at a magazine editor and missed him and killed a publisher. But we remember with charity that his intentions were good. – Mark Twain

(of Hedda Hopper) Her virtue was that she said what she thought, her vice that what she thought didn't amount to much. – Peter Ustinov

The tabloids are just porn that any kid off the street can go and buy for 50p. – Holly Valance

In the hierarchy of predatory animals, journalists are the carrion eaters. – Jacques Welter

Journalism: an ability to meet the challenge of filling the space. – Rebecca West

(of James Gordon Bennett) A midnight ghoul preying on rottenness and repulsive filth. – Walt Whitman

The public have an insatiable curiosity to know everything. Except what is worth knowing. Journalism, conscious of this, and having tradesman-like habits, supplies their demands. – Oscar Wilde

As for modern journalism, it is not my business to defend it. It justifies its own existence by the great Darwinian principle of the survival of the vulgarist. – Oscar Wilde, *The Critic As Artist*

Bad manners make a journalist. – Oscar Wilde

(Editor) Frank Harris is invited to all of the great houses in England – once. – Oscar Wilde

The nicest thing I can say about Frances Farmer is that she is unbearable. – William Wyler

I hate journalists. There is nothing in them but tittering jeering emptiness. They have all made what Dante calls the Great Refusal. The shallowest people on the ridge of the earth. – W. B. Yeats

Radio and Television

I welcome him like I welcome cold sores. – Paula Abdul on her fellow *American Idol* judge, Simon Cowell

Can you imagine Simon (Cowell) as a kid? His imaginary friends probably never wanted to play with him. – Paula Abdul

Noel Edmonds has been nominated for a BAFTA. Boy, he must feel five feet tall. – Paul Adams

The X Factor is a rubbish part of our culture; the sooner we bin it the better. – Damon Albarn

(to Jenni Falconer) You can do anything you like on this show. It's not like GMTV where you just have to be dull. – Simon Amstell, *Never Mind The Buzzcocks*

Theatre is life. Cinema is art. Television is furniture. – Anon

Cilla Black's cackling laugh sounds like the entire River Mersey disappearing down a giant plughole. – Anon

Running the marathon is no great hardship compared to the tortuous ordeal of being interviewed afterwards by Sally Gunnell. – Anon

The secret of Matthew Kelly's appeal remains a closely guarded secret. – Anon

Richard Madeley has the looks and personality of a shop-window dummy. – Anon

Tests have proven that the best way to get your children to go to bed early is to tell them they can stay up and watch Graham Norton. – Anon

Sir Alan Sugar has the looks and charm of a warthog long since ostracized by polite warthog society. – Anon

Dale Winton: camper than a row of tents. – Anon

According to the *Sun*, Noel Edmonds has developed a crush on Natasha Kaplinsky. He said, "When I was on BBC Breakfast, I just stared at her for about ten seconds – I go purely on looks." Bad luck Noel: so does she. – Alexander Armstrong, *Have I Got News For You*

I have come to the feeling about television the way I do about hamburgers: I eat a lot of hamburgers and I don't remember a single one of them. – John Barrow

Whoever told Simon Cowell he had ears? He can't even dress properly. People who should be selling fruit and veg are talking about art, and music is art. – Boy George

Stephen Fry: The original Cinderella stories were quite gruesome. When the ugly sisters tried to slip into the slipper, they cut off their toes and bunions to try and squeeze in, and the slippers filled with blood.
Jo Brand: They probably got that idea from Trinny and Susannah. – *QI*

David Blunkett is doing *Celebrity Wife Swap*. He gets the wife, and the other bloke gets the dog. – Rory Bremner

(of *The Apprentice*) Alan Sugar shrieks like a huge indignant hedgehog at the point of climax. – Charlie Brooker

In many ways, *Big Brother* is the present day equivalent of a 1980s Club 18-30 Holiday – flirting, sunbathing, silly little organised games, and lots of people you'd like to remove from the gene pool with a cricket bat. – Charlie Brooker, *the Guardian*

(of *Celebrity Big Brother*) Jade (Goody), Jo (O'Meara) and Danielle (Lloyd) – collectively the world's thickest coven – are relentlessly haranguing blameless Bollywood star Shilpa Shetty over an endless series of imaginary crimes. I don't think they're racist, just unbelievably dumb. They're motivated by an intense, aching jealousy they're simply too stupid to process. – Charlie Brooker, *the Guardian*

Right now, the theme is *Sex In The 80s*, which must've been an exceptionally hard sell round Channel 4 Towers. Mullets! Tits! Duran Duran! More tits! Bigger mullets! Ha ha ha! All you need is a few seconds of voiceover babble about "changing attitudes" and "social upheaval" laid over the top and hey presto: you've justified everything. It's not just a load of tit shots – it's a sociological investigation. With tit shots. – Charlie Brooker, *the Guardian*

24 now seems to consist of endless Space Invader waves of sharp-suited suicide bombers, overseen by a furious Middle East maniac who closely resembles a bald Dean Gaffney (which goes some way to explaining his fury). – Charlie Brooker, *the Guardian*

Noel Edmonds looks just the sort of chap to chip in, "You can tell it's only ketchup" halfway through a horror movie. – Craig Brown

I watched a rerun on television of a 1960s comedy programme called *Mr Ed*, which was about a talking horse. Judging by the quality of the jokes, I would guess that Mr Ed wrote his own material. – Bill Bryson, *The Lost Continent*

I'm just grateful that Simon Bates is too hideous for TV. – Garry Bushell

(of Ian Hislop) A potato-headed smug-bucket. – Garry Bushell

Jan (Leeming) says she'll take her clothes off for £250,000. Can we have a whip round and pay her not to? It could put you off dried fruit for life. – Garry Bushell

Graham Norton puts the flaw in dance floor. – Garry Bushell

Des O'Connor is suffering from a hernia. Is it any wonder? He's been carrying Melanie Sykes for years. – Garry Bushell

Des O'Connor is to host *Countdown*. Is that a good idea? Des is seventy-four. Does he really want to do a show where you press a button and watch thirty seconds of your life tick away? – Garry Bushell

Kate Thornton, a woman whose broadcasting career is more mysterious than the Turin Shroud. – Garry Bushell

One man's perversion is another man's Phil Donahue Show. – Johnny Carson

Fox News gives you both sides of every story – the President's side and the Vice President's side. – Stephen Colbert

(of Simon Cowell) He of the tight smile, the high waistband and the oil slick charm. – Patrick Collins

(Dan) Maskell won immoderate praise by rousing himself two or three times an hour to murmur "Oooooh! I say!" or "What a peach of a volleh!" The Americans could never grasp the concept of a tennis commentator who specialised in sepulchral silence. And they were not alone. – Patrick Collins

Eddie Waring divided his descriptive talents between Rugby League and *It's A Knockout* and few could discern the difference. Waring was a northern cliché who tried far too hard to project his own idiosyncrasies. — Patrick Collins

Trinny (Woodall) is thin with very short legs, no boobs . . . she's as flat as a prairie. — Susannah Constantine

My biggest regret in life is saving David Frost from drowning. — Peter Cook

Paula (Abdul)'s a pain in the ass. She's just one of those irritating people. I keep my time with her to a minimum. — Simon Cowell

Big Brother is not reality anymore. You don't get ten normal people to do it. You get ten crap actors in the house. — Simon Cowell

Mr (David) Letterman is rather difficult to work for (as a guest) because he expects you to be funny, and frequently, but not quite as funny as he is. — Quentin Crisp

(of Jade Goody in *Big Brother*) How stupid was she? Very. She uses common knowledge when she means general knowledge, East Angular when she means East Anglia, insomina when she means insomnia, escape goat when she means scapegoat. She thought Sherlock Holmes was the son of Mother Theresa, who she thought was a German nurse. She thought there were seasides in Birmingham. Asked to name two vegetables growing in the garden, she came up with "strawberries and spuds". What possibly can the future hold for one so thick-skinned/thick? A career in TV, of course. — thecustard.tv

I'm Kirstie Allsopp. I wasn't born, I was knitted. — *Dead Ringers*

David Dickinson, the love child of Peter Stringfellow and a mahogany hat stand. — *Dead Ringers*

(of Noel Edmonds on *Deal Or No Deal*) Twenty-two identical sealed boxes. A tiny, tiny beard. And no questions, except one. Where the hell do I buy my shirts? — *Dead Ringers*

(of *Fame Academy*) Tonight we've got twelve contestants, three judges, two viewers. — *Dead Ringers*

Hugh Fearnley-Whittingstall, the secret love child of Alan Davies and Dougal from *The Magic Roundabout*. — *Dead Ringers*

Hello, you're watching *Newsnight Review*, so you've probably lost your remote control. – *Dead Ringers*

Bill Oddie, the missing link between man and shrub. – *Dead Ringers*

If wallpaper could speak, it would say, "Hello, I'm Nick Ross." – *Dead Ringers*

Television . . . is a medium of entertainment which permits millions of people to listen to the same joke at the same time, and yet remain lonesome. – T. S. Eliot

CBS News today has fired four employees for wildly fabricating a news story. The good news: they all got jobs over at Fox. – Craig Ferguson

Jack Lord has made hairspray for men acceptable. That is his obsession; wind-proof hair. He never worries about his face. His plastic surgeon in Beverly Hills does that – every five years. – Totie Fields

(of Michael Buerk) A miserable old bat. – Anna Ford

In 1982 I played a character in *Blade Runner* that hunts down and kills bloodthirsty humanoid life forms known as replicants. I want to say we were ahead of our time – it was four years before anybody had ever heard of Jerry Springer. – Harrison Ford

Stick ten 3ft 6in hurdles in front of Colin Jackson and even now, judging by his shape, he will glide over them with grace and speed. Getting from the start of a sentence to the end without stumbling is another matter, beyond his comfort zone. Faced with having to talk the talk rather than walk the walk, he falls to the ground in a heap of mangled syntax and twisted malapropisms. – Alan Fraser, on the athlete-turned-BBC television commentator

Sean Lock (to Alan Davies): Aren't you supposed to be an actor?
Stephen Fry: Have you <u>seen</u> *Jonathan Creek*? – *QI*

I wish there were a knob on the TV to turn up the intelligence. There's a knob called "brightness", but that doesn't work. – Gallagher

(of *Celebrity Fit Club*) You know what Rik Waller's body fat was? Sixty percent. I looked that up. That is the same per cent as a pork scratching. – Ricky Gervais

Television: a three-to-four-to-five-hour experience with nothingness. – Frederic Glezer

Dorothy: Now look, all this nonsense has to stop, Rose. What we saw was not a UFO.
Rose: Well, it wasn't a plane. Planes aren't that thin, or that bright.
Dorothy: Neither is Oprah Winfrey, but that doesn't make her a flying saucer. – *The Golden Girls*

Television has raised writing to a new low. – Samuel Goldwyn

Terry Bradshaw certainly adds some intelligence to the profession. When he was in high school, he nearly froze to death at the drive-in movie waiting to see *Closed for the Winter*. – Argus Hamilton

Can you bloody imagine it? He'd be scary. He would roar around London in a Lamborghini with a huge mayoral flagpole, shooting cyclists. – Richard Hammond on the thought of Jeremy Clarkson standing for Mayor of London

(of TV pop talent shows) From a musical point of view, these shows do not have any value. I totally believe they have devalued us, taken us back to light entertainment and voyeurism. – Brent Hansen, MTV executive

(of *Pop Idol* wannabes) I wish them the very best of luck in their careers . . . in McDonald's. – Dan Hawkins

I can't watch TV longer than five minutes without praying for nuclear holocaust. – Bill Hicks

Newsreader Moira Stuart has the type of face that would look at home peering over a five-barred gate. – Stafford Hildred

Celebrity Fit Club: they're not celebrities, they're not fit and there's no club. – Harry Hill

(of David Frost) The man who wears his hair back to front. – Frankie Howerd

(of *Sunrise*, Sky News) According to the adverts it's the show that "serves up a bit of everything". No wonder Eamonn Holmes joined. – Ian Hyland

John McCririck looks like a hedge dragged through a man backwards. – Clive James

Murray (Walker) sounds like a blindfolded man riding a unicycle on the rim of the pit of doom. – Clive James

(Terry) Wogan's is a bionic smile if I ever saw one. My guess is that the BBC built him in their own workshops. – Clive James

The X Factor is a cruise ship show. I've got nothing against the people who go on – good luck to them – but I hate how they're treated. They're given an awful sense of stardom and pressure straight away but they're only successful until the next series. – Elton John

The hideous Howard Stern has boasted about not having had his nose fixed. Why didn't he have his taste fixed? You could look up "bad taste" and "deliberately bigoted misinformation" in the dictionary, and Howard's ugly puss would be in there, illustrating the definition. – Jed Johnson

The last time I watched BBC World, a presenter was announcing the forthcoming transmission of a programme about a subject so obscure I wasn't sure if it was a place or an illness. Not only are the subjects dull, but some of the presenters are so unemotional they look capable of removing the pathos from the closing moments of *La Bohème*. – Dylan Jones

Tess Daly is a good example of the young crowd of presenters who are pretty useless. – Ulrika Jonsson

(of David Dimbleby) If degrees were handed out for bumptiousness, he would emerge with first-class honours. – John Junor

Television, despite its enormous presence, turns out to have added pitifully few lines to the communal memory. – Justin Kaplan

Cilla Black has quit *Blind Date* after eighteen years. She says the show's become more like work than fun. Now you know what it's like to watch it, Cilla. – Patrick Kielty

Good taste would likely have the same effect on Howard Stern that daylight has on Dracula. – Ted Koppel

Seeing a murder on television can help work off one's antagonisms. And if you haven't any antagonisms, the commercials will give you some. – Ernie Kovacs (to Clive Anderson) There's nothing better in showbiz than someone else's show being cancelled, as you'll find out at the end of this series. – Mark Lamarr

Dave Gahan of Depeche Mode has a pierced perineum, which is the bit between the scrotum and the arsehole. Just think Sharon Osbourne in between Louis Walsh and Simon Cowell. – Mark Lamarr, *Never Mind The Buzzcocks*

David Hasselhoff: more wooden than Pinocchio with a stiffie. – Mark Lamarr, *Never Mind The Buzzcocks*

It is easy to laugh at David Hasselhoff's pomposity. But first of all you should laugh at his hair. Then you should laugh at his face, his teeth, his name, his hair again, his acting ability, his singing ability and his grasp of his place in the scheme of things. – Mark Lamarr, *Never Mind The Buzzcocks*

Last year, David Hasselhoff was arrested in California for drink driving but the officers recognized him from *Baywatch* and so they let him off with a caution . . . to drink more and drive faster. They even threw in a map of notorious local death traps. – Mark Lamarr, *Never Mind The Buzzcocks*

The FX Channel has come out with a new drama called *Nip/Tuck*. They say it's the first TV show about plastic surgery. Really? What was *Baywatch*? – Jay Leno

NBC is going to do a reality show with soccer star David Beckham and his wife, Posh Spice of the Spice Girls. The goal is to combine the popularity of NBC with the attendance of US soccer and the relevance of the Spice Girls to create the lowest-rated show in history. – Jay Leno

Valentine's Day is the day you should be with the person you love the most. I understand Simon Cowell spent the day alone. – Jay Leno

Monica Lewinsky is hosting a new reality show for Fox. The show is called *Mr Personality*, where a woman will try to choose between twenty men who all have masks on and Monica Lewinsky offers dating advice. Well, who better to offer advice on choosing a guy without seeing his face than Monica Lewinsky? – Jay Leno

Rush Limbaugh is back at work. Doctors said his rehab was successful, but it could be weeks before he's a hundred percent self-righteous. – Jay Leno

The big rumour in Washington is that President (George W.) Bush is about to hire Tony Snow of Fox News to be his new press secretary. His job will be to defend everything the President does, so it's basically a lateral move. It's basically the same thing he's doing now. – Jay Leno

I never watch the *Dinah Shore Show* – I'm a diabetic. – Oscar Levant

(of Ant and Dec) A double act with two straight men. – Victor Lewis-Smith

(of Chris Morris) Imitation is the sincerest form of being an untalented thieving bastard. – Victor Lewis-Smith

In the US, shooting crap means gambling, whereas in the UK, it means Louis Theroux is back making another pointless documentary. – Victor Lewis-Smith

(of Craig Kilborn) As dumb as a post. – Beth Littleford

Heather Mills McCartney has been signed up to star in the American version of *Strictly Come Dancing*. She'll be the one doing the pogo. – Richard Littlejohn

(of fellow Fox Sports analyst Terry Bradshaw) He's like the big brother I never wanted. – Howie Long

Television has no regard for the absence or presence of talent: it merely makes you "famous". – Joanna Lumley

The difference between writing a book and being on television is the difference between conceiving a child and having a baby made in a test tube. – Norman Mailer

I would rather sleep in a bunk-bed under Oprah! – *Married . . . With Children*

If the television craze continues with the present level of programmes, we are destined to have a nation of morons. – Daniel Marsh

I find television very educational. Every time someone switches it on I go into another room and read a good book. – Groucho Marx

Erik Estrada – the only actor who can show all thirty-two teeth while *crying*. – Edwin McCain

60 Minutes is to journalism what *Charley's Aunt* is to criminology. – John McNulty

(to Lorraine Kelly) What plans do you have for the menpause? – Mrs Merton

(on the epidemic of TV celebrity shows) They're doing a new show, *Celebrity Corpse*, where you dig up someone after five years and try to guess who they were. – Paul Merton

John Peel could be a grumpy, cantankerous old sod. – Chris Moyles

I've experienced a great deal of enjoyment when it hasn't worked out for Johnny Vaughan. I've never met him, but he's been dismissive of me, so I love it when his ratings plummet. I'd love to push him out of the radio business. I won't rest until he's off the dial. The only good thing about him is that he's got better legs than Lauren Laverne. – Chris Moyles

(of David Frost) He rose without a trace. – Kitty Muggeridge

Television was not invented to make human beings vacuous, but is an emanation of their vacuity. – Malcolm Muggeridge

I have had my television aerials removed. It is the moral equivalent of a prostate operation. – Malcolm Muggeridge

Neighbours is like National Service in Australia. Draft dodgers are all backpacking across Europe. – Al Murray

I have tried to analyse just what it is about (BBC newsreader) Fiona Bruce that makes me hit the off button before she utters a single word. Is it her flirtatious, conspiratorial smile? Her habit of stressing the wrong words in every sentence? The exaggeratedly slow bedtime-story tone that prevents any headline from sounding more serious than a broken nail? – Philip Norman

The BBC's political editor, Nick Robinson, gives Westminster reporting all the gravitas of the comedian Harry Hill. – Philip Norman

Like Anne Robinson in a Korean restaurant, it'll be dog eat dog. – Graham Norton

The producers of *Sesame Street* say they have decided not to ask Russell Crowe to appear on the show because they don't think he's a good role model. Crowe's upset because he really wanted to host the episodes sponsored by the letters "F" and "U". – Conan O'Brien

A couple of hours ago, President (George W.) Bush arrived back in the United States after a controversial trip to England. The President said he was looking forward to seeing his loved ones. Of course he was talking about the reporters at Fox News. – Conan O'Brien

NBC announced they're going to take the show *Joey* off the air until after the Olympics. The good news is they're talking about the 2012 Olympics. – Conan O'Brien

Sally Jesse Raphael announced that after nineteen years her show has been cancelled. Executives decided to cancel her show after they realized it was still on the air. – Conan O'Brien

CBS news anchor Dan Rather has interviewed Iraqi dictator Saddam Hussein. When asked what it was like to talk to a crazy man, Saddam said, "It's not so bad." – Conan O'Brien

Legendary newsman Mike Wallace announced that he is retiring from *60 Minutes* at the age of eighty-eight. When asked why, Wallace said he wants to spend more time with his grandchildren now that they have also retired. – Conan O'Brien

Mike Wallace says that *60 Minutes* now refers to how long it takes him to pee. – Conan O'Brien

Ages ago, Louis Walsh said he hated me and he thought I sucked. Two years later I was in the same room as him and he didn't even have the balls to introduce himself to me. He said "Hello" to every single member of my family except me. I think he's a spineless prick. – Kelly Osbourne

Simon (Cowell) is a pompous little prick who walks like he has a stick stuck up his arse. – Sharon Osbourne

He likes manufactured shit. He wouldn't like a woman with an identity of her own who could answer back. He thinks all women should be like blow-up dolls, have big tits and do whatever he says. – Sharon Osbourne attacking Simon Cowell after he had described her daughter Kelly as "ugly"

(of Charlotte Church's TV chat show) I saw the new show and I think if I was her producer I would have a word with her . . . She need not swear so much, she need not remind us all the time that she's Welsh. – Michael Parkinson

My broadcast partners are Joe Theismann and Dick Vitale, so I am unaccustomed to public speaking. – Mike Patrick

They travel the globe to tell the audience of the dangers of climate change, while leaving a vapour trail which will make the problem even worse. – Jeremy Paxman, on the BBC's environment correspondents

Jan Leeming is one of the most whingeing, self-obsessed people ever seen on TV. No wonder her five husbands all made a run for it. – Allison Pearson

(of Alan Sugar) A self-styled ogre whose views are as outdated as one of his clunky old computers. – Allison Pearson

Inviting Kate Thornton to host a talent show was like asking a water buffalo to perform *Swan Lake*. For many (*X Factor*) contestants, it wasn't singing in front of the panel that was the ordeal. It was the sympathetic chat with the ghastly Miss Thornton afterwards. – Allison Pearson

I thought Tony Blackburn was the Antichrist – a totally created person, jollity and friendliness at the flick of a switch. – John Peel

(of Chris Moyles) Dave Lee Travis in waiting. – John Peel

I would sooner kiss Garrison Savannah's arse than speak to Julian Wilson. – Jenny Pitman, racehorse trainer, declining an interview with the BBC's racing presenter.

(Chris) Evans is caught in some Eighties time warp, as dated as a Sony Walkman in an iPod world. – Amanda Platell

Clearly newsreader Natasha Kaplinsky is to become the acceptable face of BBC dumbing down. They certainly don't come much dumber. – Amanda Platell

(of *Celebrity Wrestling*) Lobotomised monkeys would find it insulting to their intelligence. – Julia Raeside

(to Radio 4's *Today* presenter Sarah Montague) You're the closest thing this programme has to a pin-up. – Garry Richardson

(to David Letterman) Why are you always speeding? It's not like you've got people holding their breath till you get there. – Don Rickles

In the next episode of Anna Nicole Smith's reality series, she talks about the worst four years of her life. Third grade. – Joan Rivers

(to Anne Robinson) Is it true that you make your own yoghurt – you get a pint of milk and stare at it? – Ted Robbins

Who's judging *American Idol*? Paula Abdul! Paula Abdul judging a singing contests is like Christopher Reeve judging a dance contest. – Chris Rock

Diddy David Hamilton has a hair-do which makes him look like a newly thatched cottage. – Jean Rook

GMTV bone brain Fiona Phillips is moving to Italy after watching Tuscany on telly. Great. But shame she wasn't watching *Lost In Space*. – Ally Ross

Dumpy Kate Thornton presents a TV travel show, so does that make her a rough guide? – Ally Ross

The smallest bookstore still contains more ideas of worth than have been presented in the entire history of television. – Andrew Ross

(to Damon Albarn) I'd love to see you host a talk show. It would be rubbish but I'd watch. – Jonathan Ross

Kim and Aggie: cleaners who became celebrities. Like the Cheeky Girls in reverse. – Jonathan Ross

Michael Fish has retired. He's got the weather almost right for the last time. Don't mention the hurricane. *He* didn't. – Jonathan Ross

(of Fiona Phillips on *Strictly Come Dancing*) It was like someone trying to move a fridge. It was like she'd never learned to walk. – Jonathan Ross

(of Michael Parkinson) That guy was like some kind of disapproving father. He's a nut. I felt like he was berating me for being naked in the movie. – Meg Ryan

(of Johnny Carson) He's an anaesthetist: Prince Valium. – Mort Sahl

(to Pamela Anderson) I commend you on all you've done for PETA, wrestling the one-eyed trouser snake with your bare hands, gently cuddling it in your arms, and nurturing it back to health. – Sarah Silverman

Four days of daytime TV is my personal limit. If I see another triumph over weight loss, I think I'll kill myself. – *Six Feet Under*

What do ITV and fish fingers have in common? – After two or three minutes, you have to turn them over. – Frank Skinner

Top hats look 100 percent ridiculous on anybody, but on, for example, Willie Carson, it's like attaching a factory chimney to a bungalow. – Giles Smith

Reality shows are all the rage on TV at the moment. But that's not reality, it's just another aesthetic form of fiction. – Steven Soderbergh

(of *Big Brother*) The show is compulsive viewing, but then so were public hangings in years gone by. – Jaci Stephen

The most frightening thing on television since Anthea Turner revealed she had a sister. – Suggs

Sophie Anderton has all the credentials to be a reality TV star – vanity, vacuousness and the right vital statistics. – David Thomas

I don't care which house I live in, so long as you aren't in it. – Ingrid Tarrant to estranged husband Chris

The TV business is a cruel and shallow money trench, a long plastic hallway where thieves and pimps run free and good men die like dogs. – Hunter S. Thompson

(of *American Idol*) I ranked the contestants with three levels: gay, very gay, and Clay Aiken. – Triumph, the Insult Comic Dog

(of Rosie O'Donnell) She's a mental midget, a low-life. – Donald Trump

Malcolm Muggeridge: a garden gnome expelled from Eden. – Kenneth Tynan

There are days when any electrical appliance in the house, including the vacuum cleaner, seems to offer more entertainment possibilities than the TV set. – Harriet Van Horne

(of Simon Cowell) I do believe that his world is about to come crashing down around him very soon. At least I hope so, I hate him. – Rik Waller

(of Simon Cowell) It's all me, me, me – that's the way he is on and off the show. Sometimes I think he is so arrogant and pompous. He is so argumentative, but he doesn't have any musical integrity. He is outdated in his musical tastes. – Louis Walsh, on judging *The X Factor*

Whenever it (television) is on, it's like having somebody in my house that I want to get rid of and they won't leave. I hate the sound of it. All that noise and light coming from a piece of furniture. – John Waters

People are forever asking: "What's Pamela Anderson like?" Like I give a shit! – Ruby Wax, looking back on her TV series

The A & E Network says it will begin airing past episodes of *The Sopranos* without the violence, nudity or bad language. In other words, you'll be able to watch the entire first season in less than thirty minutes. – Mark Wheeler

(of television) It used to be that we in films were the lowest form of art. Now we have something to look down on. – Bill Wilder

Jane Fonda and Ted Turner broke up. Jane found God and Ted found it wasn't him. – Robin Williams

The cruellest thing that has happened to Lincoln since he was shot by Booth was to fall into the hands of Carl Sandburg. – Edmund Wilson on a TV miniseries about the life of Abraham Lincoln

(of Barbara Walters) A hyena in syrup. – Yevgeny Yevtushenko

MILITARY

Battles are sometimes won by generals; wars are nearly always won by sergeants and privates. – F. E. Adcock

(of US soldier Benjamin Franklin Butler) A man whom all the waters of Massachusetts Bay cannot wash back into decency. – Anon

If he was not a great man, he was at least a great poster. – Margot Asquith, of Field Marshall Lord Kitchener whose face appeared on First World War recruitment posters with the slogan 'Your Country Needs You'

(on T. E. Lawrence "of Arabia") He was always backing into the limelight. – Lord Berners

(of Viscount Montgomery) In defeat unbeatable; in victory unbearable. – Winston Churchill

(of French Marshal Jean-Jacques Joffre) The only time he ever put up a fight in his life was when we asked him for his resignation. – Georges Clemenceau

(of the Duke of Wellington) Waterloo was a battle of the first rank won by a captain of the second. – Victor Hugo (of Hugh S. Johnson) The General is suffering from mental saddle sores. – Harold Ickes

(General Douglas) MacArthur is the type of man who thinks that when he gets to heaven, God will step down from the great white throne and bow him into His vacated seat. – Harold Ickes

(of General Alexander Haig) One thing I don't want around me is an intellectual military. I don't have to worry about you on that score. – Henry Kissinger

(of French marshal Ferdinand Foch) Only a frantic pair of moustaches. – T. E. Lawrence

My dear McClellan, If you don't want to use the army I should like to borrow it for a while. – Abraham Lincoln in a letter to General George B. McClellan, mocking the latter's inactivity during the American Civil War

General McClellan is an admirable Engineer, but he seems to have a special talent for the stationary engine. – Abraham Lincoln (McClellan was originally an officer of the Corps of Engineers)

(of General Douglas Haig) He was brilliant to the top of his army boots. – David Lloyd George

(of Lord Kitchener) One of the revolving lighthouses which radiate momentary gleams of revealing light and then suddenly relapse into complete darkness. There are no intermediate stages. – David Lloyd George

(of General Douglas MacArthur) Never trust a man who combs his hair straight from his left armpit. – Alice Roosevelt Longworth

As for her harrowing account of her captivity, she claimed she feared she was being sized up for her coffin by a woman using a tape measure. Looking at Ms Turney's hips, it's more likely the measurements were for some XXL trousers. – Amanda Platell, on controversial British naval hostage Faye Turney who was held by the Iranians in 2007

(of General Philip H. Sheridan) The general is a stumpy, quadrangular little man, with a forehead of no promise and hair so short that it looks like a coat of black paint. – George Strong (of General Douglas MacArthur) I fired him because he wouldn't respect the authority of the President. I didn't fire him because he was a dumb son-of-a-bitch, although he was, but that's not against the law for generals. If it was, half to three-quarters of them would be in jail. – Harry S. Truman

(of US soldier Benedict Arnold) From some traits of his character which have lately come to my knowledge, he seems to have been so hackneyed in villainy, and so lost to all sense of honour and shame that while his facilities will enable him to continue his sordid pursuits, there will be no time for remorse. – George Washington

He never commanded more than ten men in his life – and he ate three of them! – General Weston, after former Arctic explorer Adolphus W. Greely was made a general

After (the Duke of) Wellington had left me, I entirely forgot him: nay, before. – Harriette Wilson

MOVIES

Katharine Hepburn has a cheekbone like a death's head allied to a manner as sinister and aggressive as crossbones. – James Agate

Surely nobody but a mother could have loved Bette Davis at the height of her career. – Brian Aherne

An associate producer is the only guy in Hollywood who will associate with the producer. – Fred Allen

Charlie Chaplin was a second-rate bicycle-acrobat who should have kept his mouth shut. – Kingsley Amis

Who can forget Mel Gibson in *Hamlet*? Though many have tried. – Harry Andrews

Arnold Schwarzenegger's acting is limited. He has an inability to pick up light objects, such as a telephone, in any sort of naturalistic way. – Nigel Andrews

Gary Cooper had two emotions: "hat on" and "hat off". – Anon

Zsa Zsa Gabor has proved beyond doubt that diamonds are the hardest things in the world – to get back. – Anon ex-boyfriend

Hugh Grant has the range of a paper airplane. – Anon

To call Charlton Heston wooden would be to risk a lawsuit from the Forestry Commission. – Anon

Victor Mature sneers and curls his upper lip so often, it gives the impression he had it permanently waved. – Anon

Margaret Rutherford's appearance suggests an overstuffed electric chair. Her writhing stare could reduce a rabid dog to a foaming jelly. – Anon

If you cross agent Ray Stark, you'd better make sure he's dead first. – Anon

What's pink, enormous, disgusting and hangs out of Michael Winner's trunks? Michael Winner. – Anon

The first rule for a young director to follow is not to direct like Michael Winner. The second and third rules are the same. – Anon

Michael Winner's films are atrocious, but they are not the worst thing about him. – Anon

When Al Jolson attends a wedding he wants to be the bride and when he attends a funeral he wants to be the corpse. – Lou Anthony

You could never do two films in a row with David Puttnam. You have to go and bathe your wounds in between. – Michael Apted

Tom Cruise is to hunks what Velveeta is to cheese. – Emile Ardolino

(to Michael Winner) A man who believes it's better to be relentless than smart and, may I say, that's a very relentless jacket. – Alexander Armstrong

(of Jean-Claude Van Damme) Acting is not his forte. Neither is being humble. – Rosanna Arquette

When you talk about a great actor, you're not talking about Tom Cruise. – Lauren Bacall

(of Maurice Chevalier) A great artiste, but a small human being. – Josephine Baker

Katharine Hepburn isn't really stand-offish. She ignores everyone equally. – Lucille Ball

(of Bette Davis) When I get hold of her, I'll tear every hair out of her moustache! – Tallulah Bankhead

Bette Davis and I are good friends. There's nothing I wouldn't say to her face – both of them. – Tallulah Bankhead

Pola Negri couldn't act her way out of a paper bag. – Tallulah Bankhead

I suppose Kirk Douglas looks all right if your tastes happen to run to septuagenarians with blow-waves and funny stretch marks round the ears. – Lynn Barber

Nowadays, Robert Redford's skin looks like a child's sandpit after heavy rain. – Lynn Barber

I couldn't stand Chris O'Donnell when we met on the set of *Batman Forever*. He was such a jock, such a frat boy, the kind of guy who expects you to be impressed by the labels on his clothes. – Drew Barrymore

(of Hollywood) The people are unreal. The flowers are unreal, they don't smell. The fruit is unreal, it doesn't taste of anything. The whole place is a glaring, gaudy, nightmarish set. – Ethel Barrymore

Diana is a horse's arse, quite a pretty one, but still a horse's arse. – John Barrymore, father of Diana Barrymore

Half the people in Hollywood are dying to be discovered and the other half are afraid they will be. – Lionel Barrymore

(of Margaret O'Brien) If that child had been born in the Middle Ages, she'd have been burned as a witch. – Lionel Barrymore

Marilyn Monroe was smart for only ten minutes in her entire life. And that was the time it took her to sign with Twentieth Century-Fox. – Anne Baxter

I knew Elizabeth Taylor when she didn't know where her next husband was coming from. – Anne Baxter

(of Katharine Hepburn) She has a face that belongs to the sea and the wind, with large rocking horse nostrils and teeth that you just know bite an apple every day. – Cecil Beaton

(of Marilyn Monroe) A broad with a big future behind her. – Constance Bennett

In Hollywood, it's like being in a cage. They thrust the parts through the bars and you take what they give you. – Ingrid Bergman (of Joan Crawford) I'm a little repulsed by her shining lips, like balloon tyres in wet weather. – John Betjeman

One wishes that Julie Andrews didn't always give the impression that she had just left her horse in the hallway. – Michael Billington

Bo Derek is a simple girl at heart, and only realists, puritans and most other sections of society would suggest that she is totally without charm and possesses an IQ slightly higher than her chest measurement. – Anne Billson

Charlie Chaplin's films are about as funny as getting an arrow through the neck and then discovering there was a gas bill tied to it. – *Blackadder*

(of Joan Collins) A hymn to overstatement if ever there was one. – Mr Blackwell

Elizabeth Taylor looks like two small boys fighting under a mink blanket. – Mr Blackwell

Renee Zellweger looks like a painted pumpkin on a pogo stick. – Mr Blackwell

When Lauren Bacall displays her sense of humour, it's like you're witnessing a solar eclipse or some rare event. – Sally Blane

Working with Cher was like being in a blender with an alligator. – Peter Bogdanovich

Some people just court celebrity for the sake of it. People like Tom Cruise. You won't ever catch me jumping up and down on *Oprah* going on about how I love this woman. I think the man's lost it. – Jon Bon Jovi

Genetic defect, serial bee-stings or, whisper it softly, collagen, I know not, but, whatever the cause of (Jennifer) Garner's pout, the overall effect is that her top lip now enters the room several seconds before the rest of her. – Matthew Bond

Brad Pitt is handsome but not that talented. And he admits he goes through four cartons of cigarettes a week. Need I say less? – Helena Bonham Carter

(of Richard Burton) He's like all these drunks. Impossible when he's drunk and only half there when he's sober. – John Boorman

(of Mel Gibson) He seems to think he's Lee Marvin – except he's two feet shorter and about one third the talent. – John Boorman

Peter Sellers was his own worst enemy, although there was plenty of competition. – Roy Boulting

(of ageing actress Yvonne Arnaud) Such a pretty face – and now there's another face around it. – Lillian Braithwaite

Mr (James) Dean appears to be wearing my last year's wardrobe and using my last year's talent. – Marlon Brando

(to Val Kilmer) You are confusing your talent with the size of your paycheck. – Marlon Brando

(of Frank Sinatra) He's the kind of guy that when he dies, he's going to go to heaven and give God a bad time for making him bald. – Marlon Brando

Maggie Smith used to have excellent skin but in a few more years they'll have to unfold it to find out who she used to be. – Jeremy Brett

(of Esther Williams) Wet she's a star, dry she ain't. – Fanny Brice

Steve McQueen's features resembled a fossilized wash rag. – Alan Brien

Evelyn (Brent)'s idea of acting was to march into a scene, spread her legs and stand flat-footed and read her lines with masculine defiance. – Louise Brooks

(Marlene) Dietrich? That contraption! She was one of the beautiful-but-dumb girls, like me, but she belonged to the category of those who thought they were smart and fooled other people into believing it. – Louise Brooks

(of Shirley Temple) A swaggering, tough little slut. – Louise Brooks

If Hollywood keeps gearing movie after movie to teenagers, next year's Oscar will develop acne. – Mel Brooks

Mel Tolkin looks like a stork that dropped a baby and broke it and is coming to explain to the parents. – Mel Brooks

Nicollette Sheridan? Personality of Spam. – Julie Brown

(of Serge Gainsbourg) A human ash-tray with duvet-sized bags between his hallucinogenic blue eyes. – Tina Brown

Cecil B. De Mille was De phoney and De hypocrite of all time. – Yul Brynner

Suicide is much easier and more acceptable in Hollywood than growing old gracefully. – Julie Burchill

(of Elizabeth Taylor) She has an insipid double chin, her legs are too short, and she has a slight pot belly. – Richard Burton

I amended the actor's cliché to "Never work with children, animals, or Denholm Elliott!" – Gabriel Byrne

(of Bette Midler) She's not a bad person, but stupid in terms of grey matter. I mean, I like her, but I like my dog, too. – James Caan

Hollywood's a very weird place. I think there's less of everything except for attitude. – Dean Cain

(of Basil Rathbone) He has a face like two profiles stuck together. – Mrs Patrick Campbell

Tallulah (Bankhead) is always skating on thin ice, and everyone wants to be there when it breaks. – Mrs Patrick Campbell

Watching the non-dancing, non-singing Fred Astaire is like watching a grounded skylark. – Vincent Canby

(of Otto Preminger) I don't think he could direct his nephew to the bathroom. – Dyan Cannon

(of Greta Garbo) Dry and draughty, like an abandoned temple. – Truman Capote

Life is difficult enough without Meryl Streep movies. And she looks like a chicken. – Truman Capote

There was an allegation that Albert Einstein wanted to take over Hollywood. Now how would you find someone with brains trying to run Hollywood? – Johnny Carson

Gloria Swanson was hideously boring and looked like a ferret. – Barbara Cartland

Ricardo Montalban is to improvised acting what Mount Rushmore is to animation. – John Cassavetes

(of Hollywood) Its idea of production value is spending a million dollars dressing up a story that any good writer would throw away. Its vision of the rewarding movie is a vehicle for some glamour-puss with two expressions and eighteen changes of costume, or for some male idol of the muddled millions with a permanent hangover, six worn-out acting tricks, the build of a lifeguard, and the mentality of a chicken-strangler. – Raymond Chandler

(of Hollywood people) Some are able and humane men and some are low-grade individuals with the morals of a goat, the artistic integrity of a slot machine, and the manners of a floorwalker with delusions of grandeur. – Raymond Chandler

(of Charlie Chaplin) He has no sense of humour, particularly about himself. – Lita Grey Chaplin

(Humphrey) Bogart's a helluva nice guy until 11.30 p.m. After that he thinks he's Bogart. – Dave Chasen

I would like to suggest to Miss Vanessa Redgrave that her winning an Academy Award is not a pivotal moment in history, does not require a proclamation, and a simple thank you would have sufficed. – Paddy Chayefsky

Jamie Lee Curtis has trouble learning her lines because English is not her first language. She doesn't, unfortunately, have a first language. – John Cleese

Last month Catherine Zeta Jones raised a few eyebrows with her flirty behaviour with veteran actor Sean Connery, a man old enough to be her husband. – Martin Clunes

(of George Peppard) He's arrogant, the sort of man who expects women to fall at his feet at the slightest command; who throws his weight around. He gives the impression that he's the star, what he says goes and that nobody else is very important. – Joan Collins

(of *Lord of the Rings*) I read the book, I read the script, I saw the movie, and I still don't understand it. – Sean Connery

Mary Pickford was the girl every young man wanted to have . . . as his sister. – Alistair Cooke

Hollywood glamour is a highly perishable coating which disappears after the first wash. – Gary Cooper

(to Claudette Colbert) I'd wring your neck, if you had one. – Noël Coward

I acted opposite Keir Dullea, a merely visually talented performer. I was later informed that he'd worked in the States as a carpenter, which did much to explain his wooden performance. – Noël Coward

(to Peter O'Toole) If you'd been any prettier it would have been *Florence of Arabia*. – Noël Coward

Faye Dunaway says she is being haunted by my mother's ghost. After her performance in *Mommie Dearest*, I can understand. – Christina Crawford

(of Bette Davis) I don't see how she built a career out of a set of mannerisms instead of acting ability. Take away the pop eyes, the cigarette and those funny clipped words, and what have you got? She's a phoney. – Joan Crawford

I didn't know Judy Garland well, but after watching her in action I didn't want to. – Joan Crawford

(of Elizabeth Taylor) A spoiled, indulgent child, a blemish on public decency. – Joan Crawford

(of Joan Crawford) Towards the end of her life she looked like a hungry insect magnified a million times – a praying mantis that had forgotten how to pray. – Quentin Crisp

(of Lana Turner) Probably the very worst actress that ever made it to the top. – John Cromwell

There's nothing I wouldn't do for Bob (Hope), and there's nothing he wouldn't do for me. And that's the way we go through life – doing nothing for each other. – Bing Crosby

I go horse riding a lot. I'd rather shovel horse manure than listen to that Hollywood bulls**t. – Mary Crosby

(of Loretta Young) Whatever it was that this actress never had, she still hasn't got it. – Bosley Crowther

If I had my way, I'd load all those Hollywood producers into a truck and drive them into the middle of the Pacific. – Tony Curtis

Hollywood is one of the few places on earth where a person with absolutely no talent can make a million dollars, and where a guy who is loaded with talent can starve to death. – Dan Dailey

(of Jayne Mansfield) A Marilyn Monroe gone to seed. – Dan Dailey

Joan Collins is to acting what her sister Jackie is to literature. – *Daily Express*

Louis B. Meyer's arm around your shoulder meant his hand was closer to your throat. – Jules Dassin

(Laurence) Olivier brandished his technique like a kind of stylistic alibi. In catching the eye, he frequently disengaged the brain. – Russell Davies

(of Sylvester Stallone) His big asset: a face that would look well upon a three-toed sloth. – Russell Davies

Keanu Reeves? I couldn't cast someone who sounds like a small Polynesian island. – Terence Davies

(of Theda Bara) She was divinely, hysterically, insanely malevolent. – Bette Davis

(of Constance Bennett) Her face was her talent, and when it dropped, so did her career, right out of sight. – Bette Davis

Why am I so good at playing bitches? I think it's because I'm not a bitch. Maybe that's why Miss (Joan) Crawford always plays ladies. – Bette Davis

The best time I ever had with Joan Crawford was when I pushed her down the stairs in *Whatever Happened to Baby Jane?* – Bette Davis

Joan Crawford has slept with every male star at MGM except Lassie. – Bette Davis

(of Joan Crawford) Those eyebrows wound up looking like African caterpillars. – Bette Davis

Joan (Crawford) always cries a lot. Her tear ducts must be close to her bladder. – Bette Davis

Lillian Gish ought to know about close-ups. Jesus, she was around when they invented them! – Bette Davis

I always admire Katharine Hepburn's cheekbones – more than her films. – Bette Davis

(of Katharine Hepburn) She sounds more and more like Donald Duck. – Bette Davis (of Miriam Hopkins) God was very good to the world. He took her from us. – Bette Davis

(of Jayne Mansfield) Dramatic art, in her opinion, is knowing how to fill a sweater. – Bette Davis

(of Glenda Jackson) She has a face to launch a thousand dredgers. – Jack De Manio

I'm George Lucas. You know, lots of people say to me, "George, why do you keep going back and tampering with the old *Star Wars* movies we love and keep creating crappy new ones we hate?" You know what I say to them? "You're fired!" – *Dead Ringers*

In his bodybuilding days Arnold Schwarzenegger was known as the Austrian Oak. Then he started acting and was known as . . . the Austrian Oak. – Jack Dee

Robert Redford's acting is as close to neutral as any I remember. He holds the camera for an eternity with his level gaze and then doesn't deliver anything. – David Denby

(of Alec Baldwin) He has eyes like a weasel. – Sandy Dennis

Whatever happened to John Travolta? I heard he joined some cult and got fat. Or he married and had a child. Which amounts to the same thing. – Gerard Depardieu

Poor Elsa (Lanchester). She left England because it already had a queen – Victoria. And she wanted to be queen of the Charles Laughton household once he became a star, but he already had the role. – Marlene Dietrich

I acted vulgar. Madonna *is* vulgar. – Marlene Dietrich

A day away from Tallulah (Bankhead) is like a month in the country. – Howard Dietz

Mickey Rooney's favourite exercise is climbing tall people. – Phyllis Diller

Bette Midler's got big tits but thank God she's got them, because she hasn't got anything else. – Divine

Barbra Streisand's face looks as though a truck ran into it. – Divine

(of wife Catherine Zeta-Jones) It's probably her greatest performance ever because she's playing a chef – and she can't boil water! – Michael Douglas

Jodie Foster is very, very, very bossy. And then some. – Robert Downey Jr

(of Hugh Grant) A self-important, boring, flash-in-the-pan Brit. – Robert Downey Jr

Descendants of the ancient Mayans in Guatemala say Mel Gibson's new movie *Apocalypto* is racist. Mayan cultural leaders object to the movie portraying their ancestors as brutal savages who sacrificed humans. They say it will only serve to promote negative stereotypes about their culture. Mel says he's sorry if anyone is offended, but he was drunk when he made the movie. – Paul Dudley

Nelson Eddy: the ham of hams. – Allan Dwan

Zsa Zsa Gabor had three or four operations on her nose and it got worse every time. It looks like an electric plug that you put in a wall. – Anita Ekberg

Kill Bill. Is it based on Hillary Clinton's diaries by any chance? – Dame Edna Everage

(to Jane Seymour) Tell me the secret of your successful marriages. – Dame Edna Everage

I heard on the news last night that they shot two innocent people in Hollywood. You know, that's surprising. I didn't know there were two innocent people in Hollywood. – Chris Farley

I hated everything about Hollywood. The brassy lingo. The lack of sensitivity and individuality. The gristmill philosophy. The yes-men. The crude and influential giants. The Seventh Avenue intrigue. The cruel caste system. The fakery. I hated everything except the money. – Frances Farmer

He was an aloof, remote person, intent on being Cary Grant playing Cary Grant playing Cary Grant. – Frances Farmer

I wouldn't want to be a dog, a horse, or a woman around Howard Hawks. – William Faulkner

The only way to make a film with Peter Sellers is to let him direct, write and produce it as well as star in it. – Charles Feldman

Tom Cruise and Nicole Kidman say their split is amicable, and they want everyone to know that after the divorce is final, their two adopted children will be returned to the prop department at Universal Studios. – Tina Fey

In order to feel safer on his private jet, John Travolta has purchased a bomb-sniffing dog. Unfortunately for the actor, the dog came six movies too late. – Tina Fey

Loretta Young was sickeningly sweet, a pure phoney. Her two faces sent me home angry and crying several times. – Virginia Field

Hollywood is the gold cap on a tooth that should have been pulled out years ago. – W. C. Fields

(of Mae West) A plumber's idea of Cleopatra. – W. C. Fields

Debbie Reynolds was indeed the girl next door. But only if you lived next door to a self-centred, totally driven, insecure, untruthful phoney. – Eddie Fisher

Don Johnson wins the Eddie Murphy prize for milking celebrity as far as it will go. – Helen Fitzgerald

Isn't Hollywood a dump – in the human sense of the word? A hideous town, pointed up by the insulting gardens of the rich, full of the human spirit at a new low of debasement. – F. Scott Fitzgerald

We were all like off an assembly line. I was being marketed as a future movie star. The roles that I played gave me no outlet for expression. When I was in New York at acting school, I was playing wonderful scenes and parts and just thoroughly enjoying the experience of acting. Suddenly, Hollywood had nothing to do with that, and I hated it. – Jane Fonda

Acting with (Laurence) Harvey is like acting by yourself – only worse. – Jane Fonda

(of Robert Redford) Secretly, I think Bob is afraid of women. He likes to tell them what to do. He likes them to be subservient. He treated me as if I were an extra or something. – Jane Fonda

(of her sister, Olivia De Havilland) I regret that I remember not one act of kindness from her all through my childhood. – Joan Fontaine

Joan Crawford had perfect posture, but it was rather intimidating. She looked as if she'd swallowed a yardstick. – Glenn Ford

Next to privacy, the rarest thing in Hollywood is a wedding anniversary. – Gene Fowler

There are two things I would never do – climb Mount Everest and work with Val Kilmer again. – John Frankenheimer

(of Barbra Streisand) She's so distasteful. – Zsa Zsa Gabor

Today you see Julia Roberts and Cameron Diaz running around looking unkempt in jogging trousers, they look like bag ladies, like homeless people. – Valentino Garavini

Clark Gable is the kind of guy who, if you say, "Hiya, Clark, how are you?", is stuck for an answer. – Ava Gardner

When Frank Sinatra was down he was sweet, but when he got back up he was hell. – Ava Gardner

Frank (Sinatra) and I were always great in bed. The trouble usually started on the way to the bidet. – Ava Gardner

(of Frank Sinatra's marriage to Mia Farrow) I always knew Frank would end up in bed with a boy. – Ava Gardner

That silly horse, Jeanette MacDonald, yakking away at wooden-peg (Nelson) Eddy with all that glycerine running down her Max Factor. – Judy Garland

My daughter (Liza Minnelli) has got a voice like chalk on a blackboard. – Judy Garland

Lana Turner's a nice girl, but it's like sitting in a room with a beautiful vase. – Judy Garland

Mel Gibson has to be the centre of attention, otherwise he gets very unhappy and leaves. – Janeane Garofalo

(of Ralph Richardson) I don't know his name but he's got a face like half a teapot. – King George VI

I'm glad you got that ugly bloke Jude Law off. Bit of glamour now on the show. That's why I'm here. I've said to him, "Jude, have something done. It's not you that's got to look at it, mate. That's why the work's drying up." – Ricky Gervais to David Letterman

Dear Ingrid (Bergman). Speaks five languages and can't act in any of them. – John Gielgud (of film-maker Michael Moore) If you're going to dedicate your career to ranting about the excesses of American capitalism, you probably shouldn't weigh four hundred and fifty pounds. – Greg Giraldo

The only thing worse than not being nominated for an Oscar would have been to be nominated and then losing to Cher. That would have been embarrassing. – Lillian Gish

Burgess (Meredith) and I had a lot in common when we got married. I loved him and he loved him. – Paulette Goddard

(of Louis B. Meyer) The only reason so many people showed up at his funeral was because they wanted to make sure he was dead. – Sam Goldwyn

It took longer to make one of Mary Pickford's contracts than it did to make one of Mary's pictures. – Sam Goldwyn

(of Kirk Douglas) Boastful, egotistical, resentful of criticism . . . if anyone dare give it. – Sheilah Graham

(Sam) Goldwyn was a monster. You really were a property. As a piece of script was.   Farley Granger

There have been times when I've been ashamed to take the money. But then I think of some of the movies that have given (Laurence) Olivier cash for his old age, and I don't feel so bad. – Stewart Granger

Julia Roberts is very big-mouthed. Literally, physically, she has a very big mouth. When I was kissing her, I was aware of a faint echo. – Hugh Grant

Ken Russell is an arrogant, self-centred, petulant individual. – Bob Guccione

Julie Andrews is like a nun with a switchblade. – Leslie Halliwell

(of Blake Edwards) A man of many talents, all of them minor. – Leslie Halliwell

CBS News reported on the Beer Drinkers' Diet, which allows people to lose weight by drinking more beer. It's well known in Hollywood. The reason it took Charlie Sheen so long to get sober is because he didn't want to break training. – Argus Hamilton

Oliver Stone is a heavy-handed propagandist, and the women in his films make Barbie look like Sylvia Plath. – Jane Hamsher

I believe that God felt sorry for actors, so he created Hollywood to give them a place in the sun and a swimming pool. The price they had to pay was to surrender their talent. – Cedric Hardwicke

(to Richard Chamberlain) You're doing it the wrong way round, my boy. You're a star and you don't know how to act. – Cedric Hardwicke

(of Michael Caine) An over-fat, flatulent, sixty-two-year-old windbag, a master of inconsequence now masquerading as a guru, passing off his vast limitations as pious virtues. – Richard Harris

In my scenes with Bo Derek, I had to imagine I was not there as her acting coach. – Richard Harris, who played Derek's father in *Tarzan*

Charlton Heston is good at portraying arrogance and ambition. But in the same way that a dwarf is good at being short. – Rex Harrison

(to Capucine) If you were more of a woman, I would be more of a man. Kissing you is like kissing the side of a beer bottle. – Laurence Harvey

The source of Woody Allen's popularity has always escaped me; I find him a very thin slice of Harold Lloyd on rye. – Robert Hatch

(of Kim Novak) I worked one day with her and quit. – Henry Hathaway

(of Cecil B. De Mille) I learned an awful lot from him by doing exactly the opposite. – Howard Hawks

There is not enough money in Hollywood to lure me into making another film with Joan Crawford. – Sterling Hayden

Goldie Hawn has the general squeaky-voiced persona of a vaguely disturbed chipmunk. – Sue Heal

Firing people came as naturally as breathing to Harry Cohn, more naturally in fact. – Ben Hecht

To bring a sense of perfection to Hollywood is to go bagging tigers with a fly swatter. – Ben Hecht

I'm a Hollywood writer, so I put on my sports jacket and take off my brain. – Ben Hecht

Tallulah (Bankhead) was sitting in a group of people, giving the monologue she always thought was conversation. – Lillian Hellman (of Norma Shearer) A face unclouded by thought. — Lillian Hellman

(of a Hollywood adaptation) You write a book like that you're fond of over the years, then you see that happen to it, it's like pissing in your father's beer. — Ernest Hemingway

Any picture in which Errol Flynn is the best actor is its own worst enemy. — Ernest Hemingway

(to Dorothy Arzner) Isn't it wonderful you've had such a great career when you had no right to have a career at all? — Katharine Hepburn

(of Sharon Stone) It's a new low for actresses when you have to wonder what's between her ears instead of her legs. — Katharine Hepburn

You can't direct a (Charles) Laughton picture. The best you can hope for is to referee. — Alfred Hitchcock

In Hollywood it's OK to be subtle, so long as you make it obvious. — Alfred Hitchcock

(of Michael Moore) Europeans think Americans are fat, vulgar, greedy, stupid, ambitious, and ignorant, and so on. And they've taken as their own, as their representative American, someone who actually embodies all of those qualities. — Christopher Hitchens

Pierce Brosnan always reminds me of the models in men's knitwear catalogues. — Paul Hoggart

Richard E. Grant always plays the same basic character, simply varying the degree of intensity with which he rolls his eyeballs. — Paul Hoggart

Billy Wilder has a mind full of razor blades. — William Holden

You can calculate Zsa Zsa Gabor's age by the rings on her fingers. — Bob Hope

(of Harry Cohn) You had to stand in line to hate him. — Hedda Hopper

I've read that (Dirk) Bogarde's cruel streak can be attributed to his fight for acceptance as an actor, as a homosexual man, and as a writer. And all the time I thought it was just because he's quite an unpleasant fellow. — Michael Hordern

(Hollywood) films are being made as though they were written by computer. They think, "What has sold before? Films with this? Films with that?" They think that if they have those elements, they have a winner. There is no desire to create. – Bob Hoskins

(Francis Ford) Coppola couldn't piss in a pot. – Bob Hoskins

I did not give Lee Majors his start in acting – you can't pin that one on me. – Rock Hudson

Clark Gable's ears make him look like a taxicab with both doors open. – Howard Hughes

(of George C. Scott) My opinion of him as an actor is much higher than my opinion of him as a man. – John Huston

Christian Slater needs something extra special for real stardom. They call it talent. – Tom Hutchinson

There have always been mixed opinions about Charles Bronson. Some people hate him like poison and some people just hate him regular. – Jill Ireland

(of Colin Farrell) I don't really go for people just because they're good looking. I mean, yes, he is gorgeous. But we all know that he's a tramp, and I'm not going to go there. – Jamelia

As far as talent goes, Marilyn Monroe was so minimally gifted as to be almost unemployable, and anyone who holds to the opinion that she was a great natural comic identifies himself immediately as a dunce. – Clive James

Arnold Schwarzenegger looks like a condom full of walnuts. – Clive James

I was wrong to suppose (Peter) Sellers thought the world revolved around him. He thought the cosmos did too. – Clive James

Orson Wells was clad in a black barrage balloon cleverly painted to look like a dinner jacket. – Clive James

Copulation was, I'm sure, Marilyn (Monroe)'s uncomplicated way of saying thank you. – Nunnally Johnson

(of Arnold Schwarzenegger) All that pumping iron seems to have given him an ethereal gaze and the toneless voice of an automaton. And it makes me wonder: is he really one of us? – Iain Johnstone

I can't see what Jack L. Warner can do with an Oscar – it can't say yes. – Al Jolson

(Shirley MacLaine) is as changeable as an opinion poll. She varies her statements and beliefs, she invents a new public face, according to what is currently fashionable or acceptable. – Carolyn Jones

I once bumped into Sally Field by the pool in a big Hollywood hotel, and time, it must be said, had not been kind to the former screen goddess – in fact, it hadn't even been mildly understanding. – Dylan Jones

Glamour is what Julie Andrews doesn't have. She does her duties efficiently but mechanically, like an airline stewardess. – Pauline Kael

Cecil B. De Mille made small-minded pictures on a big scale. – Pauline Kael

Sandy Dennis has made an acting style out of postnasal drip. – Pauline Kael

(of Bob Hoskins) A testicle with legs. – Pauline Kael

Robert Redford has turned almost alarmingly blond – he's gone past platinum, he must be plutonium; his hair is co-ordinated with his teeth. – Pauline Kael

(of Herman Mankiewicz) To know him was to like him. Not to know him was to love him. – Bert Kalmar

Howard Hughes was the only man I ever knew who had to die to prove that he had been alive. – Walter Kane

Sincerity in Hollywood is as rare as virginity at Malibu High School. – Hal Kanter

Vivien Leigh made life hell for everybody near her, unless they did everything she wished, as she wished, and when she wished. – Wolfe Kaufman

Harry Cohn liked to be the biggest bug in the manure pile. – Elia Kazan

Instead of sneaking in, if you want to be a US citizen, do it the right way. Have Angelina Jolie adopt you. – Jimmy Kimmel

Angelina Jolie has filed papers to adopt a Vietnamese boy. She adopted her first child in Cambodia, her second in Ethiopia, she gave birth to a third child in Namibia, now she's getting a child from Vietnam. She's working her way down the alphabet. She's at "V" now. Stay cool Yemen; she's coming. – Jimmy Kimmel

Lindsay Lohan is in rehab. She's smart, she's getting her rehab out of the way before she's legally old enough to drink. – Jimmy Kimmel

I watched *Titanic* when I got back home from the hospital, and cried. I knew then that my IQ had been damaged. – Stephen King

John Goodman isn't fat. He's in a category beyond fat. What does one call it? Whalelike. – Sam Kinison

What's the use of having a totally gorgeous body like Victoria Principal if you've got a mind like . . . Victoria Principal? – Jean Kittson

Boiled down to essentials, she (Greta Garbo) is a plain mortal girl with large feet. – Herbert Kretzmer

Sam Peckinpah is like an old dog you sometimes have to apologise for. – Kris Kristofferson

Working with Barbra Streisand is pretty stressful. It's like sitting down to a picnic in the middle of a freeway. – Kris Kristofferson

Filming with Streisand is an experience which may have cured me of movies. – Kris Kristofferson

(to Charles Dance) Charles, your fans are known as Charlie's Angels. Is this because there are only three of them? – *The Kumars At No. 42*

(of Billy Wilder) Underneath his aggressive, gruff exterior is pure Brillo. – Harry Kurnitz

Bill (W. C. Fields) never really wanted to hurt anybody. He just felt an obligation. – Gregory La Cava

I can safely say that I don't have any interest in Lindsay Lohan – nor do I understand anyone else that does. – Nick Lachey

(of Sophia Loren) Working with her was like being bombed by watermelons. – Alan Ladd

Hollywood gives a young girl the aura of one giant, self-contained orgy farm, its inhabitants dedicated to crawling into every pair of pants they can find. – Veronica Lake

Kirk (Douglas) would be the first to tell you that he's a difficult man; I would be the second. – Burt Lancaster (of Maureen O'Hara) She looked as though butter wouldn't melt in her mouth – or anywhere else for that matter. – Elsa Lanchester

(of Maggie Smith) She's better on stage, from a distance. On a screen, close up, she makes you want to dive for cover. – Elsa Lanchester

(of Estelle Winwood) I think it's so quaint that she's making a whole new career out of merely being very old. But I hope I never live so long that I get hired simply for not being a corpse! – Elsa Lanchester

They're a bunch of con artists (in Hollywood). They think they can pat me on the head and I'll kiss their asses. They just don't give a damn what is good or what is crap just so their lousy pictures make money. They're a bunch of peanut brains with no taste. – Mario Lanza

(Robert) Redford does not want to be an actor; he wants to be a movie star. – Arthur Laurents

Ava Gardner was her customary self, as amiable as an adder. – Helen Lawrenson

George Hamilton is audibly tan. – Fran Lebowitz

(of Steven Seagal) An inveterate liar who lived in a fantasy world. – Kelly LeBrock

Fred MacMurray held on to a buck like each one was an endangered species. – Mitchell Leisen

For some people, Bela Lugosi was the embodiment of dark, mysterious forces, a harbinger of evil from the world of shadow. For others he was merely a ham actor appearing in a type of film unsuitable for children and often unfit for adults. – Arthur Lennig

Harrison Ford said he and Steven Spielberg have finally signed on a script for *Indiana Jones 4*. In this one, the ancient relic is Indiana Jones. – Jay Leno

There are rumours that Madonna has been cut out of her husband's new movie. I don't want to say Madonna's a bad actress, but it turns out it was a home movie. – Jay Leno

Madonna is going to play Joan of Arc. She is playing a virgin. You thought the special effects in *Independence Day* were amazing . . . – Jay Leno

Winona Ryder's shoplifting trial was postponed. Apparently, she couldn't find anything to wear that wasn't evidence. – Jay Leno

You can see Winona Ryder is an Oscar-nominated actress. She said even though she was found guilty on two counts, it was still an honour just to be arrested. – Jay Leno

Remember the good old days when the only bomb you had to worry about on a plane was the Rob Schneider movie? – Jay Leno

Apparently Jessica Simpson is hoping to be the next Bond girl. She has a pretty good shot at it because 007 was also her S. A. T. score. – Jay Leno

Michael Caine can out-act any, well nearly any, telephone kiosk you care to mention. – Hugh Leonard

Congratulations are in order for Woody Allen – he and Soon Yi have a brand new baby daughter. It's all part of Woody's plan to grow his own wives. – David Letterman

Don't forget it's daylight saving time. You spring forward, then you fall back. It's like Robert Downey Jr getting out of bed. – David Letterman

It was so warm today that Angelina Jolie adopted Ben & Jerry. – David Letterman

Happy birthday to Burt Reynolds; seventy-one years old today. There were so many candles on Burt's cake, he had to wear a flame-retardant toupee. – David Letterman

Joan Crawford should have puppies, not children. – Oscar Levant

(of Zsa Zsa Gabor) The only person who left the Iron Curtain wearing it. – Oscar Levant

Zsa Zsa Gabor has discovered the secret of perpetual middle age. – Oscar Levant

Judy Garland: a vibrato in search of a voice. – Oscar Levant

Laurence Olivier is the most overrated actor on earth. Take away the wives and the looks, and you have John Gielgud. – Oscar Levant

Al Jolson's ego was such that when he heard applause for another star, he reacted as though he had been robbed. – Henry Levin

Louis B. Mayer is the most written-about mogul in Hollywood history. That's because happy reigns have no history. – David Lewis

Chuck Norris is an actor whose lack of expression is so profound that it could be mistaken for icily controlled technique. – Nicholas Lezard

There was no one remotely like John Huston, except, maybe, Lucifer. – Doris Lilly

Sophia Loren plays peasants. I play ladies. – Gino Lollobrigida

Hollywood is where they write the alibis before they write the story. – Carole Lombard

Clara (Bow) was the idol of the illiterate, and from her dainty lips came nothing more seductive than bubble gum. – Anita Loos

(of Louise Brooks) Her favourite form of exercise was walking off a movie set. – Anita Loos

(of Cameron Diaz) A lucky model who's been given a lot of opportunities. – Jennifer Lopez

(of Madonna) Do I think she's a great actress? No. Acting is what I do. – Jennifer Lopez

Jack Nicholson is a legend in his own lifetime and in his own mind. – Jennifer Lopez

(of Gwyneth Paltrow) I swear to God, I don't remember anything she was in. Some people get hot by association. I heard more about her and Brad Pitt than I ever heard about her work. – Jennifer Lopez

In Hollywood she's revered, she gets nominated for Oscars, but I've never heard anyone in the public or among my friends say, "Oh, I love Winona Ryder." – Jennifer Lopez

(of Gina Lollobrigida) Her personality is limited. She is good as a peasant but incapable of playing a lady. – Sophia Loren

Ginger Rogers was one of the worst, red-baiting, terrifying reactionaries in Hollywood. – Joseph Losey

(of Greta Garbo) The most inhibited person I've ever worked with. – Ernst Lubitsch

Whatever Francis (Ford Coppola) does for you always ends up benefiting Francis most. – George Lucas

Doris Day is as wholesome as a bowl of cornflakes and at least as sexy. – Dwight MacDonald

Joseph Losey is a versatile director who commands a wide range of styles for wrecking a movie. – Dwight MacDonald

(of Errol Flynn) His life was a fifty-year trespass against good taste. – Leslie Mallory

We Americans have always considered Hollywood, at best, a sinkhole of depraved venality. – David Mamet

(of Louis B. Mayer) He has the memory of an elephant and the hide of an elephant. The only difference is that elephants are vegetarians and Mayer's diet is his fellow man. – Herman J. Mankiewicz

Lana Turner could give you an eyewitness account of the Crucifixion and still put you to sleep. – Herman J. Mankiewicz

If Mel Brooks had come up in my time he wouldn't have qualified to be a busboy. – Joseph L. Mankiewicz

(of Marlon Brando) The once-beautiful, most distinguished actor of our time has turned into a self-loathing slob and left a lot of human wreckage in his wake. – Peter Manso

Co-starring with (Greta) Garbo hardly constituted an introduction. – Fredric March

Hollywood is full of pale imitations of Pamela Anderson and, worse still, Pamela Anderson herself. – Lisa Marchant

After Arnold Schwarzenegger, Dolph Lundgren is a bit of a disappointment. At least Arnold looks as if he comes supplied with batteries. – Adam Mars-Jones

The reason I drink is because when I'm sober I think I'm Eddie Fisher. – Dean Martin

(of Shirley MacLaine) The oars aren't touching the water these days. – Dean Martin

There's a statue of Jimmy Stewart in the Hollywood Wax Museum, and the statue talks better than he does. – Dean Martin

I wouldn't give you two cents for most of the actresses in Hollywood. Most of them take two hours to make up and then they can't act worth a damn. – Dewey Martin

(of Chico Marx) Now there sits a man with an open mind. You can feel the draught from here. – Groucho Marx

(of Sam Goldwyn) The only man who could throw a seven with one dice. – Harpo Marx

Dudley Moore has a club foot. That's not a problem – for him, his career, or anyone. What I object to is his club wit. – James Mason

(of Raquel Welch) Silicon from the knees up. – George Masters

I had no disagreement with Barbra Streisand. I was merely exasperated at her tendency to be a complete megalomaniac. – Walter Matthau

I'd love to work with Barbra Streisand again. In something appropriate. Perhaps *Macbeth*. – Walter Matthau

(of Spencer Tracy during filming of *Dr Jekyll and Mr Hyde*) Which part is he playing now? – Somerset Maugham

(of Joan Crawford) A mean, tipsy, powerful, rotten-egg lady. – Mercedes McCambridge

I never saw what was so great about Natalie (Wood). She was short, and lousy in bed. – Steve McQueen

I've been doing the Fonda workout: the Peter Fonda workout. That's where I wake up, take a hit of acid, smoke a joint, and run to my sister's house and ask her for money. – Kevin Meaney

(Dean) Martin's acting is so inept that even his impersonation of a lush seems unconvincing. – Harry Medved

Farrah Fawcett is uniquely suited to play a woman of limited intelligence. – Michael Medved

Raquel Welch is one of the few actresses in Hollywood history who looks more animated in still photographs than she does on the screen. – Michael Medved

I remember my brother once saying, "I'd like to marry Elizabeth Taylor," and my father said, "Don't worry, your time will come." – Spike Milligan

Faye Dunaway is a twentieth-century fox, a calculating lady who repels even as she attracts. – Bart Mills

(of Peter Bogdanovich) As a writer he's passable. As a director he's repetitive and unimaginative. As a man he has numerous insecurities which I legally don't dare elaborate on. And as a friend – he ain't. – Sal Mineo

(of Judy Garland) Mother was the real-life Wicked Witch of the West. – Liza Minnelli

In Hollywood now when people die they don't say, "Did he leave a will?" but "Did he leave a diary?" – Liza Minnelli

I gave up being serious about making pictures about the time I made a film with Greer Garson and she took 127 takes to say "no". – Robert Mitchum

I once heard a producer say about Howard Hughes: "He's entitled to his own opinion – and as many others as money can buy." – Robert Mitchum

A Steve McQueen performance lends itself to monotony. – Robert Mitchum

Hollywood ain't dog eat dog; it's man eat man. – Wilson Mizner

Hollywood is a trip through a sewer in a glass-bottomed boat. – Wilson Mizner

Hollywood is a carnival – where there are no concessions. – Wilson Mizner

Burt Lancaster couldn't pick up an ashtray before discussing his motivation for an hour or so. – Jeanne Moreau

I think it's great. Obviously to him, age doesn't matter, and to her, size doesn't matter. – Brittany Murphy, after her ex-fiance, Ashton Kutcher, began dating Demi Moore

(of Victor Mature) Hollywood's self-avowed disciple of conceit and vulgarity. – W. H. Mooring

To the unwashed public, Joan Collins is a star. But to those who know her, she's a commodity who would sell her own bowel movement. – Anthony Newley

You knew where you were with Errol (Flynn) – he always let you down. – David Niven

(of Jayne Mansfield) Miss United Dairies herself. – David Niven

George Sanders had a face, even in his twenties, which looked as though he had rented it on a long lease and had lived in it for so long he didn't want to move out. – David Niven

She (Loretta Young) was doing a scene, urging Richard the Lionheart to go to the Middle East and fight. Loretta read her line, "Richard, you gotta save Christianity", but not very convincingly. So De Mille took her aside and asked her to put some awe into her line reading. They reshot the scene and she said: "Aw, Richard, you gotta save Christianity!" – David Niven

Sean Connery has such a deep love of Scotland that he refuses to use anything other than a Scottish accent no matter what role he is taking. – Graham Norton

Several magazines have offered Ben Affleck thousands of dollars to publish pictures of his baby. Which means that the baby is the only Affleck whose picture makes money. – Conan O'Brien

In a recent interview, Kirstie Alley says she makes her new boyfriends wait six months before having sex with them. Of course, some of them insist on twelve months. – Conan O'Brien

There's a rumour going around that the reason Kirstie Alley lost so much weight was because she had her stomach stapled. When asked about it, Alley said, "That's ridiculous. I didn't have it stapled: I had it spot-welded." – Conan O'Brien

Pamela Anderson is being criticized because the other day she was spotted sunbathing topless in front of her ten-year-old son. Pam explained that she just wanted to keep him in the shade. – Conan O'Brien

It was reported today that US military bases will not show *Brokeback Mountain*. However, during interrogations, US troops will continue to show *Deuce Bigalow: European Gigolo*. – Conan O'Brien

Yesterday was "Take Your Daughter to Work Day". As a result, Michael Douglas spent the day saying, "No, she's actually my wife." – Conan O'Brien

People magazine is reporting that Angelina Jolie is pregnant. Angelina's doctor says it was the first time he's ever seen lips on an ultrasound. – Conan O'Brien

Nicole Kidman and singer Keith Urban got married in Australia. Because it took place in the southern hemisphere, their marriage will unravel counterclockwise. – Conan O'Brien

Sixty-eight-year-old Sophia Loren has been asked to pose nude for *Playboy*. She was asked by *Penthouse* . . . – Conan O'Brien

The day after Thanksgiving is the biggest shopping day of the year. In fact, it's the one day in the year that even Winona Ryder buys something. – Conan O'Brien

(of Shirley Temple) She wasn't very good. She was fine when she was six or seven. But did you notice how she couldn't act when she was fourteen? – Tatum O'Neal

There are three types of actress: the silly, the very silly, and Shirley MacLaine. – P. J. O'Rourke

Quentin Tarantino has the vocal modulation of a railway station announcer, the expressive power of a fence-post and the charisma of a week-old head of lettuce. – Fintan O'Toole

(of Hollywood actresses) You look into their eyes and there's no one at home. It's like looking at an unlit lamppost. – Peter O'Toole

(Charlton) Heston was miscast in *Khartoum*. His English accent came and went; mostly, it went. – Laurence Olivier

I'm not going to do any Madonna movies. For example, she did a movie and she played herself, then she did another movie and it sucked and she did another movie and it sucked and she did another movie and it sucked. Give her credit for trying, but why keep at it if you suck? – Kelly Osbourne

(of Drew Barrymore) She's like an apple turnover that got crushed in a grocery bag on a hot day. – Camille Paglia

Hollywood money isn't money. It's congealed snow, melts in your hand. – Dorothy Parker

Marion Davies has two expressions: joy and indigestion. – Dorothy Parker (of Katharine Hepburn) She ran the gamut of emotions from A to B. – Dorothy Parker

Joan Collins looks like she combs her hair with an egg-beater. – Louella Parsons

(to Hugh Grant) I find you a little wooden. How do you psyche yourself up? Do you go into a forest and look at some trees? – Dennis Pennis

(to Demi Moore) Would you ever consider keeping your clothes on if the script demanded it? – Dennis Pennis

Hollywood is a dreary industrial town controlled by hoodlums of enormous wealth, the ethereal sense of a pack of jackals, and taste so degraded that it befouled everything it touched. – S. J. Perelman

Working for the Marx Brothers was not unlike being chained to a galley car and lashed at ten-minute intervals. – S. J. Perelman

(of Joan Crawford) I'd rather have a cannibal for a co-star. – Anthony Perkins

(of Steven Seagal) Where some men are self-contained, he's vacuum-packed! – Anthony Perkins

Barbra Streisand: the most pretentious woman the cinema has ever known. – Jon Peters

Hollywood is a place that attracts people with massive holes in their souls. – Julia Phillips

Agent Mike Ovitz is even colder than his air-conditioned office. – Julia Phillips

(of Barbra Streisand) The sensitivity of a starving elephant. – Frank Pierson

Working with Julie Andrews is like being hit over the head by a Valentine's Day card. – Christopher Plummer

(of Faye Dunaway) She was a gigantic pain in the ass. She demonstrated certifiable proof of insanity. – Roman Polanski

Johnny Depp puts the dire in director. – Edward Porter

Directing Marilyn Monroe was like directing Lassie. You needed fourteen takes to get each one of them right. – Otto Preminger

(of Marilyn Monroe) A vacuum with nipples. – Otto Preminger

To read Shirley MacLaine's autobiography is to encounter one of the most inflated airheads ever to break free of her moorings. – John Preston

Actors are freaks in America, and Hollywood is all freaksville. – Vincent Price

As a human being, Joan Crawford is a very great actress. – Nicholas Ray

Jean Harlow was not a good actress, not even by Hollywood standards. – William Redfield

Everyone in Tinseltown is getting pinched, lifted and pulled. For many it's become a sick obsession. They lose some of their soul when they go under the knife and end up looking body snatched. – Robert Redford

Paul Newman has the attention span of a lightning bolt. – Robert Redford

Working with Glenda Jackson was like being run over by a Bedford truck. – Oliver Reed

Interviewing Warren Beatty is like asking a haemophiliac for a pint of blood. – Rex Reed

(of Marlon Brando) Most of the time he sounds like he has a mouth full of toilet paper. – Rex Reed

Producer Allan Carr's licence plate reads GREASE. He was responsible for that putrid movie and its totally unsuccessful sequel. Isn't it surprising what some people choose to advertise about themselves? – Rex Reed

Maybe those wide-eyed one-liners and pregnant pauses work on television, but if Miss (Goldie) Hawn is to have any kind of future in movies, she needs to learn something about the rudimentary techniques necessary to sustain a comic scene without putting the audience to sleep. – Rex Reed

(of Sylvester Stallone) He is to acting what Liberace was to pumping iron. – Rex Reed

(of Elizabeth Taylor) A Goodyear blimp, pumped full of chilli instead of butane gas. – Rex Reed

I can sing as well as Fred Astaire can act. – Burt Reynolds

(of Marlon Brando) He has preserved the mentality of an adolescent. When he doesn't try and someone's speaking to him, it's like a blank wall. In fact it's even less interesting because behind a blank wall you can always suppose that there's something interesting there. – Burt Reynolds

If Kathleen Turner had been a man, I would have punched her out long ago. – Burt Reynolds

In future, Kevin Costner should only appear in pictures that he directs himself. That way he can always be working with his favourite actor and his favourite director. – Kevin Reynolds

I doubt in her entire life Katharine Hepburn has ever bought lunch for herself or anyone else. – Ralph Richardson

Eddie Fisher married to Elizabeth Taylor is like me trying to wash the Empire State Building with a bar of soap. – Don Rickles

(to Frank Sinatra) Make yourself at home, Frank. Hit somebody. – Don Rickles

In the new movie *Paycheck*, Ben Affleck plays a man who loses two years of his memory. Let's hope it's the two years he was making *Pearl Harbor*. – Joan Rivers

Annette Bening is very grand and will not say hello, even though I remember when she used to serve me pizza. She's scared I'll bring it up. I just feel sorry for someone who is so miserable in their life that they won't even say hello. But don't worry, in ten years no one will want you anyway. – Joan Rivers

The DVD of Mariah Carey's movie *Glitter* is coming out with bonus features. Maybe one of them will be a plot. – Joan Rivers

Joan Collins is so old, she's at the British Museum being carbon dated. – Joan Rivers

I'd like to ask Tom Cruise what it's like looking into the eyes of a grasshopper. – Joan Rivers

A woman went to a plastic surgery and asked him to make her like Bo Derek. He gave her a lobotomy. – Joan Rivers

Bo Derek does not understand the concept of Roman numerals. She thought we fought in World War Eleven. – Joan Rivers

Jane Fonda didn't get that terrific body from exercise. She got it from lifting all that money. – Joan Rivers

Melanie Griffith is very sweet but dumb – the lights are on but the dogs aren't barking. – Joan Rivers

Each woman has done very well by him (Tom Cruise) — Nicole Kidman and Penelope Cruz. So this one, Katie Holmes, who doesn't seem to have much talent, is probably the luckiest of all. I saw her in *Batman Begins* and, let's just say, she better hang on to Tom for a while! — Joan Rivers

I saw Angelina Jolie on TV. Those lips are so big, she could whisper in her own ear. — Joan Rivers

Angelina Jolie's lips are like an infected arsehole. — Joan Rivers

One day I would like to have my body as slim as Nicole Kidman's, but I would never want to be as tall. Walking down the carpet at the Oscars in that red dress, she truly looked like a bottle of ketchup. — Joan Rivers

With *The Queen* and *Elizabeth I*, Helen Mirren has now played every queen in British history except Elton John and Ian McKellen. — Joan Rivers

Robert Redford had such a bad job. God, whoever did him should be ashamed. — Joan Rivers on Redford's alleged facelift

Is Elizabeth Taylor fat? Her favourite food is seconds. — Joan Rivers

Elizabeth Taylor is wearing Orson Welles-designed jeans. — Joan Rivers

Everyone is going on about how great Julia (Roberts) was in *Erin Brockovich*, but what did she actually do? Wear push-up bras. It wasn't great acting. — Eric Roberts

Gwyneth Paltrow is quite pretty in a British, horsey sort of way. — Julia Roberts

Cedric Hardwicke had the personality and drive of an old tortoise hunting for lettuce. — Rachel Roberts

(of Miriam Hopkins) Puerile and silly and snobbish. — Edward G. Robinson

I would rather drink latex paint than be in a movie with Steven Seagal. — Henry Rollins

Jeff Daniels, now he's extremely lucky. How else could you explain such a dull-looking and dull-acting personality — so to speak — starring in big-budgeted motion pictures? — Cesar Romero

Jean-Claude Van Damme exudes the charisma of a packet of Cup-A-Soup. — Jonathan Romney

I can't honestly say that Esther Williams ever acted in an Andy Hardy picture, but she swam in one. – Mickey Rooney

Richard E. Grant looks rather like one of those balloons you get from the National Gallery of Munch's The Scream, after it's burst. – Deborah Ross

Tom Cruise is to become a father. So we'll soon hear the pitter-patter of tiny feet . . . as Tom rushes down to the shop to get nappies. – Jonathan Ross

Hollywood isn't really about acting. It's about the publicity. It's about which idiot is going out with this one, which idiot had a baby. In real life, people have babies all the time and it's no big deal. But that's what the movie business has turned into. – Mickey Rourke

(of Harry Cohn) The softest thing about him is his front teeth. – Damon Runyon

(of critic John Simon) (He is like) a sadistic guard in a Nazi camp. – Harvey Sabinson

Hollywood follows polls like politics. They remake last year's hit. – Susan Sarandon

I still don't believe that Raquel Welch exists. She has been manufactured by the media merely to preserve the sexless plasticity of sex objects for the masses. – Andrew Sarris

Bernardo Bertolucci is more of a gangster than a movie director. – Maria Schneider

I can't imagine Rhett Butler chasing you for ten years. – David O. Selznick, rejecting Katharine Hepburn for the role of Scarlett O'Hara in *Gone With The Wind*

Bette Davis got most of her exercise by putting her foot down. – Tom Shales

David O. Selznick stormed through life demanding to see the manager. – Lloyd Shearer

Jack Lemmon has a gift for butchering good parts while managing to look intelligent, thus constituting Hollywood's abiding answer to the theatre. – Wilfrid Sheed

(of Colin Farrell) I've got three words for him: Am A. Teur. – Charlie Sheen

Rosie Perez? I don't think I could spend eight or ten weeks on a movie set with her. Her voice would drive me back to heroin. – Charlie Sheen

How does Francis Ford Coppola, one of the greatest filmmakers of our time, see Keanu Reeves's work, see what we've all seen, and say, "That's what I want in my movie?" How does Bertolucci see that and say, "That's my guy." Emilio and I sit around and just scratch our heads, thinking, "How did this guy get in?" – Charlie Sheen

Men find it tougher to adjust to success gracefully. They throw their weight around and try and make everyone else feel less than successful. Bruce Willis, for instance . . . – Cybill Shepherd

They say Tom Mix rides as if he's part of the horse, but they don't say which part. – Robert Sherwood

If he wants to see *Chicago*, I've left him two tickets; one adult, one child. – Brooke Shields, hitting back at criticism from Tom Cruise by sniping at his relationship with Katie Holmes

Charles Bronson's popularity within the movie industry is not legendary. – David Shipman

(of Marlene Dietrich) Age cannot wither her, nor custom stale her infinite sameness. – David Shipman

(of Jack L. Warner) He never bore a grudge against anyone he wronged. – Simone Signoret

Robert Altman has most of the qualifications for a major director except the supreme one of having something significant to say. – John Simon

The only real talent Miss (Doris) Day possesses is that of being absolutely sanitary: her personality untouched by human emotions, her brow unclouded by human thought, her form unsmudged by the slightest evidence of femininity. – John Simon

The insufferably smug and woodchuck-cheeked Minnie Driver proffers what the French call a *tête à gifler* – a face begging to be slapped. – John Simon

(of Shelley Duvall) The worst and most homeliest thing to hit the screens since Liza Minnelli. – John Simon (to Atom Egoyan, director of *Krapp's Last Tape*) I have seen at least twelve productions of this play, all more touching than yours. Was this deliberate or just incompetence on your part? – John Simon

Miss (Judy) Garland's figure resembles the giant economy-size tube of toothpaste in girls' bedrooms. Squeezed intemperately at all points, it acquires a shape that defies definition by the most resourceful solid geometrician. – John Simon

Since Jean-Luc Godard's films have nothing to say, we could perhaps have ninety minutes of silence instead of each of them. – John Simon

(of Glenda Jackson) She has the look of an asexual harlequin. – John Simon

You have to have a stomach for ugliness to endure Carol Kane – to say nothing of the zombie-like expressions she mistakes for acting. – John Simon

(of Diane Keaton) Her work, if that is the word for it, always consists chiefly of a dithering, blithering, neurotic coming apart at the seams – an acting style that is really a nervous breakdown in slow motion. – John Simon

(of Walter Matthau) He looked like a half-melted rubber bulldog. – John Simon

(of Melina Mercouri) Her blackly mascaraed eye-sockets gape like twin craters, unfortunately extinct. – John Simon

I always thought Liza Minnelli's face deserving – of first prize in the beagle category. It is a face going off in three directions simultaneously: the nose always en route to becoming a trunk, blubber lips unable to resist the pull of gravity, and a chin trying its damnedest to withdraw into the neck. – John Simon

Miss Minnelli has only two things going for her – a father and mother who got her there in the first place, and tasteless reviewers and audiences who keep her there. – John Simon

Barbra Streisand: a cross between an aardvark and an albino rat. – John Simon

(of Barbra Streisand) Were she to collide with a Mack truck, it is the truck that would drop dead. – John Simon

(of Orson Welles) The sad thing is that he has consistently put his very real talents to the task of glorifying his imaginary genius. – John Simon

I'll never put Tom Cruise down. He's already kinda short. – Don Simpson

(of Robert Redford) Well, at least he has finally found his true love – what a pity he can't marry himself. – Frank Sinatra

John Frankenheimer went from boy-wonder to has-been without ever passing through the stage of maturity. – Neil Sinyard

(on the crowds at Harry Cohn's funeral) It proves what they always say: give the public what they want to see, and they'll come out for it. – Red Skelton

Glenn Close is not an actress – she's an address. – Maggie Smith

Kathleen Turner's OK in stills. When she talks and moves about, she reminds me of someone who works in a supermarket. – Ann Sothern

George Lucas reminded me a little of Walt Disney's version of a mad scientist. – Steven Spielberg

If there's anything I hate it's a goddamned phony and Hollywood's filled with 'em, pretending to be what they're not and some of them never were. – Barbara Stanwyck

(of Laurence Harvey) An appalling man and, even more unforgivably, an appalling actor. – Robert Stephens

I really thought that the make-up artist for *Cinderella Man* should have won. I mean, it's hard to make Russell Crowe look like he got in a fight. – Jon Stewart at the 2006 Academy Awards

That's when I realised we were a comedy duo, when I saw *Behind Enemy Lines*. I realized Owen Wilson should never be alone. – Ben Stiller

(of Gwyneth Paltrow) She lives in rarefied air that's a little thin. It's like she's not getting quite enough oxygen. – Sharon Stone

(of Tony Curtis) A passionate amoeba. – David Susskind

(of Elizabeth Taylor) Overweight, overbosomed, overpaid, and undertalented. – David Susskind

(of Lana Turner) She is not even an actress, only a trollop. – Gloria Swanson

Peter O'Toole had a face not so much lived in as infested. – Paul Taylor

There are times when Richard Gere has the warm effect of a wind tunnel at dawn. – David Thompson

Elizabeth Taylor isn't spoiled. I have often seen her pour her own champagne for breakfast. – Mike Todd

(of Kelly Brook) To say she acts would be to overstretch the truth. – Christopher Tookey

Ms (Patsy) Kensit has all the comic timing and subtlety of an aircraft carrier. – Christopher Tookey

(of Rob Schneider) The only hope of this guy ever making a funny movie is for him to switch brains with someone who's actually talented. – Christopher Tookey

(of Daryl Hannah) I have seen her on many occasions, and she is quite simply in need of a shower or bath. – Donald Trump

(of Francis Ford Coppola) He is his own worst enemy. If he directs a little romance, it has to be the biggest, most overdone little romance in movie history. – Kenneth Turan

Marilyn (Monroe) was a very lucky young lady. If she hadn't died tragically and young, her lack of real acting talent would have shown up by forty. Until you're forty, you can coast on your looks. – Lana Turner

I thank God that neither I nor any member of my family will ever be so hard up that we have to work for Otto Preminger. – Lana Turner

(of Roman Polanski) The four-foot Pole you wouldn't want to touch with a ten-foot pole. – Kenneth Tynan

(of Warren Beatty) He's the type of man who will end up dying in his own arms. – Mamie Van Doren

Joan Crawford would have made an exemplary prison matron . . . She had the requisite sadism, paranoia and taste for violence. – Harriet Van Horne

(of Hollywood) Nobody is allowed to fail within a two-mile radius of the Beverly Hills Hotel. – Gore Vidal

(of Gary Cooper) He got a reputation as a great actor by just thinking hard about the next line. – King Vidor

(of Michelangelo Antonioni) It seems that boredom is one of the great discoveries of our time. If so, there's no question that he must be considered a pioneer. – Luchino Visconti

The only way I could force myself into kissing (Bette) Midler on-camera was to pretend that I was kissing my dog. – Ken Wahl

In one scene in *Jinxed* I have to hit her (Bette Midler) in the face and I thought, we could save some money on sound effects here. – Ken Wahl

Anita Louise: as cold as a stepmother's kiss. – Hal Wallis

(of Faye Dunaway) Even such natural activity as breathing now occasions in her a virtuoso display of overacting. Her eyebrows quiver, her eyes pop, her nostrils dilate, and the skin over her cheek-bones tightens. When she actually utters a line, it is as if a battalion of signallers have gone simultaneously berserk and are semaphoring delirious messages. – Frank Walker

In some of his last movies, Errol Flynn had to play himself. Unfortunately the role was beyond his acting abilities. – Jack L. Warner

They say Louis B. Mayer is his own worst enemy. Not while I'm still alive. – Jack L. Warner

Can you believe any girl looks at Dustin Hoffman and gets a thrill? I can't! – Ruth Waterbury

(of Otto Preminger) One of the meanest bastards who ever walked a soundstage. – Adam West

(of Jean Harlow) She's the kind of girl who climbed the ladder of success, wrong by wrong. – Mae West

(of Jayne Mansfield) When it comes to men, I heard she never turns anything down except the bedcovers. – Mae West

(of Mae West) A kind of Mt Rushmore of the cosmetician's art. – Dwight Whitney

Hollywood is a celluloid Detroit, a factory town for mass production out of which something good comes now and then. – Billy Wilder

(of Charlie Chaplin) When he found a voice to say what was on his mind, he was like a child of eight writing lyrics for Beethoven's Ninth. – Billy Wilder

The trouble with Tony Curtis is that he's interested only in tight pants and wide billing. – Billy Wilder (of Marilyn Monroe) She has breasts like granite and a brain like Swiss cheese, full of holes. – Billy Wilder

I am the only director who ever made two pictures with Marilyn Monroe. Forget the Oscar, I deserve the Purple Heart. – Billy Wilder

(of Peter Sellers) What do you mean, heart attack? You've got to have a heart before you can have an attack. – Billy Wilder

(of David Niven) An extremely mean and deeply heartless figure. – Peter Willes

Ah, Victor (Spinetti), still struggling to keep your head below water? – Emlyn Williams

Lana Turner couldn't act her way out of her form-fitting cashmeres. – Tennessee Williams

(of Sean Connery) Guys like him and (Michael) Caine talk about acting as if they knew what it was. – Nicol Williamson

Tallulah (Bankhead) talked so ceaselessly that you had to make a reservation five minutes ahead to get a word in. – Earl Wilson

Hollywood: a place where they shoot too many pictures and not enough actors. – Walter Winchell

She just behaved badly, like she was competing with me. I understand that Shirley grew up in a different era, when women had flesh under their fingernails from competing with one another, but I'm not like that. – Debra Winger on Shirley MacLaine, her co-star in *Terms of Endearment*

Paul Henreid looks as though his idea of fun would be to find a nice cold damp grave and sit in it. – Richard Winnington

They'd have to pay me an awful lot of money to work with James Cameron again. – Kate Winslet

Sean Connery can't console himself for not being a second Laurence Olivier. – Shelley Winters

Joan Crawford can chew up two directors and three producers before lunch. – Shelley Winters

At the RKO studios Hepburn was called "Katharine of Arrogance". Not without reason . . . – Estelle Winwood

My attitude about Hollywood is that I wouldn't walk across the street to pull one of those executives out of the snow if he was bleeding to death. Not unless I was paid for it. – James Woods

Mamie Van Doren often acted like Mr Ed the Talking Horse. – Paula Yates

Zsa Zsa Gabor has been married so many times she has rice marks on her face. – Henny Youngman

Goldie Hawn was landed with an idiot giggle, a remorseless inclination to squeak and if a brain hummed behind those dumbfounded eyes the secret never leaked out. – Donald Zec

One of my unfavourite directors is (Michelangelo) Antonioni, because he tells the same story all the time in the same style. To me he is like a fly that tries to go out of the window and doesn't realize there is glass, and keeps banging against it and never reaches the sky. – Franco Zeffirelli

Rudolph Valentino's acting is largely confined to protruding his large, almost occult eyes until the vast areas of white are visible, drawing back the lips of his wide, sensuous mouth to bare his gleaming teeth, and flaring his nostrils. – Adolph Zukor

Poisonous Reviews
(of *Fort Apache*) There is enough Irish comedy to make me wish Cromwell had done a more thorough job. – James Agate

(of *The Egg and I*) Marjorie Main, in an occasional fit of fine wild comedy, picks up the show and brandishes it as if she were wringing its neck. I wish to God she had. – James Agee

(of *Tycoon*) Several tons of dynamite are set off in this picture – none of it under the right people. – James Agee

(of *You Were Meant For Me*) That's what you think. – James Agee

(of Mel Gibson's *Hamlet*) To go or not to go, strewth, that is the question. – Anon

Divorce His, Divorce Hers: all the joy of standing by at an autopsy. – Anon

(of *The Three Musketeers*) Angela Lansbury wears the crown of France as though she had won it at a county fair. – Anon (of *Alone in the Dark*) So poorly built, so horribly acted and so sloppily stitched together that it's not even at the straight-to-DVD level. – Anon

(of *Battlefield Earth*) A million monkeys with a million crayons would be hard-pressed in a million years to create anything as cretinous. – Anon

(of *Fingers at the Window*) The kind of picture actors do when they need work. – Lew Ayres

(of *At Long Last Love*) Burt Reynolds sings like Dean Martin with adenoids and dances like a drunk killing cockroaches . . . If this film were any more of a dog, it would shed. – John Barbour

(of *Beyond the Poseidon Adventure*) Sally Field and Michael Caine were so damned wooden they could have floated the *Poseidon* up to the surface in ten seconds flat. – Rona Barrett

(of *Heaven's Gate*) A film so dire it deserves to be reviewed in the obituary column. – Laura Baum

(of *The Entertainer*) Has set itself to scratching the dandruff out of the mane of life. – Paul Beckley

(of *The League of Extraordinary Gentlemen*) It could be introduced as Exhibit A in the case against digital effects technology. – John Beifuss

(of *Zoom*) When it comes to action, comedy, and drama, three words apply: lamer, lamer, lamest. – James Berardinelli

First of all, I want to thank Warner Brothers. Thank you for putting me in this piece of shit, this God-awful movie . . . It's just what my career needed. – Halle Berry, accepting her Golden Raspberry Award for *Catwoman*

(of *The Man Who Fell to Earth*) Once you have pierced through its glittering veneer, you find only another glittering veneer underneath. – Michael Billington

(of *Honest*, starring pop group All Saints) The worst kind of rubbish, the kind that makes you angry you have wasted a hundred and five minutes of your life. – Peter Bradshaw

(of *Mame*) An elephantine budget matched with minuscule inagination. – Geoff Brown

Rocky Balboa isn't a response to Stallone's late-life crisis, it *is* his late-life crisis, right up there on the screen. – Ty Burr

(of *At Long Last Love*) Starring Cybill Shepherd and Burt Reynolds, who have, between them, four left feet and who sing with a gallantry that reminds me of small children taking their first solo swim across the deep end. – Vincent Canby

(of *The Godfather, Part II*) It's a Frankenstein monster stitched together from leftover parts. It talks. It moves in fits and starts but it has no mind of its own. – Vincent Canby

(of *Superman IV*) About as dreary as a summit conference in Belgium. – Brian Case

(of *Private Benjamin*) A movie you don't salute, you court martial; the script went AWOL. – Charles Champlin

(of *Lady in the Water*) It takes a real gift to make something as excruciatingly self-important as this plodding fable, a bedtime story M. Night Shyamalan reportedly wrote for his kids. Be content, they slept well. – Tom Charity

(of *Basic Instinct 2*) Dead serious and stone idiotic, the only basic instinct on evidence here is desperation. – Carina Chocano

(of *Arthur and the Invisibles*) Director Luc Besson admits he knew nothing about animation before he started this project, and it shows. – Alex Chun

(of *What's Up, Doc?*) As a pompous middle-European intellectual, Kenneth Mars mugs and drools in a manner that Jerry Lewis might find excessive. – Jay Cocks

(of *The Eiger Sanction*) All the villains have been constructed from prefabricated Bond models. – Richard Combs

Little Man is a comedy based on a single gag that's not very funny. Therefore, it's exactly one joke short of being a one-joke film. – Randy Cordova

Don't expect to be beguiled by *A Good Year*. That would be like trying to warm your hands at an artificial fireplace. – Richard Corliss

(of *Hook*) Sitting through two hours and twenty minutes is at times like running through treacle wearing flippers. – Peter Cox

(of *The Agony and the Ecstasy*) All agony, no ecstasy. – Judith Crist

(of Jessica Lange in *King Kong*) A dumb blonde who falls for a huge plastic finger. – Judith Crist

(of *The Man in the Middle*) For once (Robert) Mitchum seems to have an excuse for keeping his eyes at half-mast. – Judith Crist

(of *Marooned*) I suspect a computer fed with a dictionary could come up with better dialogue. – Judith Crist

(of *Satan Met a Lady*) One lives through it in constant expectation of seeing a group of uniformed individuals appear suddenly from behind the furniture and take the entire cast into protective custody. – Bosley Crowther

(of *Plan 9 From Outer Space*) The film has become so famous for its own badness that it's now beyond criticism. – *Cult Flicks and Trash Pics*

(of *The Da Vinci Code*) It's a truly awful book. What an achievement to make a film that is even worse. – *Daily Mail*

(of *The League of Extraordinary Gentlemen*) These guys have dumbed down a comic book. – Manohla Dargis

Duets does for karaoke bars what *Jaws* did for the ocean. It features five actors and Huey Lewis. And The News? Not so good. – Frank DeCaro

(of *Armageddon*) The movie is an assault on the eyes, the ears, the brain, common sense and the human desire to be entertained. No matter what they're charging to get in, it's worth more to get out. – Roger Ebert

I had a colonoscopy once, and they let me watch it on TV. It was more entertaining than *The Brown Bunny*. – Roger Ebert

Only enormously talented people could have made *Death to Smoochy*. Those with lesser gifts would have lacked the nerve to make a film so bad, so miscalculated, so lacking any connection with any possible audience. – Roger Ebert

On the basis of *Dirty Love*, I am not certain that anyone involved has ever seen a movie, or knows what one is. – Roger Ebert

This movie doesn't scrape the bottom of the barrel. This movie isn't the bottom of the barrel. This movie isn't below the bottom of the barrel. This movie doesn't deserve to be mentioned in the same sentence with barrels . . . The day may come when *Freddy Got Fingered* is seen as a milestone of neo-surrealism. The day may never come when it is seen as funny. – Roger Ebert

(of *Resident Evil Apocalypse*) Parents: if you encounter teenagers who say they liked this movie, do not let them date your children. – Roger Ebert

(of *Hanging Up*) Could very well be the cinematic equivalent of an unwelcome telemarketing call from a timeshare salesman. – Michael Elliott

Resurrection Man leaves you with the feeling of having been on an occasionally unguided tour of an abattoir – Richard Falcon

The only terrifying thing about *Creepshow 2* is the thought of *Creepshow 3*. – Nigel Floyd

(of *Kansas*) Like the eponymous state, this has corn as far as the eye can see. – Nigel Floyd

In *Titanic*, James Cameron had to invent a Romeo-and-Juliet-style fictional couple to heat up what was a real-life catastrophe. This seems a tiny bit like giving Anne Frank a wacky best friend to perk up the attic. – Libby Gelman-Waxner

(of *Basic Instinct 2*) Unenjoyable, unerotic, I daresay unwatchable. – Todd Gilchrist

Deuce Bigalow: European Gigolo was overlooked for an Academy Award because nobody had the foresight to invent a category for Best Running Penis Joke Delivered by a Third-Rate Comic. – Patrick Goldstein, *Los Angeles Times*, on the 2005 movie starring Rob Schneider

The Incredible Sarah is a job lot of obligatory Hollywood platitudes strung together with all the skill of Captain Hook trying to thread a needle. – Benny Green

(of *The Odessa File*) As resistable a parcel of sedative entertainment as ever induced narcolepsy in a healthy man. – Benny Green

(of *The Return of the Pink Panther*) The first film to be upstaged by its own credit titles. – Benny Green

(of *Best Defense,* starring Eddie Murphy) About as funny as getting hijacked by a group of kamikaze terrorists. – *The Guardian* (of *Arthur 2: on the Rocks*) As funny as a cerebral haemorrhage. – Wally Hammond

(of *The Missouri Breaks*) A picture of which it might be said, they shouldn't make 'em like that any more. – Richard Hatch

(of *Elektra*) Lacks thrills, narrative, emotion, believability, character development, and, frankly, watchability. – Aaron Hillis

(of an unnamed film) For the first time in my life I envied my feet. They were asleep. – Hedda Hopper

(of *Exodus*) After three and a half hours the approach seems more exhausting than exhaustive. – Penelope Houston

(of *Naked Lunch*) This is the movie of the book they said could never be filmed. They were right. – Tom Hutchinson

Cleopatra was the biggest asp disaster in the world. – Pauline Kael

(of *Dances with Wolves*) Kevin Costner has feathers in his hair and feathers in his head. – Pauline Kael

(of *Goodbye Mr Chips*) An overblown version with songs where they are not needed (and Leslie Bricusse's songs are never needed). – Pauline Kael

(of *The Sound of Music*) The Sound of Mucus. – Pauline Kael

(of Barbra Streisand in *What's Up, Doc?*) She doesn't do anything she hasn't already done. She's playing herself – and it's awfully soon for that. – Pauline Kael

(of *The Way We Were*) Not one moment of the picture is anything but garbage under the gravy of false honesty. – Stanley Kauffmann

(of *Shanghai Knights*) Here's where we get out the thesaurus and look up synonyms for "garbage". – Mike LaSalle

(of an anon film) Van Johnson does his best: appears. – Caroline A. Lejeune
Beginning pictures at the end
Is, I'm afraid, the modern trend.
But I'd find *Ruthless* much more winning
If it could end at the beginning. – Caroline A. Lejeune

(of *Material Girls*) It's sort of reassuring that although Madge (Madonna) has seemingly given up starring in bad movies, her company is still financing terrible scripts. – Lou Lumenick

(of Alfred Hitchcock's *Psycho*) I think the film is a reflection of a most unpleasant mind, a mean, sly, sadistic little mind. – Dwight Macdonald

(of *Cruise Control*) Did anyone read the script before signing on for this one? – Leonard Maltin

(of *Glen or Glenda*) This docu-fantasy about transvestism could well be the worst movie ever made. – Leonard Maltin

(of *Myra Breckenridge*) Film critic Rex Reed makes his "acting" debut as Myron. He manages to carry considerable enthusiasm into his masturbation sequence. – Michael Medved

Sarah Michelle Gellar battled countless monsters as Buffy the Vampire Slayer. Her biggest challenge in *The Return* is to keep from yawning. – John Monaghan

Except for helping you maintain a consistently slow pulse rate, *The Good Shepherd* isn't good for much. – Bill Muller

(of *Date Movie*) The writers must have forgotten the definition of parody when they threw darts on a board to come up with this script. – Rebecca Murray

The visual effect of Draco in *Dragonheart* was achieved using the same technology as that used for *Jurassic Park*, wherein hundreds of super-computers and thousands of man-hours are used to make the visual effects look every bit as realistic as 1920s bendable clay puppet technology. – Mike Nelson

(of *The Wizard of Oz*) It has dwarfs, music, Technicolour, freak characters and Judy Garland. It can't be expected to have a sense of humour as well and as for the light touch of fantasy, it weighs like a pound of fruitcake soaking wet. – *The New Republic*

(of *From Justin to Kelly*) For the panting masses of *American Idol* fans who imagine winning and going to live happily ever after in Lotusland, the message couldn't be clearer. You, too, might one day end up starring in the motion picture equivalent of Cheez Whiz. – *New York Times*

(of *Bonnie Prince Charlie*) David Niven rallying his hardy Highlanders to his standard in a voice hardly large enough to summon a waiter. – *The New Yorker*

(of *The Silver Chalice*) Paul Newman delivered his lines with the emotional fervour of a conductor announcing local stops. – *The New Yorker*

(of *The Buccaneer*) (Fredric) March came in like a lion and went out like a ham. – Frank Nugent

(of *Murder on the Orient Express*) Sidney Lumet ensures a smooth ride, but as usual takes too long to say what he means and brings the Express in twenty minutes late. – Chris Peachment

(of *The River*) This is one river that seems unlikely to run. – Chris Peachment

Clocking in at nearly three hours, *The Good Shepherd* is a numbing history of the CIA that leaves you Novocained. Jumps around in time like a frog with hiccups. – Rex Reed

(of *The Brothers Grimm*) Mr (Terry) Gilliam has no clear idea what he's doing, so the movie is nothing more than noise, costumes and disjointed special effects that do not make an acceptable substitute for the sense of tempo the rest of the film sorely lacks. – Rex Reed

(of *The Rocky Horror Picture Show*) The entire evening gave me a headache for which suicide seemed the only possible relief. – Rex Reed

(of *A Star Is Born*) Kris Kristofferson looked like the Werewolf of London stoned on cocaine and sounded like a dying buffalo. – Rex Reed

(of *Black Snake Moan*) Christina Ricci and Samuel L. Jackson . . . both sport laughable Southern accents that are about as authentic as Jamaicans playing bagpipes. – Rex Reed

(of *Glitter*) Only Mariah Carey could play herself in a movie and fuck it up. – *Retrocrush*

The Hindenburg manages to make one of the century's most sensational real-life catastrophes seem roughly as terrifying as a stubbed toe. – Frank Rich

(of *Lucky Lady*) A manic mess that tries to be all things to all people and ends up offering nothing to anyone. – Frank Rich

(of *Double Impact*) Sheldon Lettich directs with the limpness you associate with the vegetable he's nearly named after. – Jonathan Romney

Another Woman is a feel-good movie only in the sense that you feel much better when you stop watching it. – Simon Rose

Nothing can compare you for quite how bad *Gigli* is. – Jonathan Ross

I'd rather have chewed my own arm off than sit through something as putrid as *Pearl Harbor*. – Jonathan Ross

(of *Taxi*) As entertaining as watching a potato bake. – Marc Savlov

(of *The Adventures of Sherlock Holmes' Smarter Brother*) Director Gene Wilder has bitten off more than he can chew, and I can swallow. – John Simon

(of *The Arrangement*) As dead as the flower arrangement in an undertaker's parlour. – John Simon

(of Elizabeth Taylor in *The Taming of the Shrew*) Just how garish her commonplace accent, squeakily shrill voice, and the childish petulance with which she delivers her lines are, my pen is neither scratchy nor leaky enough to convey. – John Simon

David Lean's *Dr Zhivago* does for snow what his *Lawrence of Arabia* did for sand. – John Simon

(of *Material Girls*) "This thing is screwier than Courtney Love!" whimpers Hilary (Duff) in her usual Chihuahua-on-helium whine. Even she, however, manages to shine next to her aggravating older sister (Haylie), saddled as she is with all the comic timing of a mortally wounded elephant. – Neil Smith

(of *Stop! Or My Mom Will Shoot!*) A flatworm could write a better script . . . In some countries – China, I believe – running (the movie) once a week on government television has lowered the birth rate to zero. If they ran it twice a week, I believe in twenty years China would be extinct. – Sylvester Stallone, rubbishing the 1992 comedy in which he starred with Estelle Getty

Parting Shots is essentially the equivalent of vanity publishing: a film directed by Michael Winner, produced by Michael Winner, written by Michael Winner, edited by Michael Winner, and made for Michael Winner to watch, perhaps in company with Michael Winner's current girlfriend. – Mark Steyn

(of *We Are Marshall*) A depressingly mechanical sports drama that seems not to have been written and directed so much as home assembled, Ikea-style, by pictorial instruction. – Jan Stuart

(of *Vertigo*) The old master has turned out another Hitchcock-and-bull story in which the mystery is not so much who done it as who cares. – *Time* magazine

(of *Stepping Out*, starring Liza Minnelli) Putting on a sad show, courtesy of Liza with a zzzzz. – *Time Out*

(of *The Stick Up*) The worst film of this or possibly any year. – Barry Took

(of *Billy Bathgate*) Dustin Hoffman seems to have taken a correspondence course in playing gangsters from Al Pacino. – Christopher Tookey

9 Weeks put the rot back into erotica – Christopher Tookey

(of *Desperate Hours*) This film should never have been released, not even on parole. – Christopher Tookey

Forrest Gump is roughly as truthful about the world of intellectual handicap as *The Little Mermaid* is about fish. – Christopher Tookey

(of 2006 culture clash movie *Prime*) The movie eventually seems to lose interest in the subject, though quite a bit later than the audience. – Christopher Tookey

Rocky Balboa contains every boxing cliché and then some, until it's the exhausted audience that feel like throwing in the towel. – Christopher Tookey

A romantic comedy released to cash in on February 14, *The Truth About Love* made me nostalgic for the good old says of the St Valentine's Day Massacre. It is so loathsome that when, towards the end, its leading man stood on the Clifton Suspension Bridge to meditate on his future, the majority of the audience muttered: "Jump!" – Christopher Tookey (of *Because I Said So*) The script is tasteless as well as clichéd and (Diane) Keaton spends most of the movie being hysterical. When she suffers from laryngitis half way through, it's a blessed if temporary relief. – Christopher Tookey

(of *The Number 23*) Jim Carrey gives the worst performance of his, or indeed any other actor's, career. – Christopher Tookey

(of *Norbit*) The thing seems to have been edited by a blind man, which I think is taking equal opportunities a little too far. – Christopher Tookey

(of George Clooney in *The Good German*) A performance so wooden that Ben Affleck would have been an improvement. – Christopher Tookey

(of *Wild Hogs*) Lethargic direction from Walt Becker suggests his abysmal *Van Wilder: Party Liaison* was no momentary aberration. – Christopher Tookey

How's *Alexander*? Not great . . . The strain of breathing life into the dead scroll of a script makes Alexander's plan to conquer the world look easy. – Pete Travers

(of *Body of Evidence*) Madonna was guilty as hell. Her crime is that she just can't act, not with one stitch – or stitchless. – *USA Today*

Other practitioners of cinematic drivel can rest a little easier now; they can walk in the daylight with their heads held high, a smile on their lips and a song in their hearts. It's okay, they'll tell themselves. I didn't make *Alone in the Dark*. – Rob Vaux

(of *Battlefield Earth*) A crime against celluloid. – Rob Vaux

(of *A Love Song For Bobby Long*) The cast appears to have mistaken a verbose screenplay for great writing. – James Verniere

There's at least one idea out there for a thoughtful, provocative movie on the subject of human cloning. Unfortunately *Godsend* isn't it. – Jeff Vice

It takes some sort of talent to make a film as completely strident, over-bearing, heavy-handed and downright off-putting as *The Life of David Gale*, although it's not exactly clear what type of talent it requires. – Jeff Vice

(of *A Star Is Born*, starring Barbra Streisand) A bore is starred. – *Village Voice* (of *The Dukes of Hazzard*) Who can forget Jessica Simpson? You will, if you're lucky. – Pete Vonder Haar

(of *Envy*) The most telling symptom of bad comedy is pretty easy to diagnose: no laughs. – Pete Vonder Haar

(of *Leonard Part 6*) Movies this bad should be handled with Teflon gloves and a pair of tongs. – Scott Weinberg

(of *The Music Lovers*) Glenda Jackson's thunderous full-frontal, carpet-clawing caricature is a calamity of mistiming. – Mark Whitman

(of *Gigli*, starring Ben Affleck and Jennifer Lopez) Such an utter wreck of a movie you expect to see it lying on its side somewhere in rural Pennsylvania, with a small gang of engineers circling and a wisp of smoke rising from the caboose.   Stephen Whitty

(of *The Village*) Every village needs an idiot – and M. Night Shyamalan is hoping it's you. – Staci Layne Wilson

MUSIC

Anton Bruckner wrote the same symphony nine times, trying to get it right. He failed. – Edward Abbey

(of Eminem) Marshall Mathers is back worse than before, making a snore, whining in the microphone. – Christina Aguilera

(of Kelly Osbourne) She is the nastiest person I have ever, ever seen. – Christina Aguilera

When has Pink not been copying me, in her fashion and so on? It's always like "Gosh, I just wore that last week." – Christina Aguilera

(of Britney Spears) I can't believe that girl bought her own engagement ring! I've seen it, up close. It looks like she got it on QVC. I know Britney. She's not trailer trash, but she sure acts that way. – Christina Aguilera

(of Pete Doherty) Babyshambles have only ever released one song – one song! People talk about this great talent, but there's nothing to him. He's a mess. – Damon Albarn

When Jack Benny plays the violin, it sounds as if the strings are still back in the cat. — Fred Allen

(Bob Geldof is) so self-important and takes himself far too seriously. He doesn't publicise that he's got a two-million quid house in Battersea and all that. — Lily Allen

(of Madonna) The most over-rated person in pop history. — Lily Allen

(to the Kooks) Your regurgitated indie rock days are numbered so get over yourselves. — Lily Allen

There are a lot of people I know who are music geeks. They will sit there memorizing every single piece of information that they can off the back of a vinyl single so that they can impress their mates. They are always into Kraftwerk and things like that. — Lily Allen

(of the Pussycat Dolls) They take all their clothes off, don't say anything, promote womanizing and look like lapdancers. — Lily Allen

For *Everyone Says I Love You*, only Drew Barrymore's singing voice was dubbed. It was outside the limits of human tolerance. — Woody Allen

Drew Barrymore sings so badly, deaf people refuse to watch her lips move. — Woody Allen

I sometimes think I'd like opera better without the singing. — John Amis

So, Fyfe, your band (Guillemots) are famous for using odd instruments. Well, when I say famous . . . — Simon Amstell, *Never Mind The Buzzcocks*

Clive Anderson (to the Bee Gees): You're *hit* writers, aren't you? I think that's the word anyway.
Barry Gibb: That's the nice word.
Clive Anderson: We're one letter short.

(to the Bee Gees) At one time you called yourselves Les Tosseurs. Well, you'll always be tosseurs to me. — Clive Anderson

Jack Benny played Mendelssohn last night. Mendelssohn lost. — Anon

James Blunt is so annoying he makes me want to rip my eyeballs out just to have something to plug my ears with. — Anon

The Darkness are nothing more than a second-rate Queen tribute band. – Anon

What do the Queen Mother and Vanilla Ice have in common? – Artificial hip. – Anon

Madonna sings like Mickey Mouse on helium. – Anon

If white bread could sing, it would like Olivia Newton-John. – Anon

You know what I love about the Internet? We now have rappers who used to be gangsters and thugs telling us not to download music because that would be stealing. – Anon

(of Westlife) One of those bands who make you want to stamp your feet – all over them. – Anon

I want you to play tonight like you've never played before. Together! – Anon orchestra conductor

I don't mind what language an opera is sung in so long as it is a language I don't understand. – Edward Appleton

Barry Manilow said if he'd had a nose job, he'd have ruined his voice. Yet as he grows older, the nose keeps growing but the voice isn't getting any better. – Emile Ardolino

Every dude has had a fantasy about Jessica Simpson. Here's mine: Jessica, hold your sister Ashlee so I can kick her in the throat. – Dave Attell

No opera plot can be sensible, for people do not sing when they are feeling sensible. – W. H. Auden

I'd rather stick needles in my eyes than ever sing in the Eurovision Song Contest again. – Michael Ball

We idolized the Beatles, except for those of us who idolized the Rolling Stones, who in those days still had many of their original teeth. – Dave Barry

Mariah Carey gets her dressing room repainted! I would never do that. What proper singer would? – Shirley Bassey

I love Wagner, but the music I prefer is that of a cat hung up by its tail outside a window and trying to stick to the panes of glass with its claws. – Charles Baudelaire

All Bach's last movements are like the running of a sewing machine. – Arnold Bax

(of opera) If a thing isn't worth saying, you sing it. – Pierre Beaumarchais

The bagpipes sound exactly the same when you have finished learning them as when you start. – Thomas Beecham

Brass bands are all very well in their place – outdoors and several miles away. – Thomas Beecham

No operatic tenor has yet died soon enough for me. – Thomas Beecham

(to a member of the orchestra he was conducting) We can't expect you to be with us all the time, but perhaps you would be good enough to keep in touch now and again. – Thomas Beecham

Beethoven's last quartets were written by a deaf man and should only be listened to by a deaf man. – Thomas Beecham

(of Beethoven's Seventh Symphony) It's like a lot of yaks jumping about. – Thomas Beecham

(of Edward Elgar) The musical equivalent of St Pancras station. – Thomas Beecham

(of Arturo Toscanini) A glorified bandmaster. – Thomas Beecham

(to a fellow composer) I liked your opera. I think I will set it to music. – Ludwig van Beethoven

Rossini would have been a great composer if his teacher had spanked him enough on his backside. – Ludwig van Beethoven

Snow Patrol approximate the experience of being belaboured by a relentless robotic assailant armed with a sockful of saccharine and gravel. – David Bennum

Amy Winehouse: a tottering ragbag of bones, tattoos and teeth. – David Bennum

Handel is a tub of pork and beer. – Hector Berlioz

Did I tell you about my nightmare? I dreamt I was Madonna, shopping at Tiffany's, where I was trying to buy some class. – Sandra Bernhard

I look at my friendship with Madonna as like having a gallstone. You deal with it, there is pain, and then you pass it. – Sandra Bernhard

Vanilla Ice was the Pat Boone of rap. – Jello Biafra

The recording artist once named Pink will be called Beige when people realize that that's the colour you get when you mix her name with the crap she records. – Jack Black

MTV is to music what KFC is to chicken. – Lewis Black

(of Christina Aguilera) All crass and no class. – Mr Blackwell

(of Mariah Carey) Mariah, the fashion pariah, has finally found her stylistic niche, let's crown her the Queen of Catastrophic Kitsch. – Mr Blackwell

(of Cher) A bona fide fashion fiasco – from nose to toe she's the tacky tattooed terror. – Mr Blackwell

(of sisters Ashlee and Jessica Simpson) From gaudy to grim to downright frenetic, these two prove that bad taste is positively genetic. – Mr Blackwell

Britney Spears looks like an over-the-hill Lolita. – Mr Blackwell

(of Barbra Streisand) She looks like the masculine Bride of Frankenstein. – Mr Blackwell

People are sick to the teeth of processed and hyped pop bands. It is crap. – Bono

(of Wolfgang Amadeus Mozart) He was happily married – but his wife wasn't. – Victor Borge

(of Franz Liszt) It is gaudy musical harlotry, savage and incoherent bellow-ings. – *Boston Gazette*

I think Mick Jagger would be astounded and amazed if he realized to how many people he is not a sex symbol but a mother image. – David Bowie

I heard Michael Jackson is moving to France. For the first time my sympathies are with the French people. – Boy George

Elton John is like our headmaster, the grand old dame of pop, with a beautiful voice but living in an ornate bubble, full of fresh flowers, surrounded by people who nod and laugh at everything he says. – Boy George

Elton John would sing with a toilet-roll holder if he thought it would get him more publicity. – Boy George

If Madonna were a drag queen, she would be called Ruth Less. – Boy George

George Michael was so desperate to be famous, he feared that if fans discovered he was "a true Greek" it would all end in tears. – Boy George

Prince looks like a dwarf who's been dipped in a bucket of pubic hair. – Boy George

No wonder Bob Geldof's such an expert on famine – he's been dining out on "I Don't Like Mondays" for thirty years. – Russell Brand

Debussy played the piano with the lid down. – Robert Bresson

Oh my goodness! I can see a bright white light, and I can hear my friends and relatives beckoning me into the afterlife. Wait, what's that . . . a Richard Marx video? Oh no, I'm going to hell! – Julie Brown, on dying

Gracie (Allen) made a major contribution to the opera world. She stayed out of it. – George Burns

(of Lionel Richie) He's got a chin like an ironing board. – Pete Burns

Rod Stewart says the secret of looking young is drinking three glasses of wine a day. What a revelation: Rod thinks he looks young! Who sold him his mirrors? Anne Robinson? – Garry Bushell

Mick Jagger moves like a parody between a majorette girl and Fred Astaire. – Truman Capote

(of Mick Jagger) He's about as sexy as a pissing toad. – Truman Capote

(of Jennifer Lopez) I'd rather be onstage with a pig. – Mariah Carey

(of Madonna) I was a fan of hers back when she was popular. – Mariah Carey

Beethoven was so hard of hearing, he thought he was a painter. – George Carlin

If Frank Sinatra owed you a favour, you should ask him to have one of his buddies kill Andy Williams. – George Carlin

Bad things come in threes. A good example of that is Atomic Kitten. Whenever I think about Atomic Kitten, I'm saddened because I think there's a supermarket somewhere in the north that's three girls short. – Jimmy Carr

When you eat a lot of spicy food, you can lose your taste. When I was in India last summer, I was listening to a lot of Michael Bolton. – Jimmy Carr

Sting is always boasting about his eight-hour tantric sex sessions with his wife, Trudie Styler. Imagine how long he could keep it up if she was a looker. – Jimmy Carr

It's hard work reviewing a Stereophonics album. For a start, it involves having to sit all the way through a Stereophonics album. – Pete Cashmore

Beatlemania is like the frenzied dancing and shouting of voodoo worshippers and the howls and bodily writhings of converts among primitive evangelical sects in the southern states of America. – Dr F. Casson

Berlioz composes by splashing his pen over the manuscript and leaving the issue to chance. – Frederic Chopin

Alban Berg's music is a soporific, by the side of which the telephone book is a strong cup of coffee. – Samuel Chotzinoff

If a horse could sing in a monotone, the horse would sound like Carly Simon, only a horse wouldn't rhyme "yacht", "apricot", and "gavotte". – Robert Christgau

I don't know why Shirley Bassey's always so nasty about me. I mean she's a bit wrinkly, isn't she? She has a cheek, she's always drinking champagne. She needs to shut up. I have met her, she was OK, but rude. – Charlotte Church after Bassey criticized her drinking

Pete Doherty creates all this misery for himself to write songs and then doesn't even turn up to play them. And they're not that good anyway. – Charlotte Church

Pete Doherty thinks no one understands him but of course we all do. You're just being a wanker. Go home. – Charlotte Church

I can't stand Bob Dylan. He sounds like a freak. – Charlotte Church

Dizzee Rascal is a bit much for me. He sounds like a twelve-year-old boy on the brink of puberty. – Charlotte Church (of Snow Patrol) That guy's voice just drones on and on – it's like bagpipes. – Charlotte Church

(on criticism by Cheryl Tweedy) I thought, "Love, when you can sing 'Ave Maria', then have a go." – Charlotte Church

(of Mary J. Blige) Frankly, I'd rather listen to a pneumatic drill. She's nothing more than a spelling mistake – it should be Mary J. Bilge. – Jeremy Clarkson, *The World According to Clarkson*

Live Earth is committed to being the first carbon neutral music event. Hybrid cars will be used for transport, food will be served in biodegradable containers and the stage will be illuminated by the light that shines out of Bono's arse. – Jeremy Clarkson, *Have I Got News For You*

Lonnie Donegan died in 2002 and Mark Knopfler and Rolf Harris played at his tribute show. Friends say it's what he would have wanted – to be dead at the time. – Julian Clary

David Beckham should guide Posh in the direction of a singing coach because she's nowhere near as good at her job as her husband is at his. – Brian Clough

Even the deaf would be traumatized by prolonged exposure to the most hideous croak in Western culture. (Keith) Richards' voice is simply horrible. – Nick Coleman

I wonder how many Chinese had to go bald to supply Elton John with his latest hair? – Peter Cook

(of Marilyn Manson) He has a woman's name and wears make-up. How original! – Alice Cooper

Listening to the Fifth Symphony of Ralph Vaughan Williams is like staring at a cow for forty-five minutes. – Aaron Copland

If reaching a larger market means that you have to sound like Christopher Cross, then I'd rather stay where I am. – Elvis Costello

I have seen Madonna up close. Neither the music nor the image inspires my loins. – David Coverdale

People are wrong when they say opera is not what it used to be. It is what it used to be. That is what's wrong with it. – Noël Coward

I've never bought a Bob Dylan record. A singing poet? It just bores me to tears. – Simon Cowell

(of Mick Hucknall) I just find him very irritating. He's obnoxious. – Simon Cowell

(of Madonna) A housewife, who used to be good looking. – Simon Cowell

My advice would be to have a second hit and then you can have an opinion. – Simon Cowell to Jamelia after she said his protégée Leona Lewis sounded "a bit Mariah Carey circa 1990"

(of James Blunt) There's no humour in his music and there doesn't seem to be much depth. It's the sort of thing you'd write on a card if you were sending flowers. – Graham Coxon

(of Britney Spears) She can't sing, write or play an instrument to save her life. – David Crosby

Why don't you get your cock out and play snare with it? It will probably sound better. – Dave Davies to drummer Mick Avory during a Kinks' gig

(of Tina Turner) All legs and hair with a mouth that could swallow the whole stadium and the hot-dog stand. – Laura Lee Davies

Girls Aloud insist they're going to be selling just as many records next Christmas as they did this one. Well, provided they hang on to their Saturday jobs at HMV they could well be right. – *Dead Ringers*

The organizers of this week's gala, star-studded concert to remember George Harrison say it was such a success that next week they plan another one, to try and remember who Ringo Starr was. – *Dead Ringers*

How Garth Brooks achieved superstar status remains as much a mystery as the *Marie Celeste*. – Fred Dellar

Ozzy Osbourne couldn't carry a tune around in a suitcase. – Ronnie James Dio

Berlioz, musically speaking, is a lunatic; a classical composer only in Paris, the great city of quacks. – *Dramatic and Musical Review*

(of Franz Liszt) Composition indeed! Decomposition is the proper word for such hateful fungi. – *Dramatic and Musical Review* (of Christina Aguilera) She's an ungrateful, spoiled-rotten asshole. – Fred Durst

Jazz: music invented for the torture of imbeciles. – Henry van Dyke

(of Rod Stewart) He was so mean it hurt him to go to the bathroom. – Britt Ekland

(of Jennifer Lopez) Culturally and creatively, the woman is about as interesting as overheated meringue. – Barbara Ellen

Me and Mariah (Carey) did have a relationship. It didn't work. Our personalities collided. She's a diva, and I'm a little more regular, I guess. – Eminem

I can look at Insane Clown Posse and laugh. They can't do anything to me. What can they do to me? They have no credibility, no respect, no talent, they have nothing. – Eminem

(of Britney Spears) I'm not a fan of her music, that's for sure. I think it's corny as hell . . . She sucks and she can't sing. – Eminem

Michael Bolton has had nine hits this year . . . on his website. – Dame Edna Everage

(of Cher) A poor little mite wearing two bottle tops and a cobweb. – Dame Edna Everage

Far too noisy, my dear Mozart, far too many notes. – Archduke Ferdinand of Austria

In a recent interview, fifteen-year-old British opera star Charlotte Church said that New Yorkers are being overdramatic about the attacks of 9/11, and that firefighters are being treated like stars, which she "just doesn't agree with". But don't be too hard on Charlotte, because she's only fifteen, and when she grows up, she's gonna be *fat*. – Tina Fey

Ashlee Simpson did a special performance at Mall of America this week. Reports from those present say that the venue was completely packed; I mean seriously, people were like sardines, wall to wall, there had to be ten of them all pushed against the giant stage they constructed . . . in the janitor's closet. Because she sucks! – Tina Fey

(of Arnold Schoenberg) He was ignored till he began to smash the parlour furniture, throw bombs and hitch together ten pianolas, all playing different tunes, whereupon everyone began to talk about him. – Henry T. Fink

(of conductor Leopold Stokowski) He gave the impression of a glittering, multi-coloured painted shell; when one looked inside, one found an infinite emptiness. – Massimo Freccia

(of Coldplay) That lot are just a bunch of knobhead students. Chris Martin looks like a geography teacher. – Liam Gallagher

(of Arctic Monkeys) Their public persona is now of a bunch of grumpy old men. – Noel Gallagher

(of Pete Doherty) Overrated. He's marginally talented, but not anywhere near as good as me. If he wasn't shagging a supermodel, no one outside of *NME* would give a shit about him. – Noel Gallagher

He's gone to the zoo. The monkeys are bringing their kids to look at him. – Noel Gallagher on brother Liam

Liam's only got two problems: everything he says and everything he does. – Noel Gallagher taking another pop at his brother

(of Scissor Sisters) They're huge in England, but there's no accounting for bad taste as far as the English are concerned. – Noel Gallagher

Robbie Williams? You mean that fat dancer from Take That? – Noel Gallagher

As he tends to refer to himself in the third person, Robbie Williams is obviously a character that he's invented and the music he makes is shit. – Noel Gallagher

I'm one of the rare breed of rock 'n' rollers who actually does my own shopping. It doesn't freak me out going to buy a pint of milk. Not like Robbie Williams. – Noel Gallagher

Razorlight disgust me. Johnny Borrell . . . comes across as a bit of a knob. – Peaches Geldof

Madonna is mutton dressed as lamb. She's just not relevant now. – Peaches Geldof

(of Arctic Monkeys' Alex Turner) I don't think there's anything special to warrant how cocky he has become. – Peaches Geldof

Art Garfunkel makes Paul Simon look like LL Cool J. – Ian Gittins

(of Prince) Bambi with testosterone. – Owen Gleiberman

(of James Blunt) I think he sounds like some weird guy with fuzzy hair from the Seventies. – Alison Goldfrapp

We're wasting more energy than Ricky Martin's girlfriend. – Groundskeeper Willie, *The Simpsons*

The (Franz) Liszt bombast is bad; it is very bad; in fact there is only one thing worse in his music, and that is his affected and false simplicity. – Philip Hale

Snoop Dogg was arrested in Burbank recently when cops searched the rap star's car and found a handgun, cocaine and marijuana. He's in real trouble now. When you get a gift bag from the Grammy Awards, you are supposed to declare it as income. – Argus Hamilton

The prelude to Wagner's *Tristan und Isolde* reminds one of the old Italian painting of a martyr whose intestines are slowly unwound from his body on a reel. – Eduardo Hanslick

(of Pyotr Illyich Tchaikovsky's Violin Concerto) It gives us, for the first time, the hideous notion that there can be music which stinks to the ear. – Eduardo Hanslick

I met Bananarama once. They are living proof that make-up works. – Chesney Hawkes

Pete Doherty is grubbier than an overflowing wheelie bin. – *heat* magazine

(of the Beatles) Their lyrics are unrecognizable as the Queen's English. – Edward Heath

Perhaps it was because Nero played the fiddle, they burned Rome. – Oliver Herford

You know, if you play New Kids on the Block albums backwards . . . they sound better. Gives them that edge they're missing. – Bill Hicks

Irving Berlin had a voice that sounded like a hoarse tomcat with its tail in a clothes wringer. – Bob Hope

For a simple urban boy such as me, the idea of listening to three Somerset folk singers sounds like hell. — Kim Howells

I've watched Justin (Timberlake), but every single move he does is stolen. — Mick Jagger

When I realized Beyonce mimes half or three-quarters of her show, that took a lot away for me. I thought, "Are you an artist or are you an actress?" — Jamelia

Perry (Como) gave his usual impersonation of a man who has been simultaneously told to say "cheese" and shot in the back with a poisoned arrow. — Clive James

Rod Stewart has an attractive voice and a highly unattractive bottom. He now spends more time wagging the latter than exercising the former. — Clive James

Disco dancing is just the steady thump of a giant moron knocking in an endless nail. — Clive James

For the lifespan he's lasted, Chuck Berry's productivity has been nil, more or less. — Elton John

Hear'Say are the ugliest band I have ever seen. That guy Danny looks like Shrek. — Elton John

(of Madonna) Anyone who lip-synchs on stage when you pay seventy-five pounds to see them should be shot. — Elton John

He's pathetic. It's like a monkey with arthritis trying to go on stage and look young. I have great respect for the Stones but they would have been better if they'd thrown Keith (Richards) out fifteen years ago. — Elton John

Nowadays, record companies want the quick buck from the Backstreet Boys, from the N'Syncs, from the Britney Spears, from the S Club 7s, from the Steps. They've always been around. I'm not knocking the music, but it's like packets of cereal: there are too many of them, and too many of them are just average and mediocre. It's just fodder. — Elton John

(of Madonna) Armed with a wiggle and a Minnie Mouse squawk, she is coarse and charmless. — Sheila Johnson

Feargal Sharkey has a face like a bucket with a dent in it. — Allan Jones

Music in shops can do many things . . . If Radiohead are playing, it will probably make you want to go home, throw all your clothes away and ceremoniously top yourself. – Dylan Jones

Never should it be said that (Rod) Stewart hasn't done his bit for female emancipation – he's seen more sex than a policeman's torch. – Dylan Jones

During much of the Eighties, his eyes lassoed by eyeliner, and believing that an old silk jumpsuit would never let him down, (Rod) Stewart started to bear a disconcerting resemblance to Olivia Newton-John. – Dylan Jones

(of Keane) Chart-cosy, devoid of sensory-thrashing bursts of noise and with a fresh-faced lead singer who looks like he's just been scrumping for apples. – Tim Jonze

They've found a new chamber in the Great Pyramid. And here's what was on the wall: Rolling Stones Tour, 1567 BC. – Craig Kilborn

(of Michael Jackson's acquittal on child molestation charges) It's like they say, if you're rich and white, you can get away with anything. – Jimmy Kimmel

Michael Jackson offered a million bucks to some hospital in England to buy up the bones of the Elephant Man. Is that sick, or what? But it makes sense though – one freak trying to buy the remains of another freak. – Sam Kinison

(Max) Reger's name is the same backwards or forwards, and his music displays the same characteristic. – Irving Kolodin

(to Phil Collins after his Academy Award) When they read your name out, were you as surprised as everyone else? – *The Kumars At No. 42*

Peter Andre: the most unwelcome comeback since Jimi Hendrix's vomit. – Mark Lamarr, *Never Mind The Buzzcocks*

Carrie Fisher was James Blunt's landlady and let him make a single in her bathroom. If James Blunt ever asks to use your bathroom, make sure he's only having a shit. – Mark Lamarr, *Never Mind The Buzzcocks*

John Denver: cleaner than Marie Osmond's tampon. – Mark Lamarr, *Never Mind The Buzzcocks*

Bob Dylan: a tuneless, wrinkled scrotum. – Mark Lamarr, *Never Mind The Buzzcocks*

Gareth Gates went out with Jordan, which is the dictionary definition of tit for tat. – Mark Lamarr, *Never Mind The Buzzcocks*

Nicola from Girls Aloud has a fear of stickers. Psychologists have looked into this and pointed out that it's because these stickers normally say, "Girls Aloud CD Reduced To Clear." – Mark Lamarr, *Never Mind The Buzzcocks*

Barry Manilow famously wrote the words, "I can't smile, I can't sing, I'm finding it hard to do anything." Not only the lyrics to one of his biggest hits but also Geri Halliwell's CV. – Mark Lamarr, *Never Mind The Buzzcocks*

Vanilla Ice would have trouble rhyming Mercedes and ladies, even if he was run down by a Mercedes full of ladies, all of whom were waving rhyming dictionaries only containing the words "Mercedes" and "ladies". – Mark Lamarr, *Never Mind The Buzzcocks*

Enrique Iglesias: greasier than a disoriented gannet swimming away from the *Exxon Valdez* oil spill straight into Peter Stringfellow's discarded thong. – Mark Lamarr, *Never Mind The Buzzcocks*

Marilyn Manson: made entirely from Cher offcuts. – Mark Lamarr, *Never Mind The Buzzcocks*

Despite being a completely manufactured band, McFly are actually quite highly regarded by some critics. Their names are often mentioned alongside Nirvana and the Clash – usually as the answer in odd-one-out competitions. – Mark Lamarr, *Never Mind The Buzzcocks*

Pink Floyd: the highlight of Live 8, if you count mustard gas as the highlight of World War One. – Mark Lamarr, *Never Mind The Buzzcocks*

Things that are better-looking than the Spice Girls: loft lagging, a bucket of slops, and a waxwork model of Bill Bailey that's been left by the radiator. – Mark Lamarr, *Never Mind The Buzzcocks*

Shania Twain once performed at the Nobel Peace Prize Concert with Elton John and Phil Collins. You probably remember that year: they had to wrestle a Stanley knife off Nelson Mandela. – Mark Lamarr, *Never Mind The Buzzcocks*

Westlife, Darius and A1 were held up in a tailback on their way to 2002's Party In The Park. It was the first time a traffic jam had been awarded a Grammy for outstanding contribution to music. – Mark Lamarr, *Never Mind The Buzzcocks*

Wham split over the Gulf War – the gulf in talent between them. – Mark Lamarr, *Never Mind The Buzzcocks*

Joss Stone recently had to duet with Robbie Williams at the Brits. The only way I'd duet with Robbie Williams is on a tandem parachute jump. As long as I had the parachute and he had the tandem. – Mark Lamarr, *Never Mind The Buzzcocks*

(of Britney Spears) I'm more about a performance, she's more about entertainment and sex, being a sex symbol and trying to look like she's having sex. – Avril Lavigne

Luciano Pavarotti is only slightly smaller than Vermont. – Norman Lebrecht

Mariah Carey says she believes there is an orchestrated conspiracy by a large number of people to keep her career and her record sales down. I think that's called the public. – Jay Leno

Mariah Carey, who checked into hospital for extreme exhaustion, is doing better. Her condition has been upgraded from serious to slightly self-indulgent. – Jay Leno

Whitney Houston rear-ended a city bus with her sports car, but no one was hurt. She said she didn't know what happened. One minute she was concentrating on the big white line, and the next, boom! – Jay Leno

Michael Jackson is at home recovering from a broken foot. He can't perform. You know what you call a Jackson who can't perform? LaToya. – Jay Leno

They were talking about the racial composition of the jury pool for the Michael Jackson trial. They said it was twenty-five percent African-American and seventy-five percent white. Wait, I'm sorry, that's Michael Jackson . . . – Jay Leno

(of Michael Jackson's acquittal) Legal experts say the key was that the defence really didn't play the race card. Well, they didn't know which race to play! – Jay Leno

Michael Jackson announced that he wants to record a song for the victims of Hurricane Katrina. Michael said if he could touch just one child . . . – Jay Leno

Mick Jagger is now at that awkward age between being a Stone and passing one. – Jay Leno

Jennifer Lopez has got engaged again. She's an amazing woman. She has movies coming out, she has CDs, she has concerts, she has her own perfume line, yet she still finds time two or three times a year to get married. – Jay Leno

Madonna announced that she's four months pregnant. I wonder who the lucky team is. I believe the father is the Denver Nuggets. – Jay Leno

Sixty-year-old Barry Manilow is going in for hip surgery this month. That's three words you've never heard before in the same sentence: Barry, Manilow, and hip. – Jay Leno

The Rolling Stones say their current US tour is a lot harder than their first, when we had only thirteen states. – Jay Leno

The latest rumour is that Britney Spears is pregnant again. It turns out it was not planned. She said it happened from sitting on a limo seat. – Jay Leno

Michael Jackson has introduced his own line of candy. It's white chocolate with a nut inside. – David Letterman

Leonard Bernstein has been disclosing musical secrets that have been well known for over four hundred years. – Oscar Levant

Leonard Bernstein uses music as an accompaniment to his conducting. – Oscar Levant

(to George Gershwin) Play us a medley of your hit. – Oscar Levant

(of Frederick Delius) The musical equivalent of blancmange. – Bernard Levin

(of Bo Diddley) If he ever gets out of the key of E, he might be dangerous. – Jerry Lee Lewis

(of rapper Foxy Brown) We don't have a problem. I don't think about her. I don't care about her, because I don't deal with the devil. – Lil Kim

(of ZZ Top) When the hits dried up, they chained themselves to a radiator and became a Terry Waite tribute band. – Tony Livesey

(Fred) Durst is so rigorously faux-masculine that he looks like a male impersonator. Fred's a golfer and an executive. I find nothing in his voice, nothing of value, nothing of sex or art or death or love. It's a void and the truth of the matter is he hasn't really sold that much. He's not some sales phenomenon. He's a primo ass-kisser. – Courtney Love

In rock, you're nothing until you've slept with Winona Ryder. – Courtney Love

(of Grace Slick) She's like somebody's mum who'd a few too many drinks at a cocktail party. – Nick Lowe

Billy Idol: the Perry Como of Punk. – John Lydon

It seemed likely that the Spice Girls were going to get together to sing at Live 8 but the world's poor said, "No one's that hungry." – Des Lynam

(of Darius) That silly little goatee beard made him look like Acker Bilk's lovechild. – Nigel Lythgoe

(of Kym Marsh) Christmas has gone, but the goose is still fat. – Nigel Lythgoe

I am unable to see in (Bob) Dylan anything other than a youth of mediocre talent. Only a completely non-critical audience, nourished on the watery pap of pop music, could have fallen for such tenth-rate drivel. – Ewan MacColl

(note to Elton John) The easiest way for you to lose ten pounds is to just take off your wig. – Madonna

(of Sinead O'Connor) She looks like she's had a run-in with a lawnmower. She's about as sexy as a Venetian blind. – Madonna

Elvis (Presley) transcends his talent to the point of dispensing with it altogether. – Greil Marcus

Elvis Costello looks like Buddy Holly after drinking a can of STP Oil Treatment. – Dave Marsh

Fee Waybill of the Tubes had the most unique range in rock: two notes, both flat. – Dave Marsh

(of Yoko Ono) I don't think she's the brightest of buttons. – Paul McCartney

(of Robbie Williams) It's people like him who are destroying British pop culture. He has one percent of Mick Jagger's talent. He's the post 9/11 feel good factor. He doesn't mean anything. He's utterly vacant, a showbiz chancer. – Alan McGee

Kate Bush: sort of like the consequences of mating Patti Smith with a Hoover vacuum cleaner. – Dave McGee

Bananarama display the discreet choreography of a herd of clubfooted elephants. – *Melody Maker*

Michael Jackson hasn't just lost the plot, he's lost the whole library! – *Melody Maker*

Simply Red are just music for chartered accountants to court to in wine bars. – *Melody Maker*

The opera is to music what a bawdy house is to a cathedral. – H. L. Mencken

(of Elton John) He makes millions playing those old classics day in and day out, whereas my drive and passion is still about the future. – George Michael

The only thing Madonna will ever do like a virgin is give birth in a stable. – Bette Midler

I hope Harry Secombe dies before me because I don't want him singing at my funeral. – Spike Milligan

Of all the noises known to man, opera is the most expensive. – Molière

Robbie Williams has decided not to "crack" America because he likes living there without the level of fame he has here. Just as well, seeing as the Americans haven't exactly taken to his self-absorbed offerings anyway. – Suzanne Moore

Going to the opera, like getting drunk, is a sin that carries its own punishment with it. – Hannah More

Pete Doherty is a moronic slab of heroin-fuelled waste. He can't sing, can't dance, sweats a lot and has spots and dirty fingernails. – Piers Morgan

Pete Doherty's singing is a tuneless whining noise more akin to a live lobster being boiled. – Piers Morgan

Madonna prances about on stage like some ageing stripper. – Piers Morgan

If I go round to someone's house and there's an Eric Clapton record, I just walk out. – Jon Moss

Twenty years ago, Westlife would have been digging the M25. They've done well for a bunch of spud-faced, tone-deaf chancers. – Al Murray

I don't like country music, but I don't mean to denigrate those who do; and for the people who like country music, denigrate means "put down". – Bob Newhart (of Igor Stravinsky) His music used to be original. Now it's aboriginal. – Ernest Newman

Is Wagner a human being at all? Is he not rather a disease? – Friedrich Nietzsche

Yoko Ono's voice sounded like an eagle being goosed. – Ralph Novak

Christina Aguilera got married last weekend and she asked that the guests not talk to the Press about the wedding because she's shy. Then she asked the guests not to stare at her diamond-studded crotchless wedding dress. – Conan O'Brien

Rock star Adam Ant has pleaded guilty to hitting a man during a bar fight. If Adam Ant really did attack the man, it would be his first hit since 1986. – Conan O'Brien

Michael Bolton says he now wants to become an opera singer, which is great, because now my Dad and I can hate the same kind of music. – Conan O'Brien

Cher announced at a press conference that she will be doing her final concert tour. Which is odd, because most of Cher's body will be doing its first concert tour. – Conan O'Brien

Celine Dion has been forced to cancel a week of concerts in Vegas because she has developed a rare ear infection. Doctors say it's not surprising considering how much Celine Dion music she's forced to listen to. – Conan O'Brien

Celine Dion is moving to Belgium to prepare for her comeback tour. Belgium has announced it's moving to France. – Conan O'Brien

Snoop Dogg and six members of his posse were arrested after they got into a fight with police. Two officers sustained minor injuries and fifteen were hospitalized for smoke inhalation. – Conan O'Brien

Kevin Federline's rap album won't be released until next year but his record producer leaked the single to the Internet. When asked why, the producer said, "Why should I have to suffer alone?" – Conan O'Brien

After fourteen years together, Whitney Houston and Bobby Brown are getting a divorce. Apparently, they have to get a divorce because hanging out together violated their paroles. – Conan O'Brien

Rapper Ice-T announced that he is going to produce a hip-hop album for *Baywatch* actor David Hasselhoff. The album will be in stores this fall, where it will stay. – Conan O'Brien

Michael Jackson was inducted into the Rock and Roll Hall of Fame. It caused quite a controversy, because his nose isn't eligible for another fifteen years. – Conan O'Brien

Fans of Elton John were shocked when at a recent concert he said the "F word" fifteen times in under one minute. Others say that was just what "Candle in the Wind" needed. – Conan O'Brien

In Philadelphia, a kindergarten teacher found a five-year-old student with eight bags of heroin. The teachers became suspicious when they noticed the kid had a Courtney Love lunchbox. – Conan O'Brien

It's been reported that at a recording studio Madonna got into a heated argument with George Michael. Apparently they were arguing about who slept with more men. – Conan O'Brien

The Country Music Channel is coming under fire for airing a brand new video that features nudity. Normally country fans wouldn't be that upset, but the artist in the video is Willie Nelson. – Conan O'Brien

Ozzy Osbourne and his wife Sharon renewed their wedding vows in a private ceremony and the Village People played at their wedding reception. The lead singer of the Village People said it was nice for once to be the normal people at a party. – Conan O'Brien

Ozzy Osbourne announced that he's going to perform at this year's Ozzfest without getting paid. Afterwards, the concert's promoter said: "Don't tell Ozzy, but we haven't paid him for over twelve years." – Conan O'Brien

Oprah Winfrey said she realized she needed to lose weight when she went to a heavyweight fight and discovered she weighed more than the winner. Coincidentally, the same thing happened to Pavarotti at the Kentucky Derby. – Conan O'Brien

US Weekly is reporting that Jessica Simpson's ex-husband Nick Lachey is dating a former Miss Kentucky beauty pageant winner. Nick says that after being married to Jessica, he's ready for the depth and intelligence of Miss Kentucky. – Conan O'Brien

The other day Britney Spears was spotted leaving a club with her new boyfriend. As they were driving away, she vomited on the guy. Music experts are calling it Britney's best release in years. – Conan O'Brien

Over the weekend Britney Spears got two tattoos and shaved her head. The amazing thing is it's the most motherly thing she's done in two weeks! – Conan O'Brien

Singer Justin Timberlake has agreed to appear in an upcoming McDonald's commercial. McDonald's tried to get all the members of N'Sync, but most of them now work at Burger King. – Conan O'Brien

(of Freddie Aguilar, billed as "the Bob Dylan of the Philippines") This is unfair, since he's good-looking, plays the guitar well, can carry a tune, and writes songs that make sense. – P. J. O'Rourke

Christina Aguilera looks like a drag queen. – Kelly Osbourne

People like Busted are faking it. They don't even play their guitars. One of them came up to my guitar player at a TV show I was doing and asked him, "Do you have the little string?" It's called a fucking High E string and he didn't even know what it was called! If he doesn't know what the string is called, then that's basic. I know what it is and I don't even play guitar. If you look at their videos, you don't even see them playing the chords, you just see them strumming. Anyone can strum. It's pathetic. – Kelly Osbourne

(of Axl Rose) He is bald. I think he wears hair extensions. But I think his problem is, his head is shoved too far up his ass. – Kelly Osbourne

To be Ozzy Osbourne, it's not so bad. It could be worse, I could be Sting. – Ozzy Osbourne

I don't get Robbie Williams. I think he seems rude and he's always getting his knickers off. – Gwyneth Paltrow

Bob Geldof is a loss to the road-sweeping profession, as well as actually looking like something swept up. – Jilly Parkin

Years of cosmetic surgery have transformed Michael Jackson into a pubescent Elizabeth Taylor. – Allison Pearson

Beyonce is a bitch. I only hope she gets bit on the arse by whatever animal she wears. – Pink, slamming fur-wearing Beyonce Knowles

Michael Jackson's album was only called "Bad" because there wasn't enough room on the sleeve for "Pathetic". – Prince

(of Igor Stravinsky) Bach on the wrong notes. – Sergey Prokofiev

Leonard Cohen's music gives you the feeling that your dog just died. – *Q magazine*

(of Paul McCartney) He has become the oldest living cute boy in the world. – Anna Quindlen

(of Wagner's *Parsifal*) The kind of opera that starts at six o'clock and after it has been going three hours you look at your watch and it says 6.20. – David Randolph

(of the Bee Gees' 1988 album "ESP") Few people know that the CIA is planning to cripple Iran by playing this album on special loudspeakers secretly parachuted into the country. – *Record Mirror*

Frank Zappa couldn't write a decent song if you gave him a million and a year on an island in Greece. – Lou Reed

Cute people do not age well. Look at Paul McCartney. It's hard to believe he was ever the cute one among the Beatles. Who would ever have believed that someday Ringo would look better than Paul? – Beryl Reid

Ms. (Jessica) Simpson may be the last performer in America who can make Whoopi Goldberg seem like the soul of wit. – Frank Rich

(of Chuck Berry) I couldn't warm to him even if I was cremated next to him. – Keith Richards

(of Mick Jagger's knighthood) I don't want to step out on stage with someone wearing a fucking coronet and sporting the old ermine. – Keith Richards

Elton John's writing is limited to songs for dead blondes. – Keith Richards

(of George Michael) He's a wimp in disguise. He should go home and shave. – Keith Richards

Olivia Newton-John is Australia's gift to insomniacs. It's nothing but the blonde singing the bland. – Minnie Riperton

Karen Carpenter became thin enough to get buried in pleats. – Joan Rivers

Michael Jackson called me up and said, "I'm innocent, I'm innocent, I'm so happy. I feel like a kid again." – Joan Rivers

With Mick Jagger's lips, he could French kiss a moose. – Joan Rivers

Madonna has just lost thirty pounds – she shaved her legs. – Joan Rivers

It's tough to figure what is going to be harder: drying out New Orleans or Diana Ross. – Joan Rivers

I've met Britney (Spears) close-up and she's a hairy little thing. I kept looking for a zipper to help her get out of what I thought was a gorilla suit. – Joan Rivers

(of Geri Halliwell) A nutcase in a bikini who last ate a carbohydrate in 1999. – John Robinson

Eminem is the voice of a generation while Robbie Williams is just the voice of Robbie Williams. – Peter Robinson

Actually, I never liked (Bob) Dylan's kind of music before. I always thought he sounded just like Yogi Bear. – Mick Ronson

If I had a hammer, I'd use it on Peter, Paul and Mary. – Howard Rosenberg

(to Madonna) Congratulations on your little black baby David. Are you stopping there, or getting more? When I went to Africa, all I got was a wallet. – Jonathan Ross

(of Spice Girl Mel C) In her shell suit she used to look like a single mum on a council estate. – Jonathan Ross

I thought Kanye West was a tube station near Uxbridge. – Jonathan Ross

Madonna's not the first star who's spent millions rescuing a young boy from destitution and poverty – look what Robbie Williams has done for Jonathan Wilkes. – Jonathan Ross

Wagner had some wonderful moments but awful quarter hours. – Gioacchino Rossini

My voice and my attitude were there to provide the balance. That's what's missing from Van Halen when I ain't in it. I'm the fun in that band. It's not something that you can fake or that you can hire anywhere else. Classic Van

Halen makes you wanna drink, dance, and screw. And the new Van Halen encourages you to drink milk, drive a Nissan, and have a relationship. – David Lee Roth

Beethoven always sounds like the upsetting of bags – with here and there a dropped hammer. – John Ruskin

Madonna is like a McDonald's hamburger. When you ask for a Big Mac, you know exactly what you're getting. It's enjoyable, but it satisfies only for the moment. – Sade

(of Maurice Ravel) If he'd been making shell cases during the war it might have been better for music. – Camille Saint-Saens

If Cher has another facelift she'll be wearing a beard. – Jennifer Saunders

Jon Bon Jovi is the only person I've ever interviewed who managed to make an hour feel too long. – Miranda Sawyer

(of Claude Debussy's "La Mer") The audience seemed rather disappointed: they expected the ocean, something big, something colossal, but they were served instead with some agitated water in a saucer. – Louis Schneider

(of a Bartok piano concerto) I suffered more than upon any occasion in my life apart from an incident or two connected with "painless dentistry". – Percy Scholes

When (Maria) Callas carried a grudge, she planted it, nursed it, fostered it, watered it, and watched it grow to sequoia size. – Harold C. Schonberg

(of Franz Liszt) Most of all he gives me the impression of being a spoilt child. – Clara Schumann

(of Paul McCartney's desire to be seen as bohemian) He still persists in making records that have all the unhinged beatnik wildness of a Neighbourhood Watch meeting. – Victoria Segal

(of Johannes Brahms) His wantonness is not vicious. It is that of a great baby, rather tirelessly addicted to dressing himself up as Handel or Beethoven and making a prolonged and intolerable noise. – George Bernard Shaw

There are some experiences in life which should not be demanded twice from any man, and one of them is listening to the Brahms Requiem. – George Bernard Shaw

Kiri te Kanawa: a viable alternative to valium. – Ira Siff

I'm so glad Courtney Love is here; I left my crack in my other purse. – Sarah Silverman

(of Elvis Presley) His kind of music is deplorable, a rancid-smelling aphrodisiac. – Frank Sinatra

Pavarotti is a UN ambassador – hopefully to nowhere where there's famine. That would be a cruel joke. Unless they're sending him as a bouncy castle to cheer things up a bit. – Linda Smith

The first time I saw Cher I thought she was a hooker. – Ronnie Spector

(of Chris Martin) A man with the face of an Internet dweeb and the dress sense of a teacher. – Mimi Spencer

Harpists spend ninety percent of their lives tuning their harps and ten percent playing out of tune. – Igor Stravinsky

Vivaldi is greatly overrated – a dull fellow who could compose the same form over and so many times over. – Igor Stravinsky

I can compare "Le Carnival Romain" by Berlioz to nothing but the caperings and gibberings of a big baboon, over-excited by a dose of alcoholic stimulus. – George Templeton Strong

Michael Jackson now looks like a Barbie doll that has been whittled at by a malicious brother. – Thomas Sutcliffe

Tom Jones has earned a permanent niche in the annals of nursing-home rock. – John Swenson

Frederick Delius: a provincial Debussy. – A. J. P. Taylor

Brahms has no charm for me. I find him cold and obscure, full of pretensions, but without any real depth. – Pyotr Illyich Tchaikovsky

Handel is only fourth-rate. He is not even interesting. – Pyotr Illyich Tchaikovsky

When Janet (Jackson) travels on tour and goes to a new hotel, she demands that they install a brand-new toilet for her! And they talk about Howard Hughes! At least he achieved something in the real world without an unreal brother paving the way. – Judy Tenuta

Madonna is like a breast with a boom box. – Judy Tenuta

(to Jon Bon Jovi) So you're acting now, you're in a vampire movie, yes? That's good. Finally, a role that *requires* you to suck. – Triumph, the Insult Comic Dog

A lot of people make jokes about having awards for no reason, just for the sake of having awards, and pretending they were good when they weren't. I'm not old enough to know a lot of them but even I know that Take That were bollocks. – Alex Turner, Arctic Monkeys

(of Richard Wagner's music) The effect on me has always been so powerful that one act was quite sufficient; whenever I have witnessed two acts I have gone away physically exhausted; and whenever I have ventured an entire opera the result has been the next thing to suicide. – Mark Twain

Wagner's music is better than it sounds. – Mark Twain

Charlotte (Church) is a nasty little piece of work with a fat head. Her publicity stunts slagging everyone off haven't worked. I don't know who she and her scabby boyfriend think they are. – Cheryl Tweedy

Frankie Laine's approach to the microphone is that of an accused man pleading with a hostile jury. – Kenneth Tynan

I preferred Michael Jackson when he was black. – Gianni Versace

As for Anita's fear that she'll be assassinated, the only people who might shoot Anita Bryant are music lovers. – Gore Vidal

Rod Stewart is a man of principle: he will not go out with a woman with brown hair. – David Walliams

I'd rather eat my own shit than duet with James Blunt. – Paul Weller

There are people who are fanatical about Celine Dion. These are the same folks who mourn the demise of Watney's Red Barrel and *The Black and White Minstrel Show* and were a tad upset that Michael Bolton shaved the mullet. – Steven Wells

Musical people are so absurdly unreasonable. They always want one to be perfectly dumb at the very moment when one is longing to be absolutely deaf. – Oscar Wilde, *An Ideal Husband*

I like Wagner's music better than anybody's. It is so loud that one can talk the whole time without people hearing what one says. That is a great advantage. – Oscar Wilde

Michael Bolton sounds like he's having his teeth drilled by Helen Keller. – Jeff Wilder

(of Christina Aguilera) She looks like a cross between someone in a gay club at six in the morning and someone who's trying to save trees. – Robbie Williams

(of Sophie Ellis Bextor) She's got a face like a satellite dish and ankles like my granny's. – Robbie Williams

(of Noel Gallagher) A mean-spirited dwarf. – Robbie Williams

To Noel Gallagher, RIP. Heard your latest album – with deepest sympathy. – Robbie Williams

Kids listening to Dido, thinking, "I want to be like her", make me want to vomit. – Amy Winehouse

(of Madonna) She's an old lady, she can't shock people any more. She should get a nice band, just stand in front of them and fucking sing. – Amy Winehouse

Katie Melua must think it's her lucky day. She's singing shit new songs that her manager writes for her. – Amy Winehouse

Britney Spears is a joke now. I wish her luck with her marriage as I hope it stops her going into the studio. – Amy Winehouse

It must be great being Bryan Adams. You just carry on living in your world of three chords, a chorus and simple "Feels so right, can't be wrong" sentiments. – Jim Wirth

(of Jessica Simpson) Creating a cultural icon out of someone who goes, "I'm stupid, isn't it cute?" makes me want to throw daggers. – Reese Witherspoon

I despise Britney Spears and Christina Aguilera because they are selling sex not music. – Evan Rachel Wood

(Mick) Jagger's sold out. His music is boring and he didn't deserve his knighthood. And he still can't forgive the fact I've had more lovers than him. – Bill Wyman

Boy George reminds me of an aubergine – all shiny and plump. – Paul Young

POLITICS

(Richard) Nixon impeached himself. He gave us Gerald Ford as his revenge. – Bella Abzug

Trust J. Edgar Hoover as much as you would trust a rattlesnake with a silencer on his rattle. – Dean Acheson

(Charles) Sumner's mind had reached the calm of water which receives and reflects images without absorbing them; it contained nothing but itself. – Henry Adams

Jimmy (Carter)'s basic problem is that he's super cautious. He looks before and after he leaps. – Joey Adams

(of Henry Clay) He is, like almost all the eminent men of this country, only half educated. His morals, public and private, are loose. – John Quincy Adams

(of Andrew Jackson) A barbarian who cannot write a sentence of grammar and can hardly spell his own name. – John Quincy Adams

(of Thomas Jefferson) His attachment to those of his friends whom he could make useful to himself was thoroughgoing and exemplary. – John Quincy Adams

(of Martin Van Buren) His principles are all subordinate to his ambitions. – John Quincy Adams

(of Canadian politician Inky Mark) Frankly, if I was going to recruit somebody, I'd go further up the gene pool. – Reg Alcock

That George Washington was not a scholar is certain. That he is too illiterate, unlearned, unread for his station is equally beyond dispute. – John Adams

(of George W. Bush) He can't even speak. I just find him an embarrassment. – Robert Altman

(of Herbert Asquith) For twenty years he has held a season ticket on the line of least resistance, and has gone wherever the train of events has carried him, lucidly justifying his position at whatever point he has happened to find himself. – Leo Amery

(of Chester Arthur) First in ability on the list of second-rate men. – Anon (of Paddy Ashdown) There are two sides to every question and he always takes both. – Anon

I don't think Kenneth Baker has his hair cut; he just has an oil change. – Anon

Aneurin Bevan can hardly enter a railway train because there is no Fourth Class. – Anon

Cherie Blair has a mouth best suited to sitting on a lily pad. – Anon

You can tell when Tony Blair is lying – his lips are moving. – Anon

Rhodes Boyson looks like a character out of an unpublished novel by Charles Dickens. – Anon

When Gordon Brown leaves a room, the lights go on. – Anon

Gordon Brown is like Mr Spock without the human bits. – Anon

Bill Clinton is the Karaoke Kid – he'd sing anything to get elected. – Anon

(of Calvin Coolidge) He is so silent that he is always worth listening to. – Anon

(of Gwyneth Dunwoody) She has all the charm and finesse of a sledge-hammer. – Anon

Roosevelt proved that a man could be President for life; Truman proved that anybody could be President; and Eisenhower proved that you don't need to have a President. – Anon

(of Roy Hattersley) He won't leave any footprints on the sands of time because he is too busy covering his tracks. – Anon

Patricia Hewitt has the air of a strident headmistress, eager to inflict a detention on anyone who questions her integrity. – Anon

(Herbert) Hoover isn't a stuffed shirt. But at times he can give the most convincing impersonation of a stuffed shirt you ever saw. – Anon

Gerald Kaufman started by trying to move mountains, but ended up by merely throwing dirt. – Anon

Neil Kinnock thinks bullshit baffles brains. – Anon

(of Selwyn Lloyd) He could not tell the difference between pulling one's leg and breaking it. – Anon

John Major delivers all his statements as though auditioning for the speaking clock. – Anon

(of Robert Muldoon) The United States has Ronald Reagan, Johnny Cash, Bob Hope and Stevie Wonder. New Zealand has Robert Muldoon, no cash, no hope, and no wonder! – Anon

Robert Muldoon is a bull who carries his own china shop with him. – Anon

John Prescott keeps behaving like an untipped waiter. – Anon

You'd have thought the only way John Prescott could make a girl go weak at the knees was by sitting on her lap. – Anon

Dan Quayle looks like Robert Redford's retarded brother that they kept in the attic, and he got out somehow. – Anon

Shirley Summerskill has a face like a well-kept grave. – Anon

Margaret Thatcher objects to ideas only when others have them. – Anon

Peace, prosperity and a president smarter than his dog – already the Clinton years seem a golden age by comparison – *Arkansas Times*

(of Bill Clinton) Say what you like about the President, but we know his friends have convictions. – Dick Armey

(of Joseph Chamberlain) The manners of a cad and the tongue of a bargee. – Herbert Asquith

(of Winston Churchill) Begotten of froth out of foam. – Herbert Asquith

Sir Stafford Cripps has a brilliant mind until it is made up. – Lady Asquith

(of Winston Churchill) He would kill his own mother just so that he could use her skin to make a drum to beat his own praises. – Margot Asquith

(of David Lloyd George) He can't see a belt without hitting below it. – Margot Asquith

The trouble with Winston (Churchill) is that he nails his trousers to the mast and can't climb down. – Clement Attlee

(of Winston Churchill) I must remind the Right Honourable Gentleman that a monologue is not a decision. – Clement Attlee (of Lord Brougham) If he were a horse, nobody would buy him; with that eye no one could answer for his temper. – Walter Bagehot

(of David Owen) He has conferred on the practice of vacillation the aura of statesmanship. – Kenneth Baker

Lloyd George spent his whole life plastering together the true and the false and therefrom manufacturing the plausible. – Stanley Baldwin

(of Terry Dicks) He is undoubtedly proof that a pig's bladder on a stick can be elected as a member of parliament. – Tony Banks

Listening to Terry Dicks opining on the arts is rather like listening to Vlad the Impaler presenting *Blue Peter*. – Tony Banks

At one moment (Michael) Portillo was polishing his jackboots and planning the advance. Next thing he shows up as a TV presenter. It is rather like Pol Pot joining the Teletubbies. – Tony Banks

(of Edwina Currie) To call her bitchy is to overpraise her, because bitchiness entails some wit and brio, whereas Edwina just has a dull, knee-jerk contempt for everyone in her path. – Lynn Barber

(of George W. Bush) A pin-stripin', polo-playin', umbrella-totin' Ivy-leaguer, born with a silver spoon so far in his mouth that you couldn't get it out with a crowbar. – Bill Baxley

(Lord) Beaverbrook is so pleased to be in the government that he is like the town tart who has finally married the mayor. – Beverley Baxter

(Winston) Churchill on top of the wave has in him the stuff of which tyrants are made. – Lord Beaverbrook

I did not enter the Labour Party forty-seven years ago to have our manifesto written by Dr Mori, Dr Gallup and Mr Harris. – Tony Benn, on opinion polls

(of David Lloyd George) He spoke for a hundred and seventeen minutes, in which period he was detected only once in the use of an argument. – Arnold Bennett

Clement Attlee brings to the fierce struggle of politics the tepid enthusiasm of a lazy summer afternoon at a cricket match. – Aneurin Bevan

(of Stanley Baldwin) This second-rate orator trails his tawdry wisps of mist over the parliamentary scene. – Aneurin Bevan (of Neville Chamberlain) He has the lucidity which is the byproduct of a fundamentally sterile mind. – Aneurin Bevan

(of Neville Chamberlain) The worst thing I can say about democracy is that it has tolerated the right honourable gentleman for four and a half years. – Aneurin Bevan

(of Winston Churchill) His ear is so sensitively attuned to the bugle note of history that he is often deaf to the more raucous clamour of modern life. – Aneurin Bevan

(of Winston Churchill) He is a man suffering from petrified adolescence. – Aneurin Bevan

(of Harold Macmillan) The Prime Minister has an absolute genius for putting flamboyant labels on empty luggage. – Aneurin Bevan

I think (Stanley) Baldwin has gone mad. He simply takes one jump in the dark, looks around and then takes another. – Lord Birkenhead

(of James Garfield) He rushes into a fight with the horns of a bull and the skin of a rabbit. – Jeremiah Black

In my lifetime, we've gone from Eisenhower to George W. Bush. We've gone from John Kennedy to Al Gore. Now if that is evolution, I believe that in twelve years, we're gonna be voting for plants. – Lewis Black

I was home alone watching George W. Bush speak on television. So it was just really the two of us. And as I listened to him, I realised that one of us was nuts! And for the first time ever, I went, "Wow, it's not me!" Here's why I think there's something a little odd with George. Because a lot of the times when he speaks, his words don't match his face. Something is askew. You can't talk about the war with a smile on your face. He does it constantly. – Lewis Black

I met Dick Cheney the other night. I've never stood that close to evil. – Lewis Black

As (Arnold) Schwarzenegger has found out, the trouble with getting voted in as a joke is that sooner or later the joke gets old. – Lewis Black

(of William Pitt the Elder) He's about as effective as a cat flap in an elephant house. – *Blackadder* (of Roscoe Conkling) A becurled and perfumed grandee gazed at by the gallery-gapers. – James G. Blaine

We knew George W. Bush was in the oil business – we just didn't know it was snake oil. – Julian Bond

(of George W. Bush) He a very wise man and very strong – although perhaps not so strong as his father Barbara. – "Borat" (Sacha Baron Cohen)

John Prescott looks like a terrifying mixture of Hannibal Lecter and Terry Scott. – Gyles Brandreth

(of Margaret Beckett) Perhaps she's sucking her teeth more than usual today. – Rory Bremner, impressionist, after catching out the UK Foreign Secretary with a hoax phone call

You want to believe in Tony Blair, but rather like if you want to believe in God, there are times when he makes it very difficult to believe. – Rory Bremner

Tony Blair is so weak and vulnerable now, Madonna is thinking of adopting him. – Rory Bremner

The Conservative Party have been spectacularly helpful to me in the past. They gave me, in quick succession, John Major, William Hague, Iain Duncan Smith and Michael Howard. A comedy roll. It's a belly laugh when you think of Michael Howard saying, "It's all right, I'm not going to hurt you." – Rory Bremner

David Cameron plays by far the most convincing (Tony) Blair. The rest of us just do the voice and the mannerisms, but Cameron does the whole career. – Rory Bremner

(Benjamin) Disraeli is a self-made man who worships his creator. – John Bright

Future generations will use Blair's name as a swearword so offensive it currently has no equivalent in the English language. – Charlie Brooker

(of Jacques Chirac) Whenever I met him, I noted his smooth, meaty paw, the enormous head bending in greeting and that astonishing nose, as though moulded by a drunken potter given the simple instruction: "Arrogant Frenchman." – Philip Delves Broughton

Nearly a quarter of American men were in the Armed Forces (in 1968). The rest were in school, in prison, or were George W. Bush. – Bill Bryson, *The Life and Times of the Thunderbolt Kid*

By almost univeral agreement, the most vague and ineffectual of all (US Presidents) was Millard Fillmore, who succeeded to the office in 1850 upon the death of Zachary Taylor, and spent the next three years demonstrating how the country would have been run if they had just propped Taylor up in a chair with cushions. – Bill Bryson, *Notes From a Big Country*

John Howard is by far the dullest man in Australia. Imagine a very committed funeral home director – someone whose burning ambition from the age of eleven was to be a funeral home director, whose proudest achievement in adulthood was to be elected president of the Queanbeyan and District Funeral Home Directors' Association – then halve his personality and halve it again, and you have pretty well got John Howard. – Bill Bryson, *Down Under*

(of John Quincy Adams) His disposition is as perverse and mulish as that of his father. – James Buchanan

Bill Clinton's foreign policy experience is pretty much confined to having had breakfast once at the International House of Pancakes. – Pat Buchanan

(of Lyndon B. Johnson) He is a man of his most recent word. – William F. Buckley Jr.

I've never liked Edwina Currie; her Pooterish self-regard and her demon king eyebrows add up to an unfortunate package. – Julie Burchill

(Richard) Nixon is a man who had the morals of a private detective. – William S. Burroughs

(of Michael Dukakis) He's the stealth candidate. His campaign jets from place to place, but no issues show up on the radar screen. – George Bush

Michael Portillo is so wooden, he should be creosoted. – Garry Bushell

Ronald Reagan doesn't dye his hair, he bleaches his face. – Johnny Carson

Ronald Reagan is slightly to the right of the Sheriff of Nottingham. – Johnny Carson

Reagan's in the news again. He's at his ranch chopping wood – he's building the log cabin he was born in. – Johnny Carson

If you work for Bill Clinton, you go up and down more times than a whore's nightgown. – James Carville

(of George W. Bush) The guy's as bright as an egg timer. – Chevy Chase

(of Clement Attlee) He is a sheep in sheep's clothing. – Winston Churchill

(of Clement Attlee) A modest little man with much to be modest about. – Winston Churchill

An empty taxi arrived at 10 Downing Street, and when the door was opened, Attlee got out. – Winston Churchill

(of Stanley Baldwin) He occasionally stumbles over the truth, but he always hastily picks himself up and hurries on as if nothing had happened. – Winston Churchill

(of Stanley Baldwin) Decided only to be undecided, resolved to be irresolute, adamant for drift, solid for fluidity, all-powerful to be impotent. – Winston Churchill

I wish Stanley Baldwin no ill, but it would have been much better if he had never lived. – Winston Churchill

(of Aneurin Bevan) I've just learnt about his illness; let's hope it's nothing trivial. – Winston Churchill

(of Neville Chamberlain) He looked at foreign affairs through the wrong end of a municipal drainpipe. – Winston Churchill

(of Charles de Gaulle) He looked like a female llama surprised in her bath. – Winston Churchill

(of Charles de Gaulle) The greatest cross I have to bear is the cross of Lorraine. – Winston Churchill

(of Ramsay Macdonald) He has, more than any other man, the gift of compressing the largest amount of words into the smallest amount of thought. – Winston Churchill

(of the Labour Party) They are not fit to manage a whelk stall. – Winston Churchill

Bill Clinton is a man who thinks international affairs means dating a girl from out of town. – Tom Clancy

John Prescott and Tracey Temple had sex with the office door open, mainly so he could listen out for the pizza delivery boy. – Julian Clary, *Have I Got News For You*

(of John C. Calhoun) A rigid, fanatic, ambitious, selfishly partisan and sectional turncoat with too much genius and too little common sense, who will either die a traitor or a madman. – Henry Clay

(of Andrew Jackson) He is ignorant, passionate, hypocritical, corrupt and easily swayed by the basest men who surround him. – Henry Clay

If life were fair, Dan Quayle would be making a living asking, "Do you want fries with that?" – John Cleese

Mr (Woodrow) Wilson bores me with his fourteen points; why, God Almighty has only ten. – Georges Clemenceau

Clare Short had trouble deciding if she was a dove or a hawk, so she ended up a dork. – Martin Clunes, *Have I Got News For You*

(of Benjamin Franklin) A crafty and lecherous old hypocrite whose very statue seems to gloat on the wenches as they walk the States House yard. – William Cobbett

(of George W. Bush) I stand by this man because he stands for things. Not only for things, he stands on things. Things like aircraft carriers, and rubble, and recently flooded city squares. And that sends a strong message that no matter what happens to America she will always rebound with the most powerfully staged photo-ops in the world. – Stephen Colbert

(of George W. Bush) When the President decides something on Monday, he still believes it on Wednesday – no matter what happened Tuesday. – Stephen Colbert

(of Condoleezza Rice) Yeah, I agree, she is sexy in sort of an ice-cold praying mantis sort-of-way. – Stephen Colbert

(of William Lyne) The rogue elephant of Australian politics. – E. H. Collis

Calvin Coolidge's perpetual expression was that of someone smelling something burning on a stove. – Sherwin L. Cook

(of Herbert Hoover) That man has offered me unsolicited advice for six years, all of it bad. – Calvin Coolidge

For the Blairs' official Christmas card Cherie decided not to smile, in case they couldn't fit the card into the envelope. – Ronnie Corbett, *Have I Got News For You*

On being told he was going to be the new Home Secretary, Charles Clarke couldn't believe his ears. Well, quite frankly, none of us can believe his ears! – Ronnie Corbett, *Have I Got News For You*

Richard Nixon's motto was: "If two wrongs don't make a right, try three." – Norman Cousins

Michael Heseltine could not see a parapet without ducking beneath it. – Julian Critchley

Margaret Thatcher cannot see an institution without hitting it with her handbag. – Julian Critchley

(of Pierre Trudeau) It is better to be sincere in one language than to be a twit in two. – John Crosbie

(of Warren G. Harding) The only man, woman or child who wrote a simple declarative sentence with seven grammatical errors, is dead. – e.e. cummings

(of Teresa Gorman) Small, short-sighted, blonde, barbed – she reminds me of a bright little hedgehog. – Edwina Currie

(of Charles de Gaulle) A head like a banana and hips like a woman. – Hugh Dalton

(of Ulysses S. Grant) He does not march, nor quite walk, but pitches along as if the next step would bring him on his nose. – Richard Dana

(of Arnold Schwarzenegger) You shouldn't be governor (of California) unless you can pronounce the name of the state. – Gray Davis

I (David Cameron) come in a box so shiny and new that hopefully you won't notice I don't do anything at all. – *Dead Ringers*

(of Tony Banks) He is a man whose contribution to the arts is about the same as Bluebeard's contribution to the institution of marriage. – Terry Dicks

Randolph Churchill is like a minute insect which bites without being felt. – Benjamin Disraeli (of William Ewart Gladstone) He has not a single redeeming defect. — Benjamin Disraeli

Gladstone made his conscience not his guide, but his accomplice. — Benjamin Disraeli

A misfortune is if Gladstone fell into the Thames; a calamity would be if someone pulled him out. — Benjamin Disraeli

(of Daniel O'Connell) He has committed every crime that does not require courage. — Benjamin Disraeli

(of Sir Robert Peel) The right honourable gentleman is reminiscent of a poker. The only difference is that a poker gives off the occasional signs of warmth. — Benjamin Disraeli

(of Sir Robert Peel) The right honourable gentleman's smile is like the silver fittings on a coffin. — Benjamin Disraeli

(of Lord John Russell) If a traveller were informed that such a man was Leader of the House of Commons, he might begin to comprehend how the Egyptians worshipped an insect. — Benjamin Disraeli

When Edwina Currie goes to the dentist, he's the one who needs the anaesthetic. — Frank Dobson

No wonder that girl was licking David Mellor's toes. She was probably trying to get as far away from his face as possible. — Tommy Docherty

When Al Gore gives a fireside chat, the fire goes out. — Bob Dole

Tony Blair has done more U-turns than a dodgy plumber. — Iain Duncan Smith

Most presidents are figureheads; (George W.) Bush is a hood ornament. — Will Durst

Walter Mondale has all the charisma of a speed bump. — Will Durst

(of Thomas Dewey) He struts sitting down. — Lillian K. Dykestra

Someday our grandchildren will look up at us and say, "Where were you, Grandma, and what were you doing when you first realized that President Reagan was, er, not playing with a full deck?" — Barbara Ehrenreich

(of Nancy Reagan) A senescent bimbo with a lust for home furnishings. — Barbara Ehrenreich (of John F. Kennedy) You can always tell a Harvard man but you can't tell him much. — Dwight D. Eisenhower

Jacques Chirac can have his mouth full of jam, his lips can be dripping with the stuff, his fingers covered with it, the pot can be standing open in front of him. And when you ask him if he's a jam eater, he'll say: "Me eat jam? Never." — Valery Giscard d'Estaing

Mrs (Cherie) Blair: what a hard task she has, hasn't she? A comparatively ordinary woman in the limelight; quite bright and sweet — and she can't help her mouth, can she? — Dame Edna Everage

Does the Honourable Lady remember that she was an egg herself once? And very many members of all sides of this House regret that it was ever fertilized. — Nicholas Fairburn attacking Junior Health Minister Edwina Currie over Britain's 1988 salmonella crisis.

President (George W.) Bush wrote a letter offering his condolences to the wife of a missing Chinese fighter pilot. After Bush wrote the letter, it was quickly given to experts and then translated. Then it was translated into Chinese. — Jimmy Fallon

People are saying that Scooter Libby is taking a bullet for Dick Cheney, but I'm not sure about that. Because if Cheney wants someone to take a bullet, he usually delivers it himself. — Craig Ferguson, on the Scooter Libby scandal

(George W.) Bush doesn't know the names of countries, he doesn't know the names of foreign leaders, he can't even find the Earth on a globe. — Doug Ferrari

Tony Blair admitted during an interview this week that he has smacked his children, though only because he believed reports that they were carrying weapons of mass destruction. — Tina Fey

(George W.) Bush's overall approval ratings have hit an all-time low. If Bush's numbers don't improve, he could become the first President held back and forced to repeat his presidency. — Tina Fey

While speaking in North Carolina, President (George W.) Bush said the economy is strong and the best is yet to come. Adding, "Also the war's going great, we don't torture people, I'm eleven feet tall, and if you don't believe me, you can ask my unicorn." — Tina Fey

U2 lead singer Bono met with President (George W.) Bush at the White House. Bono urged the President to help the world's poor. Bush urged Bono to get back with Cher. – Tina Fey

California governor Arnold Schwarzenegger's popularity has been slipping in recent months as residents slowly begin to realize they elected Arnold Schwarzenegger to be their governor. – Tina Fey

Allowing Gordon Brown into No. 10 would be like letting Mrs Rochester out of the attic. He has no empathy with people and you need that to be Prime Minister. – Frank Field

(of Norman Tebbit) It is not necessary that every time he rises he should give his famous imitation of a semi-house-trained polecat. – Michael Foot

Jimmy Carter wants to speak loudly and carry a fly swatter. – Gerald Ford

(of Bill Clinton) When I was President, I said I was a Ford, not a Lincoln. Well, what we have now is a convertible Dodge. – Gerald Ford

I can still remember the first time I ever heard Hubert Humphrey speak. He was in the second hour of a five-minute talk. – Gerald Ford

George W. Bush: this is a guy who could not find oil in Texas. – Al Franken

(of Margaret Thatcher) Attila the Hen. – Clement Freud

Gerald Ford looks like the guy in a science fiction movie who is the first to see the Creature. – David Frye

David Cameron is no different from Tony Blair. He's like a songwriter who's eternally ripping off someone else's song and just changing the odd line a little. – Noel Gallagher

America is a beautiful woman and George W. Bush her oafish husband. Nobody understands what she sees in him until they recognize it was an arranged marriage. – Mike Gallay

(of George W. Bush) One thing I've learned in my life is never to trust anyone who thinks he exclusively has God on his side, especially when he is President of the United States. – Richard Gere

(of Lord Derby) When he rises to speak, he does not know what he is going to say. When he is speaking he does not know what he is saying, and when he sits down he does not know what he has said. – William Ewart Gladstone

Having gratefully accepted his subsidiary role, Mr (Tony) Blair has been cast as a poodle by Mr Bush, whose famous remark "Yo, Blair!" betrayed all the President's disdain for his simpering acolyte. – Stephen Glover

James G. Blaine wallowed in corruption like a rhinoceros in an African pool. – E.L. Godkin

(of Ronald Reagan) The youthful sparkle in his eyes is caused by contact lenses, which he keeps highly polished. – Sheila Graham

(James) Garfield has shown that he is not possessed of the backbone of an angleworm. – Ulysses S. Grant

Dan Quayle is more stupid than Ronald Reagan put together. – Matt Groening

(Lord Derby) is a very weak-minded fellow I am afraid, and, like the feather pillow, bears the marks of the last person who has sat on him. – General Douglas Haig

(of Tony Blair) He may be a liar, but he's the people's liar. – Andy Hamilton

(of Michael Howard) It's hard to find a more disliked man than (Tony) Blair – but the Tories did. – Andy Hamilton

(of Michael Howard) Instead of his "what you see is what you get" slogan, a better catchphrase would be "I'm not quite as creepy as I come across." – Andy Hamilton

President Clinton and Hillary met with Queen Elizabeth II at Buckingham Palace. She looked resplendent in her purple robes and diamond tiara. Now that she's been elected Senator, she can throw out those black pantsuits once and for all. – Argus Hamilton

Bill Clinton changed his schedule Friday to go with Hillary to Selma to help her draw a crowd for a church appearance on Sunday. Then he will accompany her to the Bridge Crossing Jubilee. In exchange he gets the next six Saturdays unsupervised. – Argus Hamilton

The USS John F. Kennedy aircraft carrier sailed to Florida for decommissioning this week. Jack, Bobby, Joe and Joe Kennedy Jr have US ships named after them. Whenever the commanding officer comes aboard ship, he is announced by a rape whistle. – Argus Hamilton

The Tory Conference are not an attractive lot, are they? I mean, if all those people were born in the same village, you'd blame pollution, wouldn't you? — Jeremy Hardy, *The News Quiz*

(of David Cameron) He is an out-and-out opportunist. I don't believe he believes anything. — Robin Harris

(of John Quincy Adams) It is said he is a disgusting man to do business. Coarse, dirty, clownish in his address and stiff and abstracted in his opinions, which are drawn from books exclusively. — William Henry Harrison

(of Donald Rumsfeld) A posturing old bully. — Max Hastings

George W. Bush has achieved the unusual feat of being simultaneously sinister and ridiculous. — Roy Hattersley

Malcolm Fraser could be described as the cutlery man of Australian politics. He was born with a silver spoon in his mouth, speaks with a forked tongue, and knifes his colleagues in the back. — Bob Hawke

My new take on the London Olympics is that Tony Blair left them for Gordon Brown as a house-warming present. A bit like a dead rat under the floorboards. — Paul Hayward

(of Richard Crossman) He had a heavyweight intellect with a lightweight judgement. — Denis Healey

(of Geoffrey Howe) Being attacked in the House by him is like being savaged by a dead sheep. — Denis Healey

(of Sir Keith Joseph) A mixture of Rasputin and Tommy Cooper. — Denis Healey

Margaret Thatcher: a bargain-basement Boadicea. — Denis Healey

(of Margaret Thatcher) The Prime Minister has given the French President a piece of her mind, not a gift I would receive with alacrity. — Denis Healey

(of George Bush) We need a President who's fluent in at least one language. — Buck Henry

Paddy Ashdown transformed a party without a leader into a party without a leader. — Michael Heseltine.

(of John Prescott) A lager lout. — Michael Heseltine

(of Neil Kinnock) The self-appointed king of the gutter. – Michael Heseltine

I decided the worst thing you can call Paul Keating, quite frankly, is Paul Keating. – John Hewson

If ignorance goes to forty dollars a barrel, I want drilling rights to George Bush's head. – Jim Hightower

(of George W. Bush) We now have an American leader who makes Ronald Reagan positively Einstein-like. – Ian Hislop

(of Ronald Reagan) The first man in twenty years to make presidency a part-time job, a means of filling up a few of those otherwise blank days of retirement. – Simon Hoggart

Harry S. Truman rules the country with an iron fist, the same way he plays the piano. – Bob Hope

(of Franklin D. Roosevelt) He would rather follow public opinion than lead it. – Harry Hopkins

(of William Jennings Bryan) One could drive a schooner through any part of his argument and never scrape against a fact. – David Houston

(of Ronald Reagan) In the heart of a political lifetime, he innocently squirrels away tidbits of misinformation and then, sometimes years later, casually drops them into his public discourse, like gumballs in a quiche. – Lucy Howard

(of Tony Blair) The deals-on-wheels Prime Minister. – Michael Howard

(of Tony Blair) I have a big dossier of his past, and I did not even have to sex it up. – Michael Howard

I'm just sick and tired of presidents who jog. Remember, if Bill Clinton wins, we're going to have another four years of his white thighs flapping in the wind. – Arianna Huffington

(of Alastair Campbell) He suggests, preposterously, that I sneer at ministers – he knows a great deal about that because he's done it for a long time. – John Humphrys

(of Huey Long) He is suffering from halitosis of the intellect. That's presuming he has intellect. – Harold Ickes

(of Alastair Campbell, Tony Blair's chief spin doctor) He presided over an appalling period in government communication. – Bernard Ingham

Calling George W. Bush shallow is like calling a dwarf short. – Molly Ivins

(of Henry Clay) He is certainly the basest, meanest scoundrel that ever disgraced the image of God. Nothing is too mean or low for him to condescend to. – Andrew Jackson

I didn't shoot Henry Clay and I didn't hang John Calhoun. – Andrew Jackson, on things that he had left undone

(of George Bush senior) Every sentence he manages to utter scatters its component parts like pond water from a verb chasing its own tail. – Clive James

(of John Adams) He is distrustful, obstinate, excessively vain, and takes no counsel from anyone. – Thomas Jefferson

(of Gordon Brown) My lies are silk while his are made of polyester. – Alan Johnson

Gerry Ford is a nice guy but he played too much football with his helmet off. – Lyndon B. Johnson

(of John F. Kennedy) The enviably attractive nephew who sings an Irish ballad for the company and then winsomely disappears before the table clearing and dishwashing begin. – Lyndon B. Johnson

Al Gore has less star quality than head lice. – Joe Joseph

Mike Codd will be lucky to get a job cleaning shithouses if I ever become Prime Minister. – Paul Keating

Peter Costello is all tip and no iceberg. – Paul Keating

(to Malcolm Fraser) You look like an Easter Island statue with an arse full of razor blades. – Paul Keating

(of John Hewson) Like a lizard on a rock – alive, but looking dead. – Paul Keating

(of John Hewson) He's like a stone statue in the cemetery. – Paul Keating

(on being verbally attacked by John Hewson) Like being flogged with a warm lettuce. – Paul Keating (of John Howard) I am not like the Leader of the Opposition. I did not slither out of the Cabinet room like a mangy maggot. – Paul Keating

John Howard has more hide than a team of elephants. – Paul Keating

John Howard is a coconut glued to his seat. – Paul Keating

(of Andrew Peacock) What we have here is an intellectual rust bucket. – Paul Keating

(of Andrew Peacock) A gutless spiv . . . a painted, perfumed gigolo . . . the Liberal Party ought to put him down like a faithful dog because he is of no use to it and of no use to the nation. – Paul Keating

(of Andrew Peacock) I suppose that the Honourable Gentleman's hair, like his intellect, will recede into the darkness. – Paul Keating

(of Ian Sinclair) What we have as a leader of the National Party is a political carcass with a coat and tie on. – Paul Keating

(of George W. Bush) It's funny to watch this clueless man go through the motions. – Garrison Keillor

(of Bob Dole) He has never met a tax he hasn't hiked. – Jack Kemp

It's unlikely George W. Bush will attempt to read the twelve-thousand-page document, as there's a serious risk that his finger would wear away. – Charles Kennedy, *Have I Got News For You*

Ronald Reagan must love poor people because he's creating so many more of them. – Edward Kennedy

Do you realize the responsibility I carry? I'm the only person between (Richard) Nixon and the White House. – John F. Kennedy, 1960

(of George W. Bush) Being lectured by the President on fiscal responsibility is a little bit like Tony Soprano talking to me about law and order. – John Kerry

Today was Arnold Schwarzenegger's inauguration as Governor of California. Arnold was told to "Raise your right hand and butcher the English language after me." – Craig Kilborn

(of John Major) He is a ditherer and a dodger, a ducker and weaver. – Neil Kinnock

(of Jimmy Carter) He is your typical smiling, brilliant, back-stabbing, bullshitting southern nut-cutter. – Lane Kirkland

George W. Bush is clearly the best thing to happen to political humorists since . . . well, since Bill Clinton. – Daniel Kurtzman

(of Winston Peters) He's probably been delayed by a full-length mirror. – David Lange

(of William Taft) He looked at me as if I was a side dish he hadn't ordered. – Ring Lardner

In Pierre Elliott Trudeau, Canada has at last produced a political leader worthy of assassination. – Irving Layton

(of George Washington) A sordid, ambitious, vain, proud, arrogant, and vindictive knave. – General Charles Lee

When (Henry) Kissinger can get the Nobel Peace Prize, what is there left for satire? – Tom Lehrer

(George W.) Bush said today he is being stalked. He said wherever he goes, people are following him. Finally someone told him, "Psst, that's the Secret Service." – Jay Leno

Ted Kennedy said Iraq is George W. Bush's Vietnam. Which is very unfair. There is a huge difference. Bush knew how to get out of Vietnam. – Jay Leno

Gerald Ford was the only person to become President without winning an election . . . besides President Bush. – Jay Leno

We make fun of George W. Bush, but this morning he was at work bright and early. OK, he was early. – Jay Leno

George W. Bush says he works out because it clears his mind. Sometimes just a little too much. – Jay Leno

President (George W.) Bush's press secretary Ari Fleischer just got married, and believe it or not, one of the wedding presents he was registered for was a DVD of *Forrest Gump*. He wanted to watch *Forrest Gump*. You'd think he'd get enough of that at work. – Jay Leno

Some members of Congress are thinking about impeaching President (George W.) Bush because he is adamant about not withdrawing troops. What are the odds of that? Two presidents in a row would be impeached for not pulling out. – Jay Leno

According to doctors, George W. Bush has the lowest heartbeat ever recorded by someone in the White House. Well, second lowest. Dick Cheney got his down to zero a couple of times. – Jay Leno

(Dick) Cheney's defence is that he was aiming at a quail when he shot the guy. Which means that Cheney now has the worst aim of anyone in the White House since Bill Clinton. – Jay Leno

Vice President Cheney tripped today. Luckily Scooter Libby was there to take the fall. – Jay Leno

President Clinton also testified before the 9/11 commission. He said he was very concerned about an attack. In fact, Clinton said he couldn't remember how many times he had told women in the White House, "Just keep your head down." – Jay Leno

In Washington, it turns out that there are still traces of anthrax in the Senate office building. Wouldn't it be ironic if, after all these years of living with Bill, Hillary winds up catching something from the Senate? – Jay Leno

Here's the basic difference between the Bush family and the Clinton family. When Bill Clinton said it was time for a cold one, he meant Hillary. – Jay Leno

Hillary Clinton said she hopes America is ready for a woman in the Oval Office. That was the great thing about her husband Bill: he was always ready for a woman in the Oval Office. – Jay Leno

According to a new study, Americans' attitudes towards overweight people are changing. They say an overwhelming majority of Americans are more accepting of heavier body types. You know what that means? Bill Clinton was a man ahead of his time. – Jay Leno

A new poll shows that American now believe that Bill Clinton is more honest than President George W. Bush. At least when Clinton screwed the nation, he did it one person at a time. – Jay Leno

Acoording to a new study, over eighteen million American men currently suffer from erectile dysfunction. And doctors say that number could double if Hillary (Clinton) gets elected. – Jay Leno

John Kerry is positioning himself for another run at the White House in 2008. Kerry said his campaign will be much better than the last one. He says this time he's going to take three positions on each issue. – Jay Leno

Monica Lewinsky has gained back all the weight she lost last year. I believe that's the cover story in *Newsweek*. In fact, she told reporters she was even considering having her jaw wired shut, but then, nah – she didn't want to give up her sex life. – Jay Leno

Monica Lewinsky told this month's *Cosmo* magazine that if it weren't for Bill Clinton, she would be a mom now, with two kids. Really? Not the way she was doing it. – Jay Leno

It's rumoured in Washington that Condoleezza Rice has a boyfriend. Allegedly, he's Canada's Foreign Minister, Peter MacKay. Since he's a diplomat and he visits her at the White House, he has to have a Secret Service code name. Do you know what his Secret Service code name is? Captain Kirk. You know why they call him that? Because he's going where no man has gone before. – Jay Leno

Defence Secretary Donald Rumsfeld has resigned. He said he wants to spend more time promoting unnecessary conflicts within his own family. – Jay Leno

Donald Rumsfeld has been let go. Insiders describe Rumsfeld's reaction as shocked and awed. How does that make Rumsfeld feel when George W. Bush tells you you're not competent enough. – Jay Leno

Donald Rumsfeld has been described as the architect of the war on Iraq. And he should be very proud, because he's built something that's going to last for years and years. – Jay Leno

Experts say Boris Yeltsin is in the difficult stage between capitalism and communism. I believe it's called alcoholism. – Jay Leno

Boris Yeltsin had his birthday today. He celebrated the usual way: face down in his cake. – Jay Leno

President (George W.) Bush says he needs a month off to unwind. Unwind? When the hell does this guy wind? – David Letterman (of George W. Bush) For those of you who wondered what a Dan Quayle presidency would have been like, now you know! – David Letterman

President (George W.) Bush now has the lowest presidential approval rating since Nixon. Now here's another coincidence. Nixon had a dog named Checkers; Bush plays checkers with his dog. – David Letterman

President Clinton apparently gets so much action that every couple of weeks they have to spray WD-40 on his zipper. – David Letterman

Clinton is a pretty shrewd man. He is now telling close friends and associates that he and Monica Lewinsky were practising for the two-man luge. – David Letterman

Over the weekend President Clinton's dog Buddy died. It is a heartbreaking thing because Buddy was a great dog. Buddy could roll over, Buddy would beg, Buddy could catch things in his mouth – wait a minute – I'm sorry, I was thinking of Monica. – David Letterman

You may think you have a stressful job, but since she's been a Senator, Hillary Clinton, they say, put on thirty pounds. In fact, she has gotten so heavy that today Bill hit on her. – David Letterman

Arnold Schwarzenegger is the first body builder to run for governor since Janet Reno. – David Letterman

Des Browne is not a man to walk past a mirror without casting it an admiring glance. – Quentin Letts

(of Menzies Campbell) His teeth whistle like a kettle and he has the neck-twitch of a Spanish gecko swallowing a mouthful of dry ants. – Quentin Letts

Gwyneth Dunwoody: a heavy roller who flattens all ministerial earthworms. – Quentin Letts

When John Prescott stands at the despatch box nowadays the galleries and the Opposition benches simply laugh. They howl their mirth as though the great galumphing fool had his trousers round his ankles. – Quentin Letts

(of John Reid) A night-club bouncer with narrow eyes, a fist fighter's twitch and a pre-emptive hint of rage. – Quentin Letts

(of John Reid) He is about as saleable as a carton of sour milk. – Quentin Letts

The Privy Council . . . is wrecked, left splintered and torn like a canvas deckchair after a visit from Cyril Smith's bottom. – Quentin Letts

(of Dwight D. Eisenhower) Once he makes up his mind, he's full of indecision. – Oscar Levant

(of Harold Macmillan) It was almost impossible to believe he was anything but a down-at-heel actor resting between engagements at the decrepit theatres of minor provincial towns. – Bernard Levin

There, but for the grace of Pierre Elliott Trudeau, sits God. – David Lewis

(of Harry S. Truman) He is a man totally unfitted for the position. His principles are elastic, and he is careless with the truth. – John L. Lewis

(of John Dean) I wouldn't waste the twenty-five cents to buy the cartridge that would propel the bullet. – G. Gordon Liddy

Would you rather go hunting with Dick Cheney or riding in a car over a bridge with Ted Kennedy? At least Cheney takes you to the hospital. – Rush Limbaugh

(of his presidential opponent Stephen A. Douglas) I did keep a grocery, and I did sell cotton, candles, and cigars, and sometimes whiskey; but I remember in those days Mr Douglas was one of my best customers. Many a time have I stood on one side of the counter and sold whiskey to Mr Douglas on the other side, but the difference between us now is this: I have left my side of the counter, but Mr Douglas still sticks to his as tenaciously as ever. – Abraham Lincoln

(of Stephen A. Douglas) His argument is as thin as the homeopathic soup that was made by boiling the shadow of a pigeon that had been starved to death. – Abraham Lincoln

(of James K. Polk) He is a bewildered, confounded, and miserably perplexed man. – Abraham Lincoln

(of George W. Bush) Man, is he over his head as the President of the United States – that's your worst combination of someone not prepared with their impulses being wrong almost every time. – Richard Linklater

(of George Bush) He's the kind of guy you'd like to have around when you want to be alone. With a little effort he could become an anonymity. – Rich Little

Margaret Beckett looks like a woman resigned to walk home alone to an empty bedsit after Grab-a-Granny night at the local disco. – Richard Littlejohn

(of John Prescott) He reacts to even the most innocuous question with an invitation to step outside. – Richard Littlejohn

John Prescott has a wholly justified inferiority complex. He's got plenty to feel inferior about. – Richard Littlejohn

(of Neville Chamberlain) He might make an adequate Lord Mayor of Birmingham in a lean year. – David Lloyd George

(of Neville Chamberlain) A retail mind in a wholesale business. – David Lloyd George

(of Winston Churchill) He has half a dozen solutions to any problem and one of them is right – the trouble is he does not know which it is. – David Lloyd George

(of Ramsay Macdonald) Sufficient conscience to bother him, but not sufficient to keep him straight. – David Lloyd George

(of Sir John Simon) The right honourable and learned gentleman has twice crossed the floor of this House, each time leaving behind a trail of slime. – David Lloyd George

(of Iain Duncan Smith) He looks like a Kinder egg with no toy inside. – Sean Lock

(of Calvin Coolidge) I do wish he didn't look as if he had been weaned on a pickle. – Alice Roosevelt Longworth

(of Eleanor Roosevelt) No woman has ever so comforted the distressed – or so distressed the comfortable. – Clare Boothe Luce

(of James Callaghan) He suffers from what you may regard as a fatal defect in a Chancellor. He is always wrong. – Iain MacLeod

(of Harold Wilson) Double-talk is his mother tongue. He is a man whose vision is limited to tomorrow's headlines. – Iain MacLeod

Anthony Eden is forever poised between a cliché and an indiscretion. – Harold Macmillan

(George W.) Bush is in command. When he heard that sectarian militias had killed Iraqis, he called for an immediate invasion of Sectaria. – Bill Maher

It is Oscar weekend. Among Best Picture nominees is *Letters From Iwo Jima*, which is a gut-wrenching tragedy about an army sent to die in a hopeless cause by a fanatical government. Or, as George W. Bush calls it, "the feel-good comedy of the year." – Bill Maher

You can tell it's spring. Laura Bush's smile is beginning to thaw. – Bill Maher

The Taliban tried to blow up Dick Cheney. He was never in danger – at the time of the attack, he was safely asleep in his coffin. – Bill Maher

Dick Cheney was in hospital again this week. He was experiencing discomfort in his leg. And the doctor asked Cheney if he stretches. Cheney said, "Are you kidding? I linked 9/11 with Saddam Hussein." – Bill Maher

I saw on the news today that one of Bill Clinton's old tormentors, a guy who wrote for the *American Spectator*, is at it again. There's a new book that says Bill Clinton has been having one-night stands . . . as he goes all around the world on his speaking tours. I don't believe it for a second. I saw President Clinton recently when he spoke on the challenges of globalization, and every person in that titty bar was spellbound. – Bill Maher

Scooter Libby was found guilty of perjury, obstruction, and making false statements – or, as the White House calls it, a press conference. – Bill Maher

(of Frank Dobson) He behaves like an agitated parrot with constipation. – John Major

(of Neil Kinnock) The chameleon of politics, consistent only in his inconsistency. – John Major

(of Margaret Thatcher) In private she was capable of changing her mind with bewildering speed until she had worked up her public opinion. Too often she conducted government by gut instinct: conviction, some said admiringly, but at any rate without mature, detached examination of the issues. – John Major

I believe that Ronald Reagan can make this country what it once was – an Arctic region covered with ice. – Steve Martin

(of Eleanor Roosevelt) She's upstairs filing her teeth. – Groucho Marx

John Major makes George Bush seem like a personality. – Jackie Mason

(of Warren G. Harding) His speeches leave the impression of an army of pompous phrases moving over the landscape in search of an idea. – William McAdoo

Richard Nixon is the kind of guy who, if you were drowning twenty feet from shore, would throw you a fifteen-foot rope. – Eugene McCarthy

(of Abraham Lincoln) The President is nothing more than a well-meaning baboon. – General George McClellan

Richard Nixon was like a kamikaze pilot who keeps apologizing for the attack. – Mary McGrory

When I arrived at the Environment Ministry in 1997, John Prescott thought biodiversity was a kind of washing powder. – Michael Meacher

Grover Cleveland sailed through American history like a steel ship loaded with monoliths of granite. – H.L. Mencken

Democracy is that system of government under which the people, having 35,717,342 native-born adult whites to choose from, including thousands who are handsome and many of whom are wise, pick out Coolidge to be head of state. – H.L. Mencken

Nero fiddled, but (Calvin) Coolidge only snored. – H. L. Mencken

(of Warren G. Harding) He writes the worst English that I have ever encountered. It reminds me of a string of wet sponges; it reminds me of tattered washing on the line; it reminds me of stale bean soup, of college yells, of dogs barking idiotically through endless nights. It is so bad that a sort of grandeur creeps into it. It drags itself out of the dark abysm of pish, and crawls insanely up to the topmost pinnacle of posh. It is rumble and bumble. It is flap and doodle. It is balder and dash. – H. L. Mencken

(of Warren G. Harding) A tin-horn politician with the manner of a rural corn doctor and the mien of a ham actor. – H. L. Mencken

(of Franklin D. Roosevelt) If he became convinced tomorrow that coming out for cannibalism would get him the votes he sorely needs, he would begin fattening a missionary in the White House backyard come Wednesday. – H. L. Mencken

(of Franklin D. Roosevelt) He had every quality that morons esteem in their heroes. – H. L. Mencken

(of Theodore Roosevelt) He hated all pretensions, save his own pretensions. – H. L. Mencken

George W. Bush studied the piano for several years before realizing that it was a musical instrument made out of wood. – Paul Merton

Nancy Reagan has agreed to be the world's first artificial heart donor. – Andrea Michaels

(of Harriet Harman) Don't give me all that crap about the feminist vote, she's hopeless. If she's honest she should campaign on the 'I'm fucking useless' vote. – Alan Milburn

Dan Quayle deserves to be Vice President like Elvis deserved his black belt in karate. – Dennis Miller

(of Margaret Thatcher) She's democratic enough to talk down to anyone. – Austin Mitchell

(of Richard Nixon) He bleeds people. He draws every drop of blood and then drops them from a cliff. He'll blame any person he can put his foot on. – Martha Mitchell

Lyndon Johnson turned out to be so many different characters he could have populated all of *War and Peace* and still had a few people left over. – Herbert Mitgang

Margaret Thatcher has the mouth of Marilyn Monroe and the eyes of Caligula. – François Mitterand

Tony Blair does the work of two men – Laurel and Hardy. – Bob Monkhouse

(of Iain Duncan Smith) He's not the most charismatic personality. In school his nickname was "Iain". – Bob Monkhouse

(to George W. Bush) The majority of Americans – the ones who never elected you – are not fooled by your weapons of mass distraction. – Michael Moore

I would like to apologize for referring to George W. Bush as a deserter. What I meant to say is that George W. Bush is a deserter, an election thief, a drunk driver, a WMD liar, and a functional illiterate. And he poops his pants. – Michael Moore (of Cherie Blair) She's not my cup of tea. If I ever see her again, it will be too soon. – Piers Morgan

(of Gordon Brown) On TV he turns into one of the Thunderbirds, speaking in a relentless monotone, performing one of the worst stage smirks I've ever seen when he thinks he should lighten up a bit. – Piers Morgan

There are some women who just make my skin crawl. Hillary Clinton, for one. I only have to look at that smug, bloated, power-crazed perma-frown to feel instantly nauseous. – Piers Morgan

(of Ruth Kelly) Every time I hear that deep, grating, nasal, hectoring, mockney twang, I feel like I did at school when someone scraped their fingernails on the blackboard. – Piers Morgan

(of Jack Straw) As his name suggests, he moves (politically) wherever the wind is blowing strongest. – Piers Morgan

New Labour strikes me as a little bit like the Venus de Milo – you have to gawp with admiration at its quality and brilliance, but it is indisputably incomplete and beginning to show more than a few signs of its age. – Rhodri Morgan

(of Australian politician Sir Henry Bolte) I doubt even the Premier's ability to handle the petty cash box at a hot-dog stand at the local Sunday School picnic. – George Moss

Hyperbole was to Lyndon Johnson what oxygen is to life. – Bill Moyers

(of Anthony Eden) He is not only a bore, but he bores for England. – Malcolm Muggeridge

(of Charles-Maurice de Talleyrand) He is a silk stocking filled with dung. – Emperor Napoleon I of France

The battle for the mind of Ronald Reagan was like the trench warfare of World War One: never have so many fought so hard for such barren terrain. – Peggy Noonan

President George W. Bush was in South Dakota today. There was an awkward moment at Mount Rushmore when he said: "Hey, look, it's those guys on the money!" – Conan O'Brien

Officials at the White House are saying that President Bush hasn't changed his schedule much since the Iraq war started. The main difference, they say, is that he's started watching the news and taping *SpongeBob*. – Conan O'Brien

Vice President Dick Cheney is donating more than two million dollars to the cardiology centre that treats him. Actually, in Cheney's case it's not really a donation, it's more of an advance. – Conan O'Brien

If I saw Mr (Charles) Haughey buried at midnight at a crossroads with a stake driven through his heart – politically speaking – I should continue to wear a clove of garlic around my neck, just in case. – Conan O'Brien

Tabloids are reporting that Senator Ted Kennedy has an illegitimate twenty-one-year-old son. Apparently, Kennedy isn't denying the report, but the kid is. – Conan O'Brien

Secretary of Defence Donald Rumsfeld announced he's stepping down. Rumsfeld said, "I made the decision after it became clear that I couldn't do my job effectively – and then I waited three years." – Conan O'Brien

California governor Arnold Schwarzenegger's approval rating is down to thirty percent. After hearing this, Arnold said, "I'm not going to act all hurt and upset because I don't have that kind of range." – Conan O'Brien

The majority of the members of the Irish parliament are professional politicians, in the sense that otherwise they would not be given jobs minding mice at crossroads. – Flann O'Brien

(of Stanley Baldwin) One could not even dignify him with the name of a stuffed shirt. He was simply a hole in the air. – George Orwell

(of Clement Attlee) He reminds me of nothing so much as a dead fish before it has had time to stiffen. – George Orwell

(of Woodrow Wilson) The air currents of the world never ventilated his mind. – Walter H. Page

(of John Adams) It has been the political career of this man to begin with hyprocisy, proceed with arrogance, and finish with contempt. – Thomas Paine

(of Edmund Burke) As he rose like a rocket, so he fell like a stick. – Thomas Paine

(on learning that Calvin Coolidge had died) How can they tell? – Dorothy Parker

(of Thomas Dewey) You really have to get to know him to dislike him. – James T. Patterson

Margaret Beckett is about as charming as Dracula's maiden auntie. – Allison Pearson

Labour is trying to blame the Conservatives for John Prescott's affair. They say it's all Margaret Thatcher's fault for banning free eye tests. – Allison Pearson

(of Herbert Hoover) He wouldn't commit himself to the time of day from a hatful of watches. – Westbrook Pegler

Nobody likes to be called a liar. But to be called a liar by Bill Clinton is really a unique experience. – Ross Perot

(of Dan Quayle) An empty suit that goes to funerals and plays golf. – Ross Perot

(of George W. Bush) He's a Boy Scout with a hormone imbalance. – Kevin Phillips

Prime Minister Tony Blair was re-elected to a record-setting third term as George Bush's bitch. – Amy Poehler

I pride myself on never having fallen for the idea that Barbara Bush was sweet and grandmotherly. I met Barbara Bush and, as I expected, she was a tank with eyes. – Paula Poundstone

All that glitters isn't (Philip) Gould. – John Prescott

(of Edward Livingstone) He is a man of splendid abilities, but utterly corrupt. Like rotten mackerel by moonlight, he shines and stinks. – John Randolph

(of Richard Rush) Never was ability so much below mediocrity so well rewarded; no, not even when Caligula's horse was made a consul. – John Randolph

(of George W. Bush) Well, I really think he shatters the myth of white supremacy once and for all. – Charlie Rangel (of Walter Mondale) I will not make age an issue of this campaign. I am not going to exploit for political purposes my opponent's youth and inexperience. – Ronald Reagan

Tony Blair has become the thieving magpie of British politics. Every idea that glistens he transfers to his own nest. – John Redwood

Richard Nixon inherited some good instincts from his Quaker forebears, but by diligent hard work, he overcame them. – James Reston

(of George W. Bush) He can't help it – he was born with a silver foot in his mouth. – Ann Richards

(of Tony Blair) An opportunist rarely matched since Jimmy Greaves was prowling penalty boxes. – Ian Ridley

(of Tony Blair) Clotheswise, he ends up looking like an IT specialist or a gay Manchester hairdresser. – Anne Robinson

(of Joseph Chamberlain) Dangerous as an enemy, untrustworthy as a friend, but fatal as a colleague. – Sir Hercules Robinson

Calvin Coolidge didn't say much, and when he did he didn't say much. – Will Rogers

(of Al Gore) Last couple of years, he's gotten as big as a house. I'm afraid lately he's been adding some rooms. He says we need to reduce carbon. He needs to reduce carbs. – Mitt Romney

(of Benjamin Harrison) He is a cold-blooded, narrow-minded, prejudiced, obstinate, timid old psalm-singing Indianapolis politician. – Theodore Roosevelt

William McKinley has no more backbone than a chocolate éclair. – Theodore Roosevelt

(of John Tyler) He has been called a mediocre man, but this is unwarranted flattery. – Theodore Roosevelt

(of Henry Addington) The indefatigable air of a village apothecary inspecting the tongue of the State. – Lord Rosebery

When Bob Dole does smile, he looks as if he's just evicted a widow. – Mike Royko

(of James G. Blaine) No man in our annals has filled so large a space and left it so empty. – Charles E. Russell

(of Tony Blair) Distinguished by his unctuous dedication to moral principles, and by his readiness to use compulsion in support of them. – Earl Russell

(of John F. Kennedy) It is said that the President is willing to laugh at himself. That is fine, but when is he going to extend that privilege to us? – Mort Sahl

(of Richard Nixon) Would you buy a second-hand car from this man? – Mort Sahl

A working man voting for Ronald Reagan is like a chicken voting for Colonel Sanders. – Paul Sarbanes

(of Ronald Reagan) We've got the kind of president who thinks arms control means some kind of deodorant. – Patricia Schroeder

Elaine: Hey, who do you think is the most unattractive world leader?
Jerry: Living or all time?
Elaine: All time.
Jerry: Well, if it's all time, then there's no contest. It begins and ends with Brezhnev.
Elaine: I dunno. You ever get a good look at De Gaulle?
George: Lyndon Johnson was uglier than De Gaulle.
Elaine: I got news for you. Golda Meir could make 'em all run up a tree.
– *Seinfeld*

Tony Blair is the ultimate air guitarist of modern political rhetoric. – Will Self

Tony Blair is a man of extraordinary affectation. – Brian Sewell

(of Margaret Thatcher) Boadicea with a handbag. – Brian Sewell

(of Theodore Roosevelt) His idea of getting hold of the right end of the stick is to snatch it from the hands of somebody who is using it effectively, and to hit him over the head with it. – George Bernard Shaw

(of Henry Dundas) The right honourable gentleman is indebted to his memory for his jests and to his imagination for his facts. – Richard Brinsley Sheridan

(of Tony Blair) Reckless with our government; reckless with his own future, position and place in history. – Clare Short

Thomas Jefferson founded the Democratic Party; Franklin Roosevelt dumbfounded it. – Dewey Short

(George W.) Bush is a mongrel. He is a cowboy. He can't even pronounce the word "nuclear". But this is the worst enemy terrorists have. And that is precisely the guy you want in charge. When the world is going nuts, you want a guy who is nuttier than them. – Gene Simmons

Jimmy Carter had the air of a man who had never taken any decisions in his life. They had always been taken for him. – Guy Simon

David Blunkett's favourite chat-up line: "Do I come here often?" – Frank Skinner

Winston (Churchill) has devoted the best years of his life to preparing his impromptu speeches. – F. E. Smith

Michael Portillo seems to have his lips on inside out. – Linda Smith

(of John Prescott) I suspect language isn't his first language. – Linda Smith

Ann Widdecombe is only audible to sheep dogs. She's like a demented Clanger. She has a swannee whistle stuck in her throat. – Linda Smith

Ann Widdecombe's confused us all by going blonde. I was watching *Question Time* thinking, "Blimey, Sue Barker's slapped on a bit of weight!" – Linda Smith

Compared to Imelda Marcos, Marie Antoinette was a bag lady. – Stephen Solarz

(of David Blunkett) He's overcome a great amount of adversity to become the one of the most horrible bastards. – Mark Steel

George W. Bush and Donald Rumsfeld are like an old couple with some holiday brochures. "Where shall we invade next? Cuba looks nice." – Mark Steel

Gerald Ford looks and talks like he just fell off Edgar Bergen's lap. – David Steinberg

John Prescott has enough spare flesh to feed the five thousand and a few of their mates. – Jaci Stephen

(of Dwight D. Eisenhower) If I talk over people's heads, Ike must talk under their feet. – Adlai Stevenson

Richard Nixon is the kind of politician who would cut down a redwood tree, then mount its stump for a speech on conservation. – Adlai Stevenson

As time goes on it has become apparent that President (George W.) Bush has developed a sophisticated exit strategy . . . for getting out of questions about an exit strategy. – Jon Stewart, on the war in Iraq

Condoleezza Rice brings an impressive résumé to her new job. The grand-daughter of a cotton farmer, the former provost of Stanford University, she is fluent in four languages, an accomplished classical pianist, and even an expert figure skater. It seems like the only thing she can't do is make peace with other nations. – Jon Stewart

Donald Rumsfeld. Love him or hate him, you've gotta admit . . . a lot of people hate him. – Jon Stewart

I'd rather vote for a chimpanzee than (George W.) Bush. – Sting

(of William Jennings Bryan) His mind was like a soup dish, wide and shallow; it could hold a small amount of nearly anything, but the slightest jarring spilled the soup into somebody's lap. – Irving Stone

(of Herbert Asquith) When one has peeled off the brown-paper wrapping of phrases and compromises, just nothing at all. – Lytton Strachey

I think the last book that Nancy (Reagan) read was *Black Beauty*. – Roger Strauss

(of Stephen A. Douglas) A noisome, squat and nameless animal. – Charles Sumner

I feel certain that Woodrow Wilson would not recognise a generous impulse if he met it in the street. – William Taft

(of Woodrow Wilson) I regard him as a ruthless hypocrite and as an opportunist, who has not convictions he would not barter at once for votes. – William Taft

(of Tony Blair) He appears to have no clear political view except that the world should be a nicer place and that he should be loved and trusted by everyone and questioned by no one. – Norman Tebbit

(of Neil Kinnock) He does have the air of a chicken pecking at a lot of corn on the ground when he is speaking. – Norman Tebbit (of Herbert Hoover) Such a little man could not have made so big a depression. – Norman Thomas

(of Hubert Humphrey) A brain-damaged old vulture. – Hunter S. Thompson

President Nixon was so crooked that he needed servants to help him screw his pants on every morning. – Hunter S. Thompson

I've been called worse things by better men. – Pierre Trudeau after Richard Nixon had called him an "asshole"

(of Dwight D. Eisenhower) This fellow doesn't know any more about politics than a pig knows about Sunday. – Harry S. Truman

(of Millard Fillmore) At a time when we needed a strong man, what we got was a man who swayed with the slightest breeze. – Harry S. Truman

(of Richard Nixon) He's one of the few in the history of the country to run for high office talking out of both sides of his mouth at the same time – and lying out of both sides. – Harry S. Truman

(of Cecil Rhodes) I admire him, I frankly confess it; and when his time comes I shall buy a piece of the rope for a keepsake. – Mark Twain

Peter Mandelson has the insolent manner of one born to the top rung but three. – Gore Vidal

I know for a fact that Mr Reagan is not clear about the difference between the Medici and the Gucci. He knows that Nancy wears one. – Gore Vidal

(of Margaret Thatcher) I cannot bring myself to vote for a woman who has been voice-trained to speak to me as though my dog has just died. – Keith Waterhouse

(of David Cameron) They say he's at ease with modern Britain, which is a Tory way of saying, "I'm not a racist." – Robert Webb

(of Woodrow Wilson) I am suspicious of a man who has a handshake like a ten-cent pickled mackerel in brown paper. – William A. White

Harold Wilson is going round the country stirring up apathy. – William Whitelaw

(of Michael Howard) He has something of the night in him. – Ann Widdecombe

Bill Clinton is most comfortable when thinking about little things – school uniforms, the minimum wage and, above all, himself. – George F. Will

You look at George W. (Bush) and you realize that some men are born great, some achieve greatness, and some get it as a graduation gift. – Robin Williams

When the media ask him (George W. Bush) a question, he answers, "Can I use a lifeline?" – Robin Williams

(of Ronald Reagan) Satire is alive and well and living in the White House. – Robin Williams

I always said little (Harry S.) Truman had a voice so high it could only be detected by a bat. – Tennessee Williams

(of Edward Heath) A shiver looking for a spine to run up. – Harold Wilson

(of Chester Arthur) A nonentity with sidewhiskers. – Woodrow Wilson

(of Ulysses S. Grant) He combined great gifts with great mediocrity. – Woodrow Wilson

(of Theodore Roosevelt) I am told he no sooner thinks than he talks, which is a miracle not wholly in accord with an educational theory of forming an opinion. – Woodrow Wilson

(of Thomas Dewey) He's the only man able to walk under a bed without hitting his head. – Walter Winchell

(of Denis Howell) He's not unlike a fifty-pence piece: double-faced, many-sided and intrinsically not worth a great deal. – Wilf Wooller

(of Canadian politician Joe Clark) No shirt is too young to be stuffed. – Larry Zolf

Republicans vs Democrats
Anti-Republican

It seems to be a law of nature that Republicans are more boring than Democrats. – Stewart Alsop

I like that about the Republicans; the evidence does not faze them, they are not bothered at all by the facts. – Bill Clinton

How did sex come to be thought of as dirty in the first place? God must have been a Republican. – Will Durst

Republicans are so empty-headed, they wouldn't make a good landfill. – Jim Hightower

(Abraham) Lincoln was right about not fooling all the people all the time. But the Republicans haven't given up trying. – Lyndon B. Johnson

I've left specific instructions that I do not want to be brought back during a Republican administration. – Timothy Leary on reincarnation

Bob Dole revealed he is one of the test subjects for Viagra. He said on Larry King, "I wish I had bought stock in it." Only a Republican would think the best part of Viagra is the fact that you could make money off of it. – Jay Leno

The number two Republican in the Senate, Mitch McConnell, underwent heart surgery last week. He's doing fine. Nothing was actually wrong with his heart – it's just that whenever a Republican is elected to a leadership position, they have to have their heart bypassed. – Jay Leno

There have been rumours swirling around Florida that Florida Governor Jeb Bush had been cheating on his wife. But he says no, that's not true – as a Republican, the only people he's been in bed with are the tobacco industry and the gun lobby. – Jay Leno

Brains, you know, are suspect in the Republican Party. – Walter J. Lippmann

What Democratic congressmen do to their women staffers, Republican congressmen do to the country. – Bill Maher

In this world of sin and sorrow there is always something to be thankful for; as for me, I rejoice that I am not a Republican. – H. L. Mencken

You have to have been a Republican to know how good it is to be a Democrat. – Jackie Onassis

If the person you are trying to diagnose politically is some sort of intellectual, the chances are two to one he is a Democrat. – Vance Packard

(of Pat Buchanan) He is racist, he's homophobic, he's xenophobic and he's a sexist. He's the perfect Republican candidate. – Bill Press

The Republicans have a habit of having three bad years and one good one, and the good one always happens to be election year. – Will Rogers

No children have ever meddled with the Republican Party and lived to tell about it. – Sideshow Bob, *The Simpsons*

Oh no, the dead have risen and they're voting Republican! – Lisa Simpson, *The Simpsons*

If the Republicans will stop telling lies about the Democrats, we will stop telling the truth about them. – Adlai Stevenson

There are some Republicans I would trust with anything – anything, that is, except public office. – Adlai Stevenson

A bureaucrat is a Democrat who holds some office that a Republican wants. – Harry S. Truman

The trouble with the Republican Party is that it has not had a new idea for thirty years. – Woodrow Wilson

You might be a Republican if you think you might remember laughing once as a kid.

You might be a Republican if you once broke loose at a party and removed your neck tie.

You might be a Republican if you've ever faxed the FBI a list of "Commies in My Neighbourhood".

You might be a Republican if you don't think *The Simpsons* is particularly funny, but you watch it because that Flanders fellow makes a lot of sense.

You might be a Republican if you've ever yelled, "Hey hippie, get a haircut."

You might be a Republican if you argue that you need two hundred handguns in case a bear ever attacks your home.

You might be a Republican if you've ever called education a luxury.

Anti-Democrat

The Democrats seem to be basically nicer people, but they have demonstrated time and again that they have the management skills of celery. They're the kind of people who'd stop to help you change a flat, but would somehow manage to set your car on fire. – Dave Barry

The principal purpose of the Democratic Party is to use the force of government to take property away from the people who earn it and give it to people who do not. – Neal Boortz

The Democratic Party is like a mule – without pride of ancestry or hope of posterity. – Edmund Burke

Democrats always assure us that deterrence will work, but when the time comes to deter, they're against it. – Ann Coulter

Democrats can't get elected unless things get worse – and things won't get worse unless they get elected. – Jeane J. Kirkpatrick

The Democrats said today that if they were in power they could get Israel to pull out of Palestine. Oh, shut up. They couldn't even get Bill to pull out of Monica.   Jay Leno

Jimmy Carter is seventy-six years old, or as Democrats call him, "their bright new star of the future". – David Letterman

The only difference between the Democrats and the Republicans is that the Democrats allow the poor to be corrupt, too. – Oscar Levant

A Democratic President is doomed to proceed to his goals like a squid, squirting darkness all about him. – Clare Boothe Luce

Compared to the Clintons, (Ronald) Reagan is living proof that a Republican with half a brain is better than a Democrat with two. – P. J. O'Rourke

You can never underestimate the ability of the Democrats to wet their finger and hold it to the wind. – Ronald Reagan

There is something about a Republican that you can only stand him for so long; and on the other hand, there is something about a Democrat that you can't stand him quite that long. – Will Rogers

You've got to be an optimist to be a Democrat, and you've got to be a humorist to stay one. – Will Rogers

I am not a member of any organized party: I am a Democrat. – Will Rogers

One of my movies was called *True Lies*. It's what the Democrats should have called their convention. – Arnold Schwarzenegger

Republicans study the financial pages of the newspaper. Democrats put them in the bottom of the bird cage. – Will Stanton

The Democratic Party can always be relied on to make a damn fool of itself at the critical time. – Ben Tillman

You might be a Democrat if you own something that says, "Dukakis for President" and still display it.

You might be a Democrat if you think the State of Florida should have tried to reform Ted Bundy.

You might be a Democrat if you think Michael Jackson is a great example of diversity.

You might be a Democrat if you believe personal injury lawyers when they say they are just trying to defend the little guy.

You might be a Democrat if you know at least one vegan.

You might be a Democrat if you trust Teddy Kennedy when he said that she was driving.

Anti-both parties

What is a Democrat? One who believes that the Republicans have ruined the country. What is a Republican? One who believes that the Democrats would ruin the country. – Ambrose Bierce

What is the difference between a Democrat and a Republican? A Democrat blows, a Republican sucks. – Lewis Black

In our two-party system, the Democrats are the party of no ideas and the Republicans are the party of bad ideas. – Lewis Black

It is easier to restrain wild donkeys (Democrats) than to raise a dead elephant (Republicans). – Arthur Hoff

Today is the anniversary of the Watergate break-in. That's the day the Republicans tried to steal the Democrats' plans. That's also the last time the Democrats had any plans worth stealing. It's also the last time a Republican President had a plan and actually carried it out. – Jay Leno

Republicans are against abortion until their daughters need one, Democrats are for abortion until their daughter wants one. – Grace McGarvie

The Democrats are the party that says government will make you smarter, taller, richer, and remove the crabgrass on your lawn. The Republicans are the party that says government doesn't work and then they get elected and prove it. – P. J. O'Rourke

The difference between a Republican and a Democrat is the Democrat is a cannibal – they have to live off each other – while the Republicans, why, they live off the Democrats. – Will Rogers

The Democrats and Republicans are equally corrupt – it's only in the amount where the Republicans excel. – Will Rogers

ROYALTY

(of his son, the future Edward VII) His intellect is of no more use than a pistol packed in the bottom of a trunk in the robber-infested Apennines. – Prince Albert

(after the death of her womanizing husband, Edward VII) Now at least I know where he is. – Queen Alexandra

Ambition radiates off (Paul) Burrell like molten lava. – Anon

(on Caroline of Brunswick, wife of George IV) She swore like an ostler and smelt like a farmyard. – Anon

Catherine the Great (of Russia) is often credited with pioneering one of the key accessories of modern woman – the toy boy. At her peak she changed men almost as frequently as other women change their hairstyle. – Anon

(on Ivan the Terrible of Russia) If any subjects incurred his displeasure, his only dilemma was whether to have them boiled alive or roasted. – Anon

Throughout the greater part of his life, George III was a kind of consecrated obstruction. – Walter Bagehot

(of Princess Anne) A bossy, unattractive, galumphing girl. – Cecil Beaton

(of Camilla, Duchess of Cornwall) The Duchess of Dowdy. – Mr Blackwell

(of Camilla, Duchess of Cornwall) She is monumentally lazy . . . a member of her family described her to me as 'the laziest woman to have been born in England in the Twentieth Century' . . . She is nervy and lacks stamina; she has never worked in her life and is terrified of being on public display. It can cause her to get bad-tempered. – Mark Bolland

(on Ludwig II of Bavaria) He was mentally gifted in the highest degree, but the contents of his mind were stored in a totally disordered fashion. – Eduard von Bomhard

The Duke of Edinburgh has perfected the art of saying hello and goodbye in the same handshake. – Jennie Bond

What the voices in Prince Charles's head are saying: So what if she's your mother, just press the pillow over her face and count to a hundred. – Frankie Boyle, *Mock the Week*

Prince Charles's primary occupation is to wait for his mother to die. – Marcus Brigstocke

(of Louis XIV of France) Strip your Louis Quatorze of his king gear, and there is nothing but a poor forked radish with a head fantastically carved. – Thomas Carlyle

No danger. For no man in England would take away my life to make you king. – Charles II to his brother, the Duke of York (the future James II), who had warned the King about travelling without guards

(of Prince Charles) To be quite frank I think he is very old fashioned and out of time. – Charles Clarke

Included in the entourage is Camilla's make-up artist, otherwise known as Ken the Plasterer. – Jeremy Clarkson on a royal tour of America

(of Charles II) One of the moral monsters of history. – Samuel Taylor Coleridge

The Duke of Windsor was an extremely dull man. He even danced a boring Charleston, which is no mean feat. – Noël Coward

Buckingham Palace says the security system works. Presumably much in the same way as Prince Charles works. – Angus Deayton, after a protester dressed as Batman scaled a Buckingham Palace balcony

Queen Elizabeth I was bald and had wooden teeth and yet somehow managed to remain a virgin. – Jack Dee

(of Henry VIII) The plain truth is that he was a most intolerable ruffian, a disgrace to human nature, and a blot of blood and grease upon the history of England. – Charles Dickens

(of the ageing Queen Charlotte, wife of George III) The bloom of her ugliness is going off. – Colonel Disbrowe

Prince William really has no personality. The guy is simply a waste of space. He could have been working long ago, or at least do something for charity. – Petra Ecclestone

(of Philip II of Spain) I cannot find it in me to fear a man who took ten years a-learning of his alphabet. – Elizabeth I

I recommended Helen Mirren (to star in *The Queen*). I said she would be ideal for any nude scenes. But, frankly, I doubt if there are any nude scenes in the Queen's life, let alone the film. – Dame Edna Everage

(of Sarah Ferguson, Duchess of York) Short on looks, absolutely deprived of any dress sense, has a figure like a Jurassic monster. – Nicholas Fairburn

(on Philippe, Duke of Orléans) His vanity seemed to render him incapable of attachment to anyone but himself. – Madame de la Fayette

There was an intruder at Prince Charles' house last night . . . with a pitchfork. He entered the home while Charles and Camilla were asleep. But no one was harmed. The intruder fled after Camilla woke up and started barking. – Craig Ferguson

Flying to an environmental award ceremony is a bit like turning up to an Oxfam award ceremony in a stretch limo. Prince Charles may as well be picking up an award for green hypocrisy. – Joss Garman on the decision by Prince Charles, who prides himself on being environmentally aware, to fly to America to receive a Global Environmental Citizen prize from Harvard

(on Chilperic, King of Neustria, France) He was extremely gluttonous, and his god was in his belly. It is impossible to imagine any vice or debauchery which this man did not practise. – Gregory of Tours (of George IV) A more contemptible, cowardly, selfish unfeeling dog does not exist than this king . . . with vices and weaknesses of the lowest and most contemptible order. − Charles Greville

(of George V) Born into the ranks of the working class, the new king's most likely fate would have been that of a street-corner loafer. − James Keir Hardie

(of James I of England) The wisest fool in Christendom. − Henri IV of France

(of Anne of Cleves) You have sent me a Flanders mare. − Henry VIII

I've never understood the attraction of royalty. This isn't the first generation. They're all a bit bonkers. They choose very strange partners, they're not managing the modern world very well. − Kim Howells, on the current British royal family

(of George IV) A man without a single claim to the gratitude of his country or the respect of posterity. − Leigh Hunt

Henry IV's feet and armpits enjoyed an international reputation. − Aldous Huxley

Prince Philip, he's a card! He has a habit of saying things like, "You're all bastards!", then, "Was that wrong? Oh, I'm sorry . . ." − Eddie Izzard

I'm prepared to take advice on leisure from Prince Philip. He's a world expert on leisure. He's been practising for most of his adult life. − Neil Kinnock

Prince William definitely isn't my type. He's too horsy looking. − Keira Knightley

(of Princess Margaret) The Billy Carter of the British monarchy. − Robert Lacey

(of Prince Harry) Not a bookish fellow and perhaps drinks more than is good for him. − Quentin Letts

He often does not go to bed for forty-eight hours, and did not take off his boots for eight weeks, behaves like a madman, makes terrible faces, barks like a dog, and, at times, says the most indecorous things. − Ludwig II of Bavaria on his equally mad brother, Otto

(of Henry VIII) A pig, an ass, a dunghill, the spawn of an adder, a basilisk, a lying buffoon, a mad fool with a frothy mouth. − Martin Luther

Queen Anne . . . when in good humour, was meekly stupid, and when in bad humour, was sulkily stupid. – Thomas Babington Macaulay

Henry VIII perhaps approached as nearly to the ideal standard of perfect wickedness as the infirmities of human nature will allow. – Sir James Mackintosh

(of the Duke of Windsor, the former Edward VIII) A pimple on the arse of the Empire. – Count Alfred de Marigny

(of George I) A dull, stupid and profligate king, full of drink and low conversation. – Justin McCarthy

(of Sarah Ferguson) She's in an old nursery rhyme, isn't she? The Duchess of York, she had ten thousand men. And when they were up, they were up . . . and when they were only halfway up, she was more than happy. – Paul Merton

I found it ironic to hear the Queen reading her speech about abolishing fox hunting to Parliament with a dead stoat wrapped around her neck. But that's not a nice way to talk about the Duke of Edinburgh. – Paul Merton

(of Princess Anne) Such an attractive lass. So outdoorsy. She loves nature in spite of what it did to her. – Bette Midler

The grovelling little bastard! – Spike Milligan, tongue firmly in cheek, after Prince Charles paid tribute to him

For fifty years or more Elizabeth Windsor has maintained her dignity, her sense of duty . . . and her hairstyle. – Helen Mirren

Princess Margaret looked like a huge ball of fur on two well-developed legs. – Nancy Mitford

(of George I) In private life he would be called an honest blockhead. – Lady Wortley Montagu

Honoured as Mother of the Year . . . Fergie is pictured in fishnets with a riding crop, an unlikely outfit for a living saint and model of maternal perfection. – Suzanne Moore, on Sarah Ferguson

Prince Charles doesn't even have to put his toothpaste on his toothbrush, yet looks like a cantankerous old man whose life is being ruined by urchins jamming potatoes up his drainpipe. – Caitlin Moran

The very idea of (Prince) Charles being king is laughable. You might as well say Ronnie Corbett will be king one day. I think that would give people more pleasure. – Morrissey

(of Queen Elizabeth II) A very pleasant middle to upper-class type lady with a talkative retired Navy husband. – Malcolm Muggeridge

He was a monster, he was destined never to finish anything in his life – not his schooling, not his marriages, not his reign – not even his pre-natal development. – Queen Nazli of Egypt on her son, Farouk I

(of George V) For seventeen years he did nothing at all but kill animals and stick in stamps. – Harold Nicolson

Prince Charles married Camilla Parker Bowles. And get this – Phil Collins was one of the guests at the royal wedding. In fact, at one point Phil Collins looked around and said, "Wow, I'm the best-looking person here." – Conan O'Brien

Prince Charles and his wife Camilla flew to Washington, DC today to meet President Bush and the First Lady. Unfortunately, during the twenty-one gun salute on the South Lawn, Camilla got frightened, bolted, and jumped over a fence. – Conan O'Brien

ABC is showing a movie about the love affair between Prince Charles and Camilla Parker Bowles, and the movie's getting bad reviews. The critics say that the guy who plays Camilla is terrible. – Conan O'Brien

According to a poll of British citizens, eighty-three percent of people say they forgive Princess Di for her infidelity. Apparently, the other seventeen percent has never gotten a look at Prince Charles. – Conan O'Brien

Prince Charles does a terrific job . . . for the Republican movement. – John O'Farrell

If it doesn't eat hay, she is not interested. – Prince Philip, of his daughter, the horse-loving Princess Royal

(of Diana, Princess of Wales) A sort of social hand grenade, ready to explode, leaving unsuspecting playboys legless and broken. – Trevor Philips

No doubt his Chateau Plonker will have an overpowering bouquet of opportunism, with strong hints of betrayal and a lingering whiff of sour grapes . . . guaranteed to leave a nasty taste in the mouth. – Amanda Platell, on a new range of wines introduced by former royal butler Paul Burrell

Fergie has been named Mother of the Year in the US. Who said the Yanks don't do irony? – Amanda Platell

(of George IV) A noble, nasty course he ran,
Superbly filthy and fastidious;
He was the world's "first gentleman",
And made the appellation hideous. – Winthrop Mackworth Praed

(of Prince Charles) Poor, pathetic creature, isn't he? A man in his fifties who still calls his mother "mummy". – Claire Rayner

Camilla (Parker Bowles) is so ugly, she has to frisk herself at airports. – Joan Rivers

Prince Charles's ears are so big he could hang-glide over the Falklands. – Joan Rivers

(of Camilla, Duchess of Cornwall) The Americans thought the bulldog clip that kept Joan Rivers' face in place had come off. – Jonathan Ross

(of Prince Charles) A rabid Tory who thinks "blacks and gays" have it easy and who would happily give up his throne to spend the rest of his life as a ski bum if he can't blast a fox to smithereens whenever he feels the urge. – Miranda Sawyer

Nowadays a parlour maid as ignorant as Queen Victoria was when she came to the throne would be classed as mentally defective. – George Bernard Shaw

(of Sarah Ferguson, Duchess of York) She's not a real princess, she's a slap-them-on-the-bottom princess. – Earl Spencer

(to Lord Louis Mountbatten) Dickie, you're so crooked that if you swallowed a nail you'd shit a corkscrew. – Sir Gerald Templer

If ever George IV had a friend, a true friend, in any social class, so we may claim that his or her name never reached our ears. – *Times* obituary

(on Don Carlos, Prince of Spain) When he passed from infancy to puberty, he took no pleasure in study nor in arms nor in horsemanship nor in any virtuous things, honest and pleasant, but only in doing harm to others. – Venetian ambassador

Queen Victoria was like a great paperweight that for half a century sat upon men's minds and when she was removed, their ideas began to flow all over the place haphazardly. – H. G. Wells

(of Mary, Queen of Scots) The most notorious whore in all the world. – Peter Wentworth

(of Elizabeth I) As just and merciful as Nero and as good a Christian as Mohammed. – John Wesley

Catherine was a great empress. She also had three hundred lovers. I did the best I could in a couple of hours. – Mae West, after playing Catherine the Great on stage

If this is the way Queen Victoria treats her convicts, she doesn't deserve to have any. – Oscar Wilde, languishing in Reading jail

When you look at Prince Charles, don't you think that someone in the Royal Family knew someone in the Royal Family? – Robin Williams

(of Charles II) Here lies our mutton-loving king,

Whose word no man relies on.
Who never said a foolish thing,
And never did a wise one.
– John Wilmot

SPORT

American Football

Lou (Holtz) is a great talker. If he were God, Moses would have to send out for more tablets. – Barry Alvarez

How do you kill a New York Giants' fan when he's been drinking? – Slam the toilet seat on his head. – Anon

The San Francisco 49ers say they are going to move. They want a new stadium that is more fan friendly. One without a scoreboard. – Jim Barach

Shannon (Sharpe) looks like a horse. I'll tell you that's an ugly dude . . . You can't tell me he doesn't look like Mr Ed. – Ray Buchanan

I would rather lose a game without Tim McKyer than win one with him. – Eddie DeBartolo

(of Tim Harris) Sometimes God gives out all the physical talent and takes away the brain. – Mike Ditka

(Alex) Karras has a lot of class. And all of it is third. – Conrad Dobler

Now available: a rare autographed photo of Terrell Owens. It's not rare because it's signed with the receiver's infamous Sharpie, it's rare because in the photograph his mouth is almost closed. – Scott Feschuk

He can be a great player in this league for a long time if he learns to say two words: "I'm full." – Jerry Glanville, on three-hundred-pound Lincoln Kennedy

I'm not saying Sean Salisbury is slow, but when he runs the ball we use a lot more film. – Dennis Green

Coach Woody Hayes doesn't know anything about drugs – he thinks uppers are dentures. – Archie Griffin

Mark Gastineau has got an IQ of about room temperature. – Dan Hampton

(of Terry Bradshaw) He's so dumb, he can't spell "cat" if you spotted him the "c" and the "a". – Thomas Henderson

If Jimmy Johnson wanted me to run twenty-six miles through hills, I would. If he wanted me to carry water bottles, I would. If he wanted me to get my hair cut like his . . . well, you have to draw the line somewhere. – Babe Laufenberg

(George) Halas was famous for being associated with only one club all his life – the one he held over your head during salary talks. – Bobby Layne

To give you an idea how bad the team is doing, he tried to run for it and lost three yards. – Jay Leno, after Arizona Cardinals' Dennis McKinley was arrested on suspicion of drug dealing

If I were the NFL commissioner, I'd put all the offensive linemen in jail for thirty days or make them spend one week with Mike Ditka. – Dexter Manley

Tom Landry is such a perfectionist that if he were married to Dolly Parton, he'd expect her to cook. – Don Meredith

There's this interior lineman who's as big as a gorilla and as strong as a gorilla. If he was as smart as a gorilla he'd be fine. – Dan Millman

If caring for a person is based on yelling and screaming, then coach (Bob) Huggins loves us very much. – Terry Nelson

The New York Giants announced that seventy-five season-ticket holders who threw snowballs during the San Diego game will be banned from attending any more Giants games. I don't think they should be rewarded for that kind of behaviour. – Conan O'Brien

Jim (Walden) has the Midas touch – everything he touches turns to mufflers. – Steve Raible

The action scenes in *Remember the Titans* were performed by actors with little football training. For many of the shots, they used the Cincinnati Bengals. – Alan Ray

Al Davis is the kind of guy who would steal your eyes and then try to convince you that you looked better without them. – Sam Rutigliano

In order to resemble William Perry, we have rented a Winnebago for our offensive line to practise against. – Steve Sloan

(of Larry Brown) He's Edward Scissorhands. He couldn't catch a cold in Alaska buck naked. – Emmitt Smith

They feature a Buddy Ryan sandwich at his restaurant. It's a little tongue and a lot of baloney. – Arnie Spanier

Twenty books have been destroyed in a fire at Auburn University's football dorm. But the real tragedy was that fifteen hadn't been coloured yet. – Steve Spurrier

The way Warren Sapp looks, there should be a McDonald's next to his house. – Michael Strahan

(of Jerry Glanville) Drop me a note if you find somebody who likes this guy. – Sam Wyche

When you tackle Earl Campbell, it reduces your IQ. – Pete Wysocki (of Ed Garvey) He does the work of three men – Larry, Curley, and Moe. – Vic Ziegel

Baseball

(of Rogers Hornsby) He was frank to the point of cruelty and subtle as a belch. – Lee Allen

(of Pepper Martin) A chunky, unshaven hobo who ran the bases like a berserk locomotive, slept in the raw, and swore at pitchers in his sleep. – Lee Allen

(of Mike Grace) Let's just say that if Disneyland is ever looking for someone to wear the Goofy costume, I've got the perfect candidate. – Larry Andersen

(of Choo Choo Coleman) He is quick on the bases, but this is an attribute that is about as essential for catchers as neat handwriting. – Roger Angell

At least the Chicago Cubs are trying. They installed a new pitching machine the other day. Unfortunately it beat them 4-1. – Anon

It was so foggy today that the Cubs couldn't even see who was beating them. – Anon

I love autumn. It gives me a chance to sit at home and watch the World Series. Kinda like the Cubs. – Anon

Now I know why there's only one "I" in "umpire". – Anon

(of Juan Berenguer) If I pulled up in front of a restaurant and he came out to park my car, I'd eat somewhere else. – Bob Brenly

(of the Chicago Cubs) There's nothing wrong with this team that more pitching, more fielding, and more hitting couldn't help. – Bill Buckner

Jose Canseco is an attention-grabbing crackpot with the credibility of a street-corner snitch. – Bryan Burwell

(of Mike Boddicker) His pitches remind me of the garbage I take out at night. – Rod Carew

Babe Herman improved greatly in his ninth season. He still hadn't caught a ball, but he was getting a lot closer. – Gordon Cobbledon

On the mound is Randy Jones, the left-hander with the Karl Marx hairdo. – Jerry Coleman

The one thing that kept Jack Perconte from being a good major-league player is performance. – Del Crandell

There'll be a man on the moon before Gaylord Perry hits a home run. – Alvin Dark, 1963. (On 20 July 1969, minutes after Apollo 11 landed on the moon, Perry hit the first, and only, home run of his career.)

The (Cincinnati) Reds media guide lists Kevin Mitchell at 210 (pounds). We have seen him now in the considerable flesh, and we can say this: that 210, it's from the chin up. – Paul Daugherty

Could be that Bill Terry's a nice guy when you get to know him, but why bother? – Dizzy Dean

Buddy Bell says the two biggest career shorteners are hustle and sweat. Oh, Buddy hustles – but he hustles at his own pace. He's a slow hustler. The biggest thing Buddy does all winter is renew his subscription to *TV Guide*. – Rich Donnelly

Van Mungo likes to drink a bit. Anything. Even hair tonic. – Leo Durocher

Hoyt Wilhelm is so old, he is likely to be the only man in baseball history to collect a pension cheque and a salary cheque at the same time. – Eddie Fisher

A smile on Gene (Mauch)'s face was as rare as a perfect game. – Tom Flaherty

(of Randy Huntley) He can catch, he can throw, and he can run, but he couldn't hit me if I walked in front of him. – Herman Franks

(of Rick Burleson) He's even tempered. He comes to the ballpark mad and stays that way. – Joe Garagiola

Billy Loes was the only player in the majors who could lose a ground ball in the sun. – Joe Garagiola

The Cleveland Indians traded infielder Stubby Clapp for a player to be named better. – Bud Geracie

(to veteran Satchel Paige) Say, Satch, tell me, was Abraham Lincoln a crouch hitter? – Lefty Gomez

Manny Ramirez is a comically awful outfielder. He is a tremendous hitter but he couldn't catch radiation poisoning at a KGB reunion banquet. – Argus Hamilton

Perhaps the problem with our ozone layer is that Rickey (Henderson)'s ego keeps punching holes in it. – Sean Horgan

(of Reggie Jackson) He'd give you the shirt off his back. Of course, he'd call a press conference to announce it. – Catfish Hunter

The first thing they do in Cleveland, if you have talent, is trade you for three guys who don't. – Jim Kern

I see that Tony Gwynn signed a contract with an incentive clause based on plate appearances . . . from the looks of Tony, he must've thought they meant dinner plates. – Jerry Klein

Chuck Hiller was a helluva hitter, but he had iron hands. You couldn't play him on rainy days – his hands would rust. – Ed Kranepool

Harvey Kuenn's face looks as if it could hold three days of rain. – Tommy Lasorda

Steve Sax plays baseball like my wife shops – all day long. – Tommy Lasorda

Darryl Strawberry is not a dog; a dog is loyal and runs after balls. – Tommy Lasorda

(of Don Zimmer) The designated gerbil. – Bill Lee

On this date in 1985, pitcher Nolan Ryan recorded his 4,000th strikeout. Four thousand strikeouts. You know what the Detroit Tigers call that? Batting practice. – Jay Leno

Major league baseball has asked its players to stop tossing baseballs into the stands during games, because they say fans fight over them and they get hurt. In fact, the Florida Marlins said that's why they never hit any home runs. It's a safety issue. – Jay Leno

Did you watch the Macy's Thanksgiving Day parade? The Fat Albert balloon sprung a leak, and at the last minute was replaced by Yankee first baseman Cecil Fielder. – David Letterman

If it's true you learn by your mistakes, Jim Frey will be the best manager ever. – Ron Luciano

If (Mo) Vaughn weighed in at 275 pounds last season, so did Rhode Island. – Mike Lupica

(Stan) Musial's batting stance looks like a small boy looking around a corner to see if the cops are coming. – Ted Lyons

The only pitcher I had left was Mike Armstrong, and the reason I didn't use him was that I wanted to win the game. – Billy Martin

When you walk by, Gaylord Perry smells like a drugstore. – Billy Martin

For a guy 6ft 8in, Dave Winfield has got the softest bat I've ever seen. – Billy Martin

Gene Mauch's stare can put you on the disabled list. – Tim McCarver

Nothing is more limited than being a limited partner of George (Steinbrenner)'s. – John McMullen

Freddie Patek is the only guy in the major leagues who needs a life preserver to get into the whirlpool bath. – Jim Murray

When (Tom) Seaver laughs, he makes dogs whine. – Lindsey Nelson

In a city that never sleeps, he did. – *Newsday*, on Roberto Alomar's miserable spell with the New York Mets

(of Mitch Williams) If you put his brain in a blue jay, the bird would fly backwards. – Al Nipper

In a recent survey, only thirteen percent of Americans said that baseball was their favourite sport. The survey was taken in the Mets dugout. – Conan O'Brien

George Steinbrenner is the salt of the earth. And the Yankee players are the open wounds of the earth. – Scott Ostler

(of Mike Anderson) His limitations are limitless. – Danny Ozark

I did not call (Darrell) Johnson an idiot. Someone else did, and I just agreed. – Jim Palmer

I taught Charlie Finley all he knows about baseball. That's why I keep asking myself where I went wrong. – Hank Peters

Leo Durocher has the ability of taking a bad situation and making it immediately worse. – Branch Rickey

(to Don Zimmer) I've reserved three seats for you at my show tonight. One for you, one for your wife, and one for your stomach. – Don Rickles

Dan Napoleon's so ugly that when a fly ball was hit toward him, it would curve away from him. – Mickey Rivers

I've never seen anyone get hit by so many balls in the field without touching them as Enos Cabell. – Frank Robinson

Hey, (Kevin) Appier, pitch faster! By the time you get done, my clothes will be out of style! – Chi Chi Rodriguez

You have to give Pete (Rose) credit for what he accomplished. He never went to college, and the only book he ever read was *The Pete Rose Story*. – Karolyn Rose, his ex-wife

(of George Steinbrenner) Every time you go into his office he greets you warmly and shakes you by the throat. – Al Rosen

Pete Rose is the most likeable arrogant person I've ever met. – Mike Schmidt

The speed gun on pitcher Tom Candiotti is like an hourglass. – Vin Scully

Mickey Hatcher is the first player to make the major leagues on one brain cell. – Roy Smalley

(of Will "the Thrill" Clark) It's hard to like a guy who wears the word "Thrill" on his helmet. – Dave Smith

Detroit fans don't know anything about baseball. They couldn't tell the difference between baseball players and Japanese aviators. – Mayo Smith

He never shuts up. The way to test a Timex watch would be to strap it to (Earl) Weaver's tongue. – Marty Springstead

(of Carl Yastrzemski) Most valuable player from the neck down. – Eddie Stanky

Dave Kingman has the personality of a tree trunk. – John Stearns

Bobby Brown reminds me of a fellow who's been hitting for twelve years and fielding one. – Casey Stengel

(of Chris Cannizzaro) I knew he couldn't hit, but no one told me he couldn't catch either. – Casey Stengel

(to Phil Rizzuto) Kid, you're too small. You ought to go out and shine shoes. – Casey Stengel

Babe Herman wore a glove for only one reason. It was a league custom. The glove would last him a minimum of six years because it rarely made contact with the ball. – Frescoe Thompson

My heel felt just like George Steinbrenner: irritating, painful, nagging, and wouldn't go away. – Mychal Thompson

Pedro Guerrero's only limitation is his ability to move around. – Joe Torre

Tommy Lasorda will eat anything as long as you pay for it. – Joe Torre

(of Phil Niekro) First I found it hard to catch him. Then I found it hard to hit him. And finally I found it hard to manage him. – Joe Torre

Mario Soto has a million-dollar arm and a ten-cent head. – Alex Trevino

(of Frank Thomas) Believe me, it's not easy to deal with an idiot. And this man over the course of the years has tried my patience. – Kenny Williams

You and Leo Durocher are on a raft. A wave comes and knocks him into the ocean. You dive in and save his life. A shark comes and takes your leg. Next day, you and Leo start out even. – Dick Young

Basketball
He made a stupid call, and it will be stupid till the day he dies. He's stupid Hank. That's his nickname. – Charles Barkley, after being ejected by referee Hank Armstrong

(to Oliver Miller) You can't even jump high enough to touch the rim unless they put a Big Mac on it. – Charles Barkley

Dennis (Rodman) has become like a prostitute, but now it's gotten ridiculous, to the point where he will do anything humanly possible to make money. – Charles Barkley

(of Kevin Willis) His upper body is built like Mt Olympia. And his lower body is built like Kathie Lee Gifford. – Charles Barkley

Dick (Motta) brings a lot to the table with his experience. It has been a learning experience already. In training camp, we learned the right way to peel bananas. – Bernie Bickerstaff

I pay (Rick) Robey more than anyone to come to my summer basketball camp. The kids can watch him play and see for themselves what not to do. – Larry Bird

Does he (Raja Bell) know me? Do I know this guy? I don't know this guy. I might have said one word to this guy. I don't know this kid . . . I don't need to know this kid. I don't want to . . . Maybe he wasn't hugged enough as a kid. – Kobe Bryant

Cotton Fitzsimmons is so short, he's the only coach in the NBA who can sleep in a pillowcase. – Skip Caray

Dick Vitale's voice could peel the skin off a potato. – Norman Chad

Like I told the team at half-time, Stevie Wonder, Roy Orbison and Ray Charles could have hit some of those shots – or at least come close. We acted like twelve people who were dropped down from outer space, put uniforms on and played like we had never seen one another before. – Jim Cleamons

(on the nose piercings of Dennis Rodman) He has so many fish hooks in his nose, he looks like a piece of bait. – Bob Costas

There's a word for a book like that: "autobiography". – Greg Cote, after a new book named Shaquille O'Neal as the best player in the history of basketball

I call Los Angeles the city of alternatives. If you don't like mountains, we got the ocean. If you don't like Knott's Berry Farm, we've got Disneyland. If you don't like basketball, we've got the Clippers. – Arsenio Hall

(of Dennis Rodman's green hair) He doesn't cut that hair, he mows it. – Chick Hearn

The LA Clippers picked high school star Darius Miles with their first choice in the NBA draft. That's the equivalent of being voted off the island. – Alex Kaseberg

The first ever basketball player has come out of the closet. Former NBA centre John Amaechi, who played for four different teams over five seasons, has publicly announced that he's a homosexual. People started to get suspicious when they found out he had no illegitimate kids. – Jimmy Kimmel

You did great, son. You scored one more point than a dead man. – Abe Lemons

The new Dennis Rodman doll is $19.95, assault and battery not included. – David Letterman

Look, guys say a lot of things and I don't put too much credence in it. Maybe they got him on a day when his milk was too warm for his Coco Puffs. – Kevin McHale, responding to an outburst by Kevin Garnett

It must have had his contract in it. – Dick Motta, Sacramento Kings' coach, after player Danny Ainge injured his back while lifting his suitcase

(of veteran coach Bill Fitch) If they can keep his wheelchair greased and his walker handy, he'll do fine. – Dick Motta

I thank my teammates for letting opponents blow by them. – Alonzo Mourning, winning the Defensive Player of the Year award

I didn't know he was that ugly. I thought he was a pretty good-looking fella when he had hair, but, oh my goodness, did that bring out all his bad features or what! He's going to be single all the rest of his life. – Don Nelson, on Dirk Nowitzki's crew cut

I asked him (Dominique Wilkins) to do some things that were difficult for him to do – like run back on defence, and pass. – Don Nelson

Me responding to (Dennis) Rodman is like talking to a Bugs Bunny doll. I don't like to talk to Looney Tunes. – Shaquille O'Neal

October 31 is the night people dress in bizarre, outlandish outfits and then make children and old people scream in horror. In most of the world, this is known as Halloween. In Southern California, it is the start of the Clippers' season. – Jerry Perisho

Dennis Rodman plays a villain in the movie *Double Team*. That's like hiring Elizabeth Taylor to play a divorcee. – Tom Powers

Billy Tubbs is what's known as a contact coach – all con and no tact. – Bob Reinhardt

Jack Simka's box score is beginning to look like his pay-check. There is a one and then a whole lot of zeroes. – Fred Roberts

(of referee Terry Durham) If I had bad breath, he would call a foul on that. – Dennis Rodman

The team is boring and lifeless. For over twenty years the Boston Celtics have stood for something. The only thing they stand for now is the anthem. – Bob Ryan

(Adolph) Rupp was unique. He wanted everybody to hate him – and he succeeded. – Bill Spivey

Vlade Divac is a quick learner, but he forgets quick, too. – Mychal Thompson

(of Dick Vitale) I know that if he shot off his mouth long enough, he'd get something right. – Billy Tubbs

The earth in LA moved more in one hour than Benoit Benjamin did all last season with the Clippers. – Peter Vecsey, after an earthquake hit Los Angeles

George McGinnis has got the body of a Greek God and the running ability of a Greek goddess. – Dick Vitale

Coach Larry Brown is like Liz Taylor. Just when you think it's over, someone new is ready to walk him down the aisle. – Donnie Walsh

Dennis Rodman's latest hairstyle looks like an inkblot test I get at my psychiatrist. – Bill Wennington

(of Isiah Thomas) Light travels faster than sound, so some people appear to be bright until you hear them speak. – Brian Williams

Charles (Barkley) once told me he would write his autobiography as soon as he could figure out who the main character would be. – Pat Williams

(of 7ft 6in Shawn Bradley) He's a lifeguard in the offseason. He can't swim, but he's great at wading. – Pat Williams

We told Stanley Roberts to go on a water diet, and Lake Superior disappeared. – Pat Williams

When Stanley Roberts was here, we had to remove an obstruction from his throat. It was a pizza. – Pat Williams

Stanley Roberts' idea of a salad is putting a piece of lettuce on a pizza. – Pat Williams

They had a big scandal at Jim Valvano's school – three players were found in the library. – Pat Williams

Boxing

I've seen George Foreman shadow boxing, and the shadow won. – Muhammad Ali

(of Joe Frazier) He's so ugly they ought to donate his face to the World Wildlife Fund. – Muhammad Ali

(of Sonny Liston) Isn't he ugly? He's too ugly to be the world's champ. The world's champ should be pretty like me. – Muhammad Ali

Sonny Liston's so ugly that when he cries the tears run down the back of his head. – Muhammad Ali

(of promoter Aileen Eaton) She's a darling woman, but I'm happy I never had to fight her. I'd rather fight Carmen Basillio or the Viet Cong. – Art Aragon

Years ago we had the Raging Bull, Jake LaMotta. Today, we've got the Raging Bullshit, Bruce Strauss. – Teddy Brenner

After boxing, I would think Mike (Tyson) will resort to what he was doing when he was growing up – robbing people. – Tommy Brooks

(Mike) Tyson is very limited. His type of boxing is OK for the back of a pub, but he's got no style, no class. He's crude and unsophisticated. – Joe Bugner

(of Audley Harrison) He's a lazy bugger who doesn't want to work, so he'll have to change. – Joe Bugner

(of Roy Jones) He doesn't know how to fight, he doesn't know how to stand and he's as wide open as the Holland Tunnel. – Al Certo

It's good that Mike Tyson has been granted parole. More steps like this must be taken to make our prisons safer places. – Greg Cote

When promoter Bob Arum pats you on the back, he's just looking for a spot to stick the knife. – Cus D'Amato

I'll shake hands with Bob Arum, but I'll take my ring off first. – Mickey Duff

(of Chris Eubank) As genuine as a three-dollar bill. – Mickey Duff

Don King is a damn sleazebag. King is nothing but a strong-arm man. He has taken his gangsterism and put it into boxing. – Dan Duva

Some people say George (Foreman) is fit as a fiddle, but I think he looks more like a cello. – Lou Duva

(Muhammad) Ali wouldn't have hit Joe Louis on the bum with a handful of rice. – Tommy Farr

(of Buster Douglas) The fella is a bore. He could be at a party and no one would know he's there. His poster could put people to sleep. – George Foreman

Mike Tyson's not all that bad. If you dig deep, dig real deep, go all the way to China, I'm sure you'll find there's a nice guy in there. – George Foreman

(of Joe Calzaghe) Basically, he's a mouthy git who's trying to be something he ain't and it looks pathetic. To be honest, I wouldn't even bother talking to him if we were in the same room. – Dean Francis

(of Muhammad Ali) He is phoney, using his blackness to get his way. – Joe Frazier

One day Don King will asphyxiate by the force of his own exhaust. – Carmen Graciano

Me and Jake LaMotta grew up in the same neighbourhood. You wanna know how popular Jake was? When we played hide-and-seek, nobody ever looked for LaMotta. – Rocky Graziano

You put your head in a noose when you sign with Don King. – Mitch Green

To hell with Bob Arum. I advise all the fighters in the world, black or white, to stay away from the sucker. – Larry Holmes

Don King doesn't care about black or white. He just cares about green. – Larry Holmes

Rocky Marciano couldn't carry my jockstrap. – Larry Holmes

I was nicknamed "Rembrandt" because I spent so much time on the canvas. – Bob Hope

Joe Bugner fought Frank Bruno like the objective of boxing was to get hit on the jaw. – Jim Jacobs

You know what animals exist in the desert. He's going to his indigenous natural habitat. What better place for night crawlers? – Don King, on learning that rival promoter Bob Arum was moving to Las Vegas

He's the first guy to drive a three-hundred-thousand-dollar car with licence plates he made himself. – Jay Leno, after Mike Tyson bought four expensive cars on his release from prison

Ricky Hatton ain't nothing but a fat man. I'm going to punch him in his beer belly when I see him. – Floyd Mayweather

Billy Wells was all chin from the waist up. – Frank Moran

I have an advantage in this fight. I have only one chin to expose. – Tommy Morrison, before his bout with George Foreman

Rick Thornberry is a poor bum whose head should be used to keep doors from slamming on a windy day. – Anthony Mundine

Frank Bruno has a chin of such pure Waterford crystal, it gives rise to the old adage that people who live in glass jaws shouldn't throw punches. The biggest danger in fighting Bruno is that you might get hit by flying glass. – Jim Murray

Promoter Don King took a ride on a dogsled. It was so cold, he had his hands in his own pockets. – Chris Myers

The well-respected professional punchbag, Julius Francis. – Matthew Norman

Mike Tyson was a referee at Wrestlemania 14, and at the end of the night he gave the crowd the finger. The weird part is it was Evander Holyfield's finger. – Conan O'Brien

(of Buster Douglas) He went to bed as a 231-pound world champion and woke up as a 270-pound parade float. – Scott Ostler

Larry Holmes is a yellow dog who is shaking at the thought of having to fight me. He'd rather retire than fight me. You can't compare me to Larry. He hasn't done anything or acted in any way that invites comparison. Boxing will be better without him. – Greg Page

Brian London possesses the most unbeautiful face – it looks as if it, at one time, fell apart and was reassembled by a drunken mechanic. – Michael Parkinson

Gerry Cooney can't fight to keep warm. – Irving Rudd

I'm not saying Tommy Hearns is a cheapskate, but he squeezes a nickel so tight, the Indian sits on the buffalo. – Irving Rudd

Don King dresses like a pimp and speechifies like a store-front preacher. – John Schulian

(of Herol "Bomber" Graham) He has turned defensive boxing into a poetic art. Trouble is, nobody ever knocked anybody out with a poem. – Eddie Shaw

(of an unnamed contender) He has everything a boxer needs except speed, stamina, a punch, and ability to take punishment. In other words, he owns a pair of shorts. – Blackie Sherrod

Tommy Morrison proved that he is an ambidextrous fighter. He can get knocked out with either hand. – Bert Sugar

I tried to stay away from (Don) King. You can't do it. It's like staying away from taxes. Sooner or later, he'll get you. – Pinklon Thomas

We all know what Don King is, but if you keep a snake in the room with the light on, you can control him. – Mike Tyson

Scott Harrison has pissed away a career then acted as if he is the victim. He doesn't have a chip on his shoulder, but a bag of King Edwards. – Frank Warren

The current version of Buster Mathis Jr boasts not just a Michelin-man waist but an *embonpoint* that would give him a better shot at starring in the next Wonderbra poster than winning a boxing title. – Richard Williams

Cricket
Shane Warne should retire and be a pantomime dame . . . made up in a great big dress with bouffant hair. – Jonathan Agnew

(of Merv Hughes) He always appeared to be wearing a tumble-dried ferret on his top lip. – Rick Broadbent

The other advantage England have got when Phil Tufnell is bowling is that he isn't fielding. – Ian Chappell

Any sport which goes on for so long that you might need a "comfort break" is not a sport at all. It is merely a means of passing the time. Like reading. – Jeremy Clarkson, *The World According to Clarkson*

Illy (Ray Illingworth) had the man-management skills of Basil Fawlty. – Darren Gough

(to Robin Smith) Does your husband play cricket as well? – Merv Hughes

There is so much coming out of his mouth, I can't hear it all. It is very motivating and makes you want to be there at the end. – Mike Hussey, Australian batsman, on sledging by England wicketkeeper Paul Nixon

(of Michael Atherton) One of the few people capable of looking more dishevelled at the start of a six-hour century than at the end of it. – Martin Johnson

(Angus) Fraser's approach to the wicket currently resembles someone who has his braces caught in the sightscreen. – Martin Johnson

Freddie Flintoff's sparkling earring looks utterly ridiculous – like an Old Etonian tie on an orang-utan. – Peter McKay

If (Ian) Botham is an English folk hero, then this must be an alarming time for the nation. – David Miller

(of Muttiah Muralitharan) At best, his action is suspicious. At worst it belongs in a darts tournament. – Michael Parkinson

I suspect he (Andre Nel) has the IQ of an empty swimming pool. – Adam Parore

(of John Snow) A fast bowler so hot-headed it was a surprise his sun hat never burst into flames. – Harry Pearson

(of Ashley Giles) Only his mother would describe him as an athlete. – Derek Pringle

W. G. Grace was by no conceivable standard a good man. He was a cheat on and off the cricket field. – C. P. Snow

(of Shane Warne) I've seen him playing football before a Test match, and believe me, his second touch was always a throw-in. – Alec Stewart

Ian Botham couldn't bowl a hoop downhill. – Fred Trueman

(of Geoffrey Boycott) I know why he's bought a house by the sea – so that he'll be able to go for a walk on the water. – Fred Trueman

There's only one head bigger than Tony Greig – and that's Birkenhead. – Fred Trueman

(of Paul Collingwood) He made a few runs in Brisbane and a double century in Adelaide, but I reckon my son could have batted on the first two days there and he's only seven. – Shane Warne

Denis Compton was the only player to call his partner for a run and wish him good luck at the same time. – John Warr

Kevin Pietersen would be deemed brash by a Texan assertiveness coach. – Simon Wilde

(of Kabir Ali) He's bowled like a camel and fielded like a drain. – Bob Willis

Jason Gillespie is a thirty-year-old in a thirty-six-year-old body. – Bob Willis

Rod Marsh: So how's your wife and my kids?
Ian Botham: The wife's fine, the kids are retarded.

Glenn McGrath: Brandes, why are you fat?
Eddo Brandes: Because every time I fuck your wife, she gives me a biscuit.

Shane Warne: I've been waiting two years to humiliate you again.
Daryll Cullinan: Looks like you spent the time eating.

Mark Waugh: What are you doing out here? There's no way you're good enough to play for England.
James Ormond: Maybe not, but at least I'm the best player in my family.

Golf

His divots go further than his drives. – Anon

He's got a swing like an octopus putting up a deckchair. – Anon

Tom Lehmann's mannerisms are reminiscent of a highly competitive turtle. – Anon

There was never much said on the course when I played with Nick (Faldo). I probably knew him twenty years before I heard him complete a sentence. – Paul Azinger

The Ryder Cup team of Americans was comprised of eleven nice guys and Paul Azinger. – Seve Ballesteros, 1991

You're not going to believe this, but a golf ball just landed on my laptop. David Duval must be on the practice range again. – Mike Bianchi, *Orlando Sentinel*

You ever watch golf on television? It's like watching flies fuck. – George Carlin

Bob Hope has a beautiful short game. Unfortunately it's off the tee. – Jimmy Demaret

(of Lew Worsham's prominent chin) He's the only guy in the world with a built-in bib. – Jimmy Demaret

He may be a great golfer, but socially he's a twenty-four-handicapper. – Gill Faldo, on ex-husband Nick

John Daly has the worst haircut I've ever seen in my life. It looks like he has a divot over each ear. – David Feherty

The only time Nick Faldo opens his mouth is to change feet. – David Feherty

(of Phil Mickelson) I don't know him but I've seen him smile, and that's quite enough to put me off wanting to know anything about him. – David Feherty

Jim Furyk has a swing like a man trying to kill a snake in a phone booth. – David Feherty

Colin Montgomerie has a face like a warthog that has been stung by a wasp. – David Feherty

(of Colin Montgomerie) I think he's the jerk of the world. – Fred Funk

Tiger Woods recently repeated his call for the PGA tour to begin the random testing of touring golfers for performance-enhancing drugs. The results won't always be pretty. The last time John Daly gave a urine sample, it had an olive in it. – Argus Hamilton

Bruce Lietzke is talking seriously about retiring from the PGA tour, which begs the question: how will anyone know? – Steve Hershey

Sammy Davis Jr hits the ball one hundred and thirty yards and his jewellery goes one hundred and fifty. – Bob Hope

There are over one hundred and fifty golf courses in the Palm Springs area and Gerry Ford is never sure which one he's going to play until his second shot. – Bob Hope

Whenever I play golf with Gerry Ford, I usually try to make it a foursome – Ford, me, a paramedic, and a faith healer. – Bob Hope

Some of these legends have been around golf a long time. When they mention a good grip, they're talking about their dentures. – Bob Hope

Doug Sanders' outfit has been described as looking like the aftermath of a direct hit on a pizza factory. – Dave Marr

He looks like somebody's always chasing him. – Gary McCord, on Miller Barber's scruffy appearance

You start your soft-boiled eggs by the time he's ready. – Johnny Miller, on Nick Faldo's slow putting

Kenneth Ferrie is a fun guy. He's like a David Feherty who can play. – Johnny Miller

Deane Beman is just another screwhead too big for his britches. – Bill Murray

You look at (Nick) Faldo and you have to resist the temptation to look at the back for the knobs. – Jim Murray

Hubert Green swings like a drunk trying to find a keyhole in the dark. – Jim Murray

Corey Pavin plays the game as if he has a plane to catch; as if he were double parked and left the meter running. Guys move slower leaving hotel fires. – Jim Murray

When (Bernhard) Langer practises on his own, he can hold up a fourball. – Dave Musgrove

(of John Daly) A mullet par excellence, big, blonde and deeply unfashionable. – Gavin Newston

It takes a lot of guts to play this game, and by looking at Billy Casper, you can tell he certainly has a lot of guts. – Gary Player on the overweight American

If Lee Trevino didn't have an Adam's apple, he'd have no shape at all. – Gary Player

(of Jose-Maria Olazabal) The man who once ruled it as smoothly as Bob Charles is presently putting more like Ray Charles. – Mark Reason

Doug Sanders looks like he took a bad trip through a paint factory. – Don Rickles

There are so many doglegs here, Lassie must have designed the course. – Bob Rosburg, on Hazeltine National Golf Club, Minnesota

Don January's playing with all the passion and verve of a meter reader. – Vin Scully

Some of these guys wouldn't pour water on you if you were on fire. – J. C. Snead

(to an unnamed golfer) You've just one problem: you stand too close to the ball – after you've hit it. – Sam Snead

I'd be surprised if more than a handful of players on the tour had Nick's phone number. – Jamie Spence on Nick Faldo's claim that a lot of players had rung him to offer him their support over his Ryder Cup row with Mark James

I'm going to go out and putt on concrete for a while. – Payne Stewart, preparing to tackle the fast Augusta National greens at the US Masters

He'll be tougher than a fifty-cent steak. – Lee Trevino, on Raymond Floyd joining the Senior Tour

At fifteen, we put down my bag to hunt for a ball, found the ball, lost the bag. – Lee Trevino, on the rough at Royal Birkdale, England

David Duval has gone from best player never to have won a major to worst player who has. – Michael Ventre

Art Rosenbaum said he wanted to get more distance. I told him to hit it and run backwards. – Ken Venturi

I've seen turtles move faster than Bernhard Langer. – Lanny Wadkins

First, hitting the ball. Second, finding out where it went. – Tom Watson, asked what would help President Gerald Ford's golf game

If conversation was fertilizer, Lee Trevino would be up to his neck in grass all the time. – Larry Ziegler

Horse Racing

Jenny Pitman reminds me of a manatee who employs a blind milliner. – Jeffrey Bernard

Who are these blokes, the jockeys? Who are they, three-foot high hobbits in a pimp's outfit! – Lee Evans

You could remove the brains from ninety percent of jockeys and they would weigh the same. – John Francome

That horse stays longer than the mother-in-law. – John Francome

Ginger McCain, trainer: Francome, you're the worst jockey in the entire world.
John Francome: No, that's too much of a coincidence.

Stewards are, on the whole, simple folk. Most of them come from a social class in which inbreeding has taken its toll. – Paul Haigh

(of fellow trainer Bob Baffert) He don't talk to me and I don't talk to him, other than that we get along real fine. – Sonny Hine

If I never hear another interview with the terminally irritating Frankie Dettori, I will not feel my life to be significantly impoverished. – Martin Kelner

Lester Piggott has a face like a well-kept grave. – Jack Leach

When interviewing Lester Piggott, an answer a third as long as the question is the standard rate of exchange. – Hugh McIlvanney

Jamie Spencer's continued determination to ride like his namesake Frank. – Tony Paley

The horse I backed was so slow, the jockey kept a diary of the trip. – Henny Youngman

My horse was so late getting home, he tiptoed into the stable. – Henny Youngman

Motor Racing

Michael (Schumacher) is the man with the most sanctions and is the most unsporting driver in the history of Formula One. Even Zinedine Zidane retired with more glory than Schumacher. – Fernando Alonso

James Hunt, he's champion of the world, right? The problem is that he thinks he's the king of the goddam world as well. – Mario Andretti

(of Andrea de Cesaris) Fast on his day. Otherwise he usually connects with the scenery. – Anon (of Bobby Hamilton Jr) He's got a 10-foot ego and a 4-foot body, and it ain't working too good right now. – Mike Bliss

Michael Schumacher's walking around with a face like a wet Monday morning. – Martin Brundle

(of Jimmy Spencer) I guess he's a "never-was". – Kurt Busch

Eddie Irvine is the classic case of the male inadequacy syndrome. – David Coulthard

Robby (Gordon)'s got a little problem going faster under caution than he does under green. – Jeff Gordon

(of Michael Schumacher) The most selfish driver I have ever worked with. He was happy enough to choose me as a partner, but when he realized I could drive quickly our friendship changed. He saw me as a threat and he didn't like it. – Johnny Herbert

(of Eddie Irvine) He's brash and can be abrasive. He goads people. He's the Ian Paisley of Formula 1. – Damon Hill

(of Nigel Mansell) Someone with about as much charisma as a damp sparkplug. – Alan Hubbard

(of Nelson Piquet) You never know what's going on in his head, and often he doesn't seem to know himself. – Nigel Mansell

(of Alain Prost) I am a better and more courageous racer than he will be if he is in Formula 1 for a lifetime. He will be more of a chauffeur, making the car work for him. – Nigel Mansell

(of Tony Stewart) He's just a fat butterball who needs his butt whipped. – Gil Martin

(of Paul Tracy) This guy has been in the grass so often the chipmunks know him by name. – Paul Page

(of Ayrton Senna) The Sao Paulo taxi driver. – Nelson Piquet

I gotta thank Ron Hornaday – for continuing to prove that he is the most disrespectful driver on the racetrack. – Scott Riggs

I couldn't hear him (Kevin Harvick). He's got that little yap-yap mouth. – Ricky Rudd (of Damon Hill) He seems to be very moody and I find it hard to get on with moody people. – Michael Schumacher

(of Nigel Mansell) He's always complaining. It is normal for him. – Ayrton Senna

Ayrton Senna had an immense number of collisions. And they could not all have been everybody else's fault. – Jackie Stewart

(of Greg Biffle) They name streets after guys like that – One Way and Dead End. – Tony Stewart

This (Tony) Stewart guy, he's coming down the back straight with his finger out the window and just giving me the bird. I'd like to take that finger and jam it right up his rear end. – Rusty Wallace

I really want to win a race this year. If I don't, then all the guys will start calling me Tim Henman. – Mark Webber

Rugby
I'd rather crawl across broken glass naked than speak to Will Carling. – Dick Best

(of the Rugby Football Union executive) Fifty-seven old farts. – Will Carling

Since Alan Solomons arrived at the club in 2004 and brought in a load of South African players, that just opened the floodgates for Northampton to be any southern hemisphere player's pension scheme. – Matt Dawson

(of Austin Healey) He is just a child, just so incredibly immature. – Nick Farr-Jones

(of Gavin Henson) His shyness is derivative of not having a high intellect. – Scott Gibbs

Austin Healey shows what a dwarf mind he possesses. – Greg Growden

(of Justin Harrison) An ape, a plank, and a plod. – Austin Healey

I think Brian Moore's gnashers are the kind you get from a DIY shop and hammer in yourself. – Paul Randall

(of Simon Geoghegan) The winger resembles Mother Brown, running with a high knee-lift and sometimes not progressing far from the spot where he started. – Mark Reason

Jack Rowell has the acerbic wit of Dorothy Parker and, according to most New Zealanders, a similar knowledge of rugby. – Mark Reason

(of David Campese) He is a parasite who feeds off my career and it's time that he got a life. How does he live with himself? How does it feel to be a man with no friends in rugby? – Wendell Sailor

I don't understand rugby at all. It's like a really boring fight that someone keeps breaking up. – Linda Smith

Gavin Henson is 6-foot 2-inches, sixteen stone and shaves his chest three times a week. Not for nothing is he known as the Welsh Lindsay Davenport. – *They Think It's All Over*

Snooker

Two-piece snooker cues are popular these days, but Alex Higgins doesn't use one because there aren't any instructions. – Steve Davis

Snooker player Stephen Hendry is the only man with a face that comes with free garlic bread. – Nick Hancock

(to Andy Hicks) You're short and bald and always will be. – Quinten Hann

Ronnie O'Sullivan's wild looks and wilder behaviour suggest he may be the Gallagher brother Liam and Noel threw out of Oasis for being too unstable. – Matthew Norman

(of Quinten Hann) He reached new levels of stupidity even by his own cretinous standards. – John Rawling

I remember when Steve Davis used to take Valium as a stimulant. – Dennis Taylor

(of snooker player Matthew Stevens) His natural expression is that of a man who may have mislaid his winning lottery ticket. – Paul Weaver

Soccer

(of Glasgow Rangers' Marco Negri) All he does is lie on the treatment table twice a day. – Dick Advocaat

It is clear that (Jose) Mourinho believes he is superior to the rest and that his success has gone to his head. – Manuel Almunia

Having to apologize to him was like having to take my pants down in front of him. – Nicolas Anelka, after a row with Real Madrid coach Vicente del Bosque

Alan Ball's voice is so high-pitched that only dogs can hear him. – Anon

Watching Peter Crouch in action is like seeing Bambi on ice. – Anon

Emile Heskey has the turning circle of a 747. – Anon

(of goalkeeper David James) Dracula is more comfortable with crosses. – Anon

They call David James "Cinderella" because he is always late for the ball. – Anon

Mickey Quinn was to dieting what Brian Sewell is to army camouflage trousers. – Anon

If you needed somebody to take a penalty kick to save your life, Chris Waddle, with his hunched shoulders and lethargic air, would rank just below Long John Silver. – Anon

(of Charlton Athletic) A teabag stays in the cup longer. – Anon

They've had to replace the new executive boxes at Nottingham Forest because they were facing the wrong way – they were facing the pitch! – Anon

Then his eyesight started to go and he took up refereeing. – Anon

(of Ray Wilkins) I call him "The Crab" because he only plays sideways. – Ron Atkinson

(of Aston Villa) Devon Loch was a better finisher. – Ron Atkinson

I always view Charlton's presence in the Premiership as rather like that of the Major's residency in *Fawlty Towers*. Bothering no one, really, they potter about, following the routines and drills, occasionally startling the other guests with an outburst but not doing much to enhance the overall glamour of the place. When they go, they won't be missed. – Danny Baker

(of Paul Gascoigne) When God gave him this enormous footballing talent he took his brain out at the same time to equal it up. – Tony Banks

England did nothing in that (2006) World Cup, so why were they bringing books out? "We got beat in the quarter-finals. I played like shit. Here's my book." Who wants to read that? – Joey Barton, upsetting Steven Gerrard, Frank Lampard, Wayne Rooney, Rio Ferdinand and Ashley Cole, all of whom penned post-World Cup books

(of Sheffield United goalkeeper Simon Tracey) He's got the brains of a rocking-horse. – Dave Bassett

The Sheffield United board have been loyal to me. When I came here they said there would be no money, and they've kept their promise. – Dave Bassett

(of David Beckham) He cannot kick with his left foot. He cannot head a ball. He cannot tackle and he doesn't score many goals. Apart from that he's all right. – George Best

(of Robbie Savage) There's more meat on a toothpick. – Alan Birchenall

(of Kenny Dalglish) He's the moaningest minnie I've ever known. – John Bond

(David) Beckham is going to be half a film actor living in Hollywood. Despite being free, no club in the world wanted him. – Ramon Calderon, Real Madrid president, after Beckham's move to LA Galaxy

I hope that one day people realize that Henri Michel is the most incompetent manager in world football. I was reading an article by Mickey Rourke, who is a guy I really like, and he referred to the people who awarded the Oscars in Hollywood as shit bags. Well, I think that Henri Michel is not far from being included in that category. – Eric Cantona, on the former French national team coach

Kenny Dalglish has about as much personality as a tennis racket. – Mike Channon

Johan Cruyff isn't worthy of consideration as a coach. He thinks he's a diva. – Javier Clemente

Trevor Brooking floats like a butterfly . . . and stings like one. – Brian Clough

I told Eddie Gray that, with his injury record, if he'd been a racehorse they'd have had him shot. – Brian Clough

(of Gary Megson) He couldn't trap a landmine. – Brian Clough

The only money Forest directors cough up is when they buy a golden goal ticket. – Brian Clough

(to Martin O' Neill) What's the point of giving you the ball when there's a genius (John Robertson) on the other wing? – Brian Clough

(of John Robertson) Whenever I felt off-colour, I'd sit next to Robbo because then I looked like Errol Flynn. – Brian Clough

Football hooligans? Well, there are ninety-two club chairmen for a start. – Brian Clough

(Craig) Bellamy is no more than a bovine, charmless, virtually friendless clown. His achievements are slender, his notoriety immense. He is the kind of player who attracts fines and enemies in equal measure; the kind whose natural expression wavers between scowl and sneer; the kind, in short, who gives professional footballers the reputation they now enjoy. – Patrick Collins

(of Alex Ferguson) To the world at large he resembles an irascible pensioner who has watched too many episodes of *The Sopranos*. – Patrick Collins

(of Neil Warnock) An irascible fellow with a taste for amateur dramatics. – Patrick Collins

I doubt if Sven-Goran Eriksson has even heard of Ian Wright. If only the rest of us could say the same. – Patrick Collins

For years I thought the club's name was Partick Thistle Nil. – Billy Connolly

(of Bruce Dyer) Having seen him finish on a day-to-day basis, I would think his last hat-trick was at primary school. – Steve Coppell

If George (Best) had been born ugly, he probably would have played till he was forty – just look at Peter Beardsley. – Pat Crerand

The extent to which George Best has fallen off the wagon was revealed today when his new liver asked for a free transfer to Paul Gascoigne. – *Dead Ringers*

And for those who missed them earlier, here are next week's Italian football results. – Hugh Dennis, *Mock the Week*, after the Italian match-fixing scandal

David James must have a brain the size of a pea! I called him a cretin a year ago, so it has taken him a whole year to find out the meaning of the word. My two-year-old daughter could learn quicker than that. – Paolo Di Canio

John Barnes's problem is that he gets injured appearing on *A Question of Sport*. – Tommy Docherty

Tony Hateley had it all. The only thing he lacked was ability. – Tommy Docherty

(of Vinnie Jones) I wouldn't only not sign him, I wouldn't let him in the ground. – Tommy Docherty

(of Ray Wilkins) He can't run, can't tackle and can't head a ball. The only time he goes forward is to toss the coin. – Tommy Docherty

(of Manchester City) There are three types of Oxo cubes. Light brown for chicken stock, dark brown for beef stock, and light blue for laughing stock. – Tommy Docherty

Wimbledon have as much charm as a broken beer bottle. – Tommy Docherty

(of Wolves) We don't use a stopwatch to judge our golden goal competition now, we use a calendar. – Tommy Docherty

(of Wolves) I just opened the trophy cabinet. Two Japanese prisoners of war came out. – Tommy Docherty

The ideal board of directors should be made up of three men: two dead and the other dying. – Tommy Docherty

After the match an official asked for two of my players to take a dope test. I offered him the referee. – Tommy Docherty

(of David Beckham) A grossly overrated player, a speechless fop with legs as bandy as a northern jockey's. – Willie Donaldson

(of Jose Mourinho) He is a little man who has suddenly been created into the owner of the world in his own head. – Edmilson

Footballers? Aren't they prima donnas? – Queen Elizabeth II

(of Steve Bruce) He needed five stitches – three in the first half and two at the interval when his brain started to seep through. – Alex Ferguson

Part of the problem is, Eric (Cantona) can't tackle. He couldn't tackle a fish supper. – Alex Ferguson

Pippo Inzaghi was born in an offside position. – Alex Ferguson

(of Arsène Wenger) He's come here from Japan and he's telling English people how to organize our football. He should keep his mouth firmly shut. – Alex Ferguson

(of Arsène Wenger) They say he's an intelligent man, right? Speaks five languages! I've got a fifteen-year-old boy from the Ivory Coast who speaks five languages! – Alex Ferguson

(of Arsène Wenger) Old vinegar face. – Alex Ferguson

Brian Clough's record speaks for itself . . . if it can get a word in. – Cris Freddi

(of David Sullivan) He doesn't know a goal-line from a clothes-line. – Barry Fry

(of Tomas Brolin) He had a bandage on his head. Perhaps one of his eyelashes had fallen out. – George Graham

As well as being England's first managerial turnip, Graham Taylor has prime ministerial qualities, combining the personality of John Major with the gift of prophecy of Neville Chamberlain. – Steve Grant

(of Darren Anderton) Old Sicknote should get a part on *Animal Hospital*. – Jimmy Greaves

Poor Fulham, with no real method up front, resembled a fire engine hurrying to the wrong fire. – Geoffrey Green

Michael Owen used to be the baby-faced assassin, (Wayne) Rooney is more like the assassin-faced baby. – *The Guardian*

Peter Beardsley is the only player who, when he appears on TV, Daleks hide behind the sofa. – Nick Hancock

There are torch-carrying search parties out looking for the bundle of promise that used to be Shaun Wright-Phillips. – Paul Hayward, *Daily Mail*

(of Thierry Henry) The whine merchant. – Matt Hughes

(of Carlton Palmer) We reckon he covers every blade of grass on the pitch – mainly because his first touch is terrible. – David Jones

(of Birmingham City chief David Sullivan) If you look into his childhood, I think you will find he wasn't breastfed . . . He is seeking attention and respect, but he's two foot two, he's got a Napoleon complex and peddles sex and sleaze for a living. Of course he wants to be heard – people like that always do. What satisfaction does he get out of selling arse ticklers and strap-ons? How does he expect respect coming from a background like that? – Simon Jordan, Crystal Palace chairman

(to Manchester United team-mate Rio Ferdinand) Just because you are paid £120,000 a week and play well for twenty minutes against Tottenham, you think you are a superstar. – Roy Keane

(Joey) Barton mentioned that he was running at six in the morning and then he wondered if me and Stevie Gerrard were doing the same. When I read that, I was thinking, "I was doing that when I was eleven." That was the difference. – Frank Lampard

(of Luis Garcia) He scores goals in big games but the next minute he looks like a pub player. – Mark Lawrenson

(of Sven-Goran Eriksson) He's got a lot of forehead. – Gary Lineker

Ruud Van Nistelrooy: why the long face? – Gary Lineker

The ever-smiling Steve McClaren is without doubt the most two-faced and false person that I have ever had the misfortune to meet in football. – Massimo Maccarone

Comparing (Paul) Gascoigne to Pelé is like comparing Rolf Harris to Rembrandt. – Rodney Marsh

The best two clubs in London are Stringfellow's and The Hippodrome. – Terry McDermott

(of Barry Fry) His management style seems to be based on the chaos theory. – Mark McGhee

(of Jason Roberts) You are talking about a man who spelt his name wrong on his transfer request. – Gary Megson

(of Craig Bellamy) A mouthy serial delinquent. – David Mellor

Ricardo Carvalho seems to have problems understanding things. Maybe he should have an IQ test. – Jose Mourinho

(of Arsène Wenger) I think he is one of these people who is a voyeur. He likes to watch other people. There are some guys who, when they are at home, have a big telescope to see what happens in other families. He speaks, speaks, speaks about Chelsea. – Jose Mourinho

(of Spurs' defensive tactics) They brought the bus and they left the bus in front of the goal. – Jose Mourinho

(of Graeme Souness) A man capable of destroying the mirror because he didnae like the way the face in it was looking at him. – Matthew Norman

Due to recent riots, an Italian soccer league is forcing teams to play games with no fans in the stadium. Which, coincidentally, is how soccer games are played here in America. – Conan O'Brien

José Mourinho recently turned down the post of Pope when he heard it was something in the way of an assistant position. – Harry Pearson

(of Dutch international Piet Fransen) Pass a ball? He'd have trouble passing wind. – Alf Ramsey

He does not look much like a male model, and his personal life, one suspects, has not presented him with too many problems of the babe-magnet variety. The Sunday red tops struggle to find many juicy revelations. Somehow, some bimbo saying, "I looked down at my breasts and there was Gary Neville" does not have a ring of authenticity. – John Rawling

(John) Hartson's got more previous than Jack the Ripper. – Harry Redknapp

(Arjen) Robben is a big actor and he did well enough to win an Oscar. – Jose Reina

(Steve) McClaren has achieved the considerable feat of making (Sven-Goran) Eriksson, who had lost the plot in his last six months, look good. – Ian Ridley

Kevin Keegan is not fit to lace George Best's drinks. – John Roberts

(of Alan Ball) With a record like his in management I would have kept quiet, yet he had the audacity to tell me how I should be doing my work. – Bobby Robson

(of Paul Gascoigne) Daft as a brush. – Bobby Robson

(of Wayne Rooney) A potato-headed granny-shagger. – Jonathan Ross

(Pat) Crerand's deceptive – he's slower than you think. – Bill Shankly

If Everton were playing down at the bottom of my garden, I'd draw the curtains. – Bill Shankly

The difference between Everton and the *Queen Mary* is that Everton carry more passengers. – Bill Shankly

There are two great teams in Liverpool – Liverpool and Liverpool Reserves. – Bill Shankly

When I've got nothing better to do, I look down the league table to see how Everton are getting along. – Bill Shankly

(of Manchester United) Matt (Busby) has got a bad back. I tell you it's two bad backs! And not much of a midfield either. – Bill Shankly

Tommy Smith would start a riot in a graveyard. – Bill Shankly

Phil Thompson tossed up with a sparrow for its legs and lost. – Bill Shankly

(of Deon Burton) After one game Barnsley wanted to sign him. After two they decided to send him back. – Jim Smith

Simon Jordan is a frustrated actor. He wants to be a media personality. – David Sullivan

If Stan Bowles could pass a betting shop like he can pass a ball he'd have no worries at all. – Ernie Tagg

Compared to my chairman at Southend, Ken Bates is Mary Poppins. – David Webb

Norman Hunter doesn't tackle opponents so much as break them down for resale as scrap. – Julie Welch

(of Peter Crouch) A basketball player. – Arsène Wenger

(of Jose Mourinho) When you give success to stupid people, it makes them more stupid sometimes and not more intelligent. – Arsene Wenger

(of Chelsea) If the way to play the game is not to play, then I will stay at home and read a book. – Arsene Wenger

Alex Ferguson's weakness is that he doesn't think he has any. – Arsène Wenger

(of Harry Kewell) A player with a heart the size of a diamond ear-stud. – Richard Williams

David Beckham is an empty shell, clothes-horse of singularly moderate talent, more of an underpants model than a proper footballer. He is that woeful thing, a celebrity. – A. N. Wilson

Steve McClaren is a number two in a number one suit. – Henry Winter on the England manager

(of Sven-Goran Eriksson) The man's like a wet fish. He's got as much passion as a tadpole. – Ian Wright

The referee was booking everyone. I thought he was filling in his lottery numbers. – Ian Wright

Tennis

My feelings are Yevgeny Kafelnikov should take his prize money when he is done here and go and buy some perspective. – Andre Agassi

(of Pete Sampras) Nobody should be ranked number one who looks like he just swung from a tree. – Andre Agassi

(of Lleyton Hewitt) The baseball cap worn back to front makes him resemble a redneck petrol pump attendant. – Anon

Perry Mason was faster around court than Greg Rusedski. – Anon

A wading pool has more depth than women's tennis. Women's tennis is in trouble. Lindsay Davenport beat the world's thirteenth-ranked player, Vera Zvonareva, in less time than it takes Andre Agassi to comb his hair . . . Earlier in the tournament Australian Sam Stosur lost to Hungarian Aniko Kapros, who serves slower than a bad restaurant. – *The Australian*

(of Martina Navratilova) In her leather-appliqued skirts and '70s wire-rim eye-glasses, she's the "Tootsie" of tennis. – Mr Blackwell

(of John McEnroe) A walking, talking, screaming, squawking metaphor for What's Wrong With Young People Today. – Julie Burchill

I'll chase that son of a bitch (Bjorn) Borg to the ends of the earth. I'll be waiting for him. I'll dog him everywhere. Every time he looks round he'll see my shadow. – Jimmy Connors

I would rather not win a single tournament than be like Lleyton (Hewitt). – Guillermo Coria

Lindsay Davenport has the turning circle of a station wagon. – Mike Dickson

I remember when Jimmy (Connors) and I went into confession and he came out a half-hour later and I said, "How'd it go?" He said, "I wasn't finished. The priest said come back next Sunday." – Chris Evert

(of Lleyton Hewitt) The constant plucking of his racket strings makes him look like a shuffling madman playing a tiny magic harp that only he can hear. – *The Guardian*

(of Marat Safin) The most unstable temperament since Henry VIII. – *The Guardian*

He's everybody's best friend in the locker room and then he steps outside the door and he's slagging everyone off. – Tim Henman, after John McEnroe said he would never win a Grand Slam event.

Look, Nastase, we used to have a famous cricket match in this country called Gentlemen versus Players. The Gentlemen were put down on the scorecard as "Mister" because they were gentlemen. By no stretch of the imagination can anybody call you a gentleman. – Wimbledon umpire Trader Horn, on being told to address Ilie Nastase as "Mister".

Like a Volvo, Bjorn Borg is rugged, has good after-sales service, and is very dull. – Clive James

(of John McEnroe) As charming as a dead mouse in a loaf of bread. – Clive James

(of John McEnroe) Hair like badly turned broccoli. – Clive James

Ilie Nastase is a Hamlet who wants to play a clown, but he is no good at it; his gags are bad, his timing is terrible and he never knows how he's going over the top – which last drawback is the kiss of death for a comic. – Clive James

(John) McEnroe respects one guy – himself, and that's it. – Luke Jensen

Maria Sharapova has lived so long in Florida that she sounds like one of those high-octane weather girls for CNN. – Martin Johnson

Today in the Australian Open, Anna Kournikova double-faulted twice and had twenty-nine unforced errors in her defeat, or, as she calls it, being in the zone. – Craig Kilborn

I have exaggerated a bit when I said that eighty percent of the top women tennis players are fat pigs. It's only seventy-five percent. – Richard Krajicek

In a major upset, softball player Jennie Finch unseated defending champ Anna Kournikova as the hottest female athlete in an espn.com poll. That's unfortunate, because this has been our only chance to call Kournikova a defending champion. – Jay Leno

(of Maria Sharapova's grunts) She sounds like a live pig being slaughtered. – Frew MacMillan

Any good male college player could beat the Williams sisters. – John McEnroe

Did you win a lottery to be linesman? – John McEnroe

(to a line judge) You can't see as well as these fucking flowers – and they're fucking plastic! – John McEnroe

(to a spectator) What other problems do you have besides being unemployed, a moron, and a dork? – John McEnroe

In the women's game, why does the pretty one always lose to the moose? – David Mitchell, *Mock the Week*

(of Tim Henman) All this selling himself as a gentleman is not true. He is the worst rubbish there is. – David Nalbandian

At Wimbledon, the ladies are simply the candles on the cake. – John Newcombe

(of Lleyton Hewitt) Imagine the love child of Jimmy Connors and the young Mike Tyson. – Matthew Norman

(Roger Federer is) an immeasurably more charming human being than McEnroe. Then again, so was Pol Pot. – Matthew Norman

Anna Kournikova has married her longtime boyfriend, Enrique Iglesias. It's the first time Anna Kournikova has shown up wearing white to an event and hasn't gone home a loser. – Conan O'Brien

Michael Chang has all the fire and passion of a public service announcement. – Alex Ramsey

The only thing faster in women's tennis than Venus Williams' serve is Anna Kournikova's exit. – Alan Ray

When Anna Kournikova wed Enrique Iglesias recently, she had all the traditional trappings. The "something borrowed" was a tennis trophy. – Alan Ray

The Williams sisters are so tough, they use a brick for a tampon. – Joan Rivers

Umpiring, the only job in the world where you can screw up on a daily basis and still have one! – Andy Roddick

(to an umpire) Have you heard of that part of the body called a spine? Get one! – Andy Roddick

(to an umpire) It's all your fault – but nothing personal. – Andy Roddick

No word yet if Kournikova will sue, but it would be the only court appearance she'd actually have a chance of winning. – Ken Rudolph, on fake topless photos of Anna Kournikova that appeared in *Penthouse*

Thanks, but no. I want to be a winner. – Maria Sharapova on being compared to Anna Kournikova

Tim Henman must be the least charismatic person in the history of sport. – Arthur Smith

(of Tim Henman) He's like a human form of beige. – Linda Smith

(of Ilie Nastase) I realize he big star now, but sometimes I feel like dog trainer who teach dog manners and graces and just when you think dog knows how he should act with nice qualities, dog make big puddle and all is wasted. – Ion Tiriac

Nastase does not have a brain; he has a bird fluttering around in his head. – Ion Tiriac

Amélie Mauresmo is one of the few women even more Amazonian than Jennifer Capriati. – Brian Viner

(of Serena Williams) She's not real any more. She doesn't really like tennis. You can tell. She's not playing from the heart. It's all contrived. She just wants to look good. – Mats Wilander

Track and Field

It should not have surprised anyone that Ben Johnson was using steroids. You don't go from 10.17 (seconds) to 9.83 on unleaded gas. – Jamie Astaphan

(of Maurice Greene) Can you really be heroic with a name like Maurice? – *The Guardian*

(of Paula Radcliffe) There's a touch of Julie Andrews syndrome. Her deal with nicey-nicey Cadbury's sums it up: fit but square. – *The Guardian*

You have to be suspicious when you line up against girls with moustaches. – Maree Holland

Despite all the suspicious rumours flying about Ben (Johnson), I kept an open mind. Now we know they weren't rumours. It's a good thing they have caught someone at the top. We are better off without him. – Eamonn Martin

The only thing that is amateur about track and field is its organization. – Craig Masback

As a runner Daley Thompson is excellent, as a jumper he is excellent, and as a thrower he is an excellent runner and jumper. – Cliff Temple

Seb (Coe) is a Yorkshireman. So he's a complete bastard and will do well in politics. – Daley Thompson

I wouldn't be surprised if one day Carl (Lewis)'s halo slipped and choked him. – Allan Wells

Others

Yachtswoman Ellen MacArthur could moan for England. – Anon

Mark Messier is probably one of the best pressure players of all time. And there would finally be someone on the team balder than me. – Dave Babych, ice hockey player

A fifteen-year-old patient yawned continuously for a period of five weeks. This feat was considered all the more remarkable since there is no record of her being a St Louis Blues season ticket holder. – *Hockey News*

The Oxford-Cambridge boat race would be much more attractive if the boats were allowed to ram each other. – Miles Kington

So Tonya Harding is embarking on a career as a recording artist. Let's hope Whitney Houston still has that bodyguard. – Bob Lacey

Lance Armstrong and Sheryl Crow have split up. Apparently Sheryl met a guy who has a car. – Jay Leno

The average female figure skater weighs ninety pounds, or as supermodels call them, big fat cows. – Jay Leno

He (Phil Taylor) was going on about how he could not get a set of table and chairs in his Bentley. He is taking the lion's share of the money because he is the best player, but I am driving around in a nine-year-old car and he's rubbing our noses in it. What does he want a Bentley for? It's pathetic. – Chris Mason, darts player

I don't know what it is, but I can't look at (wrestler) Hulk Hogan and believe that he's the end result of millions and millions of years of evolution. – Jim Murray

Tonya (Harding)'s weapon was a hubcap or, as the police report called it, "her best dinnerware." – Jerry Perisho, after the disgraced ice skater allegedly threw a hubcap at her boyfriend and punched him in the face during an argument

The only bad thing about being released by the (Ottawa) Senators is they made me keep my season tickets. – Doug Smail, ice hockey player

Then there's the luge, for which I have only one question: what drunken German gynaecologist invented that sport? What guy said, "You know what? I want to dress like a sperm, shove an ice skate in my ass, and go balls first down an ice chute. *Ja*, that would be fun!" – Robin Williams

Mr Edwards' Olympic performance was the equivalent of a first-ball duck in a Test match, two own goals in a Wembley cup final, or a first round 168 in the Open Golf Championship. – Ian Wooldridge, on inept ski jumper, Eddie "the Eagle" Edwards

We have thousands of Eddie Edwards in Norway, but we never let them jump. – Torbjorn Yggeseth

THE STAGE

Mr (John) Simon's disapproval of my plays has been a source of comfort to me over the years and his dislike of *A Delicate Balance* gives me courage to go on. – Edward Albee

Jonathan Miller is too clever by three-quarters. – Anon

(to Tennessee Williams after seeing the film version of one of his plays) Darling, they've absolutely ruined your perfectly dreadful play. – Tallulah Bankhead

(to a young actress) If you really want to help the American theatre, darling, be an audience. – Tallulah Bankhead

It seems to me that giving (critic) Clive Barnes his CBE for services to the theatre is like giving Goering the DFC for services to the RAF. – Alan Bennett

(on the eyebrows of playwright Arthur Wing Pinero) Like the skins of a small mammal, just not large enough to be used as mats. – Max Beerbohm

I see no future for A. A. Milne, whose plots are as thin as a filleted anchovy. – H. Dennis Bradley

I am more easily bored with Shakespeare and have suffered more ghastly evenings with Shakespeare than with any other dramatist I know. – Peter Brook

Critics are eunuchs at a gang-bang. – George Burns

(to Noël Coward) Your characters talk like typewriting and you yourself talk like a telegram. – Mrs Patrick Campbell

(to George Bernard Shaw) When you were quite a little boy somebody ought to have said "hush" just once. – Mrs Patrick Campbell

Andrew Lloyd Webber was born with a face like a melted Wellington boot. – Jeremy Clarkson

(to Rex Harrison) If you weren't the best light comedian in the country, all you'd be fit for would be the selling of cars in Great Portland Street. – Noël Coward

(of Harold Pinter) A sort of Cockney Ivy Compton-Burnett. – Noël Coward

(to a young actress fond of prolonged pauses) I'm a very old lady. I may die during one of your pauses. – Edith Evans

(to an actor who had given a poor performance) My dear chap! Good isn't the word! – W. S. Gilbert

Do you know how they are going to decide the Shakespeare-Bacon dispute? They are going to dig up Shakespeare and dig up Bacon; they are going to set their coffins side by side, and they are going to get (Herbert Beerbohm) Tree to recite Hamlet to them. And the one who turns in his coffin will be the author of the play. – W. S. Gilbert

(to a perspiring Herbert Beerbohm Tree after a lacklustre opening night) Your skin has been acting at any rate. – W.S. Gilbert

I don't regard (Bertolt) Brecht as man of iron-grey purpose and intellect. I think he is a theatrical whore of the first quality. – Peter Hall

(of George Bernard Shaw) The first man to have cut a swathe through the theatre and left it strewn with virgins. – Frank Harris

(of George Bernard Shaw) (An) irresponsible braggart, blaring self-trumpeter. – Henry Arthur Jones

(to Howard Dietz) I understand your new play is full of single entendre. – George S. Kaufman

(to actor William Gaxton) Watching your performance from the rear of the house. Wish you were here. – George S. Kaufman

The problem with (Andrew) Lloyd Webber's music is not that it sounds as if it were written by other composers, but that it sounds as if it were written by Lloyd Webber. – Gerald Kaufman

(George Bernard) Shaw isn't a dramatist. He is a journalist with a sense of the theatre. – Henry Arthur Jones

(of Sarah Bernhardt) A great actress, from the waist down. – Margaret Kendal

(of Ethel Merman) A brassy, brazened witch on a mortgaged broomstick. – Walter Kerr

(to an unnamed actress) Darling, I don't care what anybody says – I thought you were marvellous. – Beatrice Lillie

When I heard about *Hair*, I was kind of curious about the six naked primates on stage. So I called up the box office and they said tickets were eleven dollars apiece. That's an awful price to pay. I went into the bathroom at home and took off all my clothes and looked in the mirror for five minutes. And I said, "This isn't worth eleven dollars." – Groucho Marx

(of Samuel Beckett) A confidence trick perpetrated on the twentieth century by a theatre-hating God. – Sheridan Morley

I always said I'd like (Lionel) Barrymore's acting till the cows came home. Well, ladies and gentlemen, last night the cows came home. – George Jean Nathan

Critics? I love every bone in their heads. – Eugene O'Neill

To me, Edith (Evans) looks like something that would eat its young. – Dorothy Parker

Rex Harrison refused to play the man as a louse, which entirely robbed the play, while he was in it, of its emotional and developmental power. Rex kept saying, "I don't want to seem like a shit," so I finally said, "Why stop now?" – Terence Rattigan

I've staged shows that called for the management of a herd of buffalo, and I've shot actors out of cannons for fifty feet into the arms of an adagio dancer, but both of them were easier than saying "Good morning" to Tallulah Bankhead. – Billy Rose

Sarah Brightman couldn't act scared on the New York subway at four o'clock in the morning. – Joel Segal

(to Cedric Hardwicke) You are my fifth favourite actor, the first four being the Marx Brothers. – George Bernard Shaw

(of William Shakespeare) It would be a positive relief to dig him up and throw stones at him. – George Bernard Shaw

(to Anton Chekhov) You know I can't stand Shakespeare's plays, but yours are even worse. – Leo Tolstoy

(of Ralph Richardson) His voice is something between bland and grandiose: blandiose perhaps. – Kenneth Tynan

It is a consolation to know that such an artist as Madame (Sarah) Bernhardt has not only worn that yellow, ugly dress, but has been photographed in it. – Oscar Wilde

The first rule is not to write like Henry Arthur Jones. The second and third rules are the same. – Oscar Wilde

There is absolutely nothing wrong with Oscar Levant that a miracle cannot fix. – Alexander Woollcott

(of Mrs Patrick Campbell) An ego like a raging tooth. – W. B. Yeats

Cutting Criticisms
(of *Sweet Yesterday*) Mr Webster Booth and Miss Anne Ziegler sing delightfully and very, very often. – James Agate

Farley Granger played Mr Darcy with all the flexibility of a telegraph pole. – Brooks Atkinson

When Mr Wilbur calls his play *Halfway to Hell* he underestimates the distance. – Brooks Atkinson

(of *Twelfth Night*) Annette Crosbie played Viola like a Shetland pony. – Anon

(of *Aglavine and Selysette*) There is less in this than meets the eye. – Tallulah Bankhead

(of *Oh, Calcutta!*) The sort of show that gives pornography a bad name. – Clive Barnes

Perfectly Scandalous was one of those plays in which all the actors, unfortunately, enunciated very clearly. – Robert Benchley

(of the revival of *Godspell*) For those who missed it the first time, this is your golden opportunity: you can miss it again. – Michael Billington

(of Mae West's *Diamond Lil*) Pure trash, or rather, impure trash. – Charles Brackett

It opened at 8.40 sharp and closed at 10.40 dull. – Heywood C. Broun

Lillian Gish comes on stage as if she'd been sent for to sew rings on the new curtains. – Mrs Patrick Campbell

Mr (Orson) Welles's Brutus is like an obstetrician who very seriously visits a lady in order to placate her nerves. – Mrs Patrick Campbell, on a production of *Julius Caesar*

Unfortunately, *An Evening with Gary Lineker* is about as meaningful as night in with the Swiss Family Robinson . . . ninety spectacularly dull minutes. – James Christopher

The only moving thing about Charlton Heston's performance was his wig. – Michael Coveney

(of Lionel Bart's World War Two musical *Blitz!*) Just as long as the real thing and twice as noisy. – Noël Coward

(of a male nude scene in *The Changing Room*) I didn't pay three pounds fifty just to see half a dozen acorns and a chipolata. – Noël Coward

(after seeing Anna Neagle play Queen Victoria in *The Glorious Years*) I never realised before that Albert married beneath him. – Noël Coward

Two things should be cut: the second act and the child's throat. – Noël Coward

(of *King Lear*) Mr (Creston) Clarke played the King all evening as though under constant fear that someone else was about to play the ace. – Eugene Field

If you ask me what *Uncle Vanya* is about, I would say about as much as I can take. – Robert Garland

(of *Victory Belles*) Must be seen to be depreciated. – Robert Garland

(of *Dr Faustus*) Cedric Hardwicke conducted the soul-selling transaction with the thoughtful dignity of a grocer selling a pound of cheese. – Hubert Griffith

(of *Macbeth*) Peter O'Toole delivers every line with a monotonous tenor bark as if addressing an audience of Eskimos who have never heard of Shakespeare. – *The Guardian*

I have knocked everything in this play except the chorus girls' knees, and there God anticipated me. – Percy Hammond

The best thing about (Ian) McKellen's *Hamlet* was his curtain call. – Harold Hobson

(of *Peter Pan*) Oh for an hour of Herod! – Anthony Hope

(of *Manslaughter*) The first night's proceeds went to Justice for Women. I await a benefit in aid of Anaesthetics for Critics. – Martin Hoyle

(of *Jesus Christ Superstar*) Religion and atheism will both survive it. – Stanley Kauffmann

I don't like the play, but then I saw it under adverse conditions – the curtain was up. – George S. Kaufman

The only way this actress will get her name into the *New York Times* is if somebody shoots her. – George S. Kaufman

(of *Buttrio Square*) During the first number you hoped it would be good. After that you just hoped it would be over. – Walter Kerr

(of *Break a Leg*) I have seen stronger plots in a cemetery. – Stewart Klein

(of *Treats*) Laurence Fox produces an array of vacant, horsey expressions – at moments he would not disgrace the winner's enclosure at Aintree. – Quentin Letts

(of *Dazzling Prospect*) This pitiful little thing has to do with horse racing, and you might perhaps say that it is by Imbecility out of Staggering Incompetence. – Bernard Levin

(of *The Flower Drum Song*) An American musical so bad that at times I longed for the boy-meets-tractor theme of Soviet drama. – Bernard Levin

(of *Evita*) I shall content myself with saying that its best tune, the already famous "Don't Cry For Me, Argentina", is inferior as a melody to the ones I used when a boy to hear improvised on a saxophone outside the Albert Hall by a busker with only three fingers on his left hand. – Bernard Levin

(of Charlton Heston in *Design for a Stained Glass Window*) A pretty fellow whom the moving pictures should exultantly capture without delay, if they have any respect for the dramatic stage. – George Jean Nathan

(of *Tonight or Never*) Very well then: I say Never. – George Jean Nathan

Address Unknown has Jim Dale, but doesn't deliver. – *New York Magazine*

Frank Wildhorn's *Dracula* sucks. – *New York Magazine*

(of *The Cat and the Fiddle*) Mr (Otto) Harbach has really outdone himself in banality. – *New Yorker* (of *Give Me Yesterday*) Its hero is caused, by a novel device, to fall asleep and dream; and thus he is given yesterday. Me, I should have given him twenty years to life. – Dorothy Parker

The House Beautiful is play lousy. – Dorothy Parker

(of *The Silent Witness*) Miss (Kay) Strozzi had the temerity to wear as truly horrible a gown as ever I have seen on the American stage . . . Had she not luckily been strangled by a member of the cast while disporting this garment, I should have fought my way to the stage and done her in myself. – Dorothy Parker

If you don't knit, bring a good book. – Dorothy Parker

This wasn't just plain terrible, this was fancy terrible, this was terrible with raisins in it. – Dorothy Parker

(of *Chess*) A suite of temper tantrums all amplified to a piercing pitch that would not be out of place in a musical about one of chess's somewhat noisier fellow sports, like stock-car racing. – Frank Rich

Starlight Express is the perfect gift for the kid who has everything except parents. – Frank Rich

(of *Fedora*) It is greatly to Mrs Patrick Campbell's credit that, bad as the play was, her acting was worse. – George Bernard Shaw

(of *The Mousetrap*) A tired, old-fashioned, obvious thriller. The mystery is no longer who-did-it but who still wants to see it. – Milton Shulman

(of Diana Rigg's nude scenes in *Abelard and Heloise*) Diana Rigg is built like a brick mausoleum with insufficient flying buttresses. – John Simon

(of Denzel Washington in *Julius Caesar*) He plays Brutus as a naïve sophomore in a college comedy. – John Simon

(of *King Lear*) Jonathan Miller has turned Goneril and Regan, in near-identical ochre outfits and extravagant hairdos, into a comic version of Cinderella's ugly stepsisters. – John Simon

And now for something completely exhausted: *Spamalot*'s gags and songs are weary from their quest. – John Simon

(of *A Streetcar Named Desire*) Natasha Richardson, always a dubious actress, here proves scandalous. In the first few minutes, she has already shot all – which is to say both – her histrionic devices, consisting vocally of baby talk and simpering whines. – John Simon

(of *The Glorious Days*) There was a heated diversion of opinion in the lobbies during the interval but a small conservative majority took the view that it might be as well to remain in the theatre. – Kenneth Tynan

When you've seen all of (Eugène) Ionesco's plays, I felt at the end, you've seen one of them. – Kenneth Tynan

(of *Twentieth Century*) It's ominous when an audience leave a musical whistling the scenery. – *Variety*

(of *Hamlet*) It is a vulgar and barbarous drama . . . one would imagine this piece to be the work of a drunken savage. – Voltaire

I've seen more excitement at the opening of an umbrella. – Earl Wilson

(of *The Hero in Man*) Most of the heroes are in the audience. – Walter Winchell

The scenery was beautiful, but the actors got in front of it. – Alexander Woollcott

Number Seven opened last night. It was misnamed by five. – Alexander Woollcott

GENERAL INSULTS

PERSONALITY

I have had a perfectly wonderful evening, but this wasn't it. – Groucho Marx

Any similarity between him and a human being is purely coincidental.

Just because he goes around in circles doesn't make him a big wheel.

At least he's not obnoxious like so many other people – he's obnoxious in different and worse ways!

He must be crazy, not because he talks to himself but because he listens.

He was a solemn, unsmiling, sanctimonious old iceberg who looked like he was waiting for a vacancy in the Trinity. – Mark Twain

When he was a child, his mother wanted to hire someone to take care of him, but the Mafia charged too much.

If he were a liquid, he'd be dropping off a toilet brush.

Deep down, he's shallow.

Anyone who told him to be himself couldn't have given him worse advice.

The higher a monkey climbs, the more you see of its behind. – Joseph Stilwell

He could start a fight in an empty room.

She's so uptight you couldn't pull a needle out of her butt with a tractor. – *Roseanne*

She's happy to paint the town red with any man with a full wallet and she's happy to give him the brush when it's empty.

When they made him they broke the mould but some of it grew back.

He's just another flash in the bedpan.

People take an instant dislike to him because it saves time.

We all sprang from the apes but he didn't spring far enough.

Do you think I can buy back my introduction to you? – Groucho Marx

He could be described as charming, intelligent and witty. And perhaps one day he will be.

He has been weird the past few days. Maybe his right hand finally said no. – *Veronica Mars*

He can't be trusted: he's fishier than Lady Godiva's saddle.

He's seen it all, done it all, forgotten it all.

She was so anally retentive she couldn't sit down for fear of sucking up the furniture. – *Absolutely Fabulous*

He does have standards – they just happen to be lower than anyone else's.

Just because she's a nag doesn't mean she's got horse sense.

Fine words! I wonder where you stole them. – Jonathan Swift

He's certainly something else, but science has yet to work out precisely what.

His father looks on him as the son he never had.

You'll have to excuse my mother; she suffered a slight stroke a few years ago, which rendered her totally annoying. – *The Golden Girls*

His table manners give vultures a bad name.

He is the perfect cure for anyone with an inferiority complex.

She couldn't exude warmth if she were on fire.

He was as great as a man can be without morality. – Alexis de Tocqueville

He aims to please but he's a lousy shot.

I can't believe you took advice from her, a woman whose idea of love and compassion is letting her kids eat the fruit from her whiskey sour. – *Will and Grace*

He's as devious as a bag of weasels.

Ordinarily people live and learn – he just lives.

He's as nervous as a long-tailed cat in a room full of rocking chairs.

You never get it right, do you? You're either crawling all over them, licking their boots, or spitting poison at them like some Benzedrine puff adder. – *Fawlty Towers*

The day he was born he cried like a baby. So did his parents.

She was so hungry for publicity that she would attend the opening of an envelope.

She's such a cold person that if you kiss her too fast, you get an ice-cream headache.

The best part of him ran down his mother's legs. – Jackie Gleason

She'll tolerate any man who doesn't fit the bill, provided that he foots it.

He is so in touch with his feminine side, they are practically dating.

If he had to eat his words he'd get ptomaine poisoning.

Sometimes when I think you're the shallowest man I've ever met, you somehow manage to drain a little more out of the pool. – *Seinfeld*

He displays the tact and sensitivity of a rampaging bull elephant.

The only time he's on the level is when he's asleep.

He makes a big impression on people . . . by treading all over them.

Hey Roseanne. I just saw all the animals in the neighbourhood running in circles, so I guess that means your mother will be arriving soon. – *Roseanne*

She's been engaged more times than a telephone switchboard.

God could still use him for miracle practice.

She's so cold, she has her period in cubes.

A cherub's face, a reptile all the rest. – Alexander Pope

He used to have a handle on life but it broke.

He's a legend in his own lunchtime.

I'm actually just glad to see you. I assumed she ate her partners after mating. – *Frasier*

He doesn't suffer from insanity; he enjoys every minute of it.

You'll have to excuse him. He's going through a nonentity crisis.

Women fall at his feet – but only because of his breath.

He's going on a charm offensive. He struggles with the "charm" but he can certainly achieve the "offensive".

Nature did her best to make her a very charming woman, only poor Nature was sadly thwarted. – Geraldine Jewsbury

He lives in fear of not being misunderstood.

He is so insecure, he has more defences than Fort Knox.

We don't have to put up with your snidey remarks, your total slobbiness, your socks that set off the sprinkler system. – *Red Dwarf*

I've seen better arguments in a bowl of alphabet soup.

The going got weird, and he turned pro.

He has lost his fingertip grip on reality.

If I were the cream for that woman's coffee, I'd curdle. – Kathleen Howard, *Ball of Fire*

He has a heart of gold – yellow and hard.

The only part of him that shines is the seat of his pants.

The hand of God reaching down into the mire couldn't elevate you to the depths of degradation. – *Nothing Sacred*

She's twice the man he is.

He has an arresting personality – and should definitely be arrested for it.

He has all the maturity of wine bottled yesterday.

The kind of man . . . whom everybody speaks well of, and nobody cares about; whom all are delighted to see, and nobody remembers to talk to. – Jane Austen

She's such a heavy drinker that the last mosquito that bit her had to check into the Betty Ford Clinic.

You could throw a dart out of the window and hit someone better than him.

I never thought of him as a brother – just mom and dad's science project. – *Moonlighting*

He's such a miserable bloke he was thrown out of a Happy Eater.

He goes with the flow: he's a bed wetter.

I could dance with you until the cows come home. On second thoughts, I'd rather dance with the cows until you come home. – Groucho Marx, *Duck Soup*

He is so narrow minded, he can see through a keyhole with both eyes.

It was a great shock when he died of a heart attack because nobody thought he had a heart.

If staying here means working within ten yards of you, frankly I'd rather have a job wiping Saddam Hussein's arse! – *Bridget Jones's Diary*

If you want to complain about his behaviour, you'll have to get in line.

He's such a coward he can't even fight temptation.

He would stab his best friend for the sake of writing an epigram on his tombstone. – Oscar Wilde

Just because she is always harping on about things doesn't make her an angel.

A window of opportunity for him usually involves a brick.

He doesn't need to worry about identity theft, because no one wants to be him.

Your nickname was never Ace. Maybe Ace-hole. – *Red Dwarf*

With the right type of coaching he could be a nobody.

He should do some soul-searching. Maybe he'll find one.

He's a great advert for abortion.

He may think he's a bookworm but really he's just the ordinary kind.

You couldn't find his personality with SatNav.

My wife is an earth sign. I'm a water sign. Together we make mud. – Henny Youngman

She is so cold, your mouth sticks to her when you kiss her.

He's the type of man who leaves little to your imagination and even less to your patience.

You can never have a clash of personalities with him because he hasn't got a personality to clash with.

He is living proof that there is always someone worse off than you.

God, I hope you're not inviting that bloody, blocky, selfish, two-faced, chicken, bastard, pig-dog man, are you? – *Absolutely Fabulous*

He's about as focused as a fart.

When I think of all the people I respect the most, he's right there, serving them drinks.

He is so lazy he married a pregnant woman.

He has achieved inner peace, but still displays outer obnoxiousness.

His only hope for sexual variety is to change hands.

There goes a woman who knows all the things that can be taught and none of things that cannot be taught. – Coco Chanel

She has been married so many times that her marriage licence says "to whom it may concern".

Trying to get something of value from him is like trying to squeeze orange juice out of an apple.

He has a good personality – but not for a human being.

His personal habits are perfectly understandable . . . if he had been raised by wolves.

He's a heel without a soul.

In her single person she managed to produce the effect of a majority. – Ellen Glasgow

When he finally collects his wages of sin, they'll have to pay him double for all the extra he's put in.

He is arrogant, selfish, opinionated, rude, belligerent, mean, petty, surly and deceitful – but enough of his good points.

If there's a mental health organisation that raises money for people like you, be sure to let me know. – *As Good As It Gets*

The strongest thing about him is his breath.

You've heard the expression, "The worst is yet to come." Well, he's just arrived.

I'm not saying he's a slob, but three new species of slime mould were discovered in his bathroom.

I rang the enema helpline. They were very rude. – Jack Dee

He'll doublecross that bridge when he comes to it.

He's got just one fault – he's insufferable.

You're full of crap. You're an invertebrate scum-sucker whose moral dipstick is about two drops short of bone dry. – *The X-Files*

She's not that bad. She would give you the hair off her back.

If they can make penicillin out of mouldy bread, they can sure make something out of you. – Muhammad Ali

The only way you'd want to fall out with him is if you had the only parachute.

He's as sharp as a bag of wet mice.

He often has people in stitches – but only because he's incredibly clumsy.

If it weren't for getting silent phone calls, he'd have no social life.

He's not so much touchy as touched.

She's as deep as her dimples.

He could be a real charmer but for his personality.

He says he will be boss of the company one day – and I think one day will be long enough.

He's got one foot in the future, one foot in the past, and he's pissing on the present.

She's as fake as a tranny's fanny! – *Life On Mars*

He's as sour as milk that has been sitting in the sun for a week.

The little pig's house made of straw was more secure than he is.

He was a bit like a corkscrew. Twisted, cold and sharp. – Kate Cruise O'Brien

He's like a windscreen wiper – wet, flaccid, moving from side to side, and bowing and scraping when you look at him.

When he was born his parents checked through his birth certificate to see if they could find any loopholes.

She's very open-minded. She'll tolerate any man who doesn't fit the bill so long as he foots it.

Human beings are a disease, a cancer of this planet, you are a plague. – *The Matrix*

He never has any trouble sleeping at night, because he's unconscious most of the time anyway.

He's the decisive type. He'll always give you a definite maybe.

He may have a slick mind, but it's given him an oily tongue.

If you eliminated all the jerks from this company, it would be as crowded as the ethics room at Enron.

The less he knows on any subject, the more stubbornly he knows it.

She's a good girl by and large – well, she's certainly large and she could well be bi. – Dame Edna Everage

He's like the planet Jupiter: we know he's out there, but we're not sure what he's doing.

He pays you a compliment as if he thought you should write a receipt for it.

He's neither right-handed nor left-handed, just under-handed.

Where others have hearts, he carries a tumour of rotten principles. – Jack London

He thinks he's a great traveller just because his mind is always wandering.

He could charm an audience an hour on a stretch without ever getting rid of an idea. – Mark Twain

He displays the keen awareness of an ostrich in hiding.

I only know him superficially, but I think that's enough.

I could never understand what he saw in her until I saw her at the Caprice eating corn-on-the-cob. – Coral Browne

He has more nerve than an infected tooth.

The only prints that he will leave on the sands of time will be heel marks.

He used to be fairly indecisive, but now he's not so certain.

If Florence Nightingale had ever nursed you, she would have married Jack the Ripper instead of founding the Red Cross. – Mary Wickes, *The Man Who Came To Dinner*

One could carve a better man out of a banana.

His idea of flexitime is bending the rules until they snap.

His mother should have thrown him away and kept the stork. – Mae West, *My Little Chickadee*

That young girl is one of the least benightedly unintelligent organic life forms it has been my profound lack of pleasure not to be able to avoid meeting. – Douglas Adams

When he had a heart operation, it took eight hours – seven just to find his heart.

The only regular exercise he gets is stretching the truth.

He always tries to do the right thing, but only after he's tried everything else.

His men would follow him anywhere but only out of morbid curiosity.

He has a contagious laugh – people get sick when they hear it.

Can't we get you on *Mastermind*, Sybil? Next contestant Sybil Fawlty from Torquay, specialist subject the bleeding obvious. – *Fawlty Towers*

Being told you have his full support and backing is rather like being measured by an undertaker.

She has the sort of charm that rubs off with tissues and cold cream.

I am debarred from putting her in her place – she hasn't got one. – Edith Sitwell

He is as good as his word – and his word is no good.

I'll say this for him, he gets everywhere – like dog dirt.

He exudes all the warmth of a kettle during a power-cut.

Under no circumstances should he be allowed to breed.

I've seen lettuces with more heart than him.

He was born with a silver spoon in his mouth, and he hasn't stirred since.

He was so crooked, you could have used his spine for a safety-pin. – Dorothy L. Sayers

I've met a lot of hard-boiled eggs in my time, but you are twenty minutes. – Billy Wilder, *Ace in the Hole*

He is a well-balanced individual – he has a chip on each shoulder.

I have nothing but confidence in you. And very little of that. – Groucho Marx

They remind me of a public toilet – she's engaged and he's vacant.

She's about as cuddly as a snarling pit-bull.

He's the kind of man who picks his friends – to pieces. – Mae West

He will never be able to live down to his reputation.

His family tree is good but he is the sap.

He stands firmly on both feet in mid-air on both sides of an issue. – Homer Fergusson

She has been married so many times she has a season ticket for the registry office.

His nickname is "Caterpillar" because he got where he is by crawling.

His nickname is "Fireman" because people are always telling him to go to blazes.

His nickname is "Optician" because you give him two glasses and he makes a spectacle of himself.

His nickname is "X-Ray" because everyone can see right through him.

His nickname is "Echo" because he always has to have the last word.

His nickname is "Shoe" because people are always telling him to put a sock in it.

His nickname is "Pancake" because he's a complete tosser.

His nickname is "Needle" because he's a little prick.

His nickname is "Chauffeur" because he drives you round the bend.

His nickname is "Fly" because people are always telling him to button it.

His nickname is "Proctologist" because he's so far up the boss's backside.

His nickname is "Contortionist" because he's so far up himself.

His nickname is "String" because people are always telling him to get knotted.

Anyone who ever extends him the hand of friendship is likely to lose a couple of fingers.

I don't want to talk to you no more, you empty-headed animal food trough wiper! I fart in your general direction! Your mother was a hamster and your father smelt of elderberries. – *Monty Python and the Holy Grail*

He is someone whom the Reverend Spooner would have identified as a shining wit.

You take the lies out of him, and he'll shrink to the size of your hat; you take the malice out of him, and he'll disappear. – Mark Twain

He has a difficulty for every solution.

He may not have many faults but he certainly makes the most of the ones he has.

He is a man of splendid abilities but utterly corrupt. He shines and stinks like rotten mackerel by moonlight. – John Randolph

He's a mouse studying to be a rat.

And I want to thank you for all the enjoyment you've taken out of it. – Groucho Marx

Debating against him is no fun. Say something insulting and he looks at you like a whipped dog. – Harold Wilson

He's a man of hidden shallows.

He doesn't have ulcers, but he's a carrier.

He has sat on the fence so long that iron his entered his soul. – David Lloyd George

He has only two temperamental outbursts a year – each lasts six months.

Some people are one in a million – he was won in a raffle.

When they made him they kept the mould and threw him away.

He is a fine friend. He stabs you in the front. – L. L. Levinson

He's a prime candidate for natural deselection.

It's hard to believe he beat a million other sperm.

My prayer to God is a very short one: "Oh Lord, please make my enemies ridiculous." God has granted my wish. – Voltaire

He has every attribute of a dog except loyalty.

He's not man enough to pull on stretch socks.

That's strange. I usually get some sign when Lilith is in town – dogs forming into packs, blood weeping down the walls. – *Frasier*

Some people are has-beens. He's a never-was.

He's as anonymous as a snowball hiding behind a snowman in a snowstorm.

She tells enough white lies to ice a cake. – Margot Asquith

He's been compared to many great men. Unfavourably. But he has been compared to them.

He's just visiting this planet.

I have a mind to join a club and beat you over the head with it. – Groucho Marx

He was so crooked that when he died they had to screw him into the ground. – Bob Hope

And there he was: reigning supreme at number two.

She's got such a narrow mind, when she walks fast her earrings bang together.

He has all the virtues I dislike and none of the vices I admire. – Winston Churchill

He's acquitting himself in a way that no jury ever would.

At work he dines with the top brass – they don't trust him with the silver.

His personality is split so many ways he goes alone for group therapy.

He's not only a bachelor, he's the son of a bachelor.

He has left his body to science and science is contesting the will. – David Frost

He's the sort of man who makes his way through life like an untipped waiter.

He never chooses an opinion; he just wears whatever happens to be in style. – Leo Tolstoy

He thinks by infection, catching an opinion like a cold. – John Ruskin

He is connected to the Police Department – by a pair of handcuffs.

There's nothing wrong with him that reincarnation couldn't cure.

He's living proof that manure can grow legs and walk.

She looks at the world through green-coloured glasses. – Sonia Masello

He has reached rock bottom and started to dig.

He always thinks twice before saying nothing.

She's as tough as an ox. When she dies she'll be turned into Bovril. – Dorothy Parker

He wouldn't spot a good idea if one ran up to him, waving and shouting, "Hi, I'm a good idea."

He fills a much – needed gap.

She has the answer to everything and the solution to nothing. – Oscar Levant

If his conscience could be surgically removed, it would be a minor operation.

He's always in the right place, but at the wrong time.

He's got more issues than *National Geographic*.

He was so narrow-minded that if he fell on a pin it would blind him in both eyes. – Fred Allen

He has no more sense of direction than a bunch of firecrackers.

If he were a member of the Rat Pack, you'd want to bring in pest control.

My wife had left me, which was very painful. Then she came back to me, which was excruciating. – *Frasier*

He's so two-faced I bet he doesn't know which one to wash in the morning.

He's a self-made man – the living proof of the horrors of unskilled labour. – Ed Wynn

He's about as reliable as a punctured condom.

Some people say he's superficial – but that's just on the surface.

He's got fingers in more pies than a leper on a cookery course. – *Life On Mars*

He has a concrete mind – all mixed up and permanently set.

No one can call him a quitter – he's always fired from the job first.

He should go far – the sooner the better!

He's the kind of guy that if you kicked him in the heart, you'd break your toe.

She had an odd dry manner, something between malice and simplicity. – Hester Thrale

Somebody put a stop payment order on his reality check.

She is such a good friend that she would throw all her acquaintances into the water for the pleasure of fishing them out again. – Charles Talleyrand

He doesn't listen to his conscience because he won't take advice from a complete stranger.

His personality is infectious – but then so was the bubonic plague.

He's so unpleasant he sends get-well cards to hypochondriacs.

She has no grudge about men who love her and leave her as long as they leave her enough.

I have a soft spot for her – a swamp at the bottom of my garden.

She's the sort of woman who lives for others – you can tell the others by their hunted expression. – C. S. Lewis

Give him two glasses and he'll make a spectacle of himself.

There's nothing wrong with you that couldn't be cured with a little Prozac and a polo mallet. – Woody Allen

It only takes one drink to get him going, but he's not sure whether it's the eleventh or the twelfth.

He's in touch with reality but it's a bad connection.

He's the kind of guy who'd throw a drowning man both ends of the rope.

He's the kind of guy who'd knife you in the back and have you arrested for carrying a weapon.

His shallowness was as sparkling as the surface of a rivulet. – Mary Braddon

If she were cast as Lady Godiva, the horse would steal the show.

He's not the sort of man to trespass on your time – he encroaches on eternity.

He's not the worst person in the world, but until a worse one comes along, he'll do.

He always manages to keep his neck above water: you can tell from the colour of it.

She could carry off anything; and some people said that she did. – Ada Leverson

The reason he is so easily rattled is because he has a screw loose.

She plunged into a sea of platitudes, and with the powerful breast stroke of a channel swimmer, made her confident way towards the white cliffs of the obvious. – W. Somerset Maugham

POPULARITY

He is so unpopular that even his echo doesn't answer him.

He's about as popular as a French kiss at a family reunion.

He's as welcome as a rattlesnake at a square dance.

I worship the ground he is buried in.

Why are we honouring this man? Have we run out of human beings? – Milton Berle

He's so unpopular that when he sucks a lemon, the lemon pulls a face.

Happiness is seeing her picture on a milk carton.

I lost closer friends than "darling Georgie" the last time I was deloused. – *Blackadder*

There must be something about him that people would like, but nobody can stand close enough to him to find out.

He's a difficult man to forget. But it's definitely worth the effort.

Rimmer, did you know you're about as popular as a horny dog in a Miss Lovely Legs competition? – *Red Dwarf*

He was so unpopular that he even had to organize his own surprise birthday party.

He's really cooking with gas – it's just a pity he doesn't inhale some.

I can always tell when the mother-in-law is coming to stay, the mice throw themselves on the traps. – Les Dawson

He's about as welcome as a priest at a cub scout jamboree.

He applied to join a Lonely Hearts Club, but they wrote back and told him they weren't *that* lonely.

He'd make a lovely corpse. – Charles Dickens

He has the appeal of a sweaty sock.

He doesn't realize that there are enough people to hate in the world already without his working so hard to give us another.

I didn't attend the funeral, but I sent a nice letter saying I approved of it. – Mark Twain

She's held in high regard, particularly by the rest of the coven.

They don't make them like him anymore, and for that we are truly grateful.

Before he came along we were hungry. Now we are fed up.

He was an only child, yet he still wasn't his father's favourite.

I wish Sophia was my mother. Then I could be the one to put her in Shady Pines. – *The Golden Girls*

He has a lot of well-wishers – they'd all like to throw him down one.

I'd like to buy her something to put around her neck – a rope perhaps?

He is the reason God created the middle finger.

He's a real Don Juan with the ladies – the ladies Don Juan anything to do with him.

You are nothing! If you were in my toilet, I wouldn't bother flushing it. – *Swimming With Sharks*

He is so unpopular that when he was called for jury duty, he was found guilty.

A visit from him is about as welcome as finding out that your mother-in-law has got a twin sister.

He had a paternity suit filed against him by his own children.

He gets so far up people's noses, they can feel his shoes on their chin.

There are more people allergic to him than to pollen.

I regard you with an indifference bordering on aversion. – Robert Louis Stevenson

He is so unpopular even the Samaritans hang up on him.

Being with him is about as pleasurable as running your nose down a cactus.

He could only be missed if the minister read somebody else's eulogy.

He's a good example of why some animals eat their young.

She's a treasure. Who dug her up?

He is about as popular around here as a jar of mint sauce is to a new-born lamb.

He's about as welcome as a fox in a henhouse.

He was so unpopular he couldn't even get a date on his gravestone.

He made enemies as naturally as soap makes suds. – Percival Wilde

He's a master of worming his way out of people's confidences.

I could never learn to like her, except on a raft at sea with no other provisions in sight. — Mark Twain

You could fit all his friends into a phone box.

If popularity could be measured in miles, he'd be an inch.

Success has definitely turned his head. It's just a pity it didn't finish the job and wring his neck.

He's the most overrated human being since Judas Iscariot won the AD31 Best Disciple Competition. — *Blackadder*

Wherever he goes, people wave at him. Maybe one day they'll use all their fingers.

He's the sort of man who wins hearts wherever he goes . . . and doesn't stay.

He's about as welcome as a fart in a phone box.

The only place he's ever invited is outside.

He spent so much time trying to get rid of his halitosis, only to discover that he wasn't popular anyway.

Let's shoot him and put him out of our misery. — *M*A*S*H*

If he didn't already exist, nobody would bother inventing him.

He's alive today only because it's illegal to kill him.

She has fewer friends than Victoria Beckham has hot dinners.

I like long walks, especially when they are taken by people who annoy me. — Fred Allen

He was the warm personal charm of a millipede.

I'll never forget the first time we met — although I keep trying.

Kiss her under the mistletoe? I wouldn't kiss her under an anaesthetic.

He may be highly strung, but not high enough to suit most people.

I don't like her. But don't misunderstand me: my dislike is purely platonic. — Herbert Beerbohm Tree

He's as welcome as a turd in a swimming pool.

If his circle of friends were any smaller it would be a dot.

His new liver has rejected him, and it's a shrewd judge.

My mother-in-law fell down a wishing well. I was amazed. I never knew they worked. – Les Dawson

He's as welcome as a mouse head in a meat pie.

He had to become the outdoor type because nobody would let him inside.

There's just something I don't like about him. I can't put my finger on it, but if I did, I'd have to wash it. – *The Golden Girls*

He has a knack of making strangers immediately.

I worship the quicksand he walks on.

Some cause happiness wherever they go; others whenever they go. – Oscar Wilde

He grows on people – like a wart.

People would do anything for him, especially if it involved arranging his funeral.

He is marginally more popular than an outbreak of bird flu.

I have never killed a man, but I have read many obituaries with great pleasure. – Clarence Darrow

He throws himself into everything he does, so his colleagues have asked him to dig a deep hole.

They say you shouldn't say nothin' about the dead unless it's good. He's dead. Good. – Jackie "Moms" Mabley

MEANNESS

He is so mean, he won't let his baby have more than one measle at a time.

He's so mean he wouldn't give his daughter away at her wedding.

He's such a cheapskate that every year he offers forty thousand dollars . . . to the family of the unknown soldier.

He's the only man I ever knew who had rubber pockets so he could steal soup. – Wilson Mizner

He's so mean that he complained to the hotel where he was staying about the towels. He said they were so thick he was struggling to close his suitcase.

He is so stingy he has a burglar alarm on his garbage can.

He's so mean that when he takes a £5 note from his wallet, the Queen blinks in the light.

He is so mean, he told his children that Santa Claus was dead.

He is so mean, he told his children that the tooth fairy had been kidnapped by dental extremists.

He's tighter than a photo finish.

He's so mean that even if he were poisoned, he wouldn't die until he had reclaimed the deposit on the bottle.

He's the kind of guy who would put his wife on the dresser and kiss his wallet goodnight.

He's so mean, he's saving up for a rainy century. – Bob Zany

He is so mean that if he were a taxi driver and had Stevie Wonder in the back seat, he'd just rev up the engine for forty minutes and charge him full fare.

He is so mean that the last time he opened his wallet, the farthing was still legal currency.

He is so mean that the last time he opened his wallet, Glenn Miller was merely reported "missing".

He is so mean that the last time he opened his wallet, Charlie Chaplin had just been named "Most Promising Newcomer".

He is so mean that the last time he opened his wallet, Abraham Lincoln was still in short trousers.

He is so mean that the last time he opened his wallet was to greet the passengers on the *Mayflower*.

He is so mean that the last time he opened his wallet, it was eaten by a triceratops.

He's so mean that he takes his kids to the store's pet department and tells them it's the zoo.

She is so mean that instead of buying deodorant, she gargles disinfectant and licks her armpits.

He's tighter than a camel's arse in a sand storm.

He's a real carefree guy – he doesn't care as long as it's free.

He's so mean that when he opens his wallet, he has to fight off the moths.

He's a man of rare gifts – it's rare when he gives one.

He's so mean, the only way to get a drink out of him is to stick two fingers down his throat.

MOTORMOUTHS

He has nothing to say but that doesn't stop him saying it.

The trouble with her is that she lacks the power of conversation but not the power of speech. – George Bernard Shaw

His approach is about as subtle as a pneumatic drill.

If he blows his own trumpet much louder he won't have any breath left to call the tune.

He has a speech impediment – his foot.

Some people can speak on any subject. He doesn't need a subject.

He uses his tongue so much, he needs a retread every six months.

You know I could rent you out as a decoy for duck hunters? – Groucho Marx

If his mouth were any bigger, he could talk into his ears.

The only thing his conversation needs is a little lockjaw.

He generates more waffle than the biggest waffle-making machine in a waffle factory.

He was like a cock who thought the sun had risen to hear him crow. – George Eliot

He doesn't just hold a conversation, he strangles it.

In her case, the wages of sin will be laryngitis.

He has a waterproof voice — no one can drown it out.

He may be thoughtless but he's never speechless.

Let's give him a big hand — right across the mouth.

Generally speaking, he's generally speaking.

She never learned to swim, simply because she couldn't keep her mouth shut for that long.

Is there a rest stop between you and the end of this story? — Rich Hall

The only reason he blows his horn louder than anyone else is that he's in a thicker fog.

Success hasn't gone to his head — just to his mouth.

He never opens his mouth without subtracting from the sum of human knowledge.

He can always be relied upon to set the bull rolling.

He is the same old sausage, fizzing and sputtering in his own grease. — Henry James

Some things in life go without saying. Unfortunately he's not one of them.

He's got more neck than a giraffe.

He's like a dripping tap — you can hear him but you can't turn him off.

He likes to tell you he's positive, but really he's just wrong at the top of his voice.

You know, you haven't stopped talking since I came here. You must have been vaccinated with a phonograph needle. — Groucho Marx, *Duck Soup*

The smaller the pip, the louder the squeak.

You can guarantee that she'll be suffering from severe indiscretion after any dinner party.

When he is at a loss for words, his loss is everyone else's gain.

You can rely on her to keep your secret – the one she passes on is always her own invention.

If nagging were an Olympic sport, my Aunt Voula would win a gold medal. – *My Big Fat Greek Wedding*

I wouldn't say she's a gossip but anything she hears goes in one ear and out the telephone.

The only thing she ever gives away is secrets.

He's the sort of self-made man that can't resist passing on the recipe.

He's got a mouth on him like the Channel Tunnel.

I know she's outspoken, but by whom? – Dorothy Parker

If she bit her tongue, she'd die of acid poisoning.

Listening to him reminds me of the horns of a steer – a point here and there, and a lot of bull in between.

He doesn't have a lot to say, but unfortunately you have to listen for quite a while to find that out.

His mouth is getting too big for his muzzle.

He can compress the most words into the smallest idea of any man I know. – Abraham Lincoln

He could talk his head off and never miss it.

He is rarely at a loss for words – just for ideas to put in them.

He keeps opening things by mistake – usually his mouth.

He often behaves like he has a tiger in the tank, but the trouble is there is a donkey at the wheel.

The sharpest thing about her is her tongue.

She has a highly developed sense of rumour.

If it's true that exercise gets rid of fat, I can't understand why she's got a double chin.

He's got more front than Blackpool.

When he talks he reminds me of Moses – every time he opens his mouth the bull rushes. – Robert Orben

He always enters a room voice first.

She had a pretty gift for quotation, which is a serviceable substitute for wit. – W. Somerset Maugham

He ought to be a member of the Parole Board because he never lets anyone finish a sentence.

He's got a bigger mouth than the Mississippi.

She can talk brilliantly upon any subject, provided that she knows nothing about it. – Oscar Wilde

His vocabulary may not amount to much but it certainly has a fast turnover.

When he talks, other people get hoarse just listening.

He's not hard of hearing – just hard of listening.

He's the talk of the town – all by himself.

Your mouth is open and sound is coming out. That's never a good thing. – *Buffy the Vampire Slayer*

She's got more mouth than Julia Roberts.

His bold typeface does not conceal his incoherent words.

When there's no more to be said on a subject, you can be certain he'll still be saying it.

People know you by word of mouth – yours.

She proceeds to dip her little fountain-pen filler into pots of oily venom and to squirt the mixture at all her friends. – Harold Nicolson

His tongue works so fast he could whisk an egg with it.

He's a renewable energy source for hot-air balloons.

He has nothing to say but you have to listen a long time to discover that.

She makes it a rule never to repeat gossip: there's no need to, she always starts it.

VANITY

He has always been conceited. When he was young he joined the Navy so the world could see him.

The only big thing about him is his opinion of himself.

The last time I saw him he was walking down Lovers' Lane holding his own hand. – Fred Allen

She's not so much overdressed as wrapped up in herself.

He's so big-headed he has to wash his hair at Niagara Falls.

He never needs to go on vacation, because he's always on an ego trip.

He is so conceited that his idea of a real treat is to stand in front of the mirror and look at himself.

He's found that the best way to push himself forward is to pat himself on the back.

He's a legend in his own mirror.

He's just swallowed his pride. It'll take him a moment or two to digest it. – *The Hasty Heart*

He'll talk eloquently on any subject, provided the subject is himself.

He thinks he's out of this world – and everyone wishes he were.

He's so vain, he goes out into the garden so that the flowers can smell *him*.

Don't take any notice. He's just letting off esteem.

His opinion of himself is not just high, it's in orbit.

What time he can spare from the adornment of his person he devotes to the neglect of his duties. – William Hepworth Thompson

He's so egotistical he calls out his own name during sex.

I'd be a millionaire if I could buy him for what I think of him and sell him for what he thinks of himself.

He gets carried away with his own self-importance – but not far enough.

They are the biggest show offs since Lady Godiva entered the royal enclosure at Ascot, claiming she had literally nothing to wear. – *Blackadder*

He's so far up himself he's in danger of turning inside out.

He's so pompous he always looks as if he's auditioning to appear on a banknote.

He's full of so much crap they had to start a second pile.

No wonder he suffers from migraines – his halo is stuck on too tight.

He has a great deal of pride, but precious little to be proud of.

He is so big-headed he probably has to step into his shirts.

He is so conceited that he has a mirror on his bathroom ceiling so he can watch himself gargle.

BORES

Compared with him, Mars appears brimming with life.

An evening with him is only marginally more enjoyable than being slapped repeatedly around the face with a wet haddock.

He was the life and soul of the party, which gives you an idea of how dull it was.

She has the knack of staying longer in a couple of hours than most people do in a couple of weeks.

He is so boring he goes out and paints the town beige.

Frank, you are two of the most boring people I've ever met. – *M*A*S*H*

He's so slow that it took him twenty years of marriage to get the seven-year itch.

After five minutes of talking to him, people have been known to lose the will to live.

Talking to him is about as interesting as watching a scab form.

My wife's so boring, she could bore an arsehole on a wooden horse. – Sir Les Patterson

He is so slow that moss grows on him.

He is so slow he can't even catch his own breath.

He's so boring his dreams have Muzak.

Some people live life in the fast lane; he lives life in the bus lane.

Gee, what a terrific party. Later on we'll get some fluid and embalm each other. – Neil Simon

He is so boring, his idea of a night on the tiles actually involves grouting.

He has the charisma of a bollard.

He's the kind of bore who's here today and here tomorrow.

A conversation with him is about as invigorating as talking to a rice pudding.

He hails from Dullsville, Missouri.

He's so boring that when he watches a movie, the actors fall asleep.

The most daring thing he's ever done is to be a day overdue on his library card.

You only have to listen to him for a minute or two to realise why he's got such a wide circle of nodding acquaintances.

He bores more than the average termite.

If too much excitement can bring on a heart attack, at least you know that you're safe talking to him.

He's a walking advert for euthanasia.

He's the ideal subject for aspiring hypnotists.

Just when you think he encapsulates the limits to tedium, he goes and pushes the boundary even further.

Well, I thought my razor was dull until I heard his speech. – Groucho Marx, *Horse Feathers*

He couldn't even be the life and soul of a Tupperware party.

He has all the spark of an underwater cigarette lighter.

He doesn't need an anaesthetic to put anyone to sleep.

His life is so dull he can write his diary a week in advance.

He seems to have had a charisma bypass operation.

He's got a tongue that only runs when his brain is in neutral.

Everyone has his day and some days last longer than others. – Winston Churchill

He is so boring he can't even entertain a doubt.

His idea of a wild party is a game of Scrabble where you don't keep the score.

If he moved any slower, he'd rust.

He's about as much fun as a wet weekend in Scunthorpe.

I've seen glaciers move faster than him.

In the Formula One race of life he's the safety car.

He is an old bore. Even the grave yawns for him. – Herbert Beerbohm Tree

He's got the sort of personality that blends in anywhere . . . with the furniture.

He is wetter than a halibut's bathing costume.

He has managed to get tedium down to a fine art.

He's the sort of man you could lose in a crowd of two.

Some people stay longer in an hour than others can in a week. – William Dean Howells

He is about as interesting as watching a snail move slowly across a large rock.

Listening to his conversation is about as exciting as listening to a reading of the entire National Rail Timetable.

He's the sort of person who, if you ask him the time, tells you how the watch works.

He has all the charisma of a magnum of chloroform.

He's as worn out as a cucumber in a convent.

Quiet, will you? This man is trying to be dull. Go ahead, Frank, dull away. –
*M*A*S*H*

He's about as entertaining as watching grass grow in a window box.

We're swimming in boredom and he's handing out anchors.

Calling him dull is a gross underestimation of just how tedious he is.

He's slower than dial-up Internet.

He has the energy and drive of a snail on valium.

He has all the personality of linoleum.

He's always sharpening his sleeping skills.

He's so slow, he moves around the office the way a meal moves through a
python.

He's about as quick as a corpse.

He is no more fun than an in-growing toenail.

This party is as flat as a witch's tit.

In terms of personality and charisma, he is hard to distinguish from the tail
end of a horse.

Just a few minutes talking to him makes you want to jump for joy – off a tall
building.

I've seen more life in a tramp's vest.

He is living proof of the saying that charisma comes but once a year.

He's so slow that if he raced his pregnant wife, he'd finish third.

A chat with you, and death loses its sting. – *Blackadder*

He's slower than erosion.

He is slower than a herd of tortoises stampeding through glue.

If you only have a day to live, spend it in his company. It will seem like
forever.

He trod on a snail the other day because it was following him around; there
were two, but the other one ran off before he could catch it.

Every time I look at you I get a fierce desire to be lonesome. – Oscar Levant

This is the man who put the "small bore" into small bore rifle shooting.

He's wetter than a fish's swimsuit.

There's never a dull moment with him – it's continuous.

There are people in comas with livelier personalities than him.

He's so slow he'd have to speed up to stop.

He has about as much drive as a child's tricycle.

If you see two people talking and one looks bored, he's the other one.

He is not only dull himself, he is the cause of dullness in others. – Samuel Johnson

CLASS

If her nose were turned up any more, she'd blow her hat off every time she sneezed.

His origins are so low, you'd have to limbo under his family tree.

She's terribly class conscious. She hasn't any class and everyone's conscious of it.

The finest woman that ever walked the streets. – Mae West

The only thing that's cultured about her is her pearls.

He always has his ear to the ground – but only because he lives in the gutter.

He's such a snob he has an unlisted postcode.

If she holds her nose any higher she'll develop a double chin at the back of her neck.

She has about as much class as a bucket of phlegm.

You're so stuck-up, your finger has to make an appointment to scratch your damn head! – *The Fresh Prince of Bel Air*

He was accepted into an exclusive club – but only because they needed someone to snub.

She's lower than a flounder's nipples.

As far as he's concerned, refinement is a matter of knowing which fingers to use when you whistle for service.

He's that low he could parachute out of a snake's asshole and still have room to free-fall.

She wouldn't know Monet's "Water Lilies" unless Revlon named a nail polish after it. — *Veronica Mars*

Her family tree is nothing but a rest stop for dogs.

The only polish he has is on his shoes.

He'd steal the straw from his mother's kennel.

You are last in God's great chain. Unless there's an earwig around here you'd like to victimize. — *Blackadder*

INCOMPETENCE

You're about as useful as a one-legged man at an arse-kicking contest. — *Blackadder*

His only purpose in life is to serve as a warning to others.

He has a good family tree, but the crop is a failure.

He's completely unspoiled by failure. — Noël Coward

He has delusions of adequacy.

Xander, I know you take pride in being the voice of the common wuss, but the truth is, certain people are entitled to special privileges. They're called winners. That's the way the world works. — *Buffy the Vampire Slayer*

When the list of great men is finally read out, he will be there . . . listening.

The closest he'll ever get to becoming the toast of the town is sunburn.

He puts the "suck" into success.

His boss would gladly pay him what he's worth, but it's against the Minimum Wage Law.

The only thing he is likely to win is a Darwin Award.

The only decent impression he can do is of a man with no talent. – *Blackadder*

He was in a class of his own, but only because none of the other boys would sit near him.

He's a man with no equals – only superiors.

His talent would be indiscernible, even under a microscope.

He's a self-made man, and it's good of him to take the blame.

He is living proof that practice does not make perfect.

Failure has gone to his head.

He runs squares around the competition.

Some men are born mediocre, some men achieve mediocrity, and some men have mediocrity thrust upon them. – Joseph Heller

He couldn't hit sand if he fell off a camel.

He couldn't hit water if he fell out of a boat.

He couldn't pour water out of a boot with instructions on the heel.

He couldn't scratch his ass with a hand full of fish hooks.

He couldn't score in a brothel.

Some people make their mark on life, he's just left a stain.

At least he's original – he makes a new mistake every day.

He has that rare gift of trying to make his way in the world by pushing all the doors marked "Pull".

This is a man who had greatness thrust upon him – and ducked.

His life coach committed suicide.

If God tried to help him, we'd have an eight-day week.

Your services might be as useful as a barber's shop on the steps of a guillotine. – *Blackadder*

He's a man of hidden talents – and as soon as we find one we'll let you know.

He would be out of his depth in a puddle.

He's not only the sort of man who can't finish things he tackles – he can't even start most of them.

In the drive of life, he'll never get a ticket for speeding.

When his window of opportunity opened, he had the blinds drawn.

He has an inferiority complex, but not a very good one.

He's the sort of guy who gives failures a bad name.

His existence has yet to create the slightest ripple on the millpond of achievement.

When opportunity knocked, he was out the back and didn't hear a thing.

What are his chances of being a success? He doesn't have a fart's prayer in a hurricane.

Personally I thought you were the least convincing female impressionist since Tarzan went through Jane's handbag and ate her lipstick. – *Blackadder*

He is in the twilight of a mediocre career.

The only skill he has ever developed is the art of being obnoxious.

He was as useful in a crisis as a sheep. – Dorothy Eden

He's about as much use as piss on a forest fire.

He started at the bottom and stayed there.

I wouldn't say he was useless, but he's been fired more times than Custer's pistol.

He's been sacked more times than Rome.

Everyone is gifted: some just open the package sooner.

Like a death at a birthday party, you ruin all the fun,

Like a sucked and spat out Smartie, you're no use to anyone. – John Cooper Clarke

He's as useless as rubber lips on a woodpecker.

He's about as much use as a lead parachute.

He's about as much use as a can of dinosaur repellent.

He's about as much use as a chocolate teapot.

He's about as much use as an ashtray on a motorcycle.

He's about as much use as a condom machine in the Vatican.

He's about as much use as a grave robber in a crematorium.

He's about as much use as a glass hammer.

He's about as much use as a carpet fitter's ladder.

He's about as useful as a mint-flavoured suppository.

He's about as much use as a pulled tooth.

He's about as much use as a one-armed trapeze artist with an itchy arse.

He's got a wonderful head for money. There's this long slit on the top. – David Frost

He's outstanding in his field – just like a scarecrow.

He couldn't organize a piss-up in a brewery.

He couldn't lead a wasp to a pot of jam.

He couldn't direct a turd down a toilet.

His coordination was so bad that he had to pull his car to the side of the road to blow the horn.

That's OK, we can walk to the kerb from here. – Woody Allen, on bad parking, *Annie Hall*

Baldrick, in the Amazonian rain forests there are tribes of Indians as yet untouched by civilization who have developed more convincing Charlie Chaplin impressions than yours. – *Blackadder*

If they gave out medals for losers, he'd be first in the queue.

You think we watch any of your movies, Harry? I've seen better film on teeth. – *Get Shorty*

If he were on fire, he couldn't act as if he were burning.

Like acting with two hundred and ten pounds of condemned veal. – Coral Browne

They say he plays football like Rooney . . . Mickey Rooney.

Our resident coloratura, Mrs Pike, howled above the choir like a dingo with its paws caught in a trap. – Clive James, *Unreliable Memoirs*

She had a voice like a drowned sailor. It died at C.

Her voice is pure, but only because every time she sings she strains it.

When she sings people clap their hands . . . over their ears.

He has Van Gogh's ear for music.

Every time he tickles those ivories, the entire elephants' graveyard turns over. – *M*A*S*H*

She has a good voice – if you don't happen to like music.

They say she's got a promising voice; perhaps she'll take notice and promise to stop singing.

Listen Edith, I know you're singing, you know you're singing, but the neighbours may think I'm torturing you. – *All in the Family*

I've heard better sounds come from a radiator being drained.

At least with a voice like that, there's no need for the place to have a music licence.

She has a voice that could curdle milk.

She couldn't carry a tune if it had a handle.

She's touched more bum notes than a counterfeiter.

Her mouth is so big, she can sing duets by herself.

If you had been singing like this two thousand years ago, people would have stoned you. – Simon Cowell

My advice would be if you want to pursue a career in the music business, don't. – Simon Cowell

I will pay you to stop performing. – Simon Cowell

Did you really believe you could become the *American Idol*? Well, then, you're deaf. — Simon Cowell

It says here you went to the Fame high school. Did you get thrown out? — Simon Cowell

Ring your vocal coach and demand a refund. — Simon Cowell

The first thing that went through my mind was, you sound like someone who should be singing on a cruise ship. Halfway through the song, I imagined the ship sinking. — Simon Cowell

She has a fine voice. It's just a shame she has to spoil it by singing.

Her singing was so bad she made more bum notes than a judge at the Rear of the Year contest.

When she starts singing the neighbourhood cats run for cover.

She sounds so much better with her mouth closed.

She sings like a bird — a crow.

The first time I saw you on stage I realized what an amazing voice you have. I think you're so brave not to have had it trained.

He hits all the right notes — but not necessarily in the right order.

When she sings, it is like a chainsaw hitting a rusty nail.

Dancing with her was like moving a piano. — Ring Lardner

You call that dancing? I've seen people on fire move better than that! — *Red Dwarf*

STUPIDITY

He may look like an idiot and talk like an idiot but don't let that fool you. He really is an idiot. — Groucho Marx

When God was handing out brains, he was first in line but ended up holding the door open.

If he were any more stupid, he'd have to be watered twice a week.

He got into the gene pool while the lifeguard wasn't looking.

He let his mind wander – and it hasn't come back yet.

If there was a retarded Oscar, you would win hands down. – *Garden State*

When a thought crosses his mind, it's a long and lonely journey.

He was born stupid, and greatly increased his birthright. – Samuel Butler

He has two brains: one is lost, the other is out looking for it.

He is as thick as a whale omelette. – *Blackadder*

He's on permanent leave of absence from his senses.

He took an IQ test – and the results were negative.

You can see a thought form in his head and then come right out of his mouth without pausing in between.

Thinking isn't your strong suit, is it? – *Lost in Space*

He's a gross ignoramus – 144 times worse than an ordinary ignoramus.

Never mind about running a company, you wouldn't trust him to run a bath.

He has done for this firm what King Herod did for babysitting.

Good night, Rose. Go to sleep, honey. Pray for brains! – *The Golden Girls*

He has turned incompetence into an art form.

If he ever had a good idea, it would be beginner's luck.

He's so dumb that when his girlfriend said she had crabs, he bought her fishnet stockings.

One day he stopped to think and then forgot to start again.

While he was not dumber than an ox, he was not any smarter either. – James Thurber

He's depriving a village somewhere of its idiot.

He doesn't know the meaning of the word "failure", but then again he doesn't know the meaning of most words.

He has been seen tossing breadcrumbs to helicopters.

He makes Homer Simpson look like a Nobel Prize winner.

If men were dominoes, he'd be the double-blank. – P. G. Wodehouse

A thought struck him once and he was in hospital for three weeks.

The only purpose his head serves is to keep the rain off his neck.

Let's at least ask someone who's going to give us a slightly more intelligent opinion. Hello, wall! What do you think? – *Red Dwarf*

He's running low on thinking gas.

His brain is caught in his zipper.

He is rather like an inverse Einstein.

His brain is so weak, he has to wear crutches behind his ears.

You don't know squat. You know less than squat. You and squat could go see a movie, and squat could wear a T-shirt that said, "I'm with Stupid!" – *Frasier*

His heart is in the right place, but I'm not sure about his brain.

If brains were chocolate, he wouldn't have enough to fill an M&M.

If brains were lard, he couldn't grease a frying pan.

If brains were bird droppings, he'd have a clean cage.

If brains were eyebrows, he'd be well and truly plucked.

If brains were a choir, he'd be a soloist.

If brains were leather, he couldn't saddle a flea.

If brains were dynamite, he wouldn't have enough to blow his nose.

If brains were rain, he'd be a desert.

If brains were hair, he'd be Kojak.

If brains were money, he'd be a charity case.

If brains were arms, she'd be the Venus de Milo.

If brains were trees, he'd be a twig.

If brains were plumage, he'd be a single feather.

If brains were a bottle of champagne, he'd be a bubble.

If brains were rubber, he wouldn't have enough to make a pair of flippers for a budgie.

If brains were glue, he wouldn't have enough to cover the back of a postage stamp.

If brains were air miles, he wouldn't have enough to take off.

If brains were grains of sand, he wouldn't have enough to fill a thimble.

If brains were water, he wouldn't have enough to baptize a flea.

If brains were shoes, he'd go barefoot.

If brains were petrol, he wouldn't have enough to drive a Dinky Toy.

If brains were looks, he'd be the Elephant Man.

If brains were glass, he wouldn't have enough to make a monocle for the eye of a whelk.

If brains were farts, he couldn't stink out the inside of a matchbox.

If brains were taxed, he'd get a rebate.

Why don't you bore a hole in yourself and let the sap run out? – Groucho Marx, *Monkey Business*

He's at his wits' end, and it wasn't a long journey.

He's as bright as Alaska in December.

You've got the brain of a cheese sandwich. – *Red Dwarf*

He says he's got a mind of his own, but it seems to operate on a timeshare principle.

His mind is wonderfully clear . . . but only because it is not cluttered with facts.

So much goes over his head, he should be a limbo dancer.

He is useless on top of the ground; he ought to be under it, inspiring the cabbages. – Mark Twain

Nobody could read his mind. The print is too small.

He's so dense that light bends around him.

He'd entertain a new thought as if it were his mother-in-law.

Why is it that wherever I go, the resident idiot heads straight for me? — Gwynn Thomas

No one accuses him of being scatterbrained, because he's got no brains to scatter.

His family is so stupid that when they play Trivial Pursuit the dog wins.

She's such an airhead that whenever she sneezes, she loses IQ points.

I've got a woman so lame that she actually thinks that when I groan during sex it has anything to do with her. — *Married . . . With Children*

He's an experiment in artificial stupidity.

He can't count beyond ten with his shoes on.

He was born on April 2, a day late.

If there's an idea in his head, it must be in solitary confinement.

If ignorance were a disability, he'd get a full pension.

He's as dumb as a brick with an extra chromosome.

He was distinguished for ignorance; for he had only one idea and that was wrong. — Benjamin Disraeli

If his IQ were two points higher, he'd be a rock.

My doctor told me to exercise with dumbbells. Fancy going for a jog?

Some people are so dumb, they think the number before 0 is blastoff. — Dennis Miller

He couldn't get a clue during clue mating season in a field of clues if he smeared his body in musk and did the clue mating dance.

The only thing he can keep in his head is a cold.

How often the gods endow a man with a perfect profile and no brains to live up to it. — Katherine Mansfield

Someone should hit him with the clue stick.

Fortunately people like him usually manage to kill themselves before reproducing.

He has his headquarters where his hindquarters should be.

She put the "ding" in dingbat.

How your brain doesn't roll out of your earhole, I'll never know. – *Night Court*

Even if he had a brain, he'd probably take it out and play with it.

He has a natural talent for finding subliminal messages in ice cubes.

He may not be light on his feet, but he is certainly light in his head.

You are about as much use to me as a hole in the head, an affliction with which you must be familiar, never having had a brain. – *Blackadder*

He's afraid he'll void his warranty if he thinks too much.

Aliens zapped him with a stupidity ray – twice.

He is thicker than a complete set of *Encyclopedia Britannica*.

Please try not to be such a wiener-head. – Dave Barry

He doesn't know his own mind – and he hasn't missed much.

He's a miracle of nature: he has an IQ of two, yet he's still able to speak.

Some people are hard-boiled – he's just half-baked.

All his learning curves look like Mount Everest.

He's like a loaf of sliced bread – extra thick.

Clearly the full area of his ignorance is not yet mapped.

Your head is as empty as a hermit's address book. – *Blackadder*

He must have a large brain to hold so much ignorance.

He's as strong as an ox, and almost as intelligent.

He always speaks straight from the shoulder. It's a pity his words don't start from higher up.

He's about as cunning as a dodo.

He watches *Beavis and Butthead* to improve his vocabulary.

My son complains about headaches. I tell him all the time: when you get out of bed, it's feet first. – Henny Youngman

He makes a black hole look bright.

He has a soft heart and a head to match.

He blew his own brains out? He must have been an incredibly good shot.

He's not the sharpest tool in the shed . . . but he is a tool.

He always speaks his mind, so usually he's silent.

Frank, you've been pushing your stethoscope too far in your ears. I think it scratched your brain. − *M*A*S*H*

He's a peripheral visionary.

He would do better if he let his mind work as fast as his mouth.

Somebody bring me a knife, very long and razor sharp. I need to castrate the person who made this sauce and I don't want to cause any unnecessary suffering. I'm not a vindictive man, I'm not out to cause pain, but with this man's DNA in the gene pool, humanity is doomed. − *Chef!*

He couldn't tell you which way the elevator was going if you gave him two guesses.

His brain is permanently on cruise control.

Genius does what it must, talent does what it can, and he had best do what he's told.

If shit was wit, he'd be constipated.

He is stumped by anything that is child proof.

No one can drive him out of his mind − at most it would be a putt.

He is one of the few people capable of talking to plants on their own level.

He's forgotten more things than most people know, but that's the trouble − he's forgotten them.

Your brain would make a grain of sand look large and ungainly. − *Blackadder*

If his IQ were any lower, he'd trip over it.

His mind might have spontaneously combusted.

The space between his ears powers vacuum pumps.

Peg, I suspect your mind, much like the lost continent of Atlantis, no longer appears on my map. − *Married . . . With Children*

He is an idiot savant but without the "savant" part.

He's about as bright as a blackout.

When God said, "Come forth for brains," he came fifth.

A brain of feathers and a heart of lead. — Alexander Pope

He has a mechanical mind — it's a shame he forgot to wind it up this morning.

He has a mind like a steel trap — always closed.

Why don't you rub your two IQ points together and try to start a fire? — *Frasier*

She should wear a soft hat to match her head.

He's got a Teflon brain — nothing sticks.

I have seen more intelligent creatures than you lying on their backs on the bottom of ponds. I have seen more organized creatures than you running around farmyards with their heads cut off. — *Fawlty Towers*

The only things he gets from scratching his head are splinters.

The sum total of his knowledge could be written on the back of a postage stamp.

He had just enough intelligence to open his mouth when he wanted to eat, but certainly no more. — P. G. Wodehouse

He has the brain power of an iron filing.

To say he has a brain like a pea would do a disservice to garden vegetables the world over.

If wit were spit, his mouth would be drier than a shallow well in an African drought.

He's about as quick as a fortnight.

He's such a blockhead, he needs termite insurance for his brain.

Nobody says he is dumb. They just say he was sixteen years old before he learned how to wave goodbye.

He has the air of someone who has just stepped into an empty lift-shaft.

He is mentally qualified for handicapped parking.

His head would be put to better use as a paperweight.

That chip on his shoulder indicates a block of wood nearby.

Your head's just something you put your hat on, isn't it? – *The Thin Blue Line*

He couldn't be as stupid as he looks – and live.

He doesn't have two brain cells to rub together.

His open mind should be closed for repairs.

He's thicker than a donkey's dangler.

When he collects his thoughts he only needs a very small container.

His mental function can be graphed with a single dot.

Your brain's so minute, Baldrick, that if a hungry cannibal cracked your head open, there wouldn't be enough to cover a small water biscuit. – *Blackadder*

You couldn't find his IQ with a flashlight.

He has a strange growth on his neck – his head.

He parked his brain and forgot where he left it.

He must have been born when the planets were misaligned.

He's living proof that evolution *can* go in reverse.

He can venture into wild country inhabited solely by headhunters, safe in the knowledge that they wouldn't be interested in his.

He doesn't have the sense God gave an animal cracker.

He's as wise as the world is flat.

A brain isn't everything. In fact, in his case it's nothing.

His main stumbling block is the one in his head.

He has never had a headcold in his life, but that is only because diseases can't exist in a vacuum.

Putting his brain on the edge of a razor blade would be like putting a pea on a six-lane highway.

What he doesn't know would make a great book. – Sydney Smith

He's lost his marble.

He's permanently rotated ninety degrees from the rest of us.

Someone gave him a hockey puck once, and he spent the rest of the day trying to open it.

His train of thought has been derailed.

His train of thought is still boarding at the station.

He has an intellect rivalled only by that of the village idiot's more stupid brother.

He is an expert on padded cells.

All he remembers about his middle name is the first letter.

If stupidity were a crime, he would be number one on the Most Wanted list.

A mental midget with the IQ of a fence post. – Tom Waits

He had an idea once but it died of loneliness.

There is intelligent life on his planet but he isn't it.

He's an example of how the dinosaurs survived for millions of years with walnut-sized brains.

The average man has twelve million brain cells, but 11,999,999 of his are unemployed.

I don't think Constable Goody would get it if it came in a large bag marked "IT"! – *The Thin Blue Line*

His level of intelligence is such that he needs help to drool.

He doesn't have two neurons to rub together.

He says he has a mind of his own. He's welcome to it – who else would want it?

He was in line for brains, but he thought they said "pains", so he said, "No thanks."

He was in line for brains, but he thought they said "trains", so he said, "My dad just bought me one."

He was in line for brains, but he thought they said "canes", so he asked for a wooden one.

He was in line for brains, but he thought they said "drains", so he asked for one that could hold all kinds of crap.

She was in line for brains, but she thought they said "vanes", so she asked for one that would change with the wind.

Signs of his intelligence are as rare as rocking horse dung.

He couldn't count to twenty-one if he were barefoot and without pants.

If it weren't for his stupidity, he'd have no personality at all.

I'm alone in space with a man who'd lose a battle of wits with a stuffed iguana. – *Red Dwarf*

He has taken stupidity to new heights.

He should study to be a bone specialist – he has the head for it.

He keeps his brain in mint condition.

They must have done a clean boot on him.

When he stopped a man from abusing a donkey, it was merely an act of brotherly love.

He donated his brain to science before he had finished using it.

It's not just that he doesn't know anything, it's the fact that he doesn't even suspect much.

He is one brain cell away from being a talking monkey.

He has one of those mighty minds – mighty empty.

There are more marbles in a spray paint can than there are brains in his head.

There's enough sawdust between his ears to make a bed for an elephant.

The recesses of his mind are always in recess.

When he graduated from kindergarten, he was so excited he could hardly shave.

He used to be utterly clueless but he's turned that around three hundred and sixty degrees.

He has an intellect rivalled only by garden tools.

They put brighter heads than his on matchsticks.

He checked out of Hotel Brainy years ago.

If he were any smarter, he'd be retarded.

It is unclear which of Newton's three laws of motion keeps his ears apart.

He is as thick as pig dung and twice as smelly.

He has a one-track mind and the traffic on it is very light.

You've heard of class A drugs – well he's a class A idiot.

He knows so little and knows it so fluently. – Ellen Glasgow

He is a man of few words and doesn't know what either of them means.

His mind works like lightning – one brilliant flash and it's gone.

If he had half a mind to do anything, it would be a considerable improvement.

His mind displays the independent thought process of the average lemming.

Whatever anyone says to him goes in one ear and out the other because there is nothing blocking traffic.

The only time he has something on his mind is when he wears a hat.

He is an inspiration to botched lobotomy patients everywhere.

His very existence provides strong evidence for the theory of the missing link.

He must have been dropped on his head as a child.

He is the result of centuries of careful inbreeding.

She nearly lives up to her full potential as a dumb blonde.

An intellect devourer attacked him and left him starving.

The only thing he took up in school was space.

It's wrong to call him stupid. He's got more brains in his little finger than he has in his entire head.

In the shopping mall of the mind, he's in the toy store.

He has the attention span of an overripe grapefruit.

Sometimes it is difficult to tell if he has an ace up his sleeve or if the ace is missing from his deck altogether.

He used to go to school with his dog. Then they were separated. His dog graduated! — Henny Youngman

He lost his boarding pass to a higher plane.

He hasn't got enough sense to come in out of the rain.

He has a mind like a steel sieve.

He's got a marvellous substitute for his lack of brains — it's called silence.

People say he is the perfect idiot. I say that he's not perfect, but he is doing all right.

Some folks are wise and some are otherwise. — Tobias George Smollett

It would take him five minutes to boil a three-minute egg.

He never graduated from college, because he was only there for two terms — Truman's and Eisenhower's.

He's about as bright as a tulip bulb.

His mind would be unstable, even if mounted on a tripod.

His reaction time is longer than his attention span.

Guillotining him would only make an aesthetic difference.

He's always lost in thought — it's unfamiliar territory.

He was hypnotised as a child and nobody has been able to wake up.

She has a photogenic memory.

Anything preying on his mind would starve to death.

If he donated his body to science, it would set civilization back half a century.

He has the intellectual capacity of the average amoeba.

He ought to have a ''This Space To Let'' sign on his forehead.

He can be outwitted by a lettuce.

He is so stupid you can't trust him with an idea. — John Steinbeck

If you stand close enough to him, you can hear the ocean.

His mouth is in gear but his brain is in neutral.

He doesn't have the brain power to toast a crouton.

Fog rolled in the day he was born and a bit of it never rolled out.

His IQ is lower than a snake's belly.

If he had half a brain, his ass would be lopsided.

He should never worry about Alzheimer's because he doesn't have a mind to lose.

He's immune to caffeine and all other stimulants.

You could write everything he knows on the back of an envelope and still have room for your shopping list.

He skipped school only once. It turned out to be the day they taught everything.

He is not easily confused with someone intelligent.

He keeps his imagination on a long leash.

He has a pulse, but that's about all.

His brain was sold separately and they were out of stock.

Some folks seem to have descended from the chimpanzee later than others. – Kin Hubbard

If his brain were a hard drive, it would back up on a single floppy.

He's the kind of man you would use as a blueprint to build an idiot.

The closest he'll ever get to a brainstorm is a slight drizzle.

His head whistles in a crosswind.

If stupidity hurt, he'd go through life on a morphine drip.

He's so dumb he can't count his balls and get the same answer twice.

His mouth is working overtime, but his mind is on vacation.

He's immune from any serious head injury.

Some people don't hesitate to speak their minds because they have nothing to lose.

His mouth rarely makes calls to his brain.

He is so slow that he takes an hour and a half to watch *Sixty Minutes*.

Had his brain been constructed of silk, he would have been hard-pressed to find the material to make a canary a set of cami-knickers. – P. G. Wodehouse

If he was any slower, he'd be in reverse.

He's about as sharp as a beachball.

He's about as smart as bait.

In the land of the witless, the half-wit is king.

Sometimes he can even think without moving his lips.

Ignorance can be cured, stupid is forever.

If a fool and his money are easily parted, he must be bankrupt.

Ordinarily he is insane. But he has lucid moments when he is only stupid. – Heinrich Heine

He donated his brain to science but they made an early withdrawal.

When you look into his eyes, the only thing you can see is the back of his head.

He is living proof that man can live without a brain.

He's so dumb he couldn't find his butt with two hands and a periscope.

If ignorance is bliss, he must be the happiest person alive.

He's too pointless even to be called a pinhead.

A sharp tongue is no indication of a keen mind.

The eyes are open, the mouth moves, but Mr Brain has long since departed. – *Blackadder*

He had a brain transplant, but the brain rejected *him*.

His mind is so open that ideas simply pass through it.

He was born ignorant and has been losing ground ever since.

He suffers from a bad brains-to-balls ratio.

His brain is as good as new – simply because it's never been used.

He's so open-minded his brains have fallen out.

The twinkle in his eyes is actually the sun shining between his ears.

He forgot to pay his brain bill.

If the government ever declared war on stupidity, he'd get nuked.

He's afraid he'll void his warranty if he thinks too much.

He has the IQ of belly-button fluff.

Some drink from the fountain of knowledge – he just gargled.

His ignorance covers the whole world like a blanket, and there's scarcely a hole in it anywhere. – Mark Twain

If intelligence were rain, he'd be holding an umbrella.

If you gave him a penny for his thoughts, you'd get change.

I don't know what makes him so stupid, but it really works.

You've got the brain of a four-year-old boy, and I'll bet he was glad to get rid of it. – Groucho Marx

He's a person of rare intelligence – it's rare when he shows any.

He couldn't find two St Bernards if they were in the same telephone kiosk as him.

And how many books have you heard in your entire life? The same number as Champion the Wonder Horse! – *Red Dwarf*

He has an IQ of two, and it takes three to grunt.

In his optimum environment, he'd be locked in a life and death struggle with mushrooms.

He qualifies for the mental express line – five thoughts or less.

His brain is running on empty.

He's as smart as a politician is trustworthy.

He can talk to plants on their own level.

You. Have. No. Brain. No judgment calls are necessary. What you think means nothing. What you feel means nothing. – *Swimming With Sharks*

He's got a bungalow mind – nothing upstairs.

He's the world's only surviving brain transplant *donor.*

He fell out of the stupid tree and hit every branch on the way down.

In a battle of wits, he's a pacifist out of necessity.

People around him are at risk from passive stupidity.

God might still use him for miracle practice.

He has all the intellect of a jugged walrus and the social graces of a potty. – *Blackadder*

He is living proof of Einstein's theory that there is no limit to human stupidity.

He's as happy as if he had brains.

He is differently clued.

He doesn't have a brain, just a primitive nerve bundle.

His brain is suing for neglect.

His ignorance is encyclopaedic. – Abba Eban

What he lacks in intelligence, he more than makes up for in stupidity.

He suffers from diarrhoea of the mouth and constipation of ideas.

He has an intellect rivalled only by that of a cabbage.

His brain would rattle around in a gnat's navel.

He is as dense as a London fog.

He has a mind as empty as the sleeping pill concession at a honeymoon hotel.

She never lets ideas interrupt the easy flow of her conversation. – Jean Webster

He has dozens of books in his library and has finished colouring most of them.

He's not a complete idiot – some parts are missing.

When he was a baby his parents must have stood him on his soft spot.

He's not as dumb as he looks, but then again, that would be impossible.

Someone said you could write all he knows on the back of a postage stamp – and you could fold the stamp in half.

Next-day delivery in a nanosecond world. – Van Jacobson

Warning: objects in mirror are dumber than they appear.

APPEARANCE

I never forget a face, but in your case I'll make an exception. – Groucho Marx

I've hated your looks from the start they gave me.

If good looks are a curse, she's blessed.

He looks like a talent scout for a cemetery.

He's so ugly, when you walk by him, your pants start to wrinkle. – Mickey Rivers

When he walks into a room, the mice jump on chairs.

He's got a face like a window cleaner's sponge.

God made Man in his own image, and it would be a sad lookout for Christians throughout the world if God looked anything like you. – *Blackadder*

He has a face that would stop a sundial.

She thinks she's a siren, but she looks more like a false alarm.

Get that ugly, flea-ridden, stinking animal out of my garage, and tell him to take his horse with him! – *Taxi*

In his case, if love isn't blind, it is certainly in need of an eye test.

He's a sight for sore eyes – a real eyesore.

Her face was her chaperone. – Rupert Hughes

He was born ugly and built to last.

She's got a face like a box of smashed crabs.

He's a haemorrhoid on the face of the world.

I saw your mother naked and everything went black. I think my eyes were trying to protect my heart. – *Married . . . With Children*

He has a face that only a fist could love.

Somebody gave him a dirty look once and he's kept it ever since.

He's so hunchbacked he has to look up to tie his shoes.

When Ronnie was really annoyed his face swelled up and turned purple like the rear end of an amorous baboon. – Clive James, *Unreliable Memoirs*

I've seen healthier-looking corpses.

I've got nothing bad to say about him – his face says it all.

My great-aunt Elizabeth ate a box of chocolates every day of her life. She lived to be a hundred and two, and when she had been dead three days, she looked healthier than you do now. – *The Man Who Came To Dinner*

He was such an ugly baby that his incubator had tinted windows.

She's got a face like a busted wart.

He looks like death warmed up, but without the "warmed up" bit.

A blank helpless sort of face, rather like a rose before you drench it with DDT. – John Carey

He's got a face like a squeezed tea bag.

She can't be that two-faced otherwise she wouldn't be wearing that one.

He's got a face like a slapped bottom.

I've seen cuter dimples than hers on a golf ball.

An overdressed woman of forty-seven, with a hooked nose, who was always trying to get herself compromised, but was so peculiarly plain that to her great disappointment no one would ever believe anything against her. – Oscar Wilde, *The Picture of Dorian Gray*

He's so ugly that when he went for a vasectomy, the doctor said, "With a face like that, you don't need one."

He has a very sympathetic face. It has everyone's sympathy.

There's only one problem with his face – it's visible.

I was a lonely child, my sisters refused to play with me because I was so beautiful. Do you know what that's like? No, of course you don't. – *The Golden Girls*

He has one of the few faces that could actually be improved by a stocking mask.

When they said she had a face like a saint, they could only have meant a St Bernard.

He's got a face like a barrel of smashed assholes.

She was at the beauty parlour for five hours – and that was just for the estimate.

Her face reminds me of a flower – a cauliflower.

She got her good looks from her father. He's a plastic surgeon. – Groucho Marx

She should donate her body to science fiction.

I'm all for women who decide to get plastic surgery. Plastic surgery allows you the opportunity to let your outer appearance resemble your inner appearance. Fake. – Daniel Tosh

He looks as if his face was designed in a wind tunnel.

It's not just that the camera doesn't like her – it seems to be waging a hate campaign against her.

Why do you sit there looking like an envelope without any address on it? – Mark Twain

If looks maketh the man, he should sue for shoddy workmanship.

I've seen better-looking road kill.

He always sleeps with his face in the pillow in order to be kind to burglars.

Dreamboat? He's more like a shipwreck.

His face is a waste of molecules.

They say he puts on a brave face, but that's because you have to be brave to put on a face like his.

She's so ugly that when she kissed the Blarney Stone, it spat at her. – Les Dawson

Her face looks as if it's launched a thousand ships . . . by being smashed against the sides instead of a champagne bottle.

You're so ugly, you're uglier than a modern art masterpiece. – *Full Metal Jacket*

He looks as if he has just been dug up.

No wonder he's got a face like a tea bag – he's always in hot water.

A dowdy girl, with one of those characteristic British faces that, once seen, are never remembered. – Oscar Wilde, *The Picture of Dorian Gray*

He's got that faraway look. The farther he gets, the better he looks.

She should be in the movies. She looks better in the dark.

Marry me and I'll never look at another horse. – Groucho Marx, *A Day at the Races*

You look at his face and think: was anybody else hurt in the accident?

He is so ugly he couldn't even pull a muscle.

He looks like King Edward – the potato, not the monarch. – Ian Hislop

I've seen more shapely heads on a hammer.

What God has not given to Antoinette Green, Antoinette Green has had done. – Liza Minnelli, *The Sterile Cuckoo*

He always looks broke. When he buys a copy of *Big Issue*, people take it out of his hand and give him a pound.

She spends her day powdering her face till she looks like a bled pig. – Margot Asquith

Anyone who looks like him ought to be arrested for disturbing the peace.

When a photographer asked her to look straight at the camera she refused because it was her bad side.

My wife asked what it would take to make her look good. I said, "About a mile." – Henny Youngman

I've seen healthier-looking faces on a pirate flag.

He looks like an unmade bed.

The last time I saw anything resembling his face, it was being wiped.

Show them, as only you can, that the female body is not to be appreciated, but to be feared, reviled and in the case of most of you, kept totally covered at all times. – *Married . . . With Children*

Last week I stated that this woman was the ugliest woman I had ever seen. I have since been visited by her sister and now wish to withdraw that statement. – Mark Twain

The only time she had a figure was when she had mumps.

These two are a fastidious couple – she's fast and he's hideous. – Henny Youngman

She's as pretty as a picture . . . by Munch.

He had the sort of face that makes you realize God does have a sense of humour. – Bill Bryson

He's got a face like a picture – it needs hanging.

His face was filled with broken commandments. – John Masefield

He is dark and handsome. When it's dark, he's handsome.

To look at his face, you'd think his hobby was stepping on rakes.

Beauty may only be skin deep, but she's rotten to the core.

Nature played a cruel trick on her by giving her a waxed moustache. – Alan Bennett

She has a face that would fade flowers.

She looks a vision in the evening, but a sight in the morning.

He runs four miles a day and has a body like Mark Spitz. Unfortunately, he still has a face like Ernest Borgnine. – Ellen Burstyn, *Same Time, Next Year*

Some people's looks turn heads; his turn stomachs.

She looks like she dunked her face in a blender.

At first I thought he was walking a dog. Then I realized it was his date. – *Polyester*

If he wants to see a horror show, he only has to look in the mirror.

He has a good weapon against muggers – his face.

She was going to have her face lifted but when she found out the price, she let the whole thing drop.

She has a nice head on her shoulders, but it would look better on a neck.

He's a trellis for varicose veins. – Wilson Mizner

Most people need a licence to be that ugly.

At Christmas I would rather hang her and kiss the mistletoe.

She's got a face like a franked stamp.

They've got a picture of him at the hospital – it saves using the stomach pump.

She had much in common with Hitler, only no moustache. – Noël Coward

She's the only woman to have received a lifetime ban from a beauty parlour.

I've seen better-looking bodies at a car breaker's yard.

She was so ugly she could make a mule back away from an oat bin. – Will Rogers

Every time I find a girl who can cook like my mother, she looks like my father.

She is a peacock in everything but beauty. – Oscar Wilde, *The Picture of Dorian Gray*

She's had her face lifted so many times there's nothing inside her shoes.

His face is used to frighten people with hiccups.

You are without a doubt the most repulsive individual I have ever met. I would shake your hand but I fear it would come off. – *Blackadder*

They say a pretty face is a passport. Well hers expired years ago.

He has a great face for radio.

She got a mudpack and looked great for two days. Then the mud fell off. – Henny Youngman

She must use gunpowder on her face, because it looks shot.

He makes a very handsome corpse and becomes his coffin prodigiously. – Oliver Goldsmith

He used to be a model . . . for gargoyles.

Her face is not likely to turn on many voters. Except perhaps those who are members of the British Horse Society. – John Junor

She's like the Venus de Milo – very pretty but not all there.

She's got bobsled looks – going downhill fast.

Her face looks like she slept in it.

She used to be Miss World: Miss Carpet World. – Mrs Merton

I've seen better-looking bodies dragged out of a river.

She wore far too much rouge last night, and not quite enough clothes. That is always a sign of despair in a woman. – Oscar Wilde, *An Ideal Husband*

The only justification for calling herself highbrow is that she's had her face lifted so many times.

She'd had so many facelifts she pees through her ears.

Her face looked as if it had been made of sugar and someone had licked it. – George Bernard Shaw

She's got a face like a busted sofa.

Body off *Baywatch*, face off *Crimewatch*.

He's a parasite for sore eyes.

You're looking very beautiful tonight – it must be the lighting. – Dame Edna Everage

Hair

His hair was blowing in the breeze – and he was too proud to chase it.

Don't look now but something died on your head.

Where did you get your hair cut? The pet shop? – Henny Youngman

I've seen nicer hair on a mop.

Whenever he goes for a haircut, he asks for an oil change, too.

His hair looked as if it could be put to better use scouring pans.

What's going on with your hair, honey? Looks like you've got mousse and squirrel in there! – *Will and Grace*

It may be an awful haircut but it can't spoil his looks – nature did that years ago.

His hair sticks out so much at the side that people think he's turning right.

When I asked for a trim, I didn't expect to look as if you'd used a hedge-trimmer.

He uses so much gel that he can't let his hair down without three days' notice.

Why don't you get a haircut? You look like a chrysanthemum.

His hairline isn't receding – his hair is just trying to get away from his ugly face.

I've seen more hair on a pork chop.

He is so bald, Mr Clean is jealous.

He is so bald, he took a shower and got brainwashed.

He is so bald that when he put on a roll-neck sweater, people thought he was a deodorant stick.

He is so bald you can play air hockey on his head.

He is so bald you could draw a line down the middle of his head and it would look like his ass.

He is so bald he looks like a blown-up condom.

He is so bald, his only hope is that hair continues growing after death.

He is so bald, you can actually see what's on his mind.

He's not really bald – he's just got a tall face.

People are always dazzled when they see him – but only by the sun reflecting off his shiny head.

He has wavy hair – and it's waving goodbye.

His hairline has been badly hit by the recession.

The only thing Charles remembers fondly about his childhood is his hair. – *M*A*S*H*

He is so thin and bald that when his head catches the sun, he looks like an unused match.

He is so angry and bald that he is like a sore with a bare head.

I've seen more hair on a billiard ball.

He has so few hairs on his head that the teeth of his comb are set six inches apart.

He has so few hairs on his head that his comb doesn't need teeth, it just has gums.

The most expensive haircut he ever had cost ten dollars . . . and nine dollars went on the search fee.

She dyes her hair so much, her driver's licence has a colour wheel. – Joan Rivers

The only reason anyone would call her a pussycat is that she's dyed nine times.

Some women are blonde on their mother's side, some from their father's side; she is from peroxide.

She was what we used to call a suicide blonde – dyed by her own hand. – Saul Bellow

Some women have a smell under their nose – she has a moustache under hers.

Her hair is so rough, even Moses couldn't part it.

Her hair is so rough that instead of teeth her comb has dentures.

Don't point that beard at me – it might go off. – Groucho Marx

You know what you are? You're a beard with an idiot hanging off it. – *Black Books*

Skin

He's so pale, the only way he can get colour into his face is by sticking his tongue out.

He's so pale, he looks like he gave his pallbearers the slip.

He's so pale, he looks like an undertaker started work on him but was suddenly called away.

She always looks so immaculate – not a wrinkle out of place.

He's got so many freckles, his face looks like a hamburger bun.

His face is so wrinkled, he should have it pressed.

She's got the sort of neck you normally see on a carving dish at Christmas.

One more wrinkle and she'd pass for a prune.

Her skin was as white as leprosy. – Samuel Taylor Coleridge

She has so many wrinkles, she has to screw her hat on.

Her acne was so bad, blind people tried to read her face. – Joan Rivers

She has a face like a million dollars – green and wrinkled.

Eyes

He may be cross-eyed but at least he can watch TV in stereo.

(His) appearance was not prepossessing. He had but one eye, and the popular prejudice runs in favour of two. – Charles Dickens

I've seen glass eyes that are more sympathetic than his.

The bags under his eyes exceed the Pan Am allowance.

She's had her face lifted so many times that whenever she raises her eyebrows she pulls up her stockings.

She's had so much surgery done, her eyes are like George Michael's ass cheeks – they never close. – Joan Rivers

I've seen nicer eyes in a potato.

Her eyes are like pools – sunken and watery.

My wife has lovely coloured eyes. I particularly like the blue one. – Bob Monkhouse

She is so cross-eyed, she has to sit sideways at the cinema.

She is so cross-eyed that when she has sex, she thinks it's a threesome.

His nickname is "Isiah", because one eye's 'igher than the other.

Breasts

She's so flat-chested she's jealous of walls.

She's so flat-chested you could fax her.

She's so flat-chested, she's the only woman in the world with two backs.

Her breasts are so small she had to tattoo "front" on her chest.

She's got tits like a spaniel's ears.

When she doesn't wear a bra, it looks like two bulldogs fighting in a sack.

A new sports bra recently went on sale that features a special pocket to hold an iPod. In fact, I saw a woman today who looked like she was carrying at least twenty thousand songs. – Conan O'Brien

Her breasts are so big, they could shade two midgets at high noon.

With those whoppers, she should work at Burger King.

When she burned her bra, there was enough heat to power a small town in Texas for six weeks.

Her breasts are so enormous they carry a government health warning.

Her boobs are like a photo finish in a Zeppelin race.

Legs and Feet

The last time I saw legs like that, one of them had a message tied to it.

The last time I saw legs like that, they were supporting a table on *Antiques Roadshow*.

His feet are so big, his shoes need licence plates.

There's so much dry skin on his feet that it looks as if he kicks flour for a living.

She was so bow legged she couldn't stop a pig in an alleyway.

His feet are so big he can stamp out bushfires.

She has calves that only a cow would like.

She's got very sporting legs – like those of a rugby prop forward.

Are those your own feet or are you breaking them in for a clown?

Mouth

His mouth is so big he speaks in Dolby surround sound.

She's had so much bridge work that anyone who kisses her has to pay a toll.

She has such a big mouth that she goes bobbing for basketballs.

If his mouth were any bigger, he wouldn't have any face to wash.

He's got a smile like a crocodile with wind.

His tongue is so long that when it hangs out, people think it's his tie.

His teeth are like stars – they come out at night.

I've seen better teeth on a worn-out gearbox.

His teeth are so yellow, they call him the man with the golden teeth.

His teeth are like the Ten Commandments – all broken.

He snores so loudly his wife has to turn him away from the window so he doesn't inhale the curtains.

He's got a grin like a split watermelon.

The last time I saw a mouth like that, it had a hook in it.

He's got summer teeth – summer in his mouth, summer in his pocket.

She's got lips like two red slugs fighting in a bag of flour.

He had a winning smile, but everything else was a loser. – George C. Scott

She is so conceited that she has her dental X-rays retouched.

Her lips are so big that when she smiles, she wets her hair.

She must have stretched her mouth so wide by putting her foot in it all the time.

Her lips remind me of petals – bicycle pedals.

I wonder what she's going to use for a mouth when the gorilla wants its arse back.

Nose

He has so many nose rings that the only thing attracted to him is a magnet.

She only walks with her nose in the air so that she doesn't have to smell herself.

His nose is so long he comes around the corner and thirty seconds later the rest of him follows.

His nose is so sharp he's not allowed to take it on airplanes.

His nose is so long it gives Pinocchio an inferiority complex.

His nose is so long he makes Pinocchio look like a cat.

His nose is so long that ants live in constant fear of him.

I'd break his nose, but I've only got two hands. – *The Odd Couple*

His nose is so big the last time I saw one like it, it was attached to an elephant.

His nose is so big you could go bowling with his boogers.

His nose is so big he needs an axe to pick it.

His nose is so big there's still snow on it in summertime.

His nose is so big it has a basement.

His nose is so big it's more muscular than he is.

His nose is so big it doesn't have veins, it has pipes.

His nose is so big he keeps knocking people off bicycles.

His nose is so big it has its own moon.

His nose is so big that the last time he sneezed two hundred people were made homeless.

His nose is so big it graduated from high school a year ahead of the rest of him.

His nose is so big he has to call it Mr Nose in front of company.

His nose is so big ships use it to find their way into harbour.

His nose is so big it seats six.

His nose is so big he has to sit in the front row of the cinema.

His nose is so big you can ski down it.

His nose is so big he has to check it in as luggage when he flies.

His nose is so big Stephen Hawking has a theory about it.

His nose is so big it puts half the street in shade.

His nose is so big it lives next door to the rest of him.

His nose is so big it won't return Steven Spielberg's calls.

His nose is so big it has its own gravity.

His nose is so big it has a spine.

His nose is so big and pointed, he doesn't just keep it to the grindstone, they use it *as* a grindstone.

He's not only got a Roman nose, it's roamin' all over his face.

With a nose like that, the first thing you want to ask her is, "Where did you park your broomstick?"

She has eyes like two limpid pools – and a nose like a diving board.

He is so constipated he farts through his nose.

Doesn't know much, but leads the league in nostril hair. – Josh Billings

Is that his nose or is he eating a banana?

Her only flair is in her nostrils. – Pauline Kael

Ears

His ears are so big he gets satellite reception.

There's enough wax in his ears to put a shine on a Chrysler.

His ears are so big he has to drive with the windows down.

His ears are so full of wax you could stick a wick in and light them.

His ears are so big, people keep asking him where Noddy is.

His ears are so big he can hear you thinking.

He could swat flies with those ears.

His ears are so big he can hear sign language.

He's got ears like a hatstand.

His ears are so big, he was Dumbo's stunt double.

With his jug ears, he looks like the FA Cup.

Weight

He is on a seafood diet: whenever he sees food he eats it.

He's so unfit. The only exercise he gets is trying to join the human race.

He's so fat, he can be his own running mate. – Johnny Carson

He has learned to take every setback in life on his chins.

His problem is that all those square meals have made him round.

I said to my girlfriend, "You shouldn't eat before you swim." She said, "Why not?" I said, "You look fat." – Jimmy Carr

He's like spoilt milk – fat and chunky.

He's the ideal weight for his height – but only if his next career move is to become a sumo wrestler.

Although no man is an island, he comes close.

He certainly watches his weight. He has it right out in front of him, where he can see it.

He has to work out to look only fat.

He has a big heart and a stomach to match.

He liked his first chin so much that he added two more.

I can see you now, bending over a hot stove. But I can't see the stove. – Groucho Marx

He used to look like a Chippendale; now he looks more like a Clydesdale.

He used to be quite athletic – big chest, hard stomach. But that's all behind him now.

I'm not saying she's overweight, but her job used to be kick starting jumbo jets. – Les Dawson

His belt is supposed to buckle, not the chair.

He was so disgusted with a magazine photo depicting him as a big fat slob that he ate the first fifty thousand copies.

He had double chins all the way down to his stomach. – Mark Twain

They say that travel broadens one. He must have been around the world.

I remember him when he only had one stomach.

He's not only larger than life, he's larger than just about everything.

He's got more chins than the Chinese telephone directory.

When it comes to discussing his obesity, people don't tiptoe around him any more – besides, it's too long a journey.

He must have had a magnificent build before his stomach went in for a career of its own. – Margaret Halsey

He's got so many double chins he looks as if he's peering over a pile of pancakes.

He's so thin that when he goes through a turnstile, nothing registers.

He's so skinny that when he turns sideways he disappears.

He's so thin he looks like a stick with ears.

He's so thin, I've seen more meat on a skeleton.

He's so thin he can put his shorts on from either end.

He's so skinny that when he wears a black suit he looks like a rolled umbrella.

He's so skinny, he looks like he went to give blood and forgot to say "when".

He's so skinny, he looks like a mummy with its wrappings off.

If he were any thinner, he'd only have one eye.

He's so weak he couldn't lick a postage stamp.

He's so weak that when he lets the bath water out, he can barely fight the current.

He's so weak he couldn't fight his way out of a wet paper bag.

He's so weak he can't even throw a tantrum.

He's so weak that if you dropped a toothpick on his foot, he'd end up with a stress fracture.

He's so weak that if he tried to whip cream, the cream would win.

Some people can tear phone books in half but he'd have trouble with a wet Kleenex.

She's got a body like a steam train engine – but without the tender behind.

She's a big-hearted girl with hips to match. – Henny Youngman

She could lose ten pounds of ugly fat just by cutting her head off.

She has so many chins that she uses a bookmark to find her mouth.

She could have been Miss World but for her two feet – twelve inches on each hip.

She says she's watching her figure – presumably through a wide-angle lens.

She says she's been watching her figure, but obviously not closely enough.

She says she's been watching her figure, but it looks as if parts of it are trying to escape.

She says she's watching her figure, but with hips like that she's the only one that is.

It's like cuddling with a butterball turkey. – Jeff Foxworthy

Some figures stop traffic – hers just blocks it.

She has a memory like an elephant and a figure to match.

Even her double chin has a double chin.

Some men climb mountains, others date 'em. – *Taxi*

Her hips are so big that at parties people put their drinks on them.

She's a real oomph girl. When she sits on a sofa, it goes oomph!

I was out with a friend and he came over with a pair of girls. I said to him, "They're like buses." He said, "What, because you wait ages and then two come along at once?" I said, "No, they *are* like buses!" – Jimmy Carr

She measures 36-24-36 . . . but that's her forearm, neck, and thigh.

She has all the grace and elegance of a beached whale.

She had a visit from the fat fairy and used all her wishes.

She had not only kept her lovely figure, she's added so much to it. – Bob Fosse

She has an hourglass figure but the sand has settled in the wrong place.

Her figure described a set of parabolas that could cause cardiac arrest in a yak. – Woody Allen

She may claim to be fit as a fiddle but her shape is more reminiscent of a double bass.

Her measurements were 38, 24, 36 . . . but not necessarily in that order.

She has flabby thighs, but fortunately her stomach covers them.

Her figure is not so much hourglass as brandy glass.

Whatever anyone says, men who like fat girls belong on a late-night Channel 4 documentary. – Chris Moyles

She worries about the calories in licking stamps and envelopes.

She is so obsessed with being thin, she worries that her tampon might make her look fat.

If she was any thinner, you could pick locks with her.

To want to be size zero, you need an IQ to match.

Height

He is so short that when it rains he is always the last one to know.

He's so short that if he pulled his socks up, he'd be blindfolded.

He's a little man, that's his trouble. Never trust a man with short legs – brains too near their bottoms. – Noël Coward

His arms are so short that he has to tilt his head to scratch his ear.

Good things may come in small packages, but so does poison.

He's so small that when he plays nine holes of golf, he birdies five and falls down four.

He's so short, he would need to grow six inches even to qualify for short person complex.

He's so small he's a waste of skin. – Fred Allen

He's so short that the last time he went camping he used a condom for a sleeping bag.

He's so short he has turn-ups on his boxer shorts.

He was so small when he was born that his father handed out cigar butts.

Clothes

He was a tubby little chap who looked as if he had been poured into his clothes and had forgotten to say "when". – P.G. Wodehouse

He likes to wear shoes that match his personality. That's why he always wears sneakers.

Looking at him, I've seen better-dressed crabs.

When I see a man of shallow understanding extravagantly clothed, I feel sorry – for the clothes. – Josh Billings

He has underwear that is older than Justin Timberlake.

You can tell he's wearing an Italian suit – by the spaghetti Bolognese all down the front.

Jealousy is a very ugly thing, Dorothy. And so are you in anything backless. – *The Golden Girls*

What a lovely dress! And obviously such an old favourite. – Dame Edna Everage

It probably cost her a lot of money to look that cheap.

Do you prefer "fashion victim" or "ensembly challenged"? – *Clueless*

That jacket would have looked better on a potato.

He's the only guy I know who does his clothes shopping at the San Diego Zoo: he puts five animals in the endangered species list with one outfit. – Bob Brenly

Does Barry Manilow know you raided his wardrobe? – *The Breakfast Club*

Either her dress is too short or she's in it too far.

She always looks stressed and worn out, and the same can be said of her clothes. – *What Not To Wear*

His socks remind me of golf wear – there's a hole in one.

She looks like she got dressed in front of an airplane propeller.

With his dress sense, the only jacket he should be seen in is a straitjacket.

I don't care what everybody says. That dress does *not* make you look like a hooker. – *Buffy the Vampire Slayer*

She bought that dress for a ridiculous figure – hers.

You've been getting dressed for three hours and you still look like a bloated citrus fruit. – *Absolutely Fabulous*

She's wearing one of those atomic outfits – it has seventy-five percent fallout.

A four-hundred-dollar suit on him would look like socks on a rooster. – Earl Long

His voice is even louder than his tie.

His shoes are so big that when he goes skiing, he doesn't need to hire any skis.

That's an interesting jacket. Does Worzel Gummidge want it back?

Communists all seem to wear small caps, a look I consider better suited to tubes of toothpaste than to people. – Fran Lebowitz

I wonder why older women feel they should dress in beige? Beige clothes, beige hair, beige skin; they look like pale liquid toffees. – Mary Wesley

A hat should be taken off when you greet a lady and left off for the rest of your life. – P. J. O'Rourke, *Modern Manners*

I've seen wounds better dressed than him.

How did you get into that dress – with a spray gun? – Bob Hope

No, there's nothing wrong with that tie except that it's not tight enough around his neck. He can still breathe.

For fifty years pyjamas were manufactured almost exclusively in broad coloured stripes which reduced men's attractiveness in the bedroom to that of multi-coloured zebras. – Mary Eden

He has a suit for every day of the year – and that's it.

I used to be just like you, I made my own clothes. And just like you, I was not very good at it. — Dame Edna Everage

She looked as if she had thrown something on . . . and missed.

That dress fits her like a glove. It's a shame it doesn't fit her like a dress.

What a lovely hat! But I may make one teensy suggestion? If it blows off, don't chase it. — Miss Piggy

If fashion law were ever enforced, he would be found guilty without any hope of parole.

She was a large woman who seemed not so much dressed as upholstered. J. M. Barrie

She was a curious woman, whose dresses always looked as if they had been designed in a rage and put on in a tempest. — Oscar Wilde, *The Picture of Dorian Gray*

What a lovely hat — and so versatile. If you tire of it, you can always use it as a flowerpot.

Whatever look she was aiming for, she missed.

Your right to wear a mint-green polyester leisure suit ends when it meets my eye. — Fran Lebowitz

She dresses like she doesn't have any gay friends.

I never saw anybody take so long to dress, and with such little result. — Oscar Wilde, *The Importance of Being Earnest*

She looked as if she'd wrinkled her clothes and ironed her face.

That's a nice top. There must be a Cortina going around without seat covers. — Jim Davidson

What a nice dress. One day it may come back into fashion.

You couldn't tell if she was dressed for an opera or an operation. — Irvin S. Cobb

The reason she reached the top is because her clothes didn't.

One cannot say she was dressed. She was clothed. And so uncertainly that it was unsure she would remain even that. — Ivy Compton-Burnett

Her clothes look good, considering the shape they're on.

A perfect saint amongst women, but so dreadfully dowdy that she reminded me of a badly bound hymn book. – Oscar Wilde, *The Picture of Dorian Gray*

They said that dress looked much better on. On what? On fire?

Her hat is a creation that will never go out of style. It will look ridiculous year after year. – Fred Allen

She looks as if she dresses with a pitchfork in the morning.

I'm trying to think of a word to describe your outfit . . . affordable. – Dame Edna Everage

Just because it's your size doesn't mean you have to wear it.

She wears her clothes as if they were thrown on with a pitchfork. – Jonathan Swift

That dress is a nice sturdy fabric. And how sensible of you to take the rings out first.

Oh, what a pretty dress – and so cheap! – Zsa Zsa Gabor

PROMISCUITY

If all the girls attending the Yale prom were laid end to end, I wouldn't be at all surprised. – Dorothy Parker

She's a carpenter's dream – flat as a board and so easy to nail.

She has been under more sailors than a nautical toilet. – *The Golden Girls*

The difference between her and a bowling ball is you can only put three fingers in a bowling ball.

She has been around the block so many times she has worn a groove.

She's the original good time that was had by all. – Bette Davis

She bangs like the toilet door on a trawler.

She's had more men than the Grand Old Duke of York.

Albert Schweitzer spent less time than her in the missionary position.

At least my mother's not on the cover of *Crack Whore* magazine. – *South Park*

If sex were fast food, there'd be an arch over her bed.

She won't stand for oral sex – she prefers to kneel down for it.

Dorothy, I don't like you being taken advantage of by some guy out of town. At least when Blanche does it, it's good for tourism. – *The Golden Girls*

Every day she goes for a tramp in the woods – and he's getting pretty exhausted by it all.

She has had more hands up her dress than the Muppets.

Her legs are open so much, her knees are in different time zones.

She used to stand by the side of the road with a sign, "Last girl before freeway."

That woman speaks eight languages and can't say "no" in any of them. – Dorothy Parker

Her idea of safe sex is a padded dashboard.

Imogene, come on! I've known you for twenty years now and all I can say is that if God were handing out sexually transmitted diseases as punishment for sex, you'd be at the free clinic all the time. – *Designing Women*

Nobody knows what her right leg would say to her left leg because they've never met.

She's had more members than the Senate.

She has been kissed as often as a police court Bible, and by much the same class of people. – Robertson Davies

She's like a TV set – any fool can turn her on.

She's like a hardware store – only ten cents a screw.

She's like a bus – only fifty cents a ride.

She's like a 747 – a three-man cock pit.

She's like a Hoover – she sucks, blows, and finally gets laid in the closet.

She's like a doorknob – everyone gets a turn.

She's like a public phone box – on every corner and costs only thirty-five cents a go.

She's like a Workmate – accepts tools of all sizes.

She's like a Christmas tree – everybody hangs balls on her.

She's like a stamp – you lick her, then stick her, then finally send her away.

She's like a railroad track – she gets laid all over the country.

She's like the Pillsbury dough boy – everybody loves to poke her.

She's like a race car driver – she burns a lot of rubbers.

She's like a moped – everybody's riding her but nobody's admitting it.

She's like peanut butter – smooth, creamy, and easy to spread.

She's like a birthday cake – everybody gets a piece.

She's like Humpty Dumpty – first she gets humped, then she gets dumped.

She's like a stiff door – a couple of bangs and she starts to loosen up.

She's like a hurricane – she blows and blows and blows.

She's like a carpet – a rough shag.

She's like a ketchup bottle – everyone gets a squeeze out of her.

She's like a chicken coop – cocks flying in and out all day.

She's like a bubblegum machine – five cents a blow.

She's like a squirrel – always got some nuts in her mouth.

She's like Blockbuster Video – everybody goes home happy.

She's like a streetlamp – you can find her turned on at night on any street corner.

She's like a restaurant – she only takes deliveries in the rear.

She's like a basketball hoop – everyone gets a shot.

She's like a turtle – once she's on her back she's fucked.

She's like a gas station – you've got to pay before you pump.

She's like a telephone – even a three-year-old could pick her up.

She's like a dollar bill – she gets passed from man to man.

She's like a pool table – give five cents and she'll rack your balls.

She's like a Chinese restaurant – $8.95, all you can eat.

She's like the Bermuda Triangle – she swallows a whole lot of seamen.

She's like an escalator – guys go up and down on her all day.

She's like a shotgun – five cocks and she's loaded.

She's like a train – guys climb on and off her all day long.

She's like a refrigerator – everyone likes to put their meat in her.

She's like a dose of diarrhoea – fast and loose.

She's like a golf course in the dark – it's hard to tell one hole from another.

She's like an ice lolly – everyone wants a lick.

She's like a national radio station – easy to pick up.

She's like a bowling ball – she gets picked up, fingered, thrown into the gutter, yet still she comes back for more.

Prostitution gives her an opportunity to meet people. – Joseph Heller

When she went to the doctor, he examined her and said, "Stay out of bed for two days."

Everyone knows you're the biggest ride outside Alton Towers. – *Birds of a Feather*

She doesn't go for a particular type – anything with an Adam's apple is her type.

My girlfriend's reading a book called *Women Who Love Too Much*, which I think should have the title shortened to *Sluts*. – Jimmy Carr

She's had more pricks than a second-hand dartboard.

She was fired from her job at the sperm bank after her boss caught her drinking on the job.

I know exactly how you feel, my dear. The morning after always does look grim if you happen to be wearing last night's dress. – Ina Claire, *Ninotchka*

She has been laid more often than badly fitted linoleum.

The last time she made love she said, 'Was it good for you?' 'Yes,' said the Navy.

Her legs are like Christmas Day and New Year's Day – always apart, and everyone gets to see her between the holidays.

Oh, knock it off, Blanche! Not all of us are classified by the Navy as a friendly port! – Dorothy, *The Golden Girls*

She's the sort of girl who doesn't stall when her boyfriend's car does.

What makes her so popular are her tight clothes and loose habits.

She's made more passes than the Denver Broncos.

She has a wash and wear bridal gown. – Henny Youngman

When you tell her she sucks, she takes it as a compliment.

She's seen more ceilings than Michelangelo.

She's a walking sperm bank.

She's kissed so many sailors, her lips move in and out with the tide.

She's offered her body to science. Time and time again. – *M*A*S*H*

She drives a car with a sunroof because there's more leg room.

Her legs are like a twenty-four-hour store – open all day and open all night.

When she was growing up, her role model was a mattress.

Remember, men, we're fighting for this woman's honour, which is probably more than she ever did. – Groucho Marx, *Duck Soup*

The only word she cries out during orgasm is "Next!"

Is your vagina in the New York City guidebook? It should be, it's always open. – *Sex and the City*

She's been mounted more times in a day than a seaside donkey at the height of the holiday season.

Her idea of fidelity is not having more than one man in the bed at the same time.

He hasn't only got a roving eye, it goes on full scale expeditions.

His eye doesn't so much wander, it does marathons.

There's a name for you ladies, but it isn't used in high society – outside of a kennel. – Joan Crawford, *The Women*

The difference between her and a 747 is that not everyone's been on a 747.

She works on the principle that girls who always do right always get left.

She wears hoop earrings so that she's got somewhere to rest her ankles.

She's been on more laps than a napkin. – Walter Winchell

The only difference between her and a deckchair is it's hard to get a deckchair's legs open.

In order to avoid being called a flirt, she always yielded easily. – Charles Maurice de Talleyrand

Her virtue was something like the nine lives of a cat.

Many a woman has a past, but I am told that she has at least a dozen. – Oscar Wilde, *Lady Windermere's Fan*

She was so bad in bed, flies used to think she was dead.

She is a virgin in a world where men will turn to soft fruit for pleasure. – *Absolutely Fabulous*

AGE

Pushing forty? She's clinging on for dear life. – Ivy Compton-Burnett

His neck is so wrinkled you could use it as a cheese grater.

His bones are so creaky that when he gets up in the morning, it sounds like he's making popcorn.

He's so old he needs a jump cable to get started.

He was either a man of about a hundred and fifty who was rather young for his years, or a man of about a hundred and ten who had been aged by trouble. – P. G. Wodehouse

If things get better with age, he's approaching excellent.

Thirty-five is a very attractive age. London society is full of women of the very highest birth who have, of their own free choice, remained thirty-five for years. Lady Dumbleton is an instance in point. To my own knowledge she has been thirty-five ever since she arrived at the age of forty, which was many years ago now. – Oscar Wilde, *The Importance of Being Earnest*

Time may heal a lot of things but it hasn't done him much good.

You know you're getting old when you get that one candle on the cake. It's like, "See if you can blow this out." – Jerry Seinfeld

He's so old and decrepit that when he is nervous he doesn't get butterflies any more, he gets moths.

You know you're getting old when you go back to your class reunion and they serve prune punch. – Chi Chi Rodriguez

It takes him longer to rest these days than it does to get tired.

He's so old he doesn't even buy green bananas any more.

That dame is older than the Continental Shelf! – *Taxi*

These days he just exhausts himself by grappling with temptation.

The gods have bestowed on him the gift of perpetual old age. – Oscar Wilde

If she was a building, she'd be condemned.

She's approaching forty – but from the wrong direction.

She may be old, but she still parties like it's 1899.

To her way of thinking, birthdays are occasions when her husband takes a day off and she takes a year off.

It's Frank's birthday, I wonder how old he is. Let's saw him in half tonight and count his rings. – *M*A*S*H*

A woman is as old as she looks before breakfast.

She could pass for a woman twice her age.

She always remembers her age exactly – she ought to, it's been the same since she was thirty-nine.

She could age herself by twenty years just by telling the truth.

She may well pass for forty-three – in the dusk, with a light behind her. – W. S. Gilbert

She finally admitted her age, although she forgot to say how many years ago she reached it.

She's chasing her lost youth but shows no sign of catching it.

She has what it takes – the only problem is she's had it too long.

She's way past her sell-by date.

Forty has been a difficult age for her to get past. In fact it's taken seven years to the best of my knowledge.

Take a close-up of a woman past sixty! You might as well use a picture of a relief map of Ireland. – Nancy Astor

A wife of forty should be like money. You should be able to change her for two of twenty.

Doesn't she look fabulous? She doesn't look a day over ninety. – Arnold Schwarzenegger on mother-in-law Eunice Kennedy Shriver, aged eighty-five

FOOD FOR THOUGHT

She did not so much cook food as assassinate it.

What's on the plate, in case I have to describe it to my doctor?

All it needs is a little salt, pepper, mustard, ketchup, sauce, flavour. – M*A*S*H

She's such a bad cook that she uses the smoke alarm as a timer.

She's such a bad cook that when she throws a dinner party, the local Fire Brigade cancel all leave.

She's such a bad cook that even the cockroaches eat out.

She's such a bad cook that dinner guests cheer if the gravy moves.

She's such a bad cook that when she makes tuna noodle surprise, the surprise is that it glows in the dark and melts the silverware.

She's such a bad cook that her family use her flapjacks as Odor Eaters.

She's such a bad cook that when her family go on a picnic, the ants bring indigestion tablets.

She's such a bad cook that her pie filling bubbles over and eats the enamel off the bottom of the oven.

She's such a bad cook that even her TV-dinners are repeats.

She's such a bad cook that her cat has only three lives left.

She's such a bad cook that last year the Health Department condemned her meatloaf.

She's such a bad cook that her family's idea of a Happy Meal is one she hasn't prepared.

She's such a bad cook her family buy Alka Seltzer in bulk.

She's such a bad cook that when she barbecues, two of her kids stand by with water cannons while the third holds the phone with 911 on speed dial.

She's such a bad cook that her microwave displays "Help!"

She's such a bad cook that the only thing you get for dessert is indigestion.

She's such a bad cook that her two best recipes are meatloaf and apple pie, but her dinner guests can't tell which is which.

She's such a bad cook that her dog goes to the neighbours' house to eat.

She's such a bad cook that her family pray *after* they eat.

She's such a bad cook she can't boil water without supervision.

She's such a bad cook that her guests check their life insurance before a dinner party.

She's such a bad cook that pest control companies keep begging her for her recipes.

She's such a bad cook that her home-made scones are considered offensive weapons.

She's such a bad cook she could burn salad.

She's such a bad cook, her caramel surprise turned out to be a nasty shock.

She's such a bad cook her gravy boat sank.

She's such a bad cook that even homeless people turn down an invitation to dinner.

She's such a bad cook she considers it a culinary triumph if the pop-tart stays in one piece.

She's such a bad cook that the authorities insist all her garbage cans are marked with biohazard symbols.

She's such a bad cook that she's used three boxes of scouring pads, a bottle of Cillit Bang and a crowbar, but that macaroni and cheese still won't let go of the pan.

She's such a bad cook that her family automatically head for the dinner table every time they hear a fire engine siren.

She's such a bad cook that ice hockey teams use her home-made burgers as pucks.

She's such a bad cook that even Oliver Twist declined seconds.

My wife is the worst cook in the world. After dinner, I don't brush my teeth, I count them. – Rodney Dangerfield

My mother is such a lousy cook that Thanksgiving at her house is a time of sorrow. – Rita Rudner

Please rearrange the contents of this plate so that someone in the latest stages of malnutrition will at least take a passing interest in it. – *Chef!*

His kitchen is famous – it's where flies go to commit suicide.

Is this rice, or were they maggots?

He's a great cook, if you happen to have lost all your tastebuds.

My wife dresses to kill. She cooks the same way. – Henny Youngman

The lamb was so rare that a decent vet could have had it back on its feet again.

The meat wasn't just overdone, it was cremated.

Yes, it was a lovely meal. Do you have a stomach pump handy?

His friends threw him a big dinner – too bad it missed.

I told you the food here should not be taken internally. – *M*A*S*H*

SNAPS

Yo Mama's so fat, when she gets on the scale it says, "To be continued."

Yo Mama's so fat she's got the only car in town with stretch marks.

Yo Mama's so fat she can't even jump to a conclusion.

Yo Mama's so fat I had to take a train and two buses just to get on her good side.

Yo Mama's so fat when a ball hit her on the head, the ball burst.

Yo Mama's so fat, when she sits around the house, she sits *around the house*.

Yo Mama's so fat she could sell shade.

Yo Mama's so fat her knickers need guy ropes.

Yo Mama's so fat that when they put her on the Cambridge diet, she ate half of Cambridge.

Yo Mama's so fat that when she has sex, she has to give directions.

Yo Mama's so fat that when she walks across the living room, the radio skips.

Yo Mama's so fat she wears a microwave as a beeper.

Yo Mama's so fat she has to wear a three-piece bathing suit.

Yo Mama's so fat her ass has its own congressman.

Yo Mama's so fat you have to take three steps back just to see all of her.

Yo Mama's so fat I ran round her twice and got lost.

Yo Mama's so fat she needs a hula hoop to keep her socks up.

Yo Mama's so fat she plays Frisbee with UFOs.

Yo Mama's so fat she gets runs in her jeans.

Yo Mama's so fat she has more rolls than the town bakery.

Yo Mama's so fat her belly button doesn't have lint, it has sweaters.

Yo Mama's so fat, she fell in love and broke it.

Yo Mama's so fat she needs one barstool for each butt cheek.

Yo Mama's so fat that when she walked down the aisle with her groom, they had to walk single file.

Yo Mama's so fat this town really *isn't* big enough for the both of us.

Yo Mama's so fat the back of her neck looks like a pack of hot dogs.

Yo Mama's so fat she has three shirt sizes: extra large, extra extra large, and "Oh my God, it's coming towards us!"

Yo Mama's so fat, even her shadow has stretch marks.

Yo Mama's so fat that when she walks, her butt claps.

Yo Mama's so fat, you could house three homeless families in one of her sweaters.

Yo Mama's so fat that when she went to a dating service, they matched her up with Pittsburgh.

Yo Mama's so fat, her belly button holds two gallons of water.

Yo Mama's so fat she plays hopscotch like this: LA, Detroit, Chicago, New York.

Yo Mama's so fat she pulls up a chair to an "all you can eat" buffet.

Yo Mama's so fat she uses pillow cases when she runs out of socks.

Yo Mama's so fat that when she steps on the scale, it says, "One at a time, please."

Yo Mama's so fat it takes five people to give her a cuddle.

Yo Mama's so fat her car is made out of spandex.

Yo Mama's so fat that at ninety degrees, she smells like bacon.

Yo Mama's so fat that if you wrung out her sweat, you'd flood Missouri.

Yo Mama's so fat she got a job as team coach – not because she knew anything about football but because she could carry twenty people (eight standing).

Yo Mama's so fat, the only thing attracted to her is gravity.

Yo Mama's so fat she sat on a rowing machine and it sank.

Yo Mama's so fat she sat on the Bible and Jesus popped out.

Yo Mama's so fat that when she lost twenty pounds, it was like the *Queen Mary* losing a deckchair.

Yo Mama's so fat, people gain weight just by watching her eat.

Yo Mama's so fat the police were going to use her as an emergency air mattress when Michael Jackson started dangling his baby.

Yo Mama's so fat she had her ears pierced by harpoon.

Yo Mama's so fat that the National Weather Agency assigns names to her farts.

Yo Mama's so fat that if she put on another two pounds she could get group insurance.

Yo Mama's so fat that when she fell down, she rocked herself to sleep trying to get up.

Yo Mama's so fat she has to pay excess baggage on her own body.

Yo Mama's so fat that her university graduation photo was an aerial shot.

Yo Mama's so fat she sat on a rainbow and made Skittles.

Yo Mama's so fat, the sidewalk screams in pain when she walks on it.

Yo Mama's so fat, the whole stadium can talk behind her back.

Yo Mama's so fat her belt size is Equator.

Yo Mama's so fat she plays marbles with planets.

Yo Mama's so fat she shows up on radar.

Yo Mama's so fat, she's the same height lying down as standing up.

Yo Mama's so fat she wakes up in sections.

Yo Mama's so fat that when she bought a housecoat, it fitted the house as well.

Yo Mama's so fat the body snatchers needed a forklift truck.

Yo Mama's so fat she needs a map to find her butt.

Yo Mama's so fat, she's got smaller women orbiting around her.

Yo Mama's so fat she's a DJ for an ice-cream van.

Yo Mama's so fat that when she walked in front of the TV, I missed three commercials.

Yo Mama's so fat she rollerskates on buses.

Yo Mama's so fat that she went to a fancy dress party in a white sheet as Alaska.

Yo Mama's so fat you could go swimming in her bra.

Yo Mama's so fat she wears a life-size horse logo on her polo shirt.

Yo Mama's so fat she was born with a silver shovel in her mouth.

Yo Mama's so fat that when she walks down the aisle of an airplane she causes turbulence.

Yo Mama's so fat that when she goes to a restaurant she doesn't get a menu, she gets an estimate.

Yo Mama's so fat she fell into the Grand Canyon and got stuck.

Yo Mama's so fat she's once, twice, three times a lady.

Yo Mama's so fat she thought Barnum and Bailey were clothing designers.

Yo Mama's so fat she was baptized at Sea World.

Yo Mama's so fat that when her pager goes off, people think she's backing up.

Yo Mama's so fat she has her own postcode.

Yo Mama's so fat that when she sits in the bath, the water in the toilet rises.

Yo Mama's so fat the circus uses her as a trampoline.

Yo Mama's so fat that when she opens the fridge, it says "I give up."

Yo Mama's so fat that yachtsmen buy her old knickers to use as sails.

Yo Mama's so fat that other folk exercise by jogging around her.

Yo Mama's so fat that when she goes to the zoo, elephants throw *her* peanuts.

Yo Mama's so fat she hasn't seen her feet for six years.

Yo Mama's so fat she uses a bed mattress as a maxipad.

Yo Mama's so fat she has stabilizers.

Yo Mama's so fat her belly jiggle is the first ever perpetual motion machine.

Yo Mama's so fat that when she ran into a wall, the wall winced.

Yo Mama's so fat, all the chairs in the house have seatbelts.

Yo Mama's so fat she wears a long-sleeved bra.

Yo Mama's so fat that when she bends over we enter Daylight Savings Time.

Yo Mama's so fat that when she goes to the movies she sits next to everyone.

Yo Mama's so fat that when she sunbathed on the beach, Greenpeace tried to push her back in the water.

Yo Mama's so fat that when a cop saw her, he yelled, "Hey, you two, break it up!"

Yo Mama's so fat she had to be cut out of a hula hoop.

Yo Mama's so fat her big toe got stuck in the catflap.

Yo Mama's so fat that if someone shined her shoes, she'd have to take their word for it.

Yo Mama's so fat, her cereal bowl is a satellite dish.

Yo Mama's so fat that instead of Levi 501s, she wears Levi 1002s.

Yo Mama's so fat her butt cheeks have different area codes.

Yo Mama's so fat that when she sings it's over for everybody.

Yo Mama's so fat she has to iron her pants on the driveway.

Yo Mama's so fat that when her family wants to watch home movies they ask her to wear white.

Yo Mama's so fat that when she swims in the sea she's a danger to shipping.

Yo Mama's so fat that NASA plans to use her to shore up the hole in the ozone layer.

Yo Mama's so fat that when she took her dress to the cleaners, they said, "Sorry, we don't do curtains."

Yo Mama's so fat that when she crosses the street, cars look out for her.

Yo Mama's so fat that after she got off the carousel, the horse limped for a week.

Yo Mama's so fat everyone can talk behind her back.

Yo Mama's so fat she's half American, half Irish and half Scottish.

Yo Mama's so fat she measures 38-26-36 . . . and that was just the left arm.

Yo Mama's so fat she makes Sumo wrestlers look anorexic.

Yo Mama's so fat it takes her two trips to go through a revolving door.

Yo Mama's so fat that when she was lying on a sunbed in her blue swimsuit, seven people came up and asked which was the shallow end.

Yo Mama's so fat it takes two months to download her picture.

Yo Mama's so fat that I've known her for thirty years but I still haven't seen *all* of her.

Yo Mama's so fat that when she fell off a boat, the captain shouted, "Land Ahoy!"

Yo Mama's so fat that when people see her they immediately think of Elizabeth Taylor, Roseanne Barr and Oprah Winfrey . . . rolled into one.

Yo Mama's so fat she sets off car alarms when she runs.

Yo Mama's so fat my dog bit her and died of high cholesterol.

Yo Mama's so fat her driver's licence says, "Picture continued on other side."

Yo Mama's so fat that when she goes to the beach she's the only one that gets a tan.

Yo Mama's so fat that when she wears leather pants, it looks like they're still on the cow.

Yo Mama's so fat she looks like a galleon in full sail.

Yo Mama's so fat her dressmaker takes her measurements in light years.

Yo Mama's so fat that she needs a watch on both arms because she covers two time zones.

Yo Mama's so fat that when she rode an elephant, it sagged in the middle.

Yo Mama's so fat, when she went to the parade everyone thought she was a float.

Yo Mama's so fat that when I got on the train last night, the sign said "Maximum Occupancy: 200 Persons or Yo Mama."

Yo Mama's so fat, raccoons build their nests in her bra.

Yo Mama's so fat she stood in front of the Hollywood sign and it just said H————d.

Yo Mama's so fat, when she farted she went into orbit.

Yo Mama's so fat that when she takes a shower, her feet don't get wet.

Yo Mama's so that when yo Papa tells her to haul ass, she has to make two trips.

Yo Mama's so fat she makes Elizabeth Taylor look like slimmer of the year.

Yo Mama's so fat that when she tiptoes, everyone yells "Stampede!"

Yo Mama's so fat that when she dances the whole town rocks – literally.

Yo Mama's so fat the only label she gets to wear is "Wide Load".

Yo Mama's so fat that when she went to buy a water bed, they simply put a blanket over the Great Lakes.

Yo Mama's so fat she uses a laptop as a cell phone.

Yo Mama's so fat that when she flew on a plane, the other two hundred passengers all had to sit on the other side of the gangway.

Yo Mama's so fat that when mosquitoes see her, they scream "Buffet!"

Yo Mama's so fat she has to get out of the car to change gears.

Yo Mama's so fat she buys clothes by the acre.

Yo Mama's so fat they had to grease a doorframe and hold a doughnut on the other side to get her through.

Yo Mama's so fat that when she went jogging in New York, the vibration was heard in Los Angeles.

Yo Mama's so fat she can't play hide and seek, just seek.

Yo Mama's so fat that when she was born she didn't get a birth certificate, she got a blueprint.

Yo Mama's so fat she doesn't have dreams, she has movies.

Yo Mama's so fat that when she cut her leg, gravy dripped out.

Yo Mama's so fat that when her schoolfriends tried to give her the bumps, three of them ended up with hernias.

Yo Mama's so fat that doctors had to hire a crane to give her a facelift.

Yo Mama's so fat that when she wears corduroy pants, the ridges don't show.

Yo Mama's so fat, when she was born she gave the hospital stretch marks.

Yo Mama's so fat her blood type is Ragu.

Yo Mama's so fat she used to be a decoy for a whaling ship.

Yo Mama's so fat that when they cremate her, the heat will double the impact of global warming.

Yo Mama's so fat that bits of her can be in four rooms at once.

Yo Mama's so fat that "Place Your Billboard Ad Here" is printed on each of her butt cheeks.

Yo Mama's so fat that when they cremate her, they can scatter her ashes in the Grand Canyon and still have plenty left over.

Yo Mama's so fat that if they scatter her ashes on a windy day, it will be like a desert storm.

Yo Mama's so fat that if they scatter her ashes at sea, they will form a new continent.

Yo Mama's so fat that instead of keeping her ashes in an urn, they'll need half a dozen buckets and a beer barrel.

Yo Mama's so fat that if you put numbers on her ass, she could stamp licence plates.

Yo Mama's so fat that when she wore a Malcolm X T-shirt, helicopters tried to land on her back.

Yo Mama's so fat you could slap her butt and ride the waves.

Yo Mama's so fat you can park a bus in the shadow of her ass.

Yo Mama's so fat that when you sat on a see-saw with her, you landed in the next state.

Yo Mama's so fat, she has to roll over four times just to get an even tan.

Yo Mama's so fat she has to put her belt on with a boomerang.

Yo Mama's so fat she's on both sides of the family.

Yo Mama's so fat that she only lost a game of hide-and-seek when she was spotted behind Mount Everest.

Yo Mama's so fat that when she wears combat trousers she looks like an entire battalion.

Yo Mama's so fat that before sex, yo Papa has to roll her in sawdust and search for the damp patch.

Yo Mama's so fat that when they call her a "tramp", it's short for trampoline.

Yo Mama's so fat there was a picture of her in a magazine . . . on pages six, seven, eight and nine.

Yo Mama's so fat, her cereal bowl came with a lifeguard.

Yo Mama's so fat that when she goes to Gap, the only thing she can fit into is the changing room.

Yo Mama's so fat that when she jumps into the pool, the other swimmers can go surfing.

Yo Mama's so fat her farts provide enough energy to heat half of Chicago.

Yo Mama's so fat that people have been known to trip over her toenail clippings.

Yo Mama's so fat that when she goes to an office, they tell her to pull up a sofa.

Yo Mama's so fat that when she walks past a streetlight, it's like a total eclipse of the sun.

Yo Mama's so fat that the contents of her bladder could match Niagara Falls.

Yo Mama's so fat that when she was diagnosed with a flesh-eating virus, doctors gave her thirty years to live.

Yo Mama's so fat she grounded the London Eye.

Yo Mama's so fat that when she went bungee jumping, she took the bridge with her.

Yo Mama's so fat, she's bigger than infinity.

Yo Mama's so fat that when she got hit by a truck, she said: "Who threw that rock?"

Yo Mama's so fat that when she sat on a TV, it turned into a flat screen.

Yo Mama's so fat that when she wore a grey dress, three airplanes tried to land on her.

Yo Mama's so fat she can be in three rooms of her house at the same time.

Yo Mama's so fat that it was her ice skating on a trip to Greenland that has caused part of the polar ice cap to break away.

Yo Mama's so fat that when her waters broke, the hospital had to call in police frogmen.

Yo Mama's so fat you need SatNav to find your way around her.

Yo Mama's so fat that seven-tenths of the Earth's surface is taken up by water and the rest is Yo Mama.

Yo Mama's so fat, I have to take three steps back just to see all of her.

Yo Mama's so fat that when she was kidnapped, her face covered every side of the milk carton.

Yo Mama's so fat, Richard Branson used one of her skirts as a hot-air balloon.

Yo Mama's so fat that when God said, "Let there be light," He told her to stand out of the way first.

Yo Mama's so fat that when she crosses the road, police have to put up diversion signs.

Yo Mama's so fat she jumped for joy and got stuck.

Yo Mama's so fat that whenever she wears high heels, she strikes oil.

Yo Mama's so fat she went on the Barry White diet.

Yo Mama's so fat that when she walks to the shops, she has to have a police motorcycle escort.

Yo Mama's so fat that when she walks across a dancefloor, the band skips.

Yo Mama's so fat, she looks like she's smuggling a Volkswagen under her dress.

Yo Mama's so fat that guys who call her a "broad" are using the term as an adjective rather than a noun.

Yo Mama's so fat that when she appeared in *Titanic*, it was as the ship.

Yo Mama's so fat that on a scale of 1 to 10 she's a 747.

Yo Mama's so fat that when she applied for a job at a strip club, they turned her down because they already had a stage.

Yo Mama's so fat that when she sat on a volcano she put it out.

Yo Mama's so fat that when she wears a yellow raincoat, New Yorkers shout "Taxi!"

Yo Mama's so fat that to run rings around her you'd have to do a marathon.

Yo Mama's so fat that when she jumped in the ocean, the whales started singing, "We are family".

Yo Mama's so fat that when she went out wearing a black dress one afternoon, all the neighbours went to bed because they thought it was night.

Yo Mama's so fat that when she stood on one end of Staten Island, the land started to tilt.

Yo Mama's so fat that wherever I look, she's there.

Yo Mama's so fat that in some atlases she's listed as the eighth continent.

Yo Mama's so fat her belly button's got an echo.

Yo Mama's so fat her photograph weighs ten pounds.

Yo Mama's so fat that when you were born, they had to send out a search party to find you.

Yo Mama's so fat she can't limbo under the Arc de Triomphe.

Yo Mama's so fat she has a bigger turning circle than a jumbo jet.

Yo Mama's so fat that when she goes on a speak your weight machine, it surrenders.

Yo Mama's so fat she is paid to lie on the beach as a coastal defence.

Yo Mama's so fat that when she wore a red dress in California, they thought it was another forest fire.

Yo Mama's so fat that instead of a cotton bud, she uses a baseball bat to clean the insides of her ears.

Yo Mama's so fat that when she crosses the road, drivers always treat her as a roundabout.

Yo Mama's so fat that every time she turns around, it's her next birthday.

Yo Mama's so fat that when she jumped from a burning building and landed in the safety net, she was still bouncing up and down three hours later.

Yo Mama's so fat that to put her hands in her pockets she has to take her pants off.

Yo Mama's so fat that when she fell from the Eiffel Tower in Paris, she rolled into Belgium, flattening several villages on the way.

Yo Mama's so fat she can use Saturn's ring as a hula hoop.

Yo Mama's so fat that when she wears a green dress she acts as a body double for Central Park.

Yo Mama's so fat, they have to run a relay race to get her belt through the loops.

Yo Mama's so fat that when she gets in the car, the tyres go flat.

Yo Mama's so fat, she puts on lipstick with a paint roller.

Yo Mama's so fat you need St Bernards to find her belly button.

Yo Mama's so fat she made Weight Watchers go blind.

Yo Mama's so fat she can pack all her belongings in her folds of skin.

Yo Mama's so fat she uses soccer balls for earrings.

Yo Mama's so fat she left the house with high heels and came back with flip flops.

Yo Mama's so fat that when the family went to the beach and you kids wanted to go in the ocean, yo Papa had to tell you, "Not right now, kids. There's not room. Mama is using it."

Yo Mama's so fat that when she sneezes, it looks like a special effect.

Yo Mama's so fat she uses a kiddie slide for a shoe horn.

Yo Mama's so fat she uses a satellite dish as a diaphragm.

Yo Mama's so fat she uses redwoods as toothpicks.

Yo Mama's so fat she uses sleeping bags as leg warmers.

Yo Mama's so fat she uses the carpet as a blanket.

Yo Mama's so fat that when you walk behind her, you don't see any sunlight.

Yo Mama's so fat, her last gynaecologist fell in and hasn't been seen for weeks.

Yo Mama's so fat that when she turns around, people throw her a "Welcome Back" party.

Yo Mama's so fat that when she sits down, the chair begs for mercy.

Yo Mama's so fat she's moving the Earth out of its orbit.

Yo Mama's so fat all her clothes have to be custom made by a contractor.

Yo Mama's so fat she whistles bass.

Yo Mama's so fat she needs a solar panel to see her reflection.

Yo Mama's so fat that the first time she had sex, the earth didn't just move for her – it moved for the whole neighbourhood.

Yo Mama's so fat you don't pinch an inch, you yank a yard.

Yo Mama's so fat, you can pinch an inch on her forehead.

Yo Mama's so fat that when she fell, no one was laughing but the ground was cracking up.

Yo Mama's so fat she showers at the local car wash.

Yo Mama's so fat they use the elastic in her underwear for bungee jumping.

Yo Mama's so fat that when she went for a swim in the ocean she caused a fifty-foot tidal wave.

Yo Mama's so fat she doesn't have a doctor, she has a groundskeeper.

Yo Mama's so fat she doesn't wear a G string, she wears an A B C D E F G string.

Yo Mama's so fat she entered a fat contest and won first, second and third.

Yo Mama's so fat she fills up the bath tub and then she turns on the water.

Yo Mama's so fat they had to change "one size fits all" to "one size fits most".

Yo Mama's so fat that when she stepped on the scale, it said, 'Please get out of the car.'

Yo Mama's so fat that when she was asked to present a new TV game show, the producers decided to call it *Fat Chance*.

Yo Mama's so fat that when yo Papa finished having sex with her and tried to roll off, he was still on her.

Yo Mama's so fat she can sit around a table all by herself.

Yo Mama's so fat, it was her resting against it that the caused the Tower of Pisa to lean.

Yo Mama's so fat that when a guy insulted her and she called him fattist, he said, "No, you're definitely fattest."

Yo Mama's so fat she can't lose weight, only find it.

Yo Mama's so fat her plastic surgeon uses scaffolding.

Yo Mama's so fat that when she walks down the street, everyone yells, "Earthquake!"

Yo Mama's so fat they had to paint a stripe down her back to tell whether she was walking or rolling.

Yo Mama's so fat that instead of a clothes horse, she looks more like a shire horse.

Yo Mama's so fat that God created her and on the seventh day rested.

Yo Mama's so fat that when she gets in a lift, it *has* to go down.

Yo Mama's so fat, when a car had to swerve to avoid hitting her on the road, it ran out of petrol.

Yo Mama's so fat she has TB: two bellies.

Yo Mama's so fat, it's quicker to run rings around Saturn than it is to run rings around her.

Yo Mama's so fat that yo papa has to kneel up in bed to see if it's daylight.

Yo Mama's so fat, the shadow of her ass weighs fifty pounds.

Yo Mama's so fat that when she stepped on the scale, she saw her phone number.

Yo Mama's so fat that when she wore a black swimsuit and jumped in the ocean, people thought she was an oil slick.

Yo Mama's so fat her fingers have cottage cheese.

Yo Mama's so fat that instead of a tape measure her waist is measured by an Ordnance Survey team.

Yo Mama's so fat that when she rested on her laurels they broke.

Yo Mama's so fat that when she tried to get an all over tan, the sun burned out.

Yo Mama's so fat she can fill a room just by walking into it.

Yo Mama's so fat that she and the water can't fit into the bathtub at the same time.

Yo Mama's so fat, she is now treated by a whole team of gynaecologists, working in relays.

Yo Mama's so fat that when she bent down to tie her shoe laces, her face got burnt from re-entry.

Yo Mama's so fat her tights don't run, they waddle.

Yo Mama's so fat she doesn't have love handles, she has a roll bar.

Yo Mama's so fat she's got a wooden leg with a kickstand.

Yo Mama's so fat she ain't reached her back pocket in years.

Yo Mama's so fat she once got a whole cow stuck in her teeth.

Yo Mama's so fat that at Halloween she says trick or meatloaf.

Yo Mama's so fat she broke a branch off the family tree.

Yo Mama's so fat, people are always saying she's going to be The Next Big Thing.

Yo Mama's so fat and slow that her college nickname wasn't "Road Runner", it was 'Road Roller'.

Yo Mama's so greedy that when she goes to an 'all you can eat' buffet, they have to install speed bumps.

Yo Mama's so greedy, I've seen her order everything on a menu except 'Thank you for dining with us.'

Yo Mama's so greedy she deep fries her toothpaste.

Yo Mama's so greedy her idea of a bit on the side is an extra plate of fries.

Yo Mama's so greedy she put herself on a light diet: as soon as it's light, she starts eating.

Yo Mama's so greedy she's not on a diet, she's on a triet – whatever you're eating, she'll try it.

Yo Mama's so greedy she stands in front of the microwave oven and yells, "Hurry!"

Yo Papa's so fat that when you climb on top of him, your ears pop.

Yo priest's so fat that when he bungee jumped he went straight to hell.

Yo bookie's so fat he has to buy clothes by the furlong.

Yo grandma was so fat that when they carried her coffin, the pallbearers had to call for backup.

Yo Mama's dog is so fat, you never have to say "Stay" because his ass never moves!

Yo Mama's so old that when she went to blow out the candles on her birthday cake, she was beaten back by the flames.

Yo Mama's so old she's got hieroglyphics on her driving licence.

Yo Mama's so old she was DJ at the Boston Tea Party.

Yo Mama's so old, the average age of her friends is deceased.

Yo Mama's so old that when she walked into an antique shop, they kept her.

Yo Mama's so old that *Jurassic Park* brought back memories.

Yo Mama's so old her birth certificate has expired.

Yo Mama's so old she can remember when *Madam Butterfly* was still a caterpillar.

Yo Mama's so old she knew Burger King when he was only a prince.

Yo Mama's so old, she doesn't leave fingerprints anymore.

Yo Mama's so old, one of her pets was on Noah's Ark.

Yo Mama's so old the only dating she gets involved in is carbon dating.

Yo Mama's so old that when she walks around with no pants on, it looks like she's wearing leather pants.

Yo Mama's so old the candles cost more than the cake.

Yo Mama's so old that when they asked her age, she said, "The Bronze Age."

Yo Mama's so old, it takes her longer to rest these days than it does to get tired.

Yo Mama's so old her blood type is discontinued.

Yo Mama's so old her birth certificate is in Roman numerals.

Yo Mama's so old she was a waitress at the Last Supper.

Yo Mama's so old she farts dust.

Yo Mama's so old she drove a chariot to school.

Yo Mama's so old, the candles on her birthday cake raised the Earth's temperature by three degrees.

Yo Mama's so old, the last period she had was the Mesozoic.

Yo Mama's so old that when she ran the 100 metres they timed her with a sundial.

Yo Mama's so old that when she was a kid, rainbows were in black and white.

Yo Mama's so old she got Adam and Eve's autograph.

Yo Mama's so old that when she was in school there was no history class.

Yo Mama's so old she can remember when New York City was just fields.

Yo Mama's so old she can remember when the Dead Sea was only sick.

Yo Mama's so old she can remember when the Grand Canyon was just a ditch.

Yo Mama's so old she's got more wrinkles than an elephant's scrotum.

Yo Mama's so old that her back goes out more than she does.

Yo Mama's so old her breasts squirt out powdered milk.

Yo Mama's so old she remembers what life was like before the Ice Age.

Yo Mama's so old, she helped draw up the plans for the Pyramids.

Yo Mama's so old it looks like the wrinkle fairy tap danced on her face.

Yo Mama's so old that when I told her to act her age, she died.

Yo Mama's so old she uses her hot flushes to heat her cup of tea.

Yo Mama's so old she co-wrote the sixth commandment.

Yo Mama's so old her first job was as Cain and Abel's baby-sitter.

Yo Mama's so old that all the names in her little black book are followed by MD.

Yo Mama's so old, it was her who called the cops when David and Goliath began to fight.

Yo Mama's so old she's got a signed copy of the Bible.

Yo Mama's so old that vultures constantly circle her house.

Yo Mama's so old that when Moses parted the Red Sea, he found her fishing on the other side.

Yo Mama's so old she needed a walking frame when Jesus was still in diapers.

Yo Mama's so old, she went to an antiques auction and three people bid for her.

Yo Mama's so old I've seen stale raisins with fewer wrinkles.

Yo Mama's so old her social security number is 000-000-001.

Yo Mama's so old she used to cut Betty Rubble's hair.

Yo Mama's so old that when I asked to see her birth certificate, she handed me a rock.

Yo Mama's so old she actually walked with dinosaurs.

Yo Mama's so old, you put her in a museum instead of an old folks' home.

Yo Mama's so old, she has the addresses of all the disciples in her little black book.

Yo Mama's so old, she was deafened by the big bang.

Yo Mama's so ugly that when she stands on the beach, the tide won't come in.

Yo Mama's so ugly that when she was born, the doctor looked at her ass then her face and said, "Twins!"

Yo Mama's so ugly she has to creep up on her makeup.

Yo Mama's so ugly that when she walks into a bank, they turn off the surveillance cameras.

Yo Mama's so ugly that even the Terminator won't say, "I'll be back."

Yo Mama's so ugly, her dentist treats her by mail order.

Yo Mama's so ugly that yo papa can screw her in any position and it's still doggie-style.

Yo Mama's so ugly, her family had to tie a steak round her neck so the dogs would play with her.

Yo Mama's so ugly that if she were a scarecrow, the corn would run away.

Yo Mama's so ugly, hotel managers use her picture to keep the rats away.

Yo Mama's so ugly that when she entered a gurning contest, they said, "Sorry, no professionals."

Yo Mama's so ugly that when the family go on vacation, they put her in a kennel.

Yo Mama's so ugly she was signed up by Hollywood . . . as Shrek's double.

Yo Mama's so ugly her shrink makes her lie face down on the couch.

Yo Mama's so ugly, they knew what time she was born because her face stopped the clock.

Yo Mama's so ugly, five peeping toms have killed themselves.

Yo Mama's so ugly, her fat butt is her good side.

Yo Mama's so ugly she could scare the moss off a rock.

Yo Mama's so ugly, it looks like she's been bobbing for French fries.

Yo Mama's so ugly she makes Camilla Parker Bowles look like Cameron Diaz.

Yo Mama's so ugly, it's seven years' bad luck just to look at her.

Yo Mama's so ugly, her birth certificate was a letter of apology from the condom factory.

Yo Mama's so ugly they rub tree branches on her face to make ugly sticks.

Yo Mama's so ugly, even a hitman wouldn't take her out.

Yo Mama's so ugly, the only way she could ever get more than one date was by buying a calendar.

Yo Mama's so ugly, yo Papa had it written into their wedding vows that they would only have sex doggie-style.

Yo Mama's so ugly she practises birth control by leaving the light on.

Yo Mama's so ugly that even Prince Charming refuses to kiss her — he'd rather live as a frog.

Yo Mama's so ugly that when she gets up in the morning, the sun goes down.

Yo Mama's so ugly she could make an onion cry.

Yo Mama's so ugly she has to fake orgasms when she masturbates.

Yo Mama's so ugly, it looks like she's wearing her face inside out.

Yo Mama's so ugly that at her wedding she didn't wear a veil, she wore a ski mask.

Yo Mama's so ugly even her shadow won't be seen with her.

Yo Mama's so ugly her husband takes her to work with him just so that he doesn't have to kiss her goodbye.

Yo Mama's so ugly vampires are too scared to suck her blood.

Yo Mama's so ugly people go as her for Halloween.

Yo Mama's so ugly she pretends she's someone else when she's having sex.

Yo Mama's so ugly, when she goes swimming in the sea even Great White Sharks turn vegetarian.

Yo Mama's so ugly that yo Papa made her convert to Islam just so she could wear a burka.

Yo Mama's so ugly that even the tide wouldn't take her out.

Yo Mama's so ugly her face is like a work of modern art: you can't tell what it is.

Yo Mama's so ugly she makes blind children cry.

Yo Mama's so ugly, yo papa throws the ugly stick and she goes and fetches it every time.

Yo Mama's so ugly, her pillows cry at night.

Yo Mama's so ugly, George Bush moved Halloween to her birthday.

Yo Mama's so ugly that when she puts on lipstick, it keeps backing down the tube.

Yo Mama's so ugly she turned a straight guy gay just by flirting with him.

Yo Mama's so ugly, her face could scare a hungry wolf off a meat truck.

Yo Mama's so ugly that when she went for a part in *Beauty and the Beast*, the producers said, "Right, now who can we get to play the Beauty?"

Yo Mama's so ugly that if her face were her fortune, she'd get a tax rebate.

Yo Mama's so ugly that when yo Papa took her to the zoo, the guy at the door said, "Thanks for bringing her back."

Yo Mama's so ugly that when she looks in the mirror, her reflection ducks.

Yo Mama's so ugly, yo Papa first met her at the pound.

Yo Mama's so ugly, I've seen better hands on a clock.

Yo Mama's so ugly that at passport control they have to receive counselling after looking at her photo.

Yo Mama's so ugly she could look at a railroad track and buckle it.

Yo Mama's so ugly it looks like she ran the 100-metre dash in a ninety-metre gym.

Yo Mama's so ugly that in strip joints they pay her to put her clothes *on*.

Yo Mama's so ugly that when she was born her mother shouted, "What a treasure!" And her father said, "Yes, now let's go and bury her!"

Yo Mama's so ugly even her keeper won't visit her.

Yo Mama's so ugly she scared the stitching out of Frankenstein.

Yo Mama's so ugly that the first time yo Papa woke up next to her, he thought the Mafia had put a horse's head in the bed.

Yo Mama's so ugly that when she visited a haunted house, they offered her a job.

Yo Mama's so ugly that when she goes on safari, the lions roll up the window.

Yo Mama's so ugly that when she moved into the street, all the neighbours chipped in for curtains.

Yo Mama's so ugly she didn't just get hit with the ugly stick, she ran through the whole forest.

Yo Mama's so ugly she used to model for death threats.

Yo Mama's so ugly it looks as if her stockings are wrinkled even when she isn't wearing any.

Yo Mama's so ugly, apes want to adopt her.

Yo Mama's so ugly she can look up a camel's butt and scare the hump off it.

Yo Mama's so ugly she has to creep up on water to get a drink.

Yo Mama's so ugly they push her face into the dough mixture when making Monster cookies.

Yo Mama's so ugly that all she needs for birth control is to leave the lights on.

Yo Mama's so ugly, people hang her picture in their cars so their radios don't get stolen.

Yo Mama's so ugly that at her wedding everybody kissed the groom.

Yo Mama's so ugly that when she took her pet poodle along to audition for Animal Actors, they signed her up too . . . as a lookalike for Mr Ed.

Yo Mama's so ugly she climbed the ugly ladder and didn't miss a step.

Yo Mama's so ugly that if a pretty face can sell beauty products, hers could sell livestock equipment.

Yo Mama's so ugly, your grandma used to feed her with a fishing rod.

Yo Mama's so ugly, when she was born the doctor smacked her face.

Yo Mama's so ugly she has to get her vibrator drunk first.

Yo Mama's so ugly she could scare the chrome off a car bumper.

Yo Mama's so ugly she made a blind man cry.

Yo Mama's so ugly she got arrested for vandalizing a mirror shop.

Yo Mama's so ugly the only guy who thinks she is a ten is her shoe salesman.

Yo Mama's so ugly that even the toilet flushes when it sees her.

Yo Mama's so ugly, it looks like her face caught fire and they put it out with a fork.

Yo Mama's so ugly that when yo Papa wants to have sex in the car, he tells her to get out.

Yo Mama's so ugly the mailman mistook her for a dog.

Yo Mama's so ugly she gave Freddy Krueger nightmares.

Yo Mama's so ugly she put the Bogey man out of business.

Yo Mama's so ugly that kids trick or treat her over the phone.

Yo Mama's so ugly that when her picture appeared in the paper, scientists thought they had found the missing link.

Yo Mama's so ugly that when she went to see a proctologist, he stuck his finger in her mouth.

Yo Mama's so ugly, people at the zoo pay NOT to see her.

Yo Mama's so ugly her mother fed her by catapult.

Yo Mama's so ugly that when she reached for the remote, it jumped off the couch.

Yo Mama's so ugly that before they make love, yo Papa takes a pain killer.

Yo Mama's so ugly that when she went for a sex change, the surgeon had to flip a coin.

Yo Mama's so ugly that if ugly were a snowflake, she'd be a blizzard.

Yo Mama's so ugly that if ugly were a grain of sand, she'd be the Sahara Desert.

Yo Mama's so ugly that if ugly were an ant, she'd be an infestation.

Yo Mama's so ugly that if ugly were a strand of hair, she'd be a full Afro.

Yo Mama's so ugly that if ugly were a brick, she'd be the Great Wall of China.

Yo Mama's so ugly that if ugly were a tree, she'd be a forest.

Yo Mama's so ugly that if ugly were a fibre of wool, she'd be a sweater.

Yo Mama's so ugly that if ugly were a coffee bean, she'd be the annual harvest of Brazil.

Yo Mama's so ugly that if ugly were a mountain, she'd be Everest.

Yo Mama's so ugly that if ugly were a crime, she'd get the electric chair.

Yo Mama's so ugly that if ugly were a blade of grass, she'd be a lawn.

Yo Mama's so ugly that if ugly were an Olympic event, she'd be the Dream Team.

Yo Mama's so ugly that if ugly were an ice cube, she'd be Antarctica.

Yo Mama's so ugly that if ugly were a candy, she'd be a family-sized bag.

Yo Mama's so ugly that if ugly were a drop of water, she'd be the Pacific Ocean.

Yo Mama's so ugly that if ugly were a locust, she'd be a plague.

Yo Mama's so ugly that if ugly were a grain of rice, she'd be a risotto.

Yo Mama's so ugly that when she worked for a dentist, none of the patients needed anaesthetic.

Yo Mama's so ugly that she once took your boxer dog to Crufts and won . . . and the dog came second.

Yo Mama's so ugly that ProLifers would make an exception in her case.

Yo Mama's so ugly that when she looked out of the window she was arrested for indecent exposure.

Yo Mama's so ugly that when she takes off her bra, it looks like she's got four big toes.

Yo Mama's so ugly her face is closed at weekends.

Yo Mama's so ugly they put her face on a box of laxatives and sold it empty.

Yo Mama's so ugly that the last time she heard a whistle, she got hit by a train.

Yo Mama's so ugly that when she threw a boomerang, it refused to come back.

Yo Mama's so ugly they printed her face on airline sick bags.

Yo Mama's so ugly she turned Medusa to stone.

Yo Mama's so ugly, Rice Krispies won't talk to her.

Yo Mama's so ugly that when she was born the doctor said, "Put her back. She ain't done yet."

Yo Mama's so ugly that even the Elephant Man makes jokes about her.

Yo Mama's so ugly that when she looks in a mirror, her reflection throws up.

Yo Mama's so ugly that if you look up "ugly" in the dictionary, there's a picture of her.

Yo Mama's so ugly, even Jehovah's Witnesses don't call on her.

Yo postman's so ugly the guard dogs needed counselling.

Yo priest's so ugly he had to give his sermon from inside the confessional box.

Yo kid sister's so ugly that when she sits on a sand dune at the beach, cats try to bury her.

Yo sister's so ugly she must have been conceived on the motorway — isn't that where most accidents happen?

Yo sister's so ugly that Durex want to use her as a poster child.

Yo girlfriend's so ugly they put her in the gorilla enclosure at the zoo to stop the gorillas jerking off.

Yo kid brother's so ugly, the kids at school started saying, "Hey Gollum, give us your autograph."

Yo dog's so ugly, they had to shave its ass and make it walk backward.

Yo Papa's so ugly, his American Express card left home without him.

Yo Mama's so stupid that when she went to hospital to give blood and was asked what type she was, she told them she was an outgoing cat-lover.

Yo Mama's so stupid that when she missed the number 30 bus, she took the number 15 twice instead.

Yo Mama's so stupid she spent two weeks in a revolving door looking for a doorknob.

Yo Mama's so stupid that she was born on Christmas Day but can never remember her birthday.

Yo Mama's so stupid she couldn't even pass a blood test.

Yo Mama's so stupid she thought hot meals were stolen food.

Yo Mama's so stupid that she sits on the TV and watches the sofa.

Yo Mama's so stupid that when she went to a movie and it said, "Under 16 not admitted", she went home and phoned fifteen friends.

Yo Mama's so stupid she once ordered sushi well done.

Yo Mama's so stupid she invented a waterproof tea bag.

Yo Mama's so stupid she thinks Tiger Woods is a forest in India.

Yo Mama's so stupid she thinks DNA is the National Dyslexics Association.

Yo Mama's so stupid she thinks private enterprise means owning your personal starship.

Yo Mama's so stupid she thinks a permutation is a surgical procedure.

Yo Mama's so stupid she bought a solar-powered torch.

Yo Mama's so stupid that she orders a cheeseburger from McDonald's and says, "Hold the cheese."

Yo Mama's so stupid she studied for a dope test.

Yo Mama's so stupid she took a hose to water the kindergarten.

Yo Mama's so stupid she invented a pencil with an eraser on each end.

Yo Mama's so stupid that when she heard ninety percent of all crimes occur around the home, she went out.

Yo Mama's so stupid she thought a lawsuit was something you wear to court.

Yo Mama's so stupid that when her computer said "Press any key to continue", she phoned support complaining she couldn't find the "any" key.

Yo Mama's so stupid she takes binoculars to watch submarine races.

Yo Mama's so stupid she once asked, "What's the number for 911?"

Yo Mama's so stupid she didn't realize Philips six-inch was a screwdriver.

Yo Mama's so stupid, she thought meow mix was a record for cats.

Yo Mama's so stupid, her dog teaches *her* tricks.

Yo Mama's so stupid that when yo papa asked her to buy a colour TV, she said, "Which colour?"

Yo Mama's so stupid she thought the board of education was a piece of wood.

Yo Mama's so stupid she thinks "aperitif" means dentures.

Yo Mama's so stupid she thinks "Nessun Dorma" is a camper van.

Yo Mama's so stupid, she died before the police arrived because she couldn't find the "11" button in "911".

Yo Mama's so stupid that when she saw a sign saying "Wet Floor", she did.

Yo Mama's so stupid she thinks the English Channel is a TV station.

Yo Mama's so stupid that when you were born, she took one look at your umbilical cord and said, "Wow, it comes with cable too!"

Yo Mama's so stupid she plays solitaire for cash.

Yo Mama's so stupid her fingers and toes are numbered.

Yo Mama's so stupid she needs a cue card to say "Huh?"

Yo Mama's so stupid she planted a dogwood tree and expected a litter of puppies.

Yo Mama's so stupid that when she found out she was pregnant she asked, "Who's the mother?"

Yo Mama's so stupid she stood on a chair to raise her IQ.

Yo Mama's so stupid she failed a survey.

Yo Mama's so stupid she thinks male zebras are the ones with the black stripes.

Yo Mama's so stupid she thinks zebras have stripes so that lions can barcode them before having them for dinner.

Yo Mama's so stupid she got locked inside a bed shop and slept on the floor.

Yo Mama's so stupid she thinks Thailand is a men's clothing shop.

Yo Mama's so stupid she thinks a polygon is a dead parrot.

Yo Mama's so stupid she considers mould to be a superior life form.

Yo Mama's so stupid she got fired from the M&M factory for throwing away all the Ws.

Yo Mama's so stupid she put her watch in the bank to save time.

Yo Mama's so stupid she thinks Moby Dick is a kind of venereal disease.

Yo Mama's so stupid she fell *up* the stairs.

Yo Mama's so stupid she once had an argument on the phone with an answering machine.

Yo Mama's so stupid she calls people to ask them their phone number.

Yo Mama's so stupid she put lipstick on her forehead because she wanted to make up her mind.

Yo Mama's so stupid she ran outside with a purse because she heard there was change in the weather.

Yo Mama's so stupid that the only time she gets the point is when she sits on a drawing pin.

Yo Mama's so stupid she uses two hands to eat with chopsticks.

Yo Mama's so stupid she needed a tutor to learn how to scribble.

Yo Mama's so stupid she asked for a refund on a jigsaw puzzle because she thought it was broken.

Yo Mama's so stupid she asked for a price check at the dollar store.

Yo Mama's so stupid her brain cells are on the endangered species list.

Yo Mama's so stupid she thinks Sherlock Holmes is a housing project.

Yo Mama's so stupid that when she went to the game, she thought a quarterback was a refund.

Yo Mama's so stupid she called it quits when her fourth child was born, because she read that every fifth child born is Chinese.

Yo Mama's so stupid she runs around the bed all night trying to catch some sleep.

Yo Mama's so stupid she ought to carry a warning label on her forehead.

Yo Mama's so stupid that when she asked me what kind of jeans I had on and I said "Guess", she said "Levis".

Yo Mama's so stupid she cooks with Old Spice.

Yo Mama's so stupid it took her a week to get rid of a twenty-four-hour virus.

Yo Mama's so stupid her brain cells die alone.

Yo Mama's so stupid, she thinks the Basque Separatists arrange the garments in Victoria's Secret.

Yo Mama's so stupid she needs an operating manual for a screwdriver.

Yo Mama's so stupid she peeked over a glass wall to see what was on the other side.

Yo Mama's so stupid she sat in a tree house because she wanted to be a branch manager.

Yo Mama's so stupid that when she asked me what "Yield" meant and I said "Slow Down", she said, "W-h-a-t d-o-e-s y-i-e-l-d m-e-a-n?"

Yo Mama's so stupid she thinks Johnny Cash is a pay toilet.

Yo Mama's so stupid she thinks $E=MC^2$ is a rap star.

Yo Mama's so stupid she thinks Condoleezza Rice is a Mexican side dish.

Yo Mama's so stupid it takes two of her to listen to music.

Yo Mama's so stupid that she lost a finger and now can't count past nine.

Yo Mama's so stupid she thought that if she woke up fast enough she could see herself sleeping.

Yo Mama's so stupid she lost her job at the hairdresser's because she kept getting "blow dry" and "blow job" mixed up.

Yo Mama's so stupid that if you told her that Papa was a rolling stone, she'd tell me Mama to put Mick Jagger on child support.

Yo Mama's so stupid she thinks innuendo is an Italian suppository.

Yo Mama's so stupid she thought menopause was a button on the stereo.

Yo Mama's so stupid she thought the Internet was something you catch fish with.

Yo Mama's so stupid, she told everyone she was illegitimate because she couldn't read.

Yo Mama's so stupid she includes a "Thank you" note with her tax returns.

Yo Mama's so stupid she couldn't see that her ass was on fire with a flashlight and a three-way mirror.

Yo Mama's so stupid she hasn't bought an electric toothbrush because she doesn't know if her teeth are AC or DC.

Yo Mama's so stupid that if you put a lens in each of her ears, you'd have a telescope.

Yo Mama's so stupid that when she wanted to tighten the clothes-line, she moved the house.

Yo Mama's so stupid she marched out of the furniture shop because she had been told never to accept suites from strangers.

Yo Mama's so stupid she thinks her twin lives in the mirror.

Yo Mama's so stupid that when her dog went missing she wouldn't put an ad in the newspaper because she said the dog can't read.

Yo Mama's so stupid she sat on a window ledge because she was afraid of being framed.

Yo Mama's so stupid she has to reach inside her bra to count to two.

Yo Mama's so stupid she took a doughnut back to the shop because it had a hole in it.

Yo Mama's so stupid she thinks the St Louis Cardinals are appointed by the Pope.

Yo Mama's so stupid, she thinks a web site is where spiders live.

Yo Mama's so stupid that on her job application where it says "emergency contact", she put "911".

Yo Mama's so stupid she was three before she got a birthmark.

Yo Mama's so stupid it took her seven hours to look up "umbrella" in the dictionary because she didn't realize it was in alphabetical order.

Yo Mama's so stupid she told me to meet her at the corner of Walk and Don't Walk.

Yo Mama's so stupid she called Dan Quayle for a spell check.

Yo Nana's so stupid she never misses an episode of her screensaver.

Yo Mama's so stupid she called the drugs hotline to order some.

Yo Mama's so stupid, blondes tell jokes about *her*.

Yo Mama's so stupid that when she gets amnesia she gets smarter.

Yo Mama's so stupid that when everyone went to a fancy dress party as an item of food, yo Papa told her to go as a strawberry fool.

Yo Mama's so stupid she tried to wake up a sleeping bag.

Yo Mama's so stupid, when she went into a think-tank, she almost drowned.

Yo Mama's so stupid, she could qualify as a houseplant if she learned to photosynthesize.

Yo Mama's so stupid she thought fruit punch was a gay boxer.

Yo Mama's so stupid, she bought herself an electric toothbrush and an electric blanket and now she's saving up for an electric chair.

Yo Mama's so stupid she invented a new type of parachute that opens on impact.

Yo Mama's so stupid, she thinks "oral sex" means talking about it.

Yo Mama's so stupid she took an umbrella to see *Rain Man*.

Yo Mama's so stupid she was electrocuted while trying to boil water in the toaster.

Yo Mama's so stupid she thinks KY jelly goes with ice cream.

Yo Mama's so stupid that she tried to drop acid but the car battery fell on her foot.

Yo Mama's so stupid that when yo Papa collapsed, she dialled 911 on the microwave.

Yo Mama's so stupid that when I saw her staring at the paper and asked her what she was doing, she replied, "Watching paper view."

Yo Mama's so stupid she got locked out of a convertible car with the top down.

Yo Mama's so stupid that when airport customs officers asked her if she had anything to declare she was arrested after saying, "Only the crack up my ass."

Yo Mama's so stupid, her shoes say TGIF — toes go in front.

Yo Mama's so stupid she visited the optometrist because she heard they look on the bright side of everything.

Yo Mama's so stupid she watches The Three Stooges and takes notes.

Yo Mama's so stupid that when she went to a football game, she drowned in a Mexican wave.

Yo Mama's so stupid that when I asked her if she wanted a game of craps, she went to fetch some toilet paper.

Yo Mama's so stupid she got in an elevator and thought it was a mobile home.

Yo Mama's so stupid that at the bottom of an application form where it says "Sign Here", she put Aquarius.

Yo Mama's so stupid that when she locked her keys in the car, it took her all day to get yo family out.

Yo Mama's so stupid that when yo Papa was drowning and yelled for a life saver, she said, "Cherry or grape?"

Yo Mama's so stupid that when she went to the store to buy her first colour TV, she asked what colours they had.

Yo Mama's so stupid she got stabbed in a shootout.

Yo Mama's so stupid she refused to buy sponge, tinned fruit and jelly because she didn't want to be trifled with.

Yo Mama's so stupid that when her computer says, "You've got mail", she runs outside to wait for the postman.

Yo Mama's so stupid she went to the 24-hour convenience store and asked what time they closed.

Yo Mama's so stupid that when I put a scratch 'n' sniff sticker on the bottom of the pool, she drowned.

Yo Mama's so stupid she uses whiteout as her toothpaste.

Yo Mama's so stupid that when I asked her to do tricks for me, she wagged her tail.

Yo Mama's so stupid she invented a silent car alarm.

Yo Mama's so stupid that when she got hit by a cup, she told the police that she'd been mugged.

Yo Mama's so stupid she sold her car for gas money.

Yo Mama's so stupid she went to a family reunion to look for a date.

Yo Mama's so stupid that she stopped making ice cubes because she forgot the recipe.

Yo Mama's so stupid she once put a stamp on a fax.

Yo Mama's so stupid she puts on a wetsuit to surf the Internet.

Yo Mama's so stupid she managed to lose her shadow.

Yo Mama's so stupid she jumped off a tower block in an attempt to fly because she'd read her maxipad had wings.

Yo Mama's so stupid that when yo Papa told her Christmas was just around the corner, she went looking for it.

Yo Mama's so stupid she thought Taco Bell was a Mexican phone company.

Yo Mama's so stupid the only thing she got on her IQ test was drool.

Yo Mama's so stupid that when she saw the headline "Knife Attack On Bus", she said, "Who'd want to stab a bus?"

Yo Mama's so stupid she tried to drown herself in a carpool.

Yo Mama's so stupid she climbed on the roof because she heard drinks were on the house.

Yo Mama's so stupid she tried to steal a free sample.

Yo Mama's so stupid, she'd have to be twice as smart to be a half-wit.

Yo Mama's so stupid that when yo Papa said it was chilly outside, she went to fetch a bowl.

Yo Mama's so stupid she thinks Christmas wrap is Snoop Dogg's holiday album.

Yo Mama's so stupid she took a ruler to bed with her to see how long she slept.

Yo Mama's so stupid she got hit by a parked car.

Yo Mama's so stupid, I saw her walking down the street yelling into an envelope and when I asked her what she was doing, she said, "Sending a voice mail."

Yo Mama's so stupid that when the judge yelled, "Order in the court," she said, "I'll have a cheeseburger and a medium Coke."

Yo Mama's so stupid she threw breadcrumbs in the toilet to feed the toilet duck.

Yo Mama's so stupid she took the Pepsi challenge and chose Cif.

Yo Mama's so stupid, I saw her in the frozen food section of the supermarket with a fishing rod.

Yo Mama's so stupid that when she read the newspaper headline "Knife Attack On Bus", she rang the depot to find out how the bus was.

Yo Mama's so stupid she took a spoon to the Superbowl.

Yo Mama's so stupid that when a job application said "sex", she wrote, "Monday, Wednesday and sometimes Saturday."

Yo Mama's so stupid that when I saw her jumping up and down and asked what she was doing, she said she drank a bottle of medicine but forgot to shake it.

Yo Mama's so stupid she went to Gap to get her teeth fixed.

Yo Mama's so stupid that when yo Papa lost his marbles, she went and bought him some new ones.

Yo Mama's so stupid that when I told her I was reading a book by Homer, she asked if I'd got anything written by Bart.

Yo Mama's so stupid that she got locked in a bathroom and wet herself.

Yo Mama's so stupid she used to stand in front of the mirror with her eyes closed so that she could see what she looked like asleep.

Yo Mama's so stupid she threw a rock at the ground and missed.

Yo Papa's so stupid that when he peed on his shoes, he thought it was raining.

Yo sister's so stupid she went to the lost and found when she missed her period.

Yo sister's so stupid that they had to burn her school down just to get her out of third grade.

Yo grandpa's so stupid he thinks Beirut is a famous baseball player.

Yo brother's so stupid he tried to strangle himself with his mobile phone.

Yo minister's so stupid he gives sermons on Genesis – Phil Collins' old band.

Yo Mama's so slutty that when she got a new mini skirt, everyone commented on her nice belt.

Yo Mama's so slutty, she's blind but seeing another man.

Yo Mama's so slutty, she's entertained more soldiers than Bob Hope.

Yo Mama's so slutty, her personalized car licence plate is VD1.

Yo Mama's so slutty, her face is on posters at the sexually transmitted diseases clinic.

Yo Mama's so slutty she's got a new tattoo on her butt: "Swollen goods not accepted, please try round the front."

Yo Mama's so slutty, she's introduced a Park and Ride scheme so that clients can leave their car outside her flat.

Yo Mama's so slutty, she buys condoms in bulk.

Yo Mama's so slutty that turning off the bedroom light means shutting the car door.

Yo Mama's so slutty the identity of yo Papa is a multiple choice question.

Yo Mama's so slutty that after sex she says, "Who are you guys?"

Yo Mama's so slutty that when she fell down on a sidewalk, by the time she'd got back up, she had made twenty dollars.

Yo Mama's so slutty she has a number dispenser on her bedpost.

Yo Mama's so slutty she walks down the street with a mattress strapped to her back, asking for volunteers.

Yo Mama's so slutty she got a job as a slot machine.

Yo Mama's so slutty that yo Papa has to disguise himself as the postman to have sex with her.

Yo Mama's so slutty she gives out frequent rider miles.

Yo Mama's so slutty that I could have been your daddy, but the guy in line behind me had the correct change.

Yo Mama's so slutty she makes Madonna look virginal.

Yo Mama's so slutty that I could have been your daddy, but the gorilla beat me up the stairs.

Yo Mama's so slutty that I could have been your daddy, but the gorilla in line in front of me didn't use a condom.

Yo Mama's so smelly the government makes her wear a Biohazard warning.

Yo Mama's so smelly even dogs won't sniff her.

Yo Mama's so smelly, a blind man walking by asked her, "How much for the shrimp platter?"

Yo Mama's so smelly she uses Right Guard and Left Guard.

Yo Mama's so smelly that farmers use her bathwater as liquid fertilizer.

Yo Mama's so smelly that when she spread her legs yo Papa got seasick.

Yo Mama's so smelly that a skunk smelled her butt and passed out.

Yo Mama's so smelly, she's worse than a vegan's fart.

Yo Mama's so smelly, her Sure deodorant is now Confused.

Yo Mama's so smelly that the only dis I'm going to give her is disinfectant.

Yo Mama's so smelly that the coroner picked her up while she was sleeping.

Yo Mama's so smelly, she made Right Guard call for backup.

Yo Mama's so smelly, dogs like to roll around on her.

Yo Mama's so smelly her bedroom is like the place where whales go to die.

Yo Mama's so smelly she made Right Guard turn left.

Yo Mama's so smelly, there's more crust in her knickers than on a loaf of bread.

Yo Mama's so smelly, her poo is glad to escape.

Yo Mama's so smelly she hums more than a humming bird.

Yo Mama's so smelly that when you were born, all the doctors and nurses had to wear oxygen masks.

Yo Mama's so smelly they had to invent Chanel No. 6.

Yo Mama's so smelly, yo Papa can't eat her pussy without a lifeguard on duty.

Yo Mama's so smelly she made the gasmask become a fashion statement.

Yo Mama's feet are so smelly she should be charged with sock abuse.

Yo Mama's so dirty she has to creep up on the bath water.

Yo Mama's so dirty she lost two stone taking a shower.

Yo Mama's so dirty you can tell her age by counting the rings around her.

Yo Mama's so dirty she actually repels mosquitoes.

Yo Mama's so dirty that even the rats shout, "Unclean! Unclean!"

Yo Mama's so dirty that grass grows in her belly button.

Yo Mama's so dirty, the last time she had a bath was to mark the end of Prohibition.

Yo Mama's so dirty that Saddam Hussein tried to import her bath water to use as chemical weapons.

Yo Mama's so dirty that when she went to the doctor, he didn't send her for a blood test, he sent her for a soil test.

Yo Mama's so dirty that when she wears a black dress people think she's naked.

Yo Mama's so dirty, her farts register eight on the Richter scale.

Yo Mama's so dirty that after you shake her hand you have to be quarantined.

Yo Mama's so dirty her tights can walk to the laundry basket by themselves.

Yo Mama's so dirty that the only reason flies were given wings was so they could beat her to the dump.

Yo Mama's so dirty that Tony Blair scared her because she thought he said he was going to be tough on grime and tough on the causes of grime.

Yo Mama's so dirty you can tell her age by the rings underneath her armpits.

Yo Mama's so dirty that even tramps won't be seen with her.

Yo Mama's so dirty that mould forms on her teeth.

Yo Mama's so dirty, mice go mud wrestling in her belly button.

Yo Mama's so dirty that when her drill sergeant said, "Hit the dirt", everyone started hitting her.

Yo Mama's so dirty, President Bush was considering dropping her farts on Iraq.

Yo Mama's so dirty she makes mud look clean.

Yo Mama's so dirty, her idea of a bubble bath is to eat baked beans for dinner.

Yo Mama's so dirty she leaves rings around the public swimming pool.

Yo Mama's house is so dirty that visitors have to wipe their feet before going back outside.

Yo Mama's house is so dirty that the cockroaches ride around in dune buggies.

Yo Mama's house is so dirty that cockroaches check in but never check out.

Yo Mama's house is so dirty the mice bring napkins so they won't have to eat off her floor.

Yo Mama's house is so dirty that when she says the toilet is *en suite*, she means you go on the suite.

Yo Mama's house is so dirty Mr Sheen killed himself.

Yo Mama's house is so dirty she has been appointed to keep the national collection of bacteria.

Yo Mama's house is so dirty, the rats are consulting their lawyer.

Yo Mama's house is so dirty that when she finally cleaned under her bed, she found Shergar, Lord Lucan and the crew of the *Marie Celeste*.

Yo Mama's so nasty I talked to her over the PC and she gave me a virus.

Yo Mama's so nasty she bit the dog and gave it rabies.

Yo Mama's so nasty there are more scabs on her than ever crossed a union picket line.

Yo Mama's so nasty she puts ice down her knickers to keep the crabs fresh.

Yo Mama's so nasty her crabs use her tampon string as a bungee cord.

Yo Mama's so nasty she's got more clap than an auditorium.

Yo Mama's so nasty her breasts give sour milk.

Yo Mama's so nasty that when she dies, she wants to be cremated and thrown in someone's face.

Yo Mama's so nasty that when she does the splits she sticks to the floor.

Yo Mama's so nasty she went swimming and made the Dead Sea.

Yo Mama's so nasty, even her scabs have scabs.

Yo Mama's so greasy that Texaco buy oil from her.

Yo Mama's so greasy her freckles slipped off.

Yo Mama's so greasy that helping her across the road was like wrestling with a bar of wet soap.

Yo Mama's so greasy she sells her sweat to the chip shop.

Yo Mama's so greasy she keeps sliding off the bed at night.

Yo Mama's so greasy she can easily slip into something more comfortable.

Yo Mama's so greasy that slugs find her trail of slime attractive.

Yo Mama's so greasy that her slip-on shoes slip right off.

Yo Mama's so greasy that the kids in the park use her as a slide.

Yo Mama's so greasy that her push-up bra couldn't stop itself.

Yo Mama's so greasy that when she goes to bed at night she wears snow chains to hold up her gown.

Yo Mama's so greasy that her leg warmers started frying.

Yo Mama's so greasy that the staff at the supermarket refer to her as a slippery customer.

Yo Mama's so greasy that it's easier to hold on to a job than it is to hold on to yo Mama.

Yo Mama's so greasy she doesn't give blood, she gives oil.

Yo Mama's so greasy that when two muggers attacked her, she gave them the slip.

Yo Mama's hair is so greasy you could fry chicken in it.

Yo Mama's hair is so greasy her centre parting slipped down to her ear.

Yo Mama's hair is so greasy her slides keep sliding off.

Yo Mama's hair is so greasy her grips won't grip.

Yo Mama's hair is so greasy her head lice choke to death.

Yo Mama's hair is so greasy she doesn't wash it with shampoo, she washes it with industrial detergent.

Yo Mama's hair is so greasy that when it is wet, it forms oil slicks.

Yo Mama's hair is so greasy that you need to wear rubber gloves before running your fingers through it.

Yo Mama's so poor burglars break into her home and *leave* money.

Yo Mama's so poor she hangs the toilet paper out to dry.

Yo Mama's so poor that after I pissed in your yard, she thanked me for watering the lawn.

Yo Mama's so poor they put her photo on food stamps.

Yo Mama's so poor she watches television on Etch-A-Sketch.

Yo Mama's so poor people rob her house for practice.

Yo Mama's so poor that she can only get to wear her best dress when the dog doesn't need its blanket.

Yo Mama's so poor that to save on water, she washes her hair when she flushes the toilet.

Yo Mama's so poor that people talk to her in Romanian.

Yo Mama's so poor that the last time your family had a hot meal was when your house was on fire.

Yo Mama's so poor that her favourite hat doubles up as a lampshade.

Yo Mama's so poor that a brick through her window would be considered a home improvement.

Yo Mama's so poor that your Kinder eggs never have any surprises in them.

Yo Mama's so poor she waves an ice cube around and calls it air conditioning.

Yo Mama's so poor the bank repossessed her cardboard box.

Yo Mama's so poor that when I saw her hobbling down the street with one shoe, I shouted, "Lost a shoe?", and she said, "No, just found one."

Yo Mama's so poor she can't even afford to go to the free clinic.

Yo Mama's so poor, when you ring the doorbell the toilet flushes.

Yo Mama's so poor the only way she can watch TV is by drilling a hole through her neighbour's wall.

Yo Mama's so poor that the garbage collectors give *her* a tip at Christmas.

Yo Mama's so poor, she can't even afford the last two letters, so she just calls herself "po".

Yo Mama's so poor, she's got more furniture on her porch than in her house.

Yo Mama's so poor that when I asked her what she was doing kicking a can down the street, she said, "Moving."

Yo Mama's so poor that you know the story about the old woman who lived in a shoe, well yo Mama lives in a flip flop.

Yo Mama's so poor that while for some people money talks, for yo Mama it doesn't even whisper.

Yo Mama's so poor that when yo brother started having epileptic fits, she used him as a dishwasher.

Yo Mama's so poor she uses tumbleweed as a Christmas tree.

Yo Mama's so poor, she's in debt to the blood bank.

Yo Mama's so poor her idea of double glazed windows is two layers of clingfilm.

Yo Mama's so poor she does her grocery shopping by rummaging through the back of the garbage truck.

Yo Mama's so poor the only drink you get offered in her house is spit.

Yo Mama's so poor I saw her wrestling a squirrel for a peanut.

Yo Mama's so poor she can't even afford to eat her words.

Yo Mama's so poor she conserves toilet paper by using both sides.

Yo Mama's so poor that when I asked her where the toilet was, she said, "Just choose a corner."

Yo Mama's so poor that instead of using a steam iron, she sits on the laundry and farts.

Yo Mama's so poor, the only time she can put chips on yo plate is when she drops it.

Yo Mama's so poor that when someone rings her doorbell, she leans out the window and says "ding-dong".

Yo Mama's so poor she uses cobwebs for curtains.

Yo Mama's so poor that when I stepped on a skateboard outside her house, she yelled, "Hey, get off the car!"

Yo Mama's so poor that instead of switching on the central heating, she kicks yo Papa in the balls and warms her hands on his breath.

Yo Mama's so poor she can't even afford to spend a penny.

Yo Mama's so poor that if you go to her home and ask to use the toilet, she says, "Sure, third tree on the right."

Yo Mama's so poor that when someone went into her living room and stood on a cigarette butt, she yelled: "Who turned off the heater?"

Yo Mama's so poor, her idea of "the good china" is a paper plate.

Yo Mama's so poor that when I walked into her house and swatted a firefly, she said, "Who turned off the lights?"

Yo Mama's so poor that when you use her bathroom, she gives you two sticks – one to hold up the ceiling and the other to fight off the cockroaches.

Yo Mama's so poor she bought a TV with only two channels – On and Off.

Yo Mama's so poor she does drive-by shootings on the bus.

Yo Mama's so poor she can't even afford to put her two cents' worth into the conversation.

Yo Mama's so poor she has to wear her McDonald's uniform to church.

Yo Mama's so poor that when she heard about the Last Supper, she thought the food stamps had run out.

Yo Mama's so poor the rats in her house go round with begging bowls.

Yo Mama's so poor that when she cut her finger, she used chewing gum as a plaster.

Yo Mama's so poor that when I threw a rock at a trash can, she popped out and said, "Who knocked?"

Yo Mama's so poor that when she throws a bone to the dog, it has to call for a fair catch.

Yo Mama's so poor that every night she goes to KFC to lick other people's fingers.

Yo Mama's so poor she can't afford a mop, so she stands on her head to clean the floor.

Yo Mama's so poor the only time she smelled hot food was when a rich man farted.

Yo Mama's so poor she eats cereal with a fork to save milk.

Yo Mama's so poor that when you go over for dinner, she just reads out the recipes.

Yo Mama's so poor she went to the wishing well and threw in an IOU.

Yo Mama's so poor, her kids were made in Taiwan.

Yo Mama's so poor that when you asked her what was for dinner, she took off her shoelaces and said, "Spaghetti."

Yo Mama's so poor she has to take the trash *in*.

Yo Mama's so poor that when I went to use her bathroom, I saw a cockroach sitting on a Pepsi can saying, "Wait your turn!"

Yo Mama's so poor that the only hot meal she had in ages was when a tramp was sick over her.

Yo Mama's so poor she can't even afford to pay attention.

Yo Mama's so poor she only got married for the rice.

Yo Mama's house is so small her front and back doors are on the same hinge.

Yo Mama's house is so small that she can't even order a large pizza.

Yo Mama's house is so small that half of the TV is in one room and half in another.

Yo Mama's house is so small that as soon as you enter it, you've just left.

Yo Mama's house is so small the front door is a cat flap.

Yo Mama's house is so small that I stepped through her front door and fell out the back.

Yo Mama's house is so small she can cut her front lawn with nail scissors.

Yo Mama's house is so small that when she left a shoe box in the yard, the council thought it was an extension.

Yo Mama's house is so small that she and yo Papa sleep in separate rooms – but in the same bed.

Yo Mama's house is so small that only one bird can sit on her roof at a time.

Yo Mama's house is so small, her cat complains that there's not enough room to swing a mouse.

Yo Mama's house is so small, you have to stand on one leg in the shower.

Yo Mama's house is so small that the living-room carpet is just a sample.

Yo Mama's house is so small, you can be upstairs and downstairs at the same time.

Yo Mama's house is so small that the bathroom tiles are just two books of postage stamps.

Yo Mama's house is so small, the three-piece suite has to be in three different rooms.

Yo Mama's house is so small the main TV set is on a cell phone.

Yo Mama's house is so small that visiting sardines complained about the cramped conditions.

Yo Mama's house is so small, the cockroaches are hunchbacked.

Yo Mama's house is so small that when she drops a Kleenex, she has wall-to-wall carpet.

Yo Mama's house is so small that when mail goes through the letterbox it hits everyone inside.

Yo Mama's house is so small, Barbie and Ken rejected it.

Yo Mama's house is so small the doormat just says WEL.

Yo Mama's house is so small you have to go outside just to change your mind.

Yo Mama's so skinny she has to stand in the same place twice to cast a shadow.

Yo Mama's so skinny her bra fits better backwards.

Yo Mama's so skinny yo Papa put a pair of antlers on her head and used her as a hat-stand.

Yo Mama's so skinny she swallowed a meatball and thought she was pregnant.

Yo Mama's so skinny you could blindfold her with dental floss.

Yo Mama's so skinny her pants have one belt loop.

Yo Mama's so skinny that when she wears a fake fur coat she looks like a pipe cleaner.

Yo Mama's so skinny, instead of calling her your parent, you call her transparent.

Yo Mama's so skinny I've seen more meat on a vegan's plate.

Yo Mama's so skinny that when she drinks a tomato juice she looks like a thermometer.

Yo Mama's so skinny that when she closes one eye she looks like a needle.

Yo Mama's so skinny she only has one stripe on her pyjamas.

Yo Mama's so skinny that when she takes a bath and lets the water out, her toes get caught in the plughole.

Yo Mama's so skinny that when she took up golf, the pro called her the thin end of the wedge.

Yo Mama's so skinny she went missing for two days before yo Papa found her standing behind the lampstand.

Yo Mama's so skinny that thirteen is unlucky for her because it's her bust size.

Yo Mama's so skinny that while the rest of your family fly abroad on vacation, she goes air mail.

Yo Mama's so skinny she doesn't show up on X-rays.

Yo Mama's so skinny she was an artist's model for L. S. Lowry.

Yo Mama's so skinny that when I gave her a piece of popcorn, she went into a coma.

Yo Mama's so skinny that the neighbour's dog buried her in the garden.

Yo Mama's so skinny she makes Olive Oyl look obese.

Yo Mama's so skinny she uses a Band Aid as a maxi-pad.

Yo Mama's so skinny that when yo Papa penetrates her, she looks like a hunchback.

Yo Mama's so skinny she looks like a mic stand.

Yo Mama's so skinny that if she turned sideways and stuck out her tongue, she'd look like a zipper.

Yo Mama's so skinny she's only held together by bacteria.

Yo Mama's so skinny she tied knots in her legs just so she could have knees.

Yo Mama's so skinny she can dodge raindrops.

Yo Mama's so skinny her nipples touch.

Yo Mama's so skinny she could wear an onion ring as a necklace.

Yo Mama's so skinny that when she farts she blows away.

Yo Mama's so skinny that if she had a yeast infection, she'd be a quarter-pounder with cheese.

Yo Mama's teeth are so yellow, I can't believe it's not butter.

Yo Mama's teeth are so yellow, cars slow down when she smiles.

Yo Mama's teeth are so yellow, when she drinks water it turns into lemonade.

Yo Mama's teeth are so yellow that when she walked into church everybody said, "I see the light!"

Yo Mama's teeth are so yellow when she smiles that you can see Dorothy skipping across them.

Yo Mama's teeth are so yellow that she got a job at the cinema spitting on popcorn.

Yo Mama's teeth are so yellow she has to brush them with a butter knife.

Yo Mama's teeth are so yellow that when the sun saw her smile, it said, "Someone's doing my job. I might as well go home."

Yo Mama's teeth are so black, you'd think she had eaten coal for dinner.

Yo Mama's teeth stick out so much it looks like her nose is playing the piano.

Yo Mama's teeth are so rotten, when she smiles they look like dice.

Yo Mama's teeth are so crooked, when she smiles it looks like her tongue is in jail.

Yo Mama's teeth are so crooked that she needs a map to find her tongue.

Yo Mama's got so many gaps in her teeth, her mouth looks like piano keys.

Yo Mama's teeth are so ugly she got pulled over for not having dental insurance.

Yo Mama's teeth are so big it looks like her mom had an affair with Mr Ed.

Yo Mama's teeth are so big that when she sneezed she bit a hole in her chest.

Yo Mama's teeth are so big her dentist charges her by the tooth.

Yo Mama's so short she has to slam-dunk her bus fare.

Yo Mama's short, she doesn't roll dice, she pushes them.

Yo Mama's so short she poses for trophies.

Yo Mama's so short that when it comes to painting her house, she can only reach the skirting board.

Yo Mama's so short she has to get to running start to get up on the toilet.

Yo Mama's so short she can do backflips under the bed.

Yo Mama's so short she's afraid to get off the carpet alone.

Yo Mama's so short she trips on her tampon string.

Yo Mama's so short she doesn't see eye to eye with anyone.

Yo Mama's so short she can hang glide on a Dorito.

Yo Mama's so short, her head smells of her feet.

Yo Mama's so short that when the doctor gave her a suppository she doubled in size.

Yo Mama's so short she does pull-ups on a staple.

Yo Mama's so short that even close up she looks far away.

Yo Mama's so short she looks people straight in the belly button.

Yo Mama's so short she can pick mushrooms without bending down.

Yo Mama's so short she's a teller at a piggy bank.

Yo Mama's so short that when she and her twin sister walk down the street, people say, "Hey, it's a pair of shorts!"

Yo Mama's so short she would drown by the time she realized it was raining.

Yo Mama's so short that Dopey, Bashful and Doc see her as a kindred spirit.

Yo Mama's so short, you can see her whole body on her driver's licence.

Yo Mama's so short that when she sneezes, she hits her head on the floor.

Yo Mama's so short she can sit on a dime and swing her legs.

Yo Mama's so short she can look a grasshopper in the eye.

Yo Mama's so short that whenever anyone goes into a bar and orders a short, the barman thinks they mean yo Mama.

Yo Mama's so short she doesn't know if she has a headache or a footache.

Yo Mama's so short she has to hold up a sign that says "Don't Spit. I Can't Swim."

Yo Mama's so short, she broke her leg jumping off the toilet.

Yo Mama's so short people think she's one of The Borrowers.

Yo Mama's so short she doesn't have legs, she has feet growing out of her ass.

Yo Mama's got so much dandruff she needs to defrost it before combing her hair.

Yo Mama's got so much dandruff that when a fly landed on her head, it said: "I ain't seen this much snow in years!"

Yo Mama's got so much dandruff that when she shakes her head outside, they have to clear the street with a snowplough.

Yo Mama's got so much dandruff it looks like she's permanently wearing a white bobble hat.

Yo Mama's got so much dandruff that her family uses it to stuff pillows and quilts.

Yo Mama's got so much dandruff they are holding the next Winter Olympics at her house.

Yo Mama's got so much dandruff she has more flakes than Cadbury's.

Yo Mama's got so much dandruff there is a crisp layer beneath the soft top layer.

Yo Mama's got so much dandruff, polar bears use her hair as camouflage.

Yo Mama's got so much dandruff, she can simulate desiccated coconut with a single scratch.

Yo Mama's got so much dandruff that yo family wear snowboots whenever she combs her hair.

Yo Mama's got so much dandruff, it looks as if she's been the victim of an air raid by a squadron of pigeons.

Yo Mama's got so much dandruff, she provided the backdrop for *White Christmas*.

Yo Mama's got so much dandruff, I've seen penguins nesting in her hair.

Yo Mama's glasses are so thick she can see into the future.

Yo Mama's glasses are so thick that when she looks on a map, she can see people waving.

Yo Mama's glasses are so thick she can burn ants with them.

Yo Mama has so many varicose veins on her body she could double as a road map.

Yo Mama has so many varicose veins she looks like a lump of Stilton cheese.

Yo Mama's breath stinks so bad that when she burps, her teeth have to duck.

Yo Mama's breath stinks so bad it made a Tic Tac run away.

Yo Mama's breath stinks so bad her mouth needs Odor Eaters.

Yo Mama's breath stinks so bad it can strip paint off the walls.

Yo Mama's breath stinks so bad that people look forward to her farts.

Yo Mama's breath stinks so bad we don't know whether she needs gum or toilet paper.

Yo Mama's breath stinks so bad it kills more household germs than bleach.

Yo Mama's breath stinks so bad it must be taking karate lessons, because it's really kicking.

Yo Mama's breath stinks so bad that people on the other end of the phone hang up.

Yo Mama's breath stinks so bad, it could prise barnacles off a ship.

Yo Mama's breath stinks so bad, rain goes back to the clouds.

Yo Mama's breath stinks so bad, she has to take prescription Tic Tacs.

Yo Mama's breath stinks so bad, it really does seem like she's talking shit.

Yo Mama's so lazy, her idea of cleaning the house is to sit in a corner and gather dust.

Yo Mama's so lazy she doesn't walk in her sleep – she hitch hikes.

Yo Mama's so lazy she thinks a two income family is where yo Papa has two jobs.

Yo Mama's so lazy only her cheques bounce.

Yo Mama's so lazy a one-legged tortoise moves more than her.

Yo Mama's so lazy she won't even raise a smile.

Yo Mama's so lazy her idea of exercise is changing channels on the TV.

Yo Mama's so lazy her nose runs more than she does.

Yo Mama's so lazy she's expected to win *American Idle*.

Yo Mama's so lazy that when they asked her if she'd run for President, she said, "Hell, I ain't runnin' for nobody!"

Yo Mama's so lazy she couldn't even be moved to tears.

Yo Mama's so lazy she's like a sack of couch potatoes.

Yo Mama's so lazy her lazy eye has spread to her entire body.

Yo Mama's so lazy she won't even exercise her human rights.

Yo Mama's so lazy even her bowels don't have movements.

Yo Mama's so lazy nothing runs in her family.

Yo Mama's so lazy she's got a remote control just to operate her remote.

Yo Mama's so hairy that when she puts her arms to her side, it looks like she has Don King in a headlock.

Yo Mama's so hairy it looks like she's got a herd of yak in her armpits.

Yo Mamas so hairy she's got afros on her nipples.

Yo Mama's so hairy you could knit her into a pair of gloves.

Yo Mama's so hairy that when her son was born, he suffered severe rugburn.

Yo Mama's so hairy, her breasts look like coconuts.

Yo Mama's so hairy you could stuff a mattress with the hair from her legs.

Yo Mama's so hairy she's got blackbirds nesting in her belly button.

Yo Mama's so hairy that when she got in my car, it looked like I had tinted windows.

Yo Mama's so hairy that native beaters had to hack their way through to reach her thighs.

Yo Mama's so hairy that when she walks the dog, people stroke *her*.

Yo Mama's so hairy that Sting has announced he wants to save her forest.

Yo Mama's so hairy, they filmed *Gorillas in the Mist* in her shower.

Yo Mama's so hairy she shaves with a weedwacker.

Yo Mama's so hairy she got a trim and lost ten pounds.

Yo Mama's so hairy, if she could fly she'd look like a magic carpet.

Yo Mama's so hairy she has dreadlocks on her back.

Yo Mama's so hairy Bigfoot took a picture of her.

Yo Mama's so hairy her breasts have sideburns.

Yo Mama's got so much hair on her upper lip she has to braid it.

Yo Mama's chest hair is so damn long it grows all the way down to her dick.

Yo Mama's got one toe and one knee and they call her Toni.

Yo Mama's got a wooden nipple and they call her Corky.

Yo Mama's got one tooth and they call her Chopper One.

Yo Mama's got no fingers but she talks about how she wanted to be with the Pointer Sisters.

Yo Mama's got no fingers but she talks about how she's gonna press charges.

Yo Mama's only got three fingers but she still says, "Gimme five!"

Yo Mama's got one arm and swims in circles.

Yo Mama's got one leg and a bicycle.

Yo Mama's got no neck but she talks about how she's all choked up.

Yo Mama's got no ears but she tries on sunglasses.

Yo Mama's only got one ear but she talks about how she wants to hear both sides of the story.

Yo Papa's bow-legged, yo Mama's knock-kneed, and when they walk down the street they spell OK.

Yo Papa's dick is so small that when he took it out in court it was rejected for lack of evidence.

Yo Papa's dick is so small he uses a thimble as a condom.

Yo Papa's dick is so small that even the Hubble Telescope couldn't spot it from sixty yards.

Yo Papa's dick is so small, he stuffs his pants with peanuts to feel good about himself.

Yo Papa's dick is so small that if he were Adam, he could have used a clover leaf to cover himself in the Garden of Eden.

EUPHEMISMS

His elevator doesn't go all the way to the top floor.

The lights are on but nobody's at home.

The oven's on, but nothing's cooking.

The radio's playing but nobody's listening.

He's a few sandwiches short of a picnic.

He's a few trees short of an orchard.

He's a few clowns short of a circus.

He's a few peas short of a pod.

He's a few currants short of a fruit cake.

He's a few guppies short of an aquarium.

He's a few feathers short of a whole duck.

He's a few flowers short of an arrangement.

He's a few spokes short of a wheel.

He's several nuts short of a full pouch.

He's a few chapters short of a novel.

He's a few pancakes short of a stack.

He's a couplet short of a sonnet.

He's a flying buttress short of a cathedral.

He's one song short of a musical.

He's one drop short of an empty bladder.

He's one span short of a bridge.

He's one tree short of a hammock.

He's one car short of a chase scene.

He's one sultana short of a total fruitcake.

He's two socks short of a pair.

He's a few crayons short of a full box.

He's a few links short of a chain.

He's a few ears short of a bushel.

He's a few straws short of a bale.

He's a few clues short of a crossword.

He's a couple of slates short of a full roof.

He's one Brady short of a Bunch.

He's a few chocolate chips short of a cookie.

He's a few pickles short of a jar.

He's a few keys short of a piano.

He's a few pixels short of a full image.

She's a few beads short of a rosary.

She's several pearls short of a necklace.

She's one tit short of an udder.

He's a pane short of a window.

He's a lettuce leaf short of a salad.

He's four bows short of a string quartet.

He's a burger short of a Happy Meal.

He's a few beers short of a six-pack.

He's several peas short of a casserole.

He's a few bricks short of a full load.

He's a goose short of a gaggle.

He's a sentence short of a paragraph.

He's a battleship short of a full fleet.

He's a sausage short of a barbecue.

He's a button short of a shirt.

He's one colour short of a rainbow.

He's one hot pepper short of an enchilada.

He's a cup and saucer short of a place setting.

He's a scallop short of a seafood platter.

He's one screw short of a final assembly.

His truck's a little short of a full load.

His golf bag does not contain a full set of irons.

His manual drive is stuck in reverse.

He's a calendar with blank squares.

One boot is stuck in the sand.

He's a BLT missing the bacon.

There's nothing between the stethoscopes.

He's a square with only three sides.

There are a few tiles missing from his space shuttle.

The spit valve has fallen off his trumpet again.

He's a statue in a world of pigeons.

He's operating in stand-by mode.

He doesn't have a round in every chamber.

His attic's a little dusty.

He is strolling through life with one shoelace untied.

There's nothing on his radar.

Oil doesn't reach his dipstick.

She types 120 words per minute, but her keyboard isn't plugged in.

He's pedalling fast, but he's not getting anywhere.

He's got plenty of bricks but no cement.

He is stuck on the down escalator of life.

He's sitting in the right pew but in the wrong church.

There's no grain in his silo.

His blender doesn't go past "mix".

He's got all of the notes but none of the music.

He's driving at night with the lights off.

He's skating on the wrong side of the ice.

He's flying on one engine.

Not all his dogs are barking.

He's knitting with only one needle.

He's a .22 calibre intellect in a .357 Magnum world.

He smells the coffee but can't find the pot.

His teapot's got a cracked lid.

Both oars in the water, but they're on the same side of the boat.

There's plenty of salt in the shaker, but no holes in the lid.

Perfect chassis, bad driver.

He's permanently out to lunch.

He is a little too tall for his blood supply.

He's playing baseball with a rubber bat.

Full throttle, dry tank.

Gasoline engine, diesel fuel.

His receiver is off the hook.

He's a titanic intellect in a world full of icebergs.

He's a violin minus a bow.

He's a PBS mind in an MTV world.

There's a loose wire in his headset.

His gavel doesn't quite hit the bench.

Her sewing machine has been out of thread for some time now.

He's goalkeeper for the darts team.

He's got a full six-pack but he lacks the plastic thingy to hold it all together.

A photographic memory, but with the lens cover left on.

His files are compressed 100 percent.

His puzzle is missing a few pieces.

He's a wind-up clock without a key.

There's no hay in the loft.

His display is always flashing 12:00.

His closet is full of hangers but no clothing.

He's not the sharpest knife in the drawer.

He's not the fizziest drink in the fridge.

He's not the brightest porch light on the block.

He's not the shiniest penny in the jar.

He's not the freshest egg in the carton.

He's not the smartest suit in the wardrobe.

He's not the coldest beer in the fridge.

He's a dim bulb in the marquee of life.

His train tracks aren't quite parallel.

His watchdog is sleeping.

He's a couple of blocks behind the parade.

He's half a bubble off plumb.

He's a day late and a dollar short.

His brain waves fall a little short of the beach.

Not all cylinders are firing.

His back burners are not fully operating.

He is bandwidth limited.

He's having a party in his head, but no one is dancing.

He has been short on oxygen one time too many.

The picture frame is empty.

The elevator to the brain suite is out of order.

There's an end of season sale at the cerebral department.

He gives a lot of bull for somebody that hasn't got any cattle.

He has a one-way ticket on the Disoriented Express.

Batteries are not included.

He missed the last train to Clue Junction.

He writes blank cheques on a closed account.

There is a bubble in his think tank.

The caboose seems to be pulling the engine.

His ski lift doesn't go to the top of the hill.

There's a kangaroo loose in his top paddock.

His server has crashed.

He's a lap behind the field.

There's a lot of feathers but not much chicken.

He's a man on a mission, but he can't find his dossier.

His clock doesn't have all its numbers.

There are too many birds on his antenna.

There are too many jokers in his deck and not enough aces

There is a vacancy at the Grey Matter Hotel.

His truck can't haul a full load.

His cart can't hold all the groceries.

The cursor is flashing but there's no response.

He has his solar panels aimed at the moon.

He cackles a lot, but nobody has seen any eggs yet.

The gates are down, the lights are flashing, but the train isn't coming.

The wheel is spinning, but the hamster is dead.

In the pinball game of life, his flippers are a little farther apart than most.

He gets his orders from another planet.

He doesn't have all the dots on his dice.

He's all crown and no filling.

He's all foam and no beer.

He's all belt and no trousers.

He's all cassette and no tape.

He's all hammer and no nail.

He's all hawk and no spit.

He's all booster and no payload.

He's all foliage and no fruit.

He's all icing and no cake.

He's all missile and no warhead.

He's all wax and no wick.

He's swimming in the shallow end of the gene pool.

He's reading from a blank disk.

His suitcase doesn't have a handle.

His leads need resoldering.

There's too much yardage between the goal posts.

He's not playing with a full deck.

He's a semitone flat on the high notes.

He's a single-cylinder brain in a V8 world.

His driveway doesn't quite reach the garage.

He's a little light in his loafers.

He's diagonally parked in a parallel universe.

He only has one oar in the water.

His head doesn't cast a shadow.

His belt doesn't go through all the loops.

His antenna doesn't pick up all the channels.

His modem lights are on but there's no carrier.

His chimney's clogged.

Room for rent, unfurnished.

The cheese slid off his cracker.

The springs in his mousetrap are rusty.

He went in for repairs but wasn't tightened with a torque wrench.

He wasn't strapped in during launch.

His amplifier is turned all the way up but all you can hear is white noise.

He doesn't have all his cornflakes in one box.

He doesn't have all his dogs on one leash.

He sat under the ozone hole too long.

His gene pool could use a filter.

He's a barnacle on the ship of progress.

He's driving down the road of life with the handbrake on.

He's a butter knife in a steak world.

He's a black-and-white mind working on a colour-coded problem.

CURSES

Ancient

Woe unto thee, thou denizen of the underworld, for thou will be smitten with all-over boils!

I pray thou shalt go on a diet of crunchy, unsweetened locusts, thou child of Jezebel!

May you beget difficult teenagers, O pile of dung!

May you become as popular as a boil on the King's backside!

Woe unto thee, O armpit of Satan, for you will be kicked by an incontinent camel!

Harken, thou of little faith, for you will be turned into a pillar of salt!

Cursed shall be your basket and your kneading-trough!

Cursed shall you be in the city, and cursed shall you be in the field!

Cursed shall be the fruit of your body, and the fruit of your ground!

Listen, O thou relative of Herod, for you will have more mothers-in-law than King Solomon!

May you melt off the earth like snow off a hillside!

May your pipe never smoke, may your teapot be broke!

May you keep to the bed till the hour that you're dead!

May your spade never dig, may your sow never pig!

May your door have no latch, may your house have no thatch!

May the devil cut the head off you and make a day's work of your neck!

May the malevolent hedgehogs soil your cornflakes!

May the worms choke your worthless butt!

May the cat eat you and may the devil eat the cat!

May you have glass legs and may the glass break!

May your pigs be set upon by ravens and torn asunder, leaving only bespecked bone and curdled fat for the rats to feast upon!

May your fields be fallow, your mares be barren, and your tongue be leaden!

A pox unto thee!

Modern

May a thousand fleas infest your groin and may your arms be too short to scratch!

May you be pursued into the mountains by sex-mad baboons!

May all your teeth fall out except the one that aches!

May your daughter's hair grow thick and abundant, all over her face!

May you squat on a cactus when caught short in the desert!

May a bird of paradise fly up your nose!

May onions grow in your navel!

May your personal organizer crash!

May you leave home without your American Express card!

May your liposuction oversuck!

May your reflection disown you!

May you find your wife in bed with your best friend – your dog!

May you put on five pounds in the first week of your diet!

May a family of ferrets nest in your pants!

May your inflatable girlfriend get a flat!

May you be stranded on a desert island with Hannibal Lecter!

May your dog eat your remote!

May all of Santa's reindeer get the shits on your roof!

May your hair fall out, and your teeth fall in!

May a mean surgeon sew up your asshole!

May the devil roast the nuts off you!

May the surgeon drop your facelift!

May your flyaway hair fly away!

May your surfing be plagued with pop-ups!

May your new car be overtaken by a mobility scooter!

May your computer save function always fail!

May a seagull snatch your toupee!

May a crazed pit-bull terrier mistake your leg for its deadly rival!

May your winning lottery ticket be lost at the dry cleaner!

May the hounds of hell gnaw at your manly part!

May a hungry python be lurking in your toilet bowl!

May your therapist have a breakdown!

May you be constipated for life!

May your membership renewal for the lap dancing club be sent to your wife by mistake!

May you be trapped in an elevator with the world farting champion!

May a swarm of bees mistake your asshole for the entrance to their hive!

May your accountant be honest!

May your video recorder suddenly revert to the Julian calendar!

May global warming flood your beach house!

May your life coach commit suicide!

May the desert winds blow an angry scorpion up your underpants!

May you win a Jade Goody lookalike contest!

May you finish second to George W. Bush in a popularity contest!

May Heather Mills ask you out on a date!

May Dick Cheney invite you on a hunting vacation!

CAUSTIC COMEBACKS

Why don't you slip into something more comfortable . . . like a coma?

Could I drop you off somewhere — say, the roof?

I'm busy now. Can I ignore you some other time?

The trouble with you is you're forgotten . . . but not gone.

When your IQ reaches fifty, you should sell.

I see you remembered to take your Stupid Pill this morning.

If I gave you two aspirins, would you go away?

I'm trying to imagine you with a personality.

Do you want me to accept you as you are or do you want me to like you?

It's a case of mind over matter — I don't mind because you don't matter.

I've only got one nerve left — and you're getting on it.

I used to think you were a gibbering idiot, but now I have a much lower opinion of you.

You're good looking in a way – way off.

Sorry, but you're obviously mistaking me for someone who gives a damn.

Of all the people I've met, you're certainly one of them.

A guy with your IQ should have a low voice too.

Moonlight becomes you; total darkness even more.

I'm paid to make an idiot out of myself. Why do you do it for free? – Henny Youngman

I've seen people like you before, but I had to pay admission.

A half-wit gave you a piece of his mind, and you kept it.

What's on your mind, if you'll forgive the exaggeration?

Any friend of yours . . . is a friend of yours.

How would you like to donate a pint of blood through your nose?

I can tell you always manage to keep your head above water – just by the colour of it.

Your hairdresser must really hate you.

You're going to take *me*? The only thing you should take is penicillin.

I feel so miserable without you, it's almost like having you here. – Stephen Bishop

You should toss out more of your funny remarks – that's all they're good for.

People can't say that you have absolutely nothing. After all, you have inferiority!

You know, there's a big difference between being "hot" and being hot and sweaty.

Fight global warming: shut your mouth.

If you're going to say something that dumb, you could at least fake a stroke.

I haven't seen anything like you since the circus left town.

Where have you been all my life – and when are you going back there?

Bring out the elephants, the clowns are already here!

Is that your face or has your neck just vomited? – Julian Clary

English is your second language, isn't it? You don't have a first.

No one can stand you, but to be fair, that's your only fault.

I'm sorry, what language are you speaking? It sounds like Bollocks. – *One Foot in the Grave*

There's a bus leaving in a few minutes. Please be under it!

For two cents, I'd give you a piece of my mind – and all of yours.

All that you are you owe to your parents. Why don't you send them a penny and square the account?

I haven't been ignoring you; I've been prioritizing you.

If I'd wanted to talk to someone like you, I'd have gone to the pet store.

I'd explain it to you, but your brain would explode.

If you think I'm going off with you, then you must be dumber than you look, and that boggles the mind.

Love the coat. You were lucky to get so much material.

It's not the ups and downs in life that bother me, but the jerks like you.

I know what sign you were born under: Red Light District.

Next time I see you, remind me not to talk to you. – Groucho Marx

I would offer to shag your brains out, but it looks as if someone has beaten me to it.

Why don't you go to the library and brush up on your ignorance?

A rejection letter from MENSA wouldn't be too much of a surprise for you, would it?

The next time you wash your neck, wring it.

I believe you can trace your ancestors back to royalty – King Kong.

I can read you like a book. I just wish I could shut you up like one.

You know, you wouldn't be a bad-looking guy . . . if it weren't for your face.

I'd love to ask how old you are, but unfortunately I know you can't count that high.

Are you out of what is left of your mind?

See no evil, hear no evil, date no evil.

At least you only charge what your free advice is worth.

As people go, I wish you would.

I'll see you in my dreams – if I eat too much.

Don't worry, I like small men. In fact you're a real bargain – fifty percent off!

If you were the last man on earth I'd demand a recount.

You're a habit I'd like to kick – with both feet.

Close your mouth before someone puts an apple in it.

You must have a large brain to hold so much ignorance.

They say all good things must come to an end and the same is true of this date.

If you had your life to live over again, do it overseas. – Henny Youngman

I've heard so much about you. What's your side of the story?

If they ever put a price on your head, take it.

Why don't you go away and play Russian roulette with all chambers fully loaded?

There are two kinds of people in the world: cool people and you.

I think of you when I am lonely. Then I am quite content to be alone.

I looked high and low for you, but I obviously didn't look low enough.

If you need me, hesitate to call.

It's not very big, is it? How do you piss without getting soaked?

You have a schoolboy complexion – it looks like it was expelled.

Good news: you are no longer beneath my contempt.

I know one should judge a man by what he really is instead of by appearances, but you are *really* ugly.

At the beautician do you use the emergency entrance?

Who is using the family brain cell at the moment? – *Blackadder*

Now do you see what happens when cousins marry?

You're in amazing condition. In fact, I never saw anyone in your condition.

Your conversation is like the waves of the sea – it makes me sick.

Who am I calling 'stupid'? I don't know. What's your name?

They say space is a dangerous place . . . especially if it's between your ears.

What do you use for contraception? Your personality?

I bet you thought it was just coincidence that your parents had the same surnames before they married?

Is that your face or did your hat melt?

Well, what you lack in size, you make up for in speed.

Why don't you talk to the wall? That's plastered as well. – Jasper Carrott

I can hardly contain my indifference.

Your trailer park called – their trash is missing.

Describing you is easy: you're tall, dark and hands.

Sorry, I don't speak retardese.

You must be older than you look. No one could get to be that stupid so quickly.

Don't be ignorant all your life. Take a day off.

I've going to have a bust made out of your head, or, possibly the other way around.

What brought you out of the woodwork?

Exactly what is it that you see in you?

Please don't talk while I'm interrupting.

There are three kinds of people in this world . . . and then there's you.

I know romance brings out the best in you – the jackass.

You know what happens when you assume? You make an ASS out of U and ME.

Was it your day off when brains were handed out?

I wish I'd known you when you were alive. – L. L. Levinson

Are those your feet or are you breaking them in for a duck?

You must be arithmetic man; you add trouble, subtract pleasure, divide attention, and multiply ignorance.

It's men like you that give the Y chromosome a bad name.

Are you taking part in one of God's experiments to see if humans can function without a brain?

You're a waste of time, space, air, flesh, and the rectum you were born from.

The jerk store called and they're running out of you.

You're the kind of person I would like to have over when I have the measles.

Why don't you broaden your mind? Put a stick of dynamite in each ear.

Excuse me, my foot has gone to sleep. Do you mind if I join it?

How many times do I have to flush you before you go away?

So that's what a mummy looks like without the bandages.

Superior? You're not superior to an amoeba with special needs. – *Life On Mars*

Just because you work in computers, I didn't expect you to have a little mouse.

Would you like some cheese and crackers to go with that whine?

You are definitely non-addictive.

You are looking nicer than usual, but that's so easy for you. – Saki

You know what I like about you? Nothing.

Let's play house. You be the door, and I'll slam you.

We know what you are: now we're just haggling over the price.

The spare tyre belongs in the car trunk, not around your waist.

If you ever become a mother, can I have one of the puppies?

Can I borrow your face for a few days? My ass is going on holiday.

People clap when they see you – their hands over their eyes.

Was that suit made to order? Where were you at the time? – Henny Youngman

Don't worry if your mind wanders – it's too weak to go far.

I'd like to introduce you to some of my friends. I want to break off with them.

Jokes fall from your lips almost as fast as hair falls from your head.

I could say nice things about you, but I'd rather tell the truth.

Have you been shopping lately? They're selling lives at the mall – you should get one.

That's a nice shirt. What brand is it? Clearance?

You promised me the earth, but all I got was a little sod.

It's been fascinating to talk to you but isn't it time you were back in the home?

Is that a new hairdo or did you just walk through a wind tunnel?

I'm now convinced it is possible to communicate with the dead, because I can hear you clearly.

Let's play horse. I'll be the front end and you can just be yourself.

You should be on the stage. The next one leaves in half an hour.

You look great. Who is your embalmer?

You have the morals of a rabbit, the character of a slug, and the brain of a platypus. – *Moonlighting*

I do understand you. I have a way with dumb animals.

Do you have to leave so soon? I was just about to poison the tea.

Blood may be thicker than water but nothing is thicker than you.

No, those pants don't make you look fatter. I mean, how could they?

Personally, I liked you better when you were on the cover of *Mad* magazine.

Things could be worse. You could be here in person.

You are the excess baggage in the airport of my life.

Why don't you stand up and give your brain a rest?

I would insult you, but you're not bright enough to notice.

Would you mind reaching into your heart and getting me a piece of ice?

You have a ready wit. Tell me when it's ready.

Trust me, the only workmate that will go to bed with you is made by Black & Decker.

Why don't you get lost somewhere where they don't have a "found" department?

I like you. I know I have no taste, but I like you.

Your mother always said you were going places real fast – too bad she didn't tell you it was in the back seat of a police patrol car.

I have a warm place for you – not in my heart, in my fireplace. – W. C. Fields

I would like the pleasure of your company, but it only gives me displeasure.

Tell me, are your family happy – or do you still live at home?

The last time I saw a face like yours, I threw it a fish.

They said your baby brother looked like you. Then they turned him right side up.

Wouldn't clues have more room to fit in your head if you got rid of some of the garbage in there?

How many rocks did they have to turn over before you crawled out?

Nice perfume, but must you marinate in it?

You're smarter than you look, but then again, you'd have to be.

You look shot – and that's what you should be.

I think the world of you, and you know what a state the world is in today.

You must be an extremely tolerant person. How else could you put up with yourself?

I stuck up for you today. Someone said you weren't fit to eat with pigs. I said you were.

I'll make you a deal: I won't tell anyone you're ugly if you don't tell anyone you're stupid.

If I gave you a going-away present, would you?

You remind me of a gun — a small bore.

You have a figure like an hourglass — it takes an hour to figure it out.

Your legs aren't half bad: they're all bad.

If I told you I had a piece of dirt in my eye, would you move?

I wouldn't say your personal hygiene leaves a little to be desired, but why don't you do yourself a favour and go through the car wash . . . without your car?

You say you've got a mind of your own. It would be nice to meet it some time.

Call out the drug squad — a hundred and seventy-five pounds of dope just walked in.

If I said anything to offend you, it was purely intentional.

Who did your hair? The council?

Let's talk again after your brain transplant.

Why don't you go to the clifftop and jump to a conclusion?

You've given me something to live for — revenge.

How can I keep a fool in suspense for twenty-four hours? I'll tell you tomorrow.

I'd like to leave you with one thought, but I'm not sure you have anywhere to put it.

Have you ever noticed that whenever you sit behind a keyboard, some idiot starts typing?

Can I borrow your brain? I'm building an idiot.

When they put teeth in your mouth, they spoiled a perfectly good bum. – Billy Connolly

They just invented a new coffin for you that goes over the head. It's for people who are dead from the neck up.

Just because you have a sunken chest doesn't make you a treasure.

It takes all kinds of people to make up the world. It's a shame you're not one of them.

You'd better not sit down: brain damage is irreversible.

Never be afraid to laugh at yourself – after all, you could be missing out on the joke of the century. – Dame Edna Everage

When you wake up in the morning without all the make-up, the perfectly styled hair, the push-up bra, the sexy heels . . . does your wife still love you?

All I can say is, you're in better company than I am.

I can feel the hot blood pounding through your varicose veins.

I hope you stay single and make some poor girl happy.

That's an interesting perfume you're wearing. Who sold it to you, a skunk?

One of us is crazy. But don't worry, I'll keep your secret.

When I want your opinion, I'll give it to you.

The Anti-Moron software on my PC went crazy when I began to read your post.

Nice dress. Are you hoping to slim into it?

I wish you were on TV so I could turn you off.

Here's twenty cents. Go call all your friends and bring me back the change.

Listen, if you ever need a friend . . . buy a dog.

If I smelled as bad as you, I wouldn't live near people. – *True Grit*

I think of you as evolution in action.

The most underdeveloped territory in the world has just been discovered, and it is under your hat.

We've been through so much together, and most of it was your fault.

You have a striking personality. How long has it been on strike?

If I don't get in touch with you in six weeks or so, please show me the same consideration.

For a minute I thought you were crazy, but I was wrong: you've been crazier for much longer than that.

The next time you have an idea . . . let it go.

You look like you could have been quite a sportsman at one time – about a hundred burgers ago.

Are you wearing a turtleneck or is that your own neck?

I hate everybody and you're next.

Aren't there any mirrors in your kennel?

You look much better with my eyes closed.

You ought to go to a photographer and get your negative personality developed.

I would tell you to stop acting like a fool, but I don't think you're acting.

You remind me of history – always repeating yourself.

You're beginning to sound reasonable. Must be time to up my medication.

I see you're in shape. It's a pity the shape is round.

Was your hairdresser exacting revenge for something?

Why don't you get a nice red lamp so men can see you from the street?

You're a difficult person to dislike, but I'm managing it.

I don't want you to turn the other cheek – it's just as ugly.

Are you breaking those teeth in for Mr Ed?

Your mind needs changing. It's filthy.

Looking through my diary, I do have a window for you – to jump out of.

I didn't recognize you for a minute. It was one of the happiest minutes I've ever spent.

You should have your face lifted – with a rope around your neck.

I won't ask you to behave like a human being, because I know you don't do impressions.

Sorry, I forgot I was talking to someone to whom Rik Mayall is a comic god.

Well today was a waste of make-up, wasn't it?

I'll try being nicer if you'll try being smarter.

I believe in the hereafter. So hereafter, don't bother me.

Is all that weight you've gained for a movie role?

I believe in the hereafter, and unfortunately for you, I know what you're here after.

Is that your face, or is your ass growing teeth?

Why am I wasting my time talking to someone whose only sexual partner is his right hand?

Are you really leaving or are you just trying to brighten up my day?

I liked you when we first met but you've talked me out of it.

You are validating my inherent mistrust of strangers.

I'll consider letting you have the last word if you guarantee it *will* be your last.

I know a dozen people who would like to meet you – a jury.

You can improve the quality of this conversation by keeping your mouth shut.

I would insult you, but you're not bright enough to notice.

When you get to the men's room, you will see a sign that says "Gentlemen": pay no attention to it. Go right on in.

You must get up really early. How else could you say so many stupid things in one day?

Please turn off your mouth, it's still running.

Last night I dreamed I saw something in front of your house that made me very happy – a removal van.

Are those your legs, or are you riding a chicken?

Well, I'd love to stay and chat, but you're a total bitch. – *Family Guy*

Quick, fetch a hammer! A fly has landed on your head.

Can I borrow your head for my rock garden?

There's something about you I like. Give me a couple of years and I'll remember it.

Will you take your clammy hands off my chair? You have the touch of a love-starved cobra.

Mr Allen, this may come as a shock to you, but there are some men who don't end every sentence with a proposition. – Doris Day, *Pillow Talk*

I'll forgive your rudeness – I know you're simply being yourself.

It was kind of you to invite me to your flat. I enjoy slumming it occasionally.

No wonder you have headaches. Your halo is on too tight.

I think you should live for the moment. But after that, I'm not so sure.

Shock me, say something intelligent.

Would you like to replace my business partner who died this morning? I'll arrange it with the undertaker.

It's getting late. I was beginning to worry. I was afraid you weren't in an accident.

I'm not your type – I have a pulse.

Sorry, I didn't recognise you with your clothes on.

Whatever is eating you must be suffering from food poisoning.

I've got a minute. Tell me everything you know.

You remind me of a goat – always butting in.

There was something about you that I liked, but you spent it.

They say no woman ever made a fool out of you. So who did?

You don't need to wear jewellery – you've already got enough rings under your eyes.

If I promise to miss you, will you go away?

I don't know what I'd do without you, but it's fun thinking about it.

Anyone who said she was crazy about you would have to be.

You should be in Hollywood. In fact, anywhere but here.

What do you do for a living? You are living, aren't you?

I'd hate to take a bite out of you. You're a cookie full of arsenic. – Burt Lancaster, *Sweet Smell of Success*

You may be a down-to-earth guy, but you're not down far enough to suit me.

Would you mind keeping your mouth shut? My houseplants are wilting.

Don't leave yet. I want to forget you exactly the way you are.

Nice jacket. Didn't they have any in your size?

Please keep talking – I need the sleep.

How did you get here? Did you wriggle off the hook?

Why don't you put an egg in your shoe and beat it?

I don't want to be in your future; it's irritating enough being in your present.

OK, so you want to go home. Do you want me to call you a broomstick?

What did you say? I can't hear over the sound of your hair falling out.

You're ideal for hot weather because you leave me cold.

I don't consider you a vulture – I consider you something a vulture would eat.

Isn't such a tiny mind lonely in such a big head?

You made a big mistake today. You got out of bed.

I'd like to hear your opinion, but isn't there already enough ignorance in the world?

If I've said anything to offend you, please tell me. I might want to do it again.

Many thanks for your note. May I recommend a good taxidermist?

I'd like to reach your mind but I have no idea where it's currently located.

I like your approach. Now let's see your departure.

Please close your mouth. It's getting hot in here.

Tell me, what holds your ears apart?

I hope you never feel the way you look.

If you can't live without me, why aren't you dead already? – Cynthia Heimel

Is that a pimple on your ass, or a brain tumour?

I know I can depend on you. You're always around when you need me.

See, you should never drink on an empty head.

Don't look out of the window. People will think it's Halloween.

Is that a beard or are you eating a muskrat?

You know, if your chat-up lines don't strike oil within the first couple of minutes, you should stop boring.

I know I'm talking like an idiot, but I have to talk that way so you can understand me.

You'd make a perfect stranger.

Talk is cheap, but so are you.

I hear you were a beautiful baby. What happened?

The outpatients are out in force tonight, I see. – Tom Lehrer

I hear you're a ladykiller – they take one look at you and die of fright.

You're nobody's fool, but perhaps someone will adopt you.

Nice to see you on your feet. Who sent the derrick?

I'd like to see you in something flowing. Why don't you jump in the river?

Is that your head, or did somebody find a way to grow hair on a meatball?

Next time you throw out your old clothes, stay in them.

I'd like to kick you in the teeth, but why improve your looks?

Just when I think you've gone as low as you can go, you find a basement door. – *Moonlighting*

I'd rather have root canal surgery without anaesthetic than go on a date with you.

Is that your face or are you trying it out for an ugly sister?

Thank you, we're all challenged by your unique point of view.

I'd like to run into you again some time – when you're walking and I'm driving.

If what you don't know can't hurt you, you're practically invulnerable.

Sit down and give your mind a rest.

Your visit has climaxed an already dull day.

You're not boring me. Just wake me up when you've finished talking.

Some people have *savoir faire*. You don't even have taxi fare.

To my regret, I shall have to decline your invitation because of a subsequent engagement. – Oscar Wilde

Wipe your nose. Your brain is leaking.

I just don't hate myself enough to go out with you.

I know you like me – I can see your tail wagging.

Is your name Dan Druff? Because you get into people's hair.

Sometimes I need what only you can provide: your absence.

There are several people in this world that I find obnoxious and you are all of them.

I've enjoyed talking to you. My mind needed the rest.

No, of course you haven't put on weight. By the way, where's your jockey?

I know you say you'd go to the end of the world for me, but would you stay there?

Does it come with an air pump?

I've had a lot to drink – you're beginning to look human.

You must have sixth sense, although there's no sign of the other five.

Your point has been received, understood and ignored.

Is that your face or an open wound?

What is this, a meeting of the ugly convention?

You have everything a man could wish for, madam, including a moustache and rippling biceps.

Some people have called you a wit – and they're half right.

After hearing you talk, I now know that the dead do contact us.

Careful now, don't let your brains go to your head.

I refuse to enter into a battle of wits with you – I will not fight with an unarmed person.

If there's never been a suicide in your family, why don't you break the monotony? – Henny Youngman

You have a very striking face. How many times were you struck?

If I gave you an eraser, would you rub yourself out?

I hear you're very kind to animals, so please give that face back to the gorilla.

Whatever is eating you must be suffering horribly.

Keep talking. One day you'll say something intelligent.

A device is yet to be invented that will measure my indifference to that remark. – M*A*S*H

I would say you were handsome but my guide dog might disagree.

If truth is stranger than fiction, you must be truth.

Is it lonely up there on your pedestal?

What's on your mind, if you'll forgive the overstatement?

What's a nice guy like you doing with a face like that?

Go on, tell them everything you know – it will only take a few seconds.

I don't think you're an idiot – but what's my opinion against thousands of others?

Every day that you breathe, you make my life harder.

Is that a recent condition or were you born that way?

Everyone has a purpose in life. Perhaps yours is watching television. – David Letterman

When you go to a mind reader, do you get half price?

You're not yourself today – I noticed the improvement straight away.

I'd rather go swimming with hungry piranha than have dinner with you.

The more I think of you, the less I think of you.

Don't feel bad. A lot of people have no talent.

I'd like to give you a going-away present but you have to do your part.

Don't you have a terribly empty feeling . . . in your head?

Keep talking. I always yawn when I'm interested.

I'd curse you to look ugly, but I think I missed the rush.

Now kindly cluck off before I extract your giblets and shove a large seasoned onion between the lips you never kiss with. – *Red Dwarf*

It's hard to get the big picture when you have such a small screen.

You bring joy to others, when you leave the room.

Sure, cream rises to the top – but so does scum.

Would you mind closing the door . . . from the outside?

Someday they're going to name a disease after you.

Stay with me; I want to be alone. – Joey Adams

This is an excellent time for you to become a missing person.

Don't go to a mind reader, go to a palmist – I know you've got a palm.

You say you fear success, but really you have nothing to worry about.

I'd rather stick pins in my eyes than go out with you.

Why don't you make like a banana and split?

If I could afford the wood, I'd have your mouth boarded up.

You make me believe in reincarnation because nobody can be as stupid as you in one lifetime.

When was the last time you were with a woman who wasn't crying or asking for payment?

How would you like to be the first person to be kicked into orbit?

I didn't understand why they called it the "rat race" until I met you.

What do you look like with your mouth shut?

Maybe if we water it, it might grow.

You must have a low opinion of people if you think they're your equals.

You used to be arrogant and obnoxious but now you're the opposite – obnoxious and arrogant.

You look like a nervous wreck – apart from the nervous bit.

Have your parents ever asked you to run away?

Did your sideshow leave town without you?

I wish you were all here. I don't like to think there is more.

Except for the day before the day I met you, this is the happiest day of my life. – *Married . . . With Children*

I'd like to help you out. Which way did you come in?

Far be it from me to suggest your family is inbred, but about those webbed feet . . . ?

Great body. Too bad its only purpose is to stop your head floating away.

Have you considered suing your brains for non-support?

I've come across rotting bodies that are less offensive than you.

Things could be worse. You could be twins.

I'm trying to see things from your point of view, but I can't stick my head that far up my ass.

I can't seem to remember your name – and please don't help me.

Nice breasts! My compliments to your surgeon.

Look at you, you look so pretty. I hardly recognized you.

Let me guess . . . you're the kid who pulled a silly face and it stayed that way.

I never forget a face, and in your case I'll remember both of them.

I can't talk to you right now. Tell me, where will you be in ten years?

They say opposites attract. I hope you meet someone who is good-looking, intelligent and refined.

You fill me with inertia. – *Bedazzled*

Some day you will find yourself – and wish you hadn't.

Are your parents siblings?

If I was stuck on a desert island with you and three wishes, I'd still have two wishes.

Do you come from a happy family or do you go home at night?

Oh dear. I've smoked fatter joints than that.

I've got some mistletoe in my back pocket. Why don't you kiss my ass?

Would you mind closing your mouth so that I can see the rest of your face?

If I throw you a stick, will you leave?

Your red shirt goes so well with your eyes.

Are you mooning me or smiling?

I'd like to break the monotony. Where's your weakest point?

Were you born stupid or have you practised hard?

How did you get here? Did someone leave your cage open?

Make a mental note . . . oh, I see you're out of paper!

Make somebody happy. Mind your own business.

I really think you'll go places – and the sooner the better.

You have a good and kind soul. It just doesn't match the rest of you. – Norm Papernick

Yeah, you're pretty . . . pretty stupid.

Instead of being born again, why don't you just grow up?

As an outsider, what do you think of the human race?

You should try to get ahead. You could certainly use one.

Where did you get your degree? The University of Duuuhhh?

When you get back home, give my regards to the warden.

I'm not trying to make a monkey out of you – I can't take the credit.

Why don't you support your local Search and Rescue Unit, and get lost?

There's one too many in this room – and I think it's you.

Whilst every guy has the right to be ugly, you seem to have abused that privilege.

As if my hangover weren't bad enough, you're still here.

Keep on talking so I'll know what you're not thinking.

I'm not as dumb as you look.

I'd listen to the snot in my hankie before I'd listen to you. – *Life On Mars*

So a thought crossed your mind? It must have been a long and lonely journey.

Are you the first in your family to be born without a tail?

When I look into your eyes, I see the back of your head.

Why don't you drink some spot remover and disappear?

When I want your opinion, I'll rattle your cage.

We all have to live with our disappointments, but it doesn't mean I have to sleep with them too.

Please breathe the other way – you're bleaching my hair.

If I never needed a brain transplant, I'd choose yours because I'd want one that had hardly been used.

Sorry if I look interested. I'm not.

The last time I saw something like you, I pinned a tail on it.

Poor Emily. It's so sad that she mixed drugs and alcohol and spent the night with you . . . when most people only die. – *Taxi*

Are you always so stupid, or is today a special occasion?

What has a tiny brain, a big mouth, and an opinion nobody cares about? – You!

Pardon the mess, she was just leaving.

Guy: Isn't it amazing? Every time I breathe in and out, someone dies somewhere in this world.
Girl: Have you tried using a mouthwash?

Guy: So how do you like your eggs in the morning?
Girl: Unfertilized.

Guy: Is this seat empty?
Girl: Yes, and this one will be too if you sit down.

Guy: Your place or mine?
Girl: Both. You're going to yours, and I'm going to mine.

Guy: I promise I'll write to you.
Girl: Are you allowed to use sharp objects where you stay?

Guy: I've got something for you.
Girl: The last time you gave me something, I had to drink cranberry juice for a week.

Guy: I'd really like to see how you look in a sexy little skirt. Is there anything you'd like to see me in?
Girl: Yeah, traction.

Guy: Do you fancy going to bed?
Girl: No, thanks. I'd rather lick my own armpits.

Guy: When can I see you again?
Girl: How about in another life?

Guy: I'm like a heat-seeking missile – I can probe your darkest recesses.
Girl: It's a shame you're also like cement – it takes you two days to get hard.

Guy (following sex): That was great. I never knew you had it in you.
Girl: That's funny, neither did I . . . but I guess size isn't everything.

Guy: You and I were meant to be together.
Girl: So are my thighs.

Guy: Would you like me to bring you breakfast in bed?
Girl: No. One pig in the blanket was enough.

Guy: You make me want to puke.
Girl: You make me think somebody already did.

Guy: It's not how big it is, it's what you can do with it that counts.
Girl: Well, you can certainly do something amazing: you can make it almost invisible to the naked eye.

Guy: What do you think of my dancing?
Girl: Are you trying to get fit or are you having one?

Guy: What would you say if I told you I had a bright idea?
Girl: Nothing. I can't talk and laugh at the same time.

Guy: So what's your sign?
Girl: No Entry.

Guy: I'm a complex guy, a man of many layers.
Girl: Yes, I can see them around your stomach.

Guy: Can I bury my head in your cleavage?
Girl: Just bury your head.

Guy: I once owned a dog that was smarter than you.
Girl: He must have taught you everything you know.

Guy: Do you want to come back to my place?
Girl: I don't know. Will two people fit under a rock?

Guy: I can fulfil your sexual fantasy.
Girl: Where's your horse, then?

Guy: How do I go about getting into your pants?
Girl: Lose a hundred and thirty pounds.

Guy: I like to think it's my vocation to make women happy in bed.
Girl: Let me guess: you deliver meals on wheels to the bed-bound?

Guy: Do you fancy coming for a walk in the woods?
Girl: What for — to meet your family?

Guy: How about a date?
Girl: Sorry, I don't date outside my species.

Guy: Do you believe in love at first sight?
Girl: No, but I do believe in total, mind-numbing indifference at first sight.

Guy: One day I'm going to be famous.
Girl: My money's on April 1.

Guy: May I have the last dance?
Girl: You've just had it.

Guy: I've got some condoms, so I think we should sleep together right now.
Girl: What's the rush? Are they close to their expiry date?

Guy: What do you mean you don't like me? What's wrong with me?
Girl: How long have you got?

Guy: What do you mean you don't like me? What's wrong with me?
Girl: Do you want me to do this alphabetically?

Guy: I know how to please a woman.
Girl: Well, please leave me alone.

Guy: Whisper those three little words that would make my day.
Girl: Go to hell.

Guy: Give me a chance and I could really light your fire.
Girl: Not with that little match you couldn't.

Guy: You could steal my heart.
Girl: I'd rather steal your kidney. I could get more for it.

Guy: You make me want to throw my arms around you.
Girl: You make me want to throw up.

Guy: I don't care. There's plenty more fish in the sea.
Girl: Not if you've got a rusty rod.

Guy: I've changed my mind.
Girl: Good. Does the new one work better?

Guy: I've got a condom with your name on it.
Girl: I don't think so. My name's not Durex Extra Small.

Guy: Nice legs. When do they open?
Girl: Nice mouth. When does it shut?

Guy: Don't go thinking about me while I'm gone.
Girl: I wasn't thinking about you while you were here.

Guy: Do you want to get out of here?
Girl: Sure. As long as you promise not to come with me.

Guy: You're one in a million.
Girl: So are your chances.

Guy: We could make sweet music.
Girl: Not on that organ.

Guy: You're insulting my intelligence.
Girl: I didn't think that was possible.

Guy: Say, haven't we met before?
Girl: Yes, I'm a nurse at the VD clinic.

Guy: What are you doing tonight?
Girl: Whatever it is, it won't be with you.

Guy: How about I turn the lights down low?
Girl: Lower, lower. I can still see you.

Guy: Is there someone else?
Girl: There must be.

Girl: If you loved me you wouldn't drink so much.
Guy: If I didn't drink so much I wouldn't love you.

Girl: I've spoken with monkeys more polite than you.
Guy: I'm glad to hear you attended your family reunion.

Girl: You know, I could make your life a living hell.
Guy: I'm not really looking for a relationship right now.

Girl: I can wrap guys around my little finger.
Guy: You could wrap quite a few around your waist.

Girl: I'll have you know I've been asked to get married more than thirty times.
Guy: Yeah, but your parents don't count.

Girl: He's so much better than you. He makes me feel eighteen again.
Guy: Is that size eighteen?

Girl: I really need somewhere to stay.
Guy: I have an attic you can hang upside down in.

Girl: Whenever I'm down in the dumps I get myself a new dress.
Guy: So that's where you get them . . .

Girl: Does this sweater make me look fat?
Guy: No, the fact that you're fat makes you look fat. That sweater makes you look purple.

Girl: There are no words for how disgusting you are.
Guy: Yes there are. You just never learned them.

Girl: I think you love Manchester United more than me!
Guy: I love Manchester City more than you!

Girl: Will I see you again?
Guy: Sorry, but I'd rather bait a crocodile with my manhood than go on another date with you.

Guy: Do you want to dance?
Girl: No.
Guy: Sorry, I think you misheard me. I said, "You look fat in those pants."

Girl: What would you guys do without us women?
Guy: Domesticate another animal.

Woman: I've just come back from the beauticians.
Friend: Pity it was closed.

Motorist: Do you know the Northampton turn-off?
Man: Know her? I married her!

Husband: I don't know why you wear a bra, you've got nothing to put in it.
Wife: You wear briefs, don't you?

Husband (looking in the mirror): How many really handsome men do you think there are in the world?
Wife: One less than you think.

Wife: Do you think I'll lose my looks as I get older?
Husband: With luck, yes.

Wife: If I dropped dead now, I'd die happy.
Husband: So would we all.

Wife: I've never been so insulted! That guy over there called me a fat, ugly, hairy whore.
Husband: You're not hairy . . .

Wife: You can't just go around treating me like some trophy wife.
Husband: Trophy wife? What contest in Hell did I win?!

Wife: How do I look with my new wardrobe?
Husband: Better with the doors shut.

Boss: Employees like that don't grow on trees, you know.
Worker: No, they normally swing from them.

Customer: Aren't you going to tell me to have a nice day?
Waiter: I don't care if you have a pulse, much less a nice day.

Lady pianist (to her house guest): I understand you love music.
Guest: Yes, but never you mind. Keep right on playing.

Woman: If I had to thank her I'd choke on the words.
Friend: Please risk it.

Aristocrat: The service at this club is terrible. Do you know who I am?
Waiter: No, sir, I do not. But I shall make inquiries and inform you directly.

Sue Ann: I have never taken "no" for an answer.
Mary: Or given it.
– *The Mary Tyler Moore Show*

Actress: What do you think is my best side?
Alfred Hitchcock: My dear, you're sitting on it.

Niles: We're a stone's throw away from one of the giants of American literature!
Roz: Not the way you throw!
– *Frasier*

Nancy: Dan, did he tell you anything? Is there another woman?
Dan: No offence, Nancy, but it's a miracle there's one.
– *Roseanne*

Maddie: I had no idea.
David: That's OK. I got lots of 'em. I'll loan you one.
- Moonlighting

Giles: Why would anyone want to harm Cordelia?
Willow: Maybe 'cause they met her?
- Buffy the Vampire Slayer

Lady Elizabeth Dryden: How can you always be poring over those musty books? I wish I were a book and then I should have more of your company.
John Dryden: Pray, my dear, if you do become a book let it be an almanack, for then I shall be able to change you every year.

Roz: I was in college, I was trying to find myself.
Niles: All you had to do was look under the nearest man.
- Frasier

Katharine Hepburn: I think I am too tall for you.
Spencer Tracy: Don't worry, Miss Hepburn, I'll soon cut you down to size.

Carlos: You don't know what it was like in prison. Twenty hours a day, eight-by-ten cell, just you and your mind.
Gabby: So, pretty much just you.
- Desperate Housewives

Jean Harlow: Is the "t" in 'Margot' pronounced?
Margot Asquith: No. The "t" is silent – as in "Harlow".

Diane: I find older men stimulating.
Sam: I hope you're not talking to me.
Diane: Well, certainly not. You're not the least bit stimulating.
- Cheers

Homer: You don't have to follow in my footsteps, son.
Bart: Don't worry – I don't even like using the bathroom after you.
- The Simpsons

Naomi Campbell: Why do they call you Posh?
Victoria Beckham: Why do they call you beautiful?

Dorothy: You know, sometimes I can't believe my ears.
Sophia: I know. I should've taped them back when you were seven.
- The Golden Girls

Nina: I hated Shakespeare in high school.
Dennis: Why? Did he write something mean in your yearbook?
– *Just Shoot Me*

Nancy Astor: Winston, if you were my husband, I should flavour your coffee
with poison.
Winston Churchill: Madam, if I were your husband I should drink it.

Karen: Candy, there's a question I've been meaning to ask that only you can
answer: is sixty sexy?
Candy: Well of course . . . Don't you remember?
– *Will and Grace*

Lewis Morris (after not being appointed Poet Laureate): It is a conspiracy of
silence against me – a conspiracy of silence. What should I do?
Oscar Wilde: Join it.

Blanche: If I wasn't such a lady I would deck you.
Dorothy: Try it and you'll be on your back so fast you'll think you're on a date.
– *The Golden Girls*

Jayne Mansfield: I have a terrific idea.
Director: Treat it gently, dear. It's in a strange place.

Kyle: I researched my family history and found that my great-great-grand-
father invented the prototype for the first shippable straw.
Max: So basically, your family has sucked for generations.
– *Living Single*

President William H. Taft: I have been talking for a quarter of an hour, but
there is so much noise that I can hardly hear myself talk.
Heckler: That's all right. You're not missing anything.

Stewie (as Brian starts singing): Who sings that?
Brian: James Taylor.
Stewie: Let's keep it that way.
– *Family Guy*

Cliff: I have impossibly high standards for a woman.
Norm: Yeah, she has to like you.
– *Cheers*

Erica: Why? Do you have a subconscious desire to harm me?
Sean: I assure you, any desire I have to harm you is totally conscious.
– *Nip/Tuck*

Anon: Have you ever played any Stockhausen?
Thomas Beecham: No, but I've stepped in it.

Karen: Oh, my God! She just asked a fairy an engine question. We're all gonna die in this car!
Will: Karen, you're not going to die. It would take a silver bullet and a wooden stake to do that.
– *Will and Grace*

Reporter: What would you do if you retired?
Charles Barkley, basketball player: If push came to shove, I could lose all self-respect and become a reporter.

Roz: It's not like she worships the devil.
Frasier: She doesn't have to! *He* worships *her*!
– *Frasier*

George S. Kaufman: I like your bald head, Marc. It feels just like my wife's behind.
Marc Connolly: So it does, George.

Blanche: But I've been disrobing in front of Dr Kagan for three years. Why would he ask you for a date when he's seen the Promised Land?
Dorothy: I don't know – too many squatters?
– *The Golden Girls*

Barbara Cartland: My dear, I'll have you know I have written a hundred and forty-five books.
Denise Robins: Oh, I see – one a year.

David: Could've fooled me.
Maddie: A gnat with a lobotomy could fool you.
– *Moonlighting*

Frasier: I do not have a fat face!
Niles: Oh please, I keep wondering how long you're going to store those nuts for winter.
– *Frasier*

Clare Boothe Luce (stepping aside in a doorway): Age before beauty.
Dorothy Parker (walking through): Pearls before swine.

Baldrick: I'm waiting for Miss Right to come along and gather me up in her arms.
Blackadder: I wouldn't be too hopeful. We'd have to get her arms out of her straitjacket first.
– *Blackadder*

Joachim von Ribbentrop, 1930s: If there is another war, the Italians will be on Germany's side.
Winston Churchill: That seems only fair; we had them last time!

Quentin: You're a bitch..
Julia: Maybe, but at least I'm not yours.
– *Nip/Tuck*

Earl of Sandwich: Sir, I do not know whether you will die on the gallows or of the pox.
John Wilkes: That will depend, my Lord, on whether I embrace your principles or your mistress.

Frasier: Honestly, Niles, have you *ever* had an unvoiced thought?
Niles: As a matter of fact, I'm having one now.
– *Frasier*

Singer: You know, my dear, I insured my voice for fifty thousand dollars.
Miriam Hopkins: That's wonderful. And what did you do with the money?

Reggie Jackson: I have a 160 IQ.
Mickey Rivers: Out of what – a thousand?

Becky: Do you remember that guy Mark?
Darlene: The stupid one.
Becky: He's not stupid, he's gorgeous! You're just jealous you can't get a guy like that.
Darlene: Well if I wait a couple of years, he'll be in my grade.
– *Roseanne*

Samuel Foote; Why do you keep singing that song?
Anon: Because it haunts me.
Samuel Foote: No wonder, since you are forever murdering it.

Sam (puckering): Do these lips remind you of anything?
Rebecca: Yeah, I think the liver in my freezer has gone bad.
– *Cheers*

Author: I hear you said that this was the worst book I ever wrote.
Douglas Jerrold: No, I didn't. I said that it was the worst book anybody ever wrote.

Dorothy (to Blanche) How long did you wait to have sex after George died?
Sophia: Till the paramedics came.
– *The Golden Girls*

Actress: I dread the thought of forty-five.
Rosalind Russell: Why, what happened to you then, dear?

Lilith: It's about an attraction that I thought was over, and now I'm beginning to think maybe it's not.
Niles: Usually in my dreams, this is where I try to run and can't.
– *Frasier*

Mrs Patrick Campbell (to theatre producer Charles Froham): Always remember, Mr Froham, that I am an artist.
Charles Froham: Your secret is safe with me.

Sam: Maybe you ought to step in here for a minute and let me show you something *I've* triumphed over.
Diane: Don't tell me you've finally mastered the stapler.
– *Cheers*

Doris Black (about Dustin Hoffman in drag): I'd like to make her look a little more attractive. How far can you pull back?
Cameraman: How do you feel about Cleveland?
– *Tootsie*

Theatre publicist: How do I get our leading lady's name in your newspaper?
George S. Kaufman: Shoot her.

Frasier: Boy, I never felt so low in my life.
Cliff: Well, Doc, if it means anything to you, I'm here for you.
Frasier: It doesn't, Cliff, but thanks.
– *Cheers*

Louie: Mr Rieger isn't here right now. Would you like to wait in my office?
Charlotte: I'd rather be the only woman on a Greek freighter!
— *Taxi*

Newsagent: Mr Monkhouse, I have as much chance of being hit by lightning
as you have of winning the Lottery.
Bob Monkhouse: You have your dream, I'll have mine.

Grace (has a sore on her lip): It's not herpes! It's not even close to herpes!
Karen: Well it's close enough to get invited to the herpes family picnic.
— *Will and Grace*

Actress (after failing to fulfil a dinner invitation): I think I was invited to your
house to dinner last Thursday night . . .
Ethel Barrymore: Oh yes? Did you come?

Maddie: David, I just don't think . . .
David (interrupting): That's OK, you look good.
— *Moonlighting*

Marie: I think for every year you age, you should add an inch to the hemline
of your dress.
Frank: Then you should be dragging around a Persian rug.
— *Everybody Loves Raymond*

Edith Summerskill: Mr Cooper, have you looked in the mirror lately and seen
the state of your nose?
Henry Cooper: Well, madam, have you looked in the mirror and seen the
state of your nose? Boxing is my excuse. What's yours?

Cordelia: Buffy, you're really campaigning for Bitch of the Year, aren't you?
Buffy: As defending champion, are you nervous?
— *Buffy the Vampire Slayer*

Party guest: Is Bach still composing?
W. S. Gilbert: No madam, he's decomposing.

Lilith: You're the only man I've ever loved!
Frasier: So are you!
— *Frasier*

Man: Where in hell have I seen you?
Archbishop Ryan: From where in hell do you come?

Edina: I mean you realize, of course, in Zen terms, everything in the Universe is just molecules, don't you? Ying and yong, ping and pong, mm? You know that, darling? These are my molecules, that's your little clump of molecules over there, sweetie. I mean in real terms there's no difference between me and the coffee, me and the table, me and a tree, me and Madonna, for God's sake.
Saffy: Except you have a fatter bottom.
– *Absolutely Fabulous*

Earl Wilson: Have you ever been mistaken for a man?
Tallulah Bankhead: No, darling. Have you?

Dr Foreman: I think your argument is specious.
Dr House: I think your tie is ugly.
– *House*

Woman: Mr President, I bet my friend that I could get you to say three words to me.
Calvin Coolidge: You lose.

Jack: Breaking news . . . I'm in love!
Will: I must have missed that, but then I don't read the farm report.
– *Will and Grace*

Reporter: Didn't you have any friends warning you not to take the job as coach of the L.A. Clippers (basketball team)?
Alvin Gentry: They all encouraged me to take the job.
Reporter: You don't have any friends, do you?

Alma: We could have tried for another baby. We could have been a family again.
Orson: I know. That's why I didn't try.
– *Desperate Housewives*

Becky: All I have to do is count to ten.
Darlene: Don't wear mittens. It'll slow you down.
– *Roseanne*

Clement Attlee (in the House of Commons washroom, as Winston Churchill positioned himself at the opposite end of the urinal): Feeling stand-offish today, are we, Winston?
Winston Churchill: That's right. Every time you see something big, you want to nationalize it.

Woody: Can I pour you a beer, Mr Peterson?
Norm: A little early, isn't it Woody?
Woody: For a beer?
Norm: No, for stupid questions.
— *Cheers*

Peggy: Tell me you love me, Al.
Al: I love football, I love beer, let's not cheapen the meaning of the word.
— *Married . . . With Children*

Oscar Wilde: Do you mind if I smoke?
Sarah Bernhardt: I don't care if you burn.

Dorothy: Why can't you sleep on the couch and give Clayton and Doug your room?
Blanche: Are you crazy? What will the neighbours think if they see two men in my bedroom?
Sophia: They'll think it's Tuesday.
— *The Golden Girls*

Sam: It just so happens that I've never met an intelligent woman I'd want to date.
Diane: Well, on behalf of all the intelligent women in the world, let me just say, "Whew!"
— *Cheers*

Club member: I've just been grossly insulted. I overheard one of that crowd saying that he would offer me £50 to resign my membership.
W. S. Gilbert: That's outrageous. You stick firm at a hundred and you'll get it.

Veronica: You wrote "slut" on my car last year at Shelly's party. Why?
Madison: Because "whore" had too many letters.
— *Veronica Mars*

Anon: I passed by your house yesterday, Oscar.
Oscar Wilde: Thank you very much.

Melchett: Some pleasant word game perhaps?
Edmund: OK, make a sentence from these words: face sodding your shut.
— *Blackadder*

Paul Bourget: I suppose life can never get entirely dull to an American, because whenever he can't strike up any other way to put in his time he can always get away with a few years trying to find out who his grandfather was.

Mark Twain: But I reckon a Frenchman's got his little standby for a dull time, too, because when all other interests fail, he can turn in and see if he can't find out who his father was.

Norm: I want something light and cold.
Carla: Sorry, it's Diane's day off.
– *Cheers*

George Bernard Shaw (inviting Winston Churchill to the opening night of *Pygmalion*): Am reserving two tickets for you for my premiere. Come and bring a friend – if you have one.
Churchill: Impossible to be present for the first performance. Will attend the second – if there is one.

Bulldog: We could still get together afterwards.
Roz: Only if I smash into your car in the parking lot.
Bulldog: Why is it the ones that want it the most put up the biggest struggle?
Roz: Because when I *do* finally give in, I want us to enjoy it. That is, if I'm not too distracted by the fact that every man on earth has died.
– *Frasier*

Author: I don't seem to write as well as I used to.
William Dean Howells: Oh, yes, you do. You write as well as ever you did. But your taste has improved.

Basil: Do you remember when we were first manacled together? We used to laugh quite a lot.
Sybil: Yes, but not at the same time, Basil.
– *Fawlty Towers*

Alan: Do you want me to report you for that earring?
Mac: Only if I can report you for that moustache.
Alan: Most women find male body piercing repugnant. I, thankfully, am completely intact.
Mac: Well, even I draw the line at piercing arseholes.
– *Green Wing*

Monica: You must be Louie.
Louie: How did you know my name?
Monica: I only had three people described to me. One was smart, one was good-looking, and one was you.
— *Taxi*

Sam Wood (directing the Marx Brothers' *A Day at the Races*): You can't make an actor out of clay.
Groucho Marx: Nor a director out of Wood!

Dan: What happened to Jimmy? I liked Jimmy.
Darlene: So did Becky, until he dumped her.
Becky: He didn't dump me!
Darlene: Get real, you hit the ground like a safe.
— *Roseanne*

Dustin Farnum: I've never been better. In the last act yesterday, I had the audience glued to their seats.
Oliver Herford: How clever of you to think of it.

Frasier (after Lilith asks him to father another child with her): Do we have to sleep together?
Lilith: I thought I'd freeze your sperm.
Frasier: Is that a yes or a no?
— *Frasier*

Isadora Duncan: You have the greatest brain in the world and I have the most beautiful body. So we ought to produce the most perfect child.
George Bernard Shaw: But what if the child inherits my body and your brain?

Baldrick: But my lord, I've been in your family since 1532!
Edmund: So has syphilis. Now get out!
— *Blackadder*

Simon Cowell: Is this something you want to pursue?
American Idol contestant: Honestly, I can take it or leave it.
Simon Cowell: Leave it.

Labour MP: Must you fall asleep while I'm speaking?
Winston Churchill: No, it is purely voluntary.

Diane: Oh no. The thing I feared most has happened.
Carla: What? Your living bra died of boredom?
– *Cheers*

Diane: He's trying to make a mountain out of a molehill.
Carla: He wants you to wear a padded bra?
– *Cheers*

Arthur Schlesinger Jr: I liked your book, Liz. Who wrote it for you?
Liz Carpenter: I'm glad you like it, Arthur. Who read it to you?

Monica: The camera adds ten pounds.
Chandler: Oh. So how many cameras are actually on you?
– *Friends*

Sybil: You're looking very happy, Basil.
Basil: Happy? Ah yes, I remember that.
– *Fawlty Towers*

Lady: There are two things I don't like about you, Mr Churchill – your politics and your moustache.
Winston Churchill: My dear madam, pray do not disturb yourself. You are not likely to come into contact with either.

Becky: Look what I found!
Darlene: Your virginity? No, wait, you left that behind the dumpster at K-Mart.
– *Roseanne*

Anon: I really can't come to your party, Mrs Parker. I can't bear fools.
Dorothy Parker: That's strange; your mother could.

Cliff: Guess what followed me home today?
Carla: A trail of slime?
– *Cheers*

Hollywood barber: How would you like your hair cut?
George S. Kaufman: In silence.

Niles: I thought you liked my Maris.
Frasier: I do, I . . . I like her from a distance. You know, the way you like the sun. Maris is like the sun. Except without the warmth.
– *Frasier*

University professor (talking about a distinguished historian): It may be doubted whether any man of our generation has plunged more deeply into the sacred fount of learning.
Abraham Lincoln: Yes, or come up drier.

Miles: You just want to cut my balls off!
Anna: Oh, I'd have to find them first!
– *This Life*

Katharine Hepburn: Thank God I don't have to act with you any more.
John Barrymore: I didn't realize you ever had, darling.

Diane: Do you know the difference between you and a fat, braying ass?
Sam: No.
Diane: The fat, braying ass would.
– *Cheers*

Actor: Has anybody got a nickel? I have to phone a friend.
George S. Kaufman: Here's a dime – phone all of them.

Loretta Swit (after Kermit fired Miss Piggy): Kermit, you can't just pick her up and throw her out in the snow.
Kermit: Not without a forklift, I can't.
– *The Muppet Show*

Colleague: Whewell's forte is science.
Sydney Smith: Yes, and his foible is omniscience.

Dan (as Becky appears, dressed for a date): Could this woman be our little Becky?
Darlene: Not all of her. If I were you, I'd check upstairs for missing Kleenex.
– *Roseanne*

Darling: I wasn't born yesterday, you know.
Blackadder: More's the pity, we could have started your personality from scratch.
– *Blackadder*

Saffy: Where's Patsy?
Edina: She's in the shop with all the dried-up things.
Saffy: Oh, should feel at home then.
– *Absolutely Fabulous*

Oscar Wilde: I wish I had said that.
James McNeill Whistler: You will, Oscar, you will.

Fat lady: You'll be hearing from my lawyers!
Al: Would that be the law offices of Haagen and Dazs?
– *Married . . . With Children*

David: Last night an idea hit me.
Maddie: Left a bruise, I hope.
– *Moonlighting*

Jimmy Greaves: What would you and Ernie have become if you hadn't been comedians?
Eric Morecambe: Mike and Bernie Winters.

Logan: Thanks for the ride. This mean you're gonna play nice now?
Veronica: Walk in front of the car. We'll see.
– *Veronica Mars*

Nina: That's it! From now on, I'm only ever going to speak when I have something truly intelligent to say.
Elliot: . . . And they never heard from her again.
– *Just Shoot Me*

William Pitt the Elder: If I cannot speak standing I will speak sitting, and if I cannot speak sitting I will speak lying.
Lord North: That he will do in whatever position he speaks.

Jack: She doesn't know I'm gay.
Grace: Has she *met* you?
– *Will and Grace*

Reporter: You just made *The Fifth Monkey*, and Kim Novak's comeback film *The Children*. Which is the most difficult to act with – monkeys or children?
Ben Kingsley: Kim Novak.

Louie: Do you know what the difference is between people like you and people like me?
Alex: Yeah, two million years of evolution.
– *Taxi*

Edina: What you don't understand is that inside of me, sweetie, inside of me, there's a thin person just screaming to get out.
Mother: Just the one, dear?
— *Absolutely Fabulous*

Lord Illingworth: Women have become too brilliant. Nothing spoils a romance so much as a sense of humour in the woman.
Mrs Allonby: Or the want of it in the man.
— Oscar Wilde, *A Woman of No Importance*

Lilah: Mind if I join you?
Wesley: On many levels, with great intensity.
— *Angel*

Frederic Leighton: My dear Whistler, you leave your pictures in such a sketchy, unfinished state. Why don't you ever finish them?
James McNeill Whistler: My dear Leighton, why do you ever begin yours?

Phoebe: What's this?
Monica: Oh, that's my bathing suit from high school.
Chandler: Oh, 'cause I thought that's what they used to cover Connecticut when it rains.
— *Friends*

Actress 1: When I walked on stage, the entire audience sat there open-mouthed.
Actress 2: Rubbish! They never all yawn at once.

Kryten: But if people see my face, what are they going to think?
Rimmer: Tell them you had an accident. Tell them you took your car to the crushers and forgot to get out.
— *Red Dwarf*

James McNeill Whistler: Don't touch that. Can't you see, it isn't dry yet?
Mark Twain: I don't mind. I have gloves on.

Elliot: Oh, Dr Cox. Does this lipstick make me look like a clown?
Dr Cox: No, it makes you look like a prostitute who caters exclusively *to* clowns.
— *Scrubs*

Peg: You haven't been very nice to my family.
Al: Neither has nature. Go bother it!
– *Married . . . With Children*

Anon: Whatever possessed you to be born in a place like Lowell, Massachusetts?
James McNeill Whistler: I wished to be near my mother.

Dorothy: I would kill Gloria if she ever wrote about my sexual escapades!
Sophia: You'd kill your sister over a pamphlet?!
– *The Golden Girls*

Mel: As the producer of this show, once more I must insist that you instruct your staff to show me a little respect.
Buddy: We're showing you as little respect as possible.
– *The Dick Van Dyke Show*

David Frost: Peter, I'm having a little dinner party on behalf of Prince Andrew and his new bride-to-be, Sarah Ferguson. I know they'd love to meet you, big fans. Be super if you could make it: Wednesday the twelfth.
Peter Cook: Hang on, I'll just check my diary . . . Oh, dear. I find I'm watching television that night.

Frank: I can be a real asset.
Hawkeye: You're only two letters off.
– *M*A*S*H*

Comte D'Orsay: I was born French, have lived French and will die French.
Benjamin Disraeli: Have you no ambition, man?

Blanche: I never had to pay a penny in backtaxes. I have a way with auditors. The last time I was audited I even got money back from the government.
Sophia: Blanche, it's not a refund when the auditor leaves two twenties on your nightstand.
– *The Golden Girls*

Lord Northcliffe: The trouble with you, Shaw, is that you look as if there were famine in the land.
George Bernard Shaw: The trouble with you, Northcliffe, is that you look as if you were the cause of it.

Nina: I like to think of my body as a temple.
Finch: Which explains why there's a line to get in on Friday nights.
— *Just Shoot Me*

Clergyman: I want to thank you for all the enjoyment you've given the world.
Groucho Marx: And I want to thank you for all the enjoyment you've taken out of the world.

Patsy: Look at my photo, the photographer really caught something there.
Saffy: Syphilis?
— *Absolutely Fabulous*

Fritz Kreisler, violinist: My fee to play at your party is $18,000.
Mrs Cornelius Vanderbilt: That's agreeable, but I hope you understand that you should not mingle with my guests.
Fritz Kreisler: Well, in that case my fee is only $500.

Sally: Mary Kelly thinks you're a complete idiot.
Patrick: Then why is she always looking at my arse when we talk?
Sally: She's lipreading.
— *Coupling*

Sam: I thought you weren't going to call me stupid now that we're being intimate.
Diane: No, I said I wasn't going to call you stupid *while* we were being intimate.
— *Cheers*

Bessie Braddock: Winston, you're drunk.
Winston Churchill: And madam, you're ugly. Tomorrow morning, however, I shall be sober.

Fat lady: How dare you say that to my face!
Al: Well, I'd say it behind your back but my car's only got half a tank of gas.
— *Married . . . With Children*

Ted (reading newspaper): Say, Murray, have you seen the spread on Sue Ann?
Murray: Yeah, but you don't notice it so much when she sits down.
— *The Mary Tyler Moore Show*

Sir! This lady is my wife. You should be ashamed.
If this lady is your wife, you should be ashamed.
— *A Night in Casablanca*

Roz: I read a study that said having frequent physical contact can actually increase your life expectancy.
Frasier: In that case, you should outlive Styrofoam.
– Frasier

He's got a great ass.
Too bad it's on his shoulders.
– Roxanne

Elaine (after Louie says his mother needs an operation): What's wrong with her?
Louie: Female problems. She's starting not to look like one.
– Taxi

Rose: Can I ask a dumb question?
Dorothy: Like no one else.
– The Golden Girls

STREET TALK

A collection of insults that have entered modern language:

Abigail – A middle-aged homosexual man who is firmly in the closet.

ABS – Asshole Behaviour Scale, used on a scale of one to ten to measure how much of an asshole some is being.

Ally McHurl – Someone with an eating disorder.

Anal retentive – A control or neatness freak.

Anorak – Someone with interests and hobbies that are generally perceived to be boring, such as trainspotting. Also a person who is obsessively knowledgeable about a particular subject.

Arselicker – Someone who tries to get into your good books for their own benefit.

Asshat – Someone has their head up their ass, thus wearing their ass as a hat.

Asswipe – A stupid person.

Auntie – An older gay man.

Bag job – A female with a nice body but an ugly face, which therefore needs a paper bag over it during sex.

Bag of old and mouldy ass – A person nursing a bad hangover.

Barbara – A pre-op transsexual.

Barfogenic – Sickening, nauseating.

Bassackwards – Someone or something that is totally screwed up.

Bean flicker – A lesbian.

Beard – A woman who goes on a date with a gay man to conceal the fact that he's gay.

Bellend – A complete idiot.

BFB – Better from behind.

Blandiose – Someone who has pretensions to grandeur but is actually bland.

Blockormore – A girl that only looks good from a block or more.

James Blunt – Derogatory rhyming slang, as in "You're a complete James Blunt."

Board with warts – A flat-chested woman.

Bowl of stupid – The breakfast of choice for idiots the world over.

Bozo – A dunce, a fool.

Bronno – An impoverished female who lives in a caravan and wears the same clothes every day.

Brown nose – Someone who crawls to you, a creep.

Bunny-boiler – An obsessive, mentally unstable woman (from Glenn Close's character in the movie *Fatal Attraction*).

Burdick – An excessively lazy person.

Butterface – A woman who is hot from the neck down, but ugly from the neck up (i.e. she is hot everywhere but-her-face).

Butters – Ugly.

Caboose like a moose – Someone with a big arse.

Candy-ass – A sissy, a wimp.

Carpet muncher – A lesbian.

CBA – Can't Be Arsed, lazy.

Chav – Sub-species of teenage boy that traditionally wears a baseball cap, Burberry and bling. (British)

Cheese weasel – Someone who is lazy and lacking responsibility, who leaves the work to others.

Chickenhead – A woman who specialises in oral sex.

Choad – A short, fat person.

Chowderhead – Someone stupid.

Chrome dome – A guy with a bald head.

Chubby chaser – A person of either sex who is attracted to someone overweight.

Chugger – One who masturbates.

Chuggernaut – One who masturbates a lot.

Clappin' – Out of date, usually referring to a person's clothes, i.e. "his pants are clappin'."

Cockholster – A sexually promiscuous woman.

Cocksucker – A mean or despicable individual.

Content-free – Lacking in substance, vacuous.

Couch potato – A lazy person who does nothing but sit on the couch and watch TV. Also known sometimes as a sofa spud.

Croc face – An elderly person.

Crud – Someone who is contemptible, disgusting.

Crud bucket – Someone who is full of crud, i.e. extremely disgusting.

Cum dumpster – A woman to have sex with and then forget; a one-night stand.

Deadass – A bore.

Debbeh – A stupid girl. (British)

Dementoid – A mentally unstable person.

Denson – A very dense person.

Dickweasel – Someone who is particularly irritating.

Ding-a-ling – A scatterbrained or eccentric person.

Dingbat – A foolish or stupid person.

Ding-dong – An empty-headed individual, a fool.

Dingleberry – An incompetent person.

Dinner whore – A girl whose goal in life is a free meal or an expensive gift.

Dirtbag – Heavy drinker with poor dress sense and often a mullet haircut. (American)

Dittohead – Someone who mindlessly agrees with someone else's opinion.

Dork – Actually a whale's penis, but used colloquially to describe an oddball with nerd-like tendencies.

Dorkette – Female dork.

Double bagger – A woman so ugly that sex with her is only possible with two bags – one over her head and a second bag over your own head in case her bag falls off.

Douchebag – A total jerk.

Dragon breath – Halitosis.

Dweeb – A studious, hard-working, but socially inept person.

E-shank – A woman who flirts online because she is not attractive enough to get a date in the real world.

E-thug – A pale-faced kid who spends all his time threatening people on Internet message boards to compensate for his lack of a life.

Earwhore – A woman that talks incessantly.

Emo – Short for "emotional", used to describe teenagers who fake their own misery. (American)

Ewalt – A guy with a huge ego but a tiny penis.

Faghag – A heterosexual woman who hangs out with gay men, e.g. Cilla Black.

Flake – A silly, incompetent person.

Flatline – Someone so stupid as to be brain-dead.

Fraudience – A group of overly enthusiastic spectators positioned to cheerlead the performer; a tactic often used by politicians.

Fruit flies – Heterosexual women who socialise extensively with gay men (see faghag).

Fuckwit – Someone who is totally clueless.

Fudge – A very stupid person, because these letters (FUDGE) will be the grades they get in their GCSE exams.

Fugly – Fucking ugly.

Gamer – Someone who is socially inept and plays video games regularly.

Garnish – An objectionable friend of a friend whose company you tolerate simply to please your friend.

Gash badger – Someone who makes coarse remarks.

Gimp – Someone who is considered uncool or stupid.

Glamour glommers – Fickle followers of fashion.

Gobshite – Someone who talks nonsense. (Irish)

Gronk – A moron, idiot, total loser.

Guido – A sad, pathetic excuse for a male, usually from the New York area. (Italian-American)

Halfpipe – An idiot, clueless person.

Hamburglar – Inept criminal (like a ham actor).

Hangin' – An adjective to describe someone with an undesirable body and bad dress sense.

Heffer – A fat girl, built like a cow.

Himbo – A male bimbo.

Hoe – A highly promiscuous person.

Hoggard – An unattractive person who looks like a pig.

Hoser – A clumsy, boorish, heavy-drinking man.

Howling – Ugly.

Hung like a Tic Tac – To have a very small penis.

Ice tart – A female groupie at ice hockey games.

Jackshitter – Someone who talks about a subject of which they know next to nothing.

Jadd – Smelly.

Jag bag – Man boobs, common in overweight males.

Jag off – A male with annoying habits. (American)

January joiner – Someone who joins a gym in January as part of a New Year's fitness kick and by February is back to being a couch potato.

Jizzmopper – Someone with a menial job.

Kentucky waterfall – Another name for the mullet hairstyle. (American)

Klutz – A clumsy person.

Lame – Boring, unadventurous.

Lamer – An Internet user who irritates others in forums etc.

Lard – A fat person who doesn't think he or she is fat.

Lard-ass – A fat person who is also useless at just about everything.

Low-bandwidth – Limited conversational ability.

Mailbox head – Someone who has an unusually square head, for example British racing driver David Coulthard.

Mall girl – A shallow shopaholic.

Meathead – A muscular guy with a short temper and a tiny intellect.

Minger – An ugly person.

Minging – Ugly.

Minglord – The master of all mingers.

Monet – Someone who, like Monet's paintings, looks great from a distance but not so good close up.

Mong – Someone who does something stupid.

Mooch – A visitor to your home who outstays his or her welcome, a freeloader.

Motherfucker – A moron.

Mouse in his pocket – Phrase to describe someone who is big and strong, but stupid.

Muffin top – The look where a woman's tight jeans make her flab hang over the waistband, in the same way that the top of a muffin spills over the edge of the paper. (Australian)

Muffing – Adjective to describe someone who smells like they haven't washed for a few months.

Mule – Rough, slovenly, uncouth.

Munter – An ugly-looking woman.

Muppet – A person who is easily manipulated.

Ned – Non-educated delinquent Scottish chav.

Noob – Someone incapable of mastering a particular skill.

Nubcake – A person lacking experience and/or common sense.

Numpty – Someone who is totally clueless, hence adjective numptyesque (Scottish).

Oinker – A fat person.

Oxygen thief – A lazy, worthless individual, whose very existence uses up oxygen that could be consumed by someone more useful.

Patsy – Someone who is easily taken advantage of.

Phrasemonger – Someone who relentlessly quotes others.

Pie merchant – Fat person, usually male.

Pikey – Anyone who lives in a caravan. (British)

Pissant – An insignificant person.

Plonker – A dimwit.

Prawn – A girl with a great body but a bad face (when you eat a prawn, you eat the body and throw away the head). (Australian)

Quegg – A school insult used to describe a boy who has yet to grow pubic hair.

Quimby – A bumbling buffoon. (from *The Simpsons*)

Rancid – Something that smells disgusting.

Rank – Ugly, gross.

Retard – A person with a mental deficiency, an idiot.

Scumbag – A person with no class.

Scuzzbucket – A contemptible, sleazy individual.

Sheepshagger – Someone who lives in the country.

Shirtlifter – A gay male.

Shitstain – A person of no merit whatsoever.

Skank – A teenage girl of dubious hygiene and morals.

Skeezer – A woman of easy virtue, a slapper.

Slaphead – Bald man.

Slump buster – An unattractive female that a baseball player has sex with in the hope of ending his playing slump. (American)

Smeghead – An idiot. (British)

Spakker – A total idiot.

Spamhead – A silly, annoying person.

Spunk bubble – A worthless person.

Swamp donkey – A very ugly, usually fat girl.

Talking hairdo – A TV journalist (usually female) who is more concerned about her appearance than the topic under debate.

Thunder thighs – A woman with broad hips and big thighs.

Tightass – Someone who is reluctant to spend money.

Tosspot – An idiot.

Trailer trash – People who live in trailers. (American)

Triple bagger – A woman so ugly that you need three paper bags in order to have sex with her – one to put over her head, a second to put over your head. in case her bag falls off, and a third bag to be sick into afterwards.

Twonk – An idiot.

Ugly as sin – Exceptionally ugly.

Verbal diarrhoea – Incessant, mindless talk.

Vidiot – Someone whose knowledge is restricted to what they see on TV.

Wang – Slang for male genitalia, so an alternative to describing someone as a dickhead, prick or knobhead etc.

Wanksta – A pathetic individual who pretends to be a gangster.

Wasbund – Insulting term applied to an ex-husband.

Wasteman – Someone who does nothing with their life.

Wearing the cheese – Moving or doing something exceptionally slowly.

Whale rider – A man who is sexually attracted to overweight women.

Window licker – A mentally retarded person.

Zero – A complete nonentity.

Zit zapper – A teenager with rampant acne.

FILHO DA PUTA! – SOME FOREIGN INSULTS AND SWEAR WORDS

Jy pis me af – You're pissing me off (Afrikaans)

Poephol – Asshole (Afrikaans)

Teef – Bitch (Afrikaans)

Debil – Idiot (Albanian)

Wajab zibik! – An infection to your dick! (Arabic)

Eem vorigas bacheek doer! – Kiss my ass! (Armenian)

Eshu koorak – Son of a donkey (Armenian)

Anavy sikim – Motherfucker (Azerbaijani)

Choodmarani – Motherfucker (Bengali)

Haramjada – Bastard (Bengali)

Laewra aga – Dickhead (Bengali)

Coochka – Bitch (Bulgarian)

Jhew lun dou – Pig cock scrotum (Chinese)

Poq gai – Go die in the street (Chinese)

Gloopan – Idiot (Croatian)

Shoopchino – Asshole (Croatian)·

Smrdljiva kurvetino! – You stinky bitch! (Croatian)

Do prdele! – Up yours! (Czech)

Din mor sutter pik i helvede – Your mother sucks cocks in hell (Danish)

Dinf far tagen den i roeven – Your father is a practising homosexual (Danish)

Du er pisse irriterende – You're a pain in the ass (Danish)

Klam – Repulsive (Danish)

Apenaaier – Monkey-fucker (Dutch)

Hoerenjong – Son of a bitch (Dutch)

Ik laat een scheet in jouw richting – I fart in your direction (Dutch)

Leeghoofd – Airhead (Dutch)

Moderneuker – Motherfucker (Dutch)

Stop het in je nauwe gaatje! – Stick it up your ass! (Dutch)

Mine vittu – Fuck off (Estonian)

Äitisi nai poroja! – Your mother copulates with reindeer! (Finnish)

Kusipää – Pisshead (Finnish)

Molopää – Dickhead (Finnish)

Conasse – Moron (French)

Fils de pute – Son of a bitch (French)

Vous m'emmerdez – You're pissing me off (French)

Va te branler – Go play with yourself (French)

Go n-ithe na péisteoga thú – May the worms eat you (Gaelic)

Plá ar do theach – A plague on your house (Gaelic)

Póg mo thóin – Kiss my ass (Gaelic)

Téigh trasna ort féin – Go fuck yourself (Gaelic)

Depp – Idiot (German)

Drecksau – Dirty pig (German)

Lech mich am Arsch – Lick my ass (German)

Schlampe – Slut (German)

Verpiss dich! – Get lost! (German)

Fila mou to kolo – Kiss my ass (Greek)

Gamiola – Woman of easy virtue (Greek)

Ben zonah – Son of a bitch (Hebrew)

Seggfej – Asshole (Hungarian)

Drusla – Slut (Icelandic)

Bangsat – Bastard (Indonesian)

Ngentot – Fart (Indonesian)

Pantat besar – Big ass (Indonesian)

Figlio di puttana – Son of a whore (Italian)

Puttana – Whore (Italian)

Vaffanculo – Go fuck yourself (Italian)

Baka – Idiot (Japanese)

Busu – Extremely ugly girl (Japanese)

Onara atama – Fart head (Japanese)

Ookiosewada! – Up yours! (Japanese)

Urusai, kono bakayaro – Shut up, you noisy idiot (Japanese)

Ja-schuck! – You bastard! (Korean)

Bohsia – Slut (Malaysian)

Butoh – Asshole (Malaysian)

Ni ma le bi – Your mother contracts turtles (Mandarin)

Drittsekk – Shitbag (Norwegian)

Fleskepanne – Meathead (Norwegian)

Runknisse – A masturbating gnome (Norwegian)

Støgging – Extremely ugly (Norwegian)

Beshoor – Stupid (Persian)

Mardar sag – Your mother is a dog (Persian)

Dupek – Asshole (Polish)

Jebiesz jeze – You fuck hedgehogs (Polish)

Skurwysyn – Son of a bitch (Polish)

Escroto – Asshole (Portuguese)

Filho da puta – Son of a bitch (Portuguese)

Foder a mona – Piss off (Portuguese)

Punheteiro – Wanker (Portuguese)

Da-te-n pula mea – Go fuck yourself (Romanian)

Moa-te pe ghiapa – Go sliding on ice to your midwife; get lost. (Romanian)

Mudack – Dumbass (Russian)

Padlo – Scoundrel (Russian)

Sooka – Bitch (Russian)

Zhopa – Asshole (Russian)

Pirnièan – Stupid person (Slovenian)

Preklet vosu! – Cursed donkey! (Slovenian)

Besame el culo – Kiss my ass (Spanish)

Hijo de mil putas – Son of a thousand bitches (Spanish)

Metete un palo por el culo – Shove a stick up your ass (Spanish)

Kuksugare – Cocksucker (Swedish)

Rövhål – Asshole (Swedish)

Oross puh – Bitch (Turkish)

Putz – Fool (Yiddish)

Schlemeil – Clumsy idiot (Yiddish)

WEAKEST LINKISMS

Who has no marbles to lose?

Who is all milk and no cornflakes?

Whose windmill is not turning?

Who's a few trucks short of a convoy?

Who's as quick as a tortoise on Prozac?

Who's as useless as a stripper in a nudist resort?

Who put the "more" into moron?

Whose brain server is permanently down?

Whose clue meter is reading zero?

Whose intelligence is their best-kept secret?

Who is all bun and no burger?

Who is more asshead than asset?

Who is a pothole on the highway of life?

Whose mouth and brain are getting divorced?

Who'd have a problem counting their legs?

Who is to intelligence what John Prescott is to hang gliding?

Who is to intelligence what Rip Van Winkle is to insomnia?

Who is to intelligence what Long John Silver is to ballroom dancing?

Who is to intelligence what King Herod was to babysitting?

Who is to intelligence what Captain Hook is to text messaging?

Who is to intelligence what Elvis was to the Slimfast diet?

Who has fallen out of the Tree of Knowledge?

Whose IQ and shoe size are the same number?

Who is the torch without a bulb?

Who here is as out of place as Paris Hilton in a nunnery?

Who here would benefit from a lobotomy?

Who is three pence short of a shilling?

Which of you is less articulate than a truck?

Who is a few strands short of a toupee?

Whose intellectual capacity wouldn't fill an egg cup?

Who is all pop-up and no text?

Who is a brick short of an outhouse?

Who's the runt of the litter?

Who's cooking on low gas?

Whose reservoir of knowledge has dried up?

Whose headlights are constantly on dim?

Whose mental power is experiencing rolling blackouts?

Who is as welcome as a whoopee cushion at a funeral service?

Who's as much use as a vegan in an abattoir?

Who would be out of their depth in the shallow end?

Who'd get shipwrecked in a rock pool?

Who's an olive short of a martini?

Who's the prune among the plums?

Who has the attention span of a goldfish?

Whose jigsaw is missing more than one piece?

Who's the red sock in your white wash?

Who's the Jade Goody among the Albert Einsteins?

Who is as thick as a club sandwich?

Who's got a rip in their marbles bag?

Who is as useful as a ballerina in a rugby scrum?

Who makes Simple Simon look educated?

Who's got varicose brains?

Who is not smarter than the average bear?

Who would come third in a duel?

Whose key does not fit the lock?

Who's the donkey in the Kentucky Derby?

Who is a singer short of a full choir?

Which of you has become hard of thinking?

Whose lot is very, very vacant?

Who could talk to a plant as an equal?

Whose absence would not make the heart grow fonder?

Who is a cymbal short of a drum kit?

Who hasn't got both their hands on the steering wheel?

Who here is the intellectual equal of a turnip?

Who is as out of place here as a lap dancer at a vicar's tea party?

Which of you was a plank of wood in a previous life?

Which of you has an empty in-tray?

Who is still working on mono in a stereo world?

Whose recipe for success has gone lumpy?

MEN BASHING

God made Adam before Eve because you always make a rough draft before the final copy.

Men are beasts, and even beasts don't behave as they do. — Brigitte Bardot

Why do men want to marry virgins? — Because they can't stand criticism.

Yeah, I did marry beneath me. Doesn't every woman. — Roseanne Barr

The fastest way to a man's heart is through his chest. — Roseanne Barr

Even if a man can hit a glass on the table four out of five times when clipping his toenails, women will never truly appreciate his skill.

What women want: to be loved, to be listened to, to be desired, to be respected, to be needed, to be trusted, and sometimes, just to be held. What men went: tickets for the World Series. — Dave Barry

Guys are simple . . . women are not simple and they always assume that men must be just as complicated as they are, only way more mysterious. The whole point is guys are not thinking much. They are just what they appear to be. Tragically. — Dave Barry

The obvious and fair solution to the housework problem is to let men do the housework for, say, the next six thousand years, to even things up. The trouble is that men, over the years, have developed an inflated notion of the importance of everything they do, so that before long they would turn housework into just as much of a charade as business is now. They would hire secretaries and buy computers and fly off to housework conferences in Bermuda, but they'd never clean anything. — Dave Barry

The sight of blonde hair knocks men three rungs down the evolutionary ladder.

What's with you men? Would hair stop growing on your chest if you asked directions somewhere? – Erma Bombeck

I don't hate men. I think men are absolutely fantastic . . . as a concept. – Jo Brand

Men build bridges and throw railroads across deserts, and yet they contend successfully that the job of sewing on a button is beyond them. – Heywood Broun

Why do women live longer than men? – Someone has to stick around and clean up the mess after them.

Why is food better than men? – Because you don't have to wait an hour for seconds.

I like a man that wears a wedding ring, because without it, they're like a shark without a fin. You pretty much gotta know they're out there. – Brett Butler

I'm a modern man. I've never had problems buying tampons. But apparently they're not a proper present. – Jimmy Carr

Men aren't necessities, they're luxuries. – Cher

The only time a man thinks about a candlelit dinner is if there has been a power failure.

Men are like bank accounts – without a lot of money, they don't generate much interest.

When a man of forty falls in love with a girl of twenty, it isn't *her* youth he is seeking but his own. – Lenore Coffee

Men were made for war. Without it they wandered greyly about, getting under the feet of the women, who were trying to organize the really important things of life. – Alice Thomas Ellis

Beware of men who cry. It's true that men who cry are sensitive to and in touch with their feelings, but the only feelings they tend to be sensitive to and in touch with are their own. – Nora Ephron, *Heartburn*

Men are like high heels – they're easy to walk on once you get used to it.

Men are like chocolates – they never last long enough and they always leave stains whenever they get hot.

Men don't realize that if we're sleeping with them on the first date, we're probably not interested in seeing them again either. – Chelsea Handler

Can you imagine a world without men? No crime and lots of happy, fat women. – Nicole Hollander

The difference between Government bonds and men is that bonds mature.

Men are simple things. They can survive a whole weekend with only three things: beer, boxer shorts and batteries for the remote control. – Diana Jordan

Men are like car alarms. They both make a lot of noise no one listens to. – Diana Jordan

A woman without a man is like a neck without a pain.

My sister gives me the creeps – all her old boyfriends. – Terri Kelly

Women speak because they wish to speak, whereas a man speaks only when driven to speech by something outside himself – like, for instance, he can't find any clean socks. – Jean Kerr

Why do women love cats? Cats are independent, they don't listen, they don't come in when you call, they like to stay out all night, and when they're home they like to be left alone and sleep. In other words, every quality that women hate in a man, they love in a cat.

A new study says that the number one quality men find attractive in a woman is her sense of humour. They especially like it when women laugh at a joke and their boobs bounce up and down. – Jay Leno

According to a recent poll, sixty percent of women believe in ghosts. That's because they've seen how quickly guys can disappear after sex. – Jay Leno

A new survey of women in their twenties says that the number one quality a woman wants in a husband is the ability to share his innermost feelings. When these same women are asked the question in their forties, they'll settle for a guy who doesn't make disgusting noises when he eats. – Jay Leno

The one thing you can be sure of about a well-dressed man is that his wife picks his clothes.

Men think monogamy is something you make dining tables out of. – Kathy Lette

Why do men prefer blondes? – Men always like intellectual company.

Man is the missing link between apes and human beings. – Konrad Lorenz

Commitment is what every woman wants; men can't even spell it.

If it can't be fixed by duct tape or WD-40, it's a female problem. – Jason Love

I wasn't sure about tattoos on my fella, but they were good during sex because it was something for me to watch. – Jane McDonald

How is a man like a snowstorm? – Because you don't know when it's coming, how many inches you'll get or how long it will stay.

Women want mediocre men, and men are working hard to be as mediocre as possible. – Margaret Mead

Men are like a fine wine. They all start out like grapes, and it's our job to stamp on them and keep them in the dark until they mature into something you'd like to have dinner with. – Kathleen Mifsud

How can you tell the difference between men's real gifts and their guilt gifts? – Their guilt gifts are more expensive.

I don't deny that an odd man here and there, if he's caught young and trained up proper, and if his mother has spanked him well beforehand, may turn out a decent being. – Lucy Maud Montgomery

It takes only four men to wallpaper a house, but you have to slice them thinly.

Although no man is an island, you can make quite an effective raft out of six. – Simon Munnery

I know many married men, I even know a few happily married men, but I don't know one who wouldn't fall down the first open coal hole running after the first pretty girl who gave him a wink. – George Jean Nathan

I love the male body, it's better designed than the male mind. – Andrea Newman

I wonder why men get serious at all. They have this delicate, long thing hanging outside their bodies which goes up and down by its own will. If I were a man, I would always be laughing at myself. – Yoko Ono

Every time a woman leaves off something she looks better, but every time a man leaves off something he looks worse. – Will Rogers, on clothes

A man becomes so accustomed to the thought of his own faults that he will begin to cherish them as charming little "personal characteristics". – Helen Rowland

A man's desire for a son is usually nothing but the wish to duplicate himself in order that such a remarkable pattern may not be lost to the world. – Helen Rowland

When a man makes a woman his wife, it's the highest compliment he can pay her, and it's usually the last. – Helen Rowland

There are only two kinds of men – the dead and the deadly. – Helen Rowland

How is a man like the weather? – Nothing can be done to change either one of them.

Don't try to teach men how to do anything in public. They can learn in private; in public they have to know. – Rita Rudner

I've finally figured that being male is the same thing, more or less, as having a personality disorder. – Carol Shields

The more I see of men, the more I admire dogs.

There are easier things in life than trying to find a nice guy . . . like nailing jelly to a tree, for example.

A woman without a man is like a fish without a bicycle. – Gloria Steinem

Men are like mascara – they run at the first sign of emotion.

When God created man she was only experimenting.

There is one thing you can give to a man who has everything – a woman to show him how it works.

Men like smart women because opposites attract.

Only a man would buy a $700 car and put a $5,000 stereo in it.

Man is the only animal that blushes. Or needs to. – Mark Twain

Men are like placemats – they show up only when there's food on the table.

A man's idea of helping with the housework is lifting his legs so his wife can hoover.

Talking with a man is like trying to saddle a cow. You work like hell, but what's the point? – Gladys Upham

Sometimes I think if there was a third sex, men wouldn't get so much as a glance from me. – Amanda Vail

The first time you buy a house you think how pretty it is and sign the cheque. The second time you look to see if the basement has termites. It's the same with men. – Lupe Velez

The difference between a new husband and a new dog is that a dog is always happy to see you and only takes a month to train.

The difference between a man and a broken clock is that even a broken clock is right twice a day.

Don't let a man put anything over on you except an umbrella. – Mae West

There is, of course, no reason for the existence of the male sex except that sometimes one needs help with moving the piano. – Rebecca West

A man's idea of a romantic evening is a candlelit football stadium.

Young men want to be faithful and are not; old men want to be faithless and cannot. – Oscar Wilde

A lot of guys think the larger a woman's breasts are, the less intelligent she is. I don't think it works like that. I think it's the opposite. I think the larger a woman's breasts are, the less intelligent the men become. – Anita Wise

Not all men are annoying. Some are dead.

WOMEN BASHING

My wife and I thought we were in love but it turned out to be benign. – Woody Allen

Give a woman an inch and she thinks she's a ruler.

A good wife always forgives her husband when she's wrong. – Milton Berle

Brigands demand your money or your life; women require both. – Samuel Butler

The only time a woman is interested in a man's company is when he owns it.

A woman will lie about anything, just to stay in practice. – Raymond Chandler

Why do women stop menstruating in their fifties? Because they need the blood for their varicose veins.

If you can stay up and listen with a fair degree of attention to whatever garbage, no matter how stupid it is that they (women) are coming out with, till ten minutes past four in the morning . . . you're in! – Peter Cook

My wife asked for plastic surgery; I cut up her credit card. – Rodney Dangerfield

He's been trying to drown his troubles for years, but she's too good a swimmer.

Women are like elephants to me: nice to look at, but I wouldn't want to own one. – W. C. Fields

No two women are alike – in fact no one woman is alike.

Men wake up as good-looking as when they went to bed. Women somehow deteriorate during the night.

Marry an outdoors woman. Then if you throw her out into the yard for the night, she can still survive. – W. C. Fields

The difference between a battery and a woman is that a battery has a positive side.

We have drugs to make women speak, but none to keep them silent. – Anatole France

He and his wife were inseparable. Sometimes it took four people to pull them apart.

A woman's mind is cleaner than a man's. She changes it more often. – Oliver Herford

If a guy doesn't climax it's his fault; if a woman doesn't climax it's his fault.

Women give us solace, but if it were not for women we should never need solace. – Don Herold

If you don't think women are explosive, try dropping one.

Women's intuition is the result of millions of years of not thinking. – Rupert Hughes

The difference between a woman and a washing machine is that when you dump a load in the washing machine, it doesn't call you the next day.

My wife made me a millionaire. I used to have three million. – Bobby Hull

A woman can hold a grudge until it dies of old age . . . and then she will have it stuffed and mounted.

If you have a choice of selling shoes to ladies or giving birth to a flaming porcupine, look into that second career. – Richard Jeni

I don't worry about terrorism. I was married for two years. – Sam Kinison

Feminism was established so as to allow unattractive women easier access to mainstream society. – Rush Limbaugh

The home shopping network! There's a good idea for women. It was a little too hard driving to the mall with a couch strapped to their ass! – *Married . . . With Children*

God created the orgasm so that women can moan even when they're happy.

Women should be obscene and not heard. – Groucho Marx

Anyone who thinks that marriage is a fifty-fifty proposition doesn't understand women or fractions. – Jackie Mason

What's the difference between a woman and a water buffalo? – About twenty-five pounds.

Women are hens, puffed-up clucking creatures; little more than egg-laying machines, woken up each morning by a persistent cock. – Al Murray

What have women and dog turds got in common? The older they get, the easier they are to pick up.

Women are nothing but machines for producing children. – Napoleon I

I have an idea that the phrase "weaker sex" was coined by some woman to disarm some man she was preparing to overwhelm. – Ogden Nash

Three of my wives were very good housekeepers. After we got divorced, they kept the house. – Willie Pep

The chief excitement in a woman's life is spotting people who are fatter than she is. – Helen Rowland

What's the best way to get a youthful figure? – Ask a woman her age.

I like women with gaps in their teeth. They are so damnably useful when it comes to scraping carrots. – Peter Tinniswood

I still see my ex-girlfriend every year at the restraining order renewal breakfast. – Christopher Titus

Receptionist: How do you write women so well?

Melvin Udall: I think of a man. Then I take away reason and accountability. That's a woman.
– As Good As It Gets

Once a woman has given you her heart you can never get rid of the rest of her body. – John Vanbrugh

A man's face is his autobiography. A woman's face is her work of fiction. – Oscar Wilde

I haven't spoken to my wife for eighteen months. I don't like to interrupt her. – Henny Youngman

Women are like shoes. They can always be replaced.

I just got back from a pleasure trip. I took my wife to the airport. – Henny Youngman

There are three types of women: the intelligent, the beautiful, and the majority.

SHAKESPEAREAN PUT-DOWNS

Methinks thou art a general offence and every man should beat thee. – *All's Well That Ends Well*

He professes not keeping of oaths; in breaking them he is stronger than Hercules. – *All's Well That Ends Well*

In his sleep he does little harm, save to his bedclothes about him. – *All's Well That Ends Well*

This woman's an easy glove, my lord; she goes off and on at pleasure. – *All's Well That Ends Well*

She is too mean to have her name repeated. – *All's Well That Ends Well*

He has everything that an honest man should not have; what an honest man should have, he has nothing. – *All's Well That Ends Well*

He's a most notable coward, an infinite and endless liar, an hourly promise-breaker, the owner of no one good quality. – *All's Well That Ends Well*

I am sure, though you know what temperance should be, you know not what it is. – *Antony and Cleopatra*

His kisses are Judas's own children. – *As You Like It*

His brain is as dry as the remainder biscuit after a voyage. – *As You Like It*

Is his head worth a hat? Or his chin worth a beard? – *As You Like It*

I do desire we be better strangers. – *As You Like It*

She's the kitchen wench, and all grease, and I know not what use to put her to but to make a lamp of her, and run from her by her own light. – *The Comedy of Errors*

No longer from head to foot than from hip to hip, she is spherical, like a globe. I could find out countries in her. – *The Comedy of Errors*

More of your conversation would infect my brain. – *Coriolanus*

The people deserve such pity of him as the wolf does of the shepherds. – *Coriolanus*

The tartness of his face sours ripe grapes. – *Coriolanus*

There is no more mercy in him than there is milk in a male tiger. – *Coriolanus*

His celestial breath was sulphurous to smell. – *Cymbeline*

She's outpriz'd by a trifle. – *Cymbeline*

This Cloten was a fool, an empty purse, there was no money in it. Not Hercules could have knocked out his brains for he had none. – *Cymbeline*

Your bait of falsehood takes this carp of truth. – *Hamlet*

Polonius: I will most humbly take my leave of you.
Hamlet: You cannot, sir, take from me anything that I will not more willingly part withal. – *Hamlet*

(You are) spacious in the possession of dirt. – *Hamlet*

My two schoolfellows. Whom I shall trust as I will adders' fangs. – *Hamlet*

Why dost thou converse with that trunk of humours, that bolting-hutch of beastliness, that swollen parcel of dropsies, that huge bombard of sack, that stuffed cloak-bag of guts, that roasted Manningtree ox with the pudding in his belly, that reverend Vice, that grey Iniquity, that father Ruffian, that Vanity in years? – *Henry IV, Part I*

There's no more valour in (him) than in a wild duck. – *Henry IV, Part I*

There's no more faith in thee than in a stewed prune. – *Henry IV, Part I*

Do thou amend thy face, and I'll amend my life. – *Henry IV, Part I*

Falstaff sweats to death and lards the lean earth as he walks along. – *Henry IV, Part I*

You might have thrust him and all his apparel into an eel-skin. – *Henry IV, Part II*

(Your) face is Lucifer's privy-kitchen, where he doth nothing but roast malt-worms. – *Henry IV, Part II*

Your means are very slender, and your waist is great. – *Henry IV, Part II*

What a disgrace it is to me that I should remember your name. – *Henry IV, Part II*

Is it not strange that desire should so many years outlive performance? – *Henry IV, Part II*

(Your) face is not worth sunburning. – *Henry V*

(You are) the scarecrow that affrights our children so. – *Henry VI, Part I*

This knave's tongue begins to double. – *Henry VI, Part II*

Seems he a dove? His feathers are but borrow'd. – *Henry VI, Part II*

No man's pie is freed from (your) ambitious finger. – *Henry VIII*

(Thou art) not at all a friend to truth. – *Henry VIII*

He was a man of an unbounded stomach. – *Henry VIII*

Where wilt thou find a cavern dark enough to mask thy monstrous visage? – *Julius Caesar*

Sell your face for five pence and 'tis dear. – *King John*

Thou art a boil, a plague-sore, or embossed carbuncle, in my corrupted blood. – *King Lear*

You are not worth the dust which the rude wind blows in your face. – *King Lear*

Get thee glass eyes: and, like a scurvy politician, seem to see the things thou dost not. – *King Lear*

He draweth out the thread of his verbosity finer than the staple of his argument. – *Love's Labour's Lost*

They have been at a great feast of languages and stolen the scraps. – *Love's Labour's Lost*

(Your) horrid image doth unfix my hair. – *Macbeth*

I had rather be married to a death's-head with a bone in his mouth. – *The Merchant of Venice*

(You) speak an infinite deal of nothing. – *The Merchant of Venice*

Wilt thou show the whole wealth of thy wit in an instant? – *The Merchant of Venice*

How shall I be revenged on him? I think the best way were to entertain him with hope till the wicked fire of lust have melted him in his own grease. – *The Merry Wives of Windsor*

His speech was like a tangled chain; nothing impaired, but all disordered. – *A Midsummer Night's Dream*

He is no less than a stuffed man. – *Much Ado About Nothing*

(You are) duller than a great thaw. – *Much Ado About Nothing*

You have such a February face, so full of frost, of storm, and cloudiness. – *Much Ado About Nothing*

May his pernicious soul rot half a grain a day! – *Othello*

(You are) an index and prologue to the history of lust and foul thoughts. – *Othello*

If you have any music that may not be heard, to 't again. – *Othello*

Your peevish chastity is not worth a breakfast in the cheapest country. – *Pericles*

Thou lump of foul deformity! – *Richard III*

Out of my sight! Thou dost infect my eyes. – *Richard III*

(You) diffus'd infection of a man! – *Richard III*

Never hung poison on a fouler toad. – *Richard III*

Thou art unfit for any place but hell. – *Richard III*

A fan to hide her face, for her fan's the fairer face! – *Romeo and Juliet*

You kiss by th' book. – *Romeo and Juliet*

I know she is an irksome brawling scold. – *The Taming of the Shrew*

His complexion is perfect gallows. – *The Tempest*

Would thou wert clean enough to spit upon. – *Timon of Athens*

Were I like thee, I'd throw away myself. – *Timon of Athens*

Thou disease of a friend! – *Timon of Athens*

Away, thou issue of a mangy dog! – *Timon of Athens*

A fusty nut with no kernel. – *Troilus and Cressida*

He has not so much brain as ear-wax. – *Troilus and Cressida*

(He) wears his wits in his belly and his guts in his head. – *Troilus and Cressida*

Would the fountain of your mind were clear again, that I might water an ass in it. – *Troilus and Cressida*

I had rather be a tick in a sheep than such a valiant ignorance. – *Troilus and Cressida*

Taste your legs, sir, put them to motion. – *Twelfth Night*

If he were opened and you find so much blood in his liver as will clog the foot of a flea, I'll eat the rest of th'anatomy. – *Twelfth Night*

(You are) a coward, a most devout coward, religious in it. – *Twelfth Night*

Observe him, for the love of mockery. – *Twelfth Night*

She hath more hair than wit, and more faults than hairs, and more wealth than faults. – *The Two Gentlemen of Verona*

A WORLD OF INSULTS

Albania
Albania is a fascinating country, but I wouldn't want to go for the *whole* weekend.

Who wears a dirty white robe and rides a pig? – Lawrence of Albania.

Armenia
Trust a snake before a Jew, a Jew before a Greek, but never trust an Armenian. French saying

One Jew can cheat ten Greeks; one Greek ten Jews; and one Armenian ten Greeks. – German saying

If you can make a good bargain with an Armenian, you can make a good bargain with the devil. – Persian saying

God made serpents and Armenians. – Turkish saying

Australia
If you find an Australian indoors, it's a fair bet that he will have a glass in his hand. – Jonathan Aitken

A Portaloo in the Pacific. – Anon

A country lying in the South Sea, whose industrial and commercial development has been unspeakably retarded by an unfortunate dispute among geographers as to whether it is a continent or an island. – Ambrose Bierce, *The Devil's Dictionary*

From time to time it sends us useful things – opals, merino wool, Errol Flynn, the boomerang – but nothing we can't actually do without. – Bill Bryson, *Down Under*

My one tip for you if you ever go to Canberra is don't leave your hotel without a good map, a compass, several days' provisions and a mobile phone with the number of a rescue service. I walked for two hours through green, pleasant, endlessly identical neighbourhoods, never entirely confident that I wasn't just going round in a large circle. – Bill Bryson, *Down Under*

I decided to come up with a new slogan for Canberra. First I wrote: "Canberra – There's Nothng To It!" and then "Canberra – Why Wait for Death?" – Bill Bryson, *Down Under*

(of St Kilda Beach, Melbourne) It's been like swimming in undiluted sewage. – Prince Charles

In America, only the successful writer is important, in France all writers are important, in England no writer is important, and in Australia you have to explain what a writer is. – Geoffrey Cottrell

Why do so many Australian men suffer from premature ejaculation? Because they have to rush back to the pub to tell their mates what happened.

Stone, paper, scissors: to most of us it's a game but to Australians it's a wedding list. – Angus Deayton

One of the strongest prejudices that one has to overcome when one visits Australia is that created by the weird jargon that passes for English in this country. – Valerie Desmond

Melbourne is the perfect place for a film about the end of the world. – Ava Gardner

Where else in the world is a generous man defined as one who would give you his arsehole and shit through his ribs? – Germaine Greer

In America, you go out, you walk across the country. You discover paradise. In Australia, you walk across the country and you find absolutely nothing. And then you die. – Robert Hughes

The only people really keeping the spirit of irony alive in Australia are taxi drivers and homosexuals. – Barry Humphries

What does an Australian say by way of foreplay? – "Brace yourself, Sheila."

Australia may be the only country in the world in which the term "academic" is regularly used as a term of abuse. – Leonie Kramer

Why did the Australian bloke cross the road? Because his dick was in the chicken. – Kathy Lette

In Australia, *not* reading poetry is the national pastime. – Phyllis McGinley

Melbourne is the kind of town that really makes you consider the question "Is there life before death?" – Bette Midler

I came to believe that it is a crime to think in Australia. – Bette Midler

New Zealand was colonized initially by those Australians who had the initiative to escape. – Robert Muldoon

An Australian relief effort is knitting sweaters to protect the fur of penguins who are being affected by an oil spill. The sweaters are being refused by many penguins who would rather die than dress casual. – Conan O'Brien

The national sport is breaking furniture. – P. J. O'Rourke, *Holidays in Hell*

Australia is still very exclusive. On the visa application they still ask if you've been convicted of a felony – although they are willing to give you a visa even if you haven't been. – P. J. O'Rourke, *Holidays in Hell*

The Australian language is easier to learn than boat talk. It has a vocabulary of about six words. – P. J. O'Rourke, *Holidays in Hell*

If it takes an IQ of sixty to tie shoelaces, why do so many Australians wear thongs?

The Australian Book of Etiquette is a very slim volume. – Paul Theroux

To Australia? Oh, don't mention that dreadful vulgar place. – Oscar Wilde, *Lady Windermere's Fan*

Belgium

Is there anything interesting about the Belgians? – Jeremy Clarkson

If you thought the last (Volkswagen) Passat was dull to behold, you really ain't seen nothing yet. This new one is sculptured dishwater. It is the motoring equivalent of Belgium: something you simply won't notice. – Jeremy Clarkson

Bolivia

Bolivians are merely metamorphosed llamas who have learned to talk but not think. – José Toribio Merino

Britain

There's nothing the British like better than a bloke who comes from nowhere, makes it, and then gets clobbered. – Melvyn Bragg

It is an interesting experience to become acquainted with a country through the eyes of the insane, and, if I may say so, a particularly useful grounding for life in Britain. – Bill Bryson, *Notes From a Small Island*

It sometimes occurs to me that the British have more heritage than is good for them. – Bill Bryson, *Notes From a Small Island*

As always, the British especially shudder at the latest American vulgarity, and then they embrace it with enthusiasm two years later. – Alistair Cooke

Stephen Fry: In the 1900 Olympics there was a sport where Britain won a gold medal, in which the only other country that competed was France. Can you imagine what that might have been?
Alan Davies: Arrogance? – *QI*

I shouldn't be saying this, high treason really, but I sometimes wonder if Americans aren't fooled by our accent into detecting a brilliance that may not be there. – Stephen Fry, on the awards success of British actors

Rain is the one thing the British do better than anybody else. – Marilyn French

What have the Channel Islands ever done for us? A couple of really expensive potatoes, a few flowers and fatty milk. – A. A. Gill

We know no spectacle so ridiculous as the British public in one of its periodical fits of morality. – Thomas Babington Macaulay

Britain is a society where the ruling class does not rule, the working class does not work, and the middle class is not in the middle. – George Mikes, *English Humour For Beginners*

We are no longer a green and pleasant land spotted with filthy places. We are a filthy island in which there is now an occasional oasis of cleanliness. – Jeremy Paxman

A soggy little island huffing and puffing to keep up with Western Europe. – John Updike

I may be naïve in hoping that remaining in Europe will make us more European, but after a thousand years of insularity from which have evolved the bingo parlour, carbonized beer and *Crossroads*, I am inclined to give it a whirl. – Keith Waterhouse, 1975

The British cook is a foolish woman, who should be turned, for her iniquities, into a pillar of that salt which she never knows how to use. – Oscar Wilde

The British public are really not equal to the mental strain of having more than one topic every three months. – Oscar Wilde, *The Picture of Dorian Gray*

To disagree with three-fourths of the British public on all points is one of the first elements of sanity, one of the deepest consolations in all moments of spiritual doubt. – Oscar Wilde

England
English coffee tastes like water that has been squeezed out of a wet sleeve. – Fred Allen

On a fine day the climate of England is like looking up a chimney, on a foul day it is like looking down. – Anon

One has not great hopes for Birmingham. I always say there is something direful in the sound. – Jane Austen

The truth is, that in London it is always a sickly season. Nobody is healthy in London, nobody can be. – Jane Austen, *Emma*

English cuisine has received a lot of unfair criticism over the years, but the truth is that it can be a very pleasant surprise to the connoisseur of severely overcooked livestock organs served in lukewarm puddles of congealed grease. – Dave Barry

The English are, I think, the most obtuse and barbarous people in the world. – Marie Henri Beyle

Had Jerusalem been built in England and the site of the Crucifixion discovered, it would promptly be built over and called the Golgotha Centre. – Alan Bennett

How lucky you English are to find the toilet so amusing. For us, it is a mundane and functional item. For you it is the basis of an entire culture. – German airman, *Blackadder*

There are worse places than Hastings . . . Beirut and Sarajevo spring to mind. – Jo Brand

Anyone from Norwich? Gimme six! – Marcus Brigstocke

English is full of booby traps for the unwary foreigner. Any language where the unassuming word "fly" signifies an annoying insect, a means of travel, and a critical part of a gentleman's apparel is clearly asking to be mangled. – Bill Bryson, *Mother Tongue*

After a fierce hurricane hit Birmingham, local officials estimate that the storm caused £800,000 worth of improvements.

The average cooking in the average hotel for the average Englishman explains to a large extent the English bleakness and taciturnity. Nobody can beam and warble while chewing pressed beef smeared with diabolical mustard. Nobody can exult aloud while ungluing from his teeth a quivering tapioca pudding. – Karel Capek

The most dangerous thing in the world is to make a friend of an Englishman, because he'll come sleep in your closet rather than spend ten shillings on a hotel. – Truman Capote

It is now so dangerous in parts of London that even the muggers go around in pairs.

In England there are sixty different religions and only one sauce. – Francesco Caracciolo

If you tell a girl you like her but she says, "I love you more like a brother," suggest a weekend in Norfolk. Unless you're from Norfolk, in which case it probably *is* your sister. – Jimmy Carr

Cannabis changed from a Class B drug to Class C, which was a nightmare for Scouse kids. They had to learn a new letter. – Jimmy Carr

I grew up in Slough in the 1970s. If you want to know what Slough was like in the 1970s, go there now. – Jimmy Carr

If Great Yarmouth was a birthday present, I'm not sure I'd bother to tear off the wrapping paper. – Stephen Cartmel

Carla: You're from England, huh?
Eric: How'd you guess?
Carla: 'Cos you sound smart even when you say stupid things. – *Cheers*

On the seventh day God didn't rest. He looked at what he had created and thought, "Oh damn it, England's gone all wrong. The sea is washing silt off the coastlines in the north and depositing it in an ugly bulbous lump near Kent." Today we call this unholy place East Anglia. – Jeremy Clarkson

Why do pigeons fly upside down over Birmingham? Because there's nothing worth crapping on.

The English contribution to world cuisine: the chip. – John Cleese

Sheep with a nasty side. – Cyril Connolly

I went to Morecambe for the week, but it was closed. – Colin Crompton

Welcome to Hastings – and you are welcome to it!

Nobody but a monumental bore would have thought of having a honeymoon at Budleigh Salterton. – Noël Coward

The English think that incompetence is the same thing as sincerity. – Quentin Crisp

People in the North die of ignorance and crisps. – Edwina Currie

Why does the River Thames run through London? – If it walked it would get mugged.

(of the Isle of Wight) All the clocks stopped in 1952. – Alan Davies

Unlike European mustards that bring out the subtle flavours of food, English mustard makes your nose bleed. – Jack Dee

That vain, ill-natured thing, an Englishman. – Daniel Defoe

Wise men affirm it is the English way
Never to grumble till they come to pay. – Daniel Defoe

England, the heart of a rabbit in the body of a lion. – Eustache Deschamps

Freedom of discussion is in England little else than the right to write or say anything which a jury of twelve shopkeepers think it expedient should be said or written. – A.V. Dicey

If any one were to ask me what in my opinion was the dullest and most stupid spot on the face of the Earth, I should decidedly say Chelmsford. – Charles Dickens

London, that great cesspool into which all the loungers of the Empire are irresistibly drained. – Arthur Conan Doyle

I sometimes think the only pleasure an Englishman has is in passing on his cold germs. – Gerald Durrell, *My Family and Other Animals*

The Englishman who has lost his fortune is said to have died of a broken heart. – Ralph Waldo Emerson

An English summer: two fine days and a thunderstorm. – English saying

It is an Englishman's privilege to grumble. – English saying

All Englishmen talk as if they've got a bushel of plums stuck in their throats, and then after swallowing them get constipated from the pips. – W. C. Fields

An Englishman absolutely believes he can warm a room by building a grate fire at the end of it. – Stephen Fiske

The English find ill health not only interesting but respectable and often experience death in an effort to avoid a fuss. – Pamela Frankau

From England, neither fair wind, nor good war. – French saying

The depressing thing about an Englishman's traditional love of animals is the dishonesty thereof – get a barbed hook into the upper lip of a salmon, drag him endlessly around the water until he loses his strength, pull him to the bank, hit him on the head with a stone, and you may well become fisherman of the year. Shoot the salmon and you'll never be asked again. – Clement Freud

Parts of London are so tough that the cats there only have six lives.

A broad definition of crime in England is that it is any lower-class activity that is displeasing to the upper class. – David Frost and Antony Jay

It takes some skill to spoil a breakfast – even the English can't do it. – J. K. Galbraith

To learn English you must begin by thrusting the jaw forward, almost clenching the teeth, and practically immobilizing the lips. In this way the English produce the series of unpleasant little mews of which their language consists. – Jose Ortega y Gasset

Bugger Bognor! – King George V

The German orginates it, the Frenchman imitates it, and the Englishman exploits it. – German saying

Among three Italians will be found two clergymen; among three Spaniards two braggarts; among three Germans two soldiers; among three Frenchmen two chefs; and among three Englishmen two whoremongers. – German saying

What do you say to a Geordie with a job? – "Big Mac, please."

I find England the English embarrassing. Fundamentally toe-curlingly embarrassing. And even though I look like one, sound like one, can imitate the social/mating behaviour of one, I'm not one. I always bridle with irritation when taken for an Englishman, and fill in those disembarkation cards by pedantically writing "Scots" in the appropriate box. – A. A. Gill, *The Angry Island*

I don't like the English. One at a time, I don't mind them. I've loved some of them. It's their collective persona I can't warm to: the lumpen and louty, coarse, unsubtle, beady-eyed, beefy-bummed herd of England. – A. A. Gill

It is related of an Englishman that he hanged himself to avoid the daily task of dressing and undressing. – Johann Wolfgang von Goethe

The biggest influence Stafford had on me was it made me want to leave Stafford. – Dave Gorman

Sylvester Stallone left the ground five minutes early to see whether his limousine was on bricks. – Alan Green, commentating at a soccer match in Liverpool

I'll only set foot in Bridlington when Hull freezes over.

The English never smash in a face. They merely refrain from asking it to dinner. – Margaret Halsey, *With Malice Toward Some*

Living in England, provincial England, must be like being married to a stupid but exquisitely beautiful wife. – Margaret Halsey

I was well warned about English food, so it did not surprise me, but I do wonder sometimes how they ever manage to prise it up long enough to get a plate under it. – Margaret Halsey

Englishwomen's shoes look as if they had been made by someone who had often heard shoes described, but had never seen any. – Margaret Halsey

The devil take these people and their language! They take a dozen monosyllabic words in their jaws, chew them, crunch them and spit them out again, and call that speaking. – Heinrich Heine

Silence can be defined as conversation with an Englishman. – Heinrich Heine

There is nothing on earth more terrible than English music, except English painting. They have no sense of sound, or eye for colour, and I sometimes wonder whether their sense of smell is not equally blunted and dulled. I should not be surprised if they cannot even distinguish between the smell of a ball of horse-dung and an orange. – Heinrich Heine

A demon took a monkey to wife – the result, by the grace of God, was the English. – Indian saying

It is good to have one foot in England; it is still better, or at least as good, to have the other out of it. – Henry James

Portsmouth is one of the most depressed towns in Southern England: a place that is arguably too full of drugs, obesity, underachievement and Labour MPs. – Boris Johnson

When two Englishmen meet their first talk is of the weather. – Samuel Johnson

London! The needy villain's general home,
The common sewer of Paris and Rome!
With eager thirst, by folly or by fate,
Sucks in the dregs of each corrupted state. – Samuel Johnson

Pass a law to give every single whingeing bloody Pommie his fare home to England. Back to the smoke and the sun shining ten days a year and shit in the streets. Yer can have it. – Thomas Keneally, Australian writer

England has become a squalid, uncomfortable, ugly place . . . an intolerant, racist, homophobic, narrow-minded, authoritarian, rat-hole run by vicious, suburban-minded, materialistic philistines. – Hanif Kureishi, 1988

The Englishman respects your opinions, but he never thinks of your feelings. – Wilfred Laurier

(of London) A place you go to get bronchitis. – Fran Lebowitz

By no stretch of the imagination is Manchester a picturesque city. – Chris Lethbridge

Eat in most restaurants in England and pretty soon your head will no longer be on speaking terms with your stomach. – Kathy Lette

Newcastle people are so hard up they hold in their piss until they go on holiday. – Sean Lock

(of space) Once you get up there, there's nothing really there. It's a bit like Norfolk. – Sean Lock

London, dirty little pool of life. – B. M. Malabari

I like to go to Liverpool, just to visit my hubcaps. – Bernard Manning

The British Empire was created as a by-product of generations of desperate Englishmen roaming the world in search of a decent meal. – Bill Marsano

The English, who eat their meat red and bloody, show the savagery that goes with such food. – J. O. de la Mettrie

When it's three o'clock in New York, it's still 1938 in London. – Bette Midler

The English have no soul; they have the understatement instead. – George Mikes, *How To Be An Alien*

In England it is bad manners to be clever, to assert something confidently. It may be your personal view that two and two make four, but you must not state it in a self-assured way, because this is a democratic country and others may be of a different opinion. – George Mikes, *How To Be An Alien*

What distinguishes Cambridge from Oxford, broadly speaking, is that nobody who has been to Cambridge feels impelled to write about it. – A. A. Milne

English women are elegant until they are ten years old. – Nancy Mitford

Most Scousers have hilarious chips on both shoulders the size of the Grand Canyon. – Piers Morgan

Mayonnaise never reached Stockport for a number of years, and nor did periods. – Paul Morley, on sex education

A ready means of being cherished by the English is to adopt the simple expedient of living a long time. I have little doubt that if, say, Oscar Wilde had lived into his nineties, instead of dying in his forties, he would have been considered a benign, distinguished figure suitable to preside at a school prize-giving or to instruct and exhort scout masters at their jamborees. He might even have been knighted. – Malcolm Muggeridge

The cold of the polar regions was nothing to the chill of an English bedroom. – Fridtjof Nansen

What do you call a Scouser in a detached house? – A burglar.

The English have no exalted sentiments. They can all be bought. – Napoleon I

Cold-blooded queers with nasty complexions and terrible teeth who once conquered half the world but still haven't figured out central heating. They warm their beers and chill their baths and boil all their food. – P. J. O'Rourke

The English are not happy unless they are miserable. – George Orwell

There's nothing like an English weirdo. We come up with the best nutters of any country. – Sharon Osbourne

The only bright lights in Grantham on a Saturday night are red, amber, and green.

Go to London. I guarantee you'll either be mugged or not appreciated. Catch the train to London, stopping at Rejection, Disappointment, Backstabbing Central and Shattered Dreams Parkway. – Alan Partridge, *I'm Alan Partridge*

There is such a thing as too much couth. – S. J. Perelman

(of Nottingham) There are no theatres, no cinemas, hardly anything. All Nottingham has is Robin Hood . . . and he's dead. – Bryan Roy

An Englishman does everything on principle: he fights you on patriotic principles; he robs you on business principles; he enslaves you on imperial principles. – George Bernard Shaw

English cuisine is so generally threadbare that for years there has been a gentlemen's agreement in the civilized world to allow the Brits pre-eminence in the matter of tea – which, after all, comes down to little more than the ability to boil water. – Wilfrid Sheed

The Englishman is never content but when he is grumbling. – Scottish saying

In North London they erect blue plaques in honour of famous entertainers; in South London they put up yellow signs saying, "Did anyone see this murder?" – Arthur Smith

Do you know that if you hold a shell suit up to your ear you can hear Romford? – Linda Smith

It must be acknowledged that the English are the most disagreeable of all the nations of Europe, more surly and morose, with less disposition to please, to exert themselves for the good of society, to make small sacrifices, and to put themselves out of their way. – Sydney Smith

What a pity it is that we have no amusements in England but vice and religion. – Sydney Smith

The moment the very name of Ireland is mentioned, the English seem to bid adieu to common feeling, common prudence, and common sense, and to act with the barbarity of tyrants, and the fatuity of idiots. – Sydney Smith

The only good thing about Luton is that, with a motorway, a railway and an airport, it's easy to get away from quickly.

There's a hole in the world
Like a great black pit,
And the vermin of the world
Inhabit it . . .
And it goes by the name of London. – Stephen Sondheim, *Sweeney Todd*

I know why the sun never sets on the British Empire: God wouldn't trust an Englishman in the dark. – Duncan Spaeth

London seems so dirty and overpriced and seedy: a city in which parking meters have replaced sparrows and terror has replaced wonder. – Imogen Stubbs

The national sport of England is obstacle racing. People fill their rooms with useless and cumbersome furniture, and spend the rest of their lives trying to dodge it. – Herbert Beerbohm Tree

The English think soap is civilization. – Heinrich von Treitschke

What do you call a Liverpool woman who has had six abortions? – Crime Prevention Officer.

An Englishman will burn his bed to catch a flea. – Turkish saying

London, black as crows and noisy as ducks, prudish with all the vices in evidence, everlastingly drunk, in spite of ridiculous laws about drunkenness, immense, though it is really basically only a collection of scandal-mongering boroughs, vying with each other, ugly and dull, without any monuments except interminable docks. – Paul Verlaine

We'd like to apologize to viewers in the north. It must be awful for them. – *Victoria Wood – As Seen On TV*

The way to endure summer in England is to have it framed and glazed in a comfortable room. – Horace Walpole

In England we have come to rely upon a comfortable time-lag of fifty years or a century intervening between the perception that something ought to be done and a serious attempt to do it. – H. G. Wells

The English country gentleman galloping after a fox – the unspeakable in pursuit of the uneatable. – Oscar Wilde

The English public always feels perfectly at ease when a mediocrity is talking to it. – Oscar Wilde

The English public takes no interest in a work of art until it is told that the work in question is immoral. – Oscar Wilde

The English have a miraculous power to change wine into water. – Oscar Wilde

Thinking is the most unhealthy thing in the world, and people die of it just as they die of any other disease. Fortunately, in England at any rate, thought is not catching. – Oscar Wilde, *The Decay of Lying*

How do you make a Scouser run faster? Stick a video player under his arm.

If you live in Birmingham, then being awake is not necessarily a desirable state. – Tony Wilson

The English have an extraordinary ability for flying into a great calm. – Alexander Woollcott

This melancholy London – I sometimes imagine that the souls of the lost are compelled to walk through its streets perpetually. One feels them passing like a whiff of air. – W. B. Yeats

Scotland

The Scotsman is one who keeps the Sabbath and everything else he can lay his hands on. – American saying

The scotch egg is such a Scottish food. It's as though a great Scottish chef said, "I need a tasty snack. Let's take an egg . . . and wrap it in meat!" – Bill Bailey

The great thing about Glasgow now is that if there is a nuclear attack it'll look exactly the same afterwards. – Billy Connolly

How do you take a census in Scotland? Throw 10p in the street. – English joke

The difference between a Scotsman and a canoe is that a canoe tips occasionally. – English joke

The difference between a Scotsman and a coconut is that you can get a drink out of a coconut. – English joke

How do you disperse an angry Scottish mob? Pass round a collection box. – English joke

Who invented the copper wire? Two Scotsmen fighting over a penny. – English joke

Nobody knows what the original people of Scotland were: cold is probably the best-informed guess, and wet. – A. A. Gill

You can have more fun at a Glasgow funeral than at an Edinburgh wedding. – Glaswegian joke

The Irish gave the bagpipes to the Scots as a joke, but the Scots haven't seen the joke yet. – Oliver Herford

The noblest prospect which a Scotchman ever sees is the high road that leads him to England. – Samuel Johnson

Oats: a grain which in England is generally given to a horse, but in Scotland it supports the people. – Samuel Johnson

Their learning is like bread in a besieged town: every man gets a little, but no man gets a full meal. – Samuel Johnson

Much may be made of a Scotchman, if he be caught young. – Samuel Johnson

In Glasgow, any cat with a tail is a visitor.

I have been trying all my life to like Scotchmen, and am obliged to desist from the experiment in despair. – Charles Lamb

Sour, stingy, depressing beggars who parade around in schoolgirls' skirts with nothing on underneath. Their fumbled attempt at speaking the English language has been a source of amusement for five centuries, and their idiot music has been dreaded by those not blessed with deafness for at least as long. – P. J. O'Rourke

Every Scotsman's fantasy is to have two women – one cleaning, the other dusting.

That garret of the earth, the knuckle-end of England, that land of Calvin, oat-cakes and sulphur. – Sydney Smith

It requires a surgical operation to get a joke well into a Scotsman's understanding. – Sydney Smith

The vice of meanness, condemned in every other country, is in Scotland translated into a virtue called "thrift". – David Thomson

A Scot is the only man on earth who would step over the bodies of a dozen bronzed naked beauties just to get to a glass of whiskey.

Wales

The best thing to come out of Wales is the M4. – English joke

What's the most common lie a Welshman tells? – I was only trying to help that sheep over the fence. – English joke

A Welshman prays on his knees on a Sunday and on his friends the rest of the week. – English saying

Loquacious dissemblers, immoral liars, stunted, bigoted, dark, ugly, pugnacious little trolls. – A. A. Gill

The Welsh are a nation of male-voice choir lovers whose only hobbies are rugby and romantic involvement with sheep. – Lenny Henry

The Welsh are not meant to go out in the sun. They start to photosynthesize. – Rhys Ifans

The earth contains no race of human beings so totally vile and worthless as the Welsh. – Walter Savage Landor

Each section of the British Isles has its own way of laughing, except Wales, which doesn't. – Stephen Leacock

The ordinary women of Wales are generally short and squat, ill-favoured and nasty. – David Mallet

Show a Welshman a thousand and one exits, one of which is marked "Self-Destruction", and he'll go right through that one. – Joseph L. Mankiewicz

They are treacherous to each other as well as to foreigners, covet freedom, neglect peace, are warlike and skilful in arms, and are eager for revenge. – Walter Map

The Welsh are so damn Welsh that it looks like affectation. – Sir Alexander Raleigh

They are irritating and annoying. They are always so pleased with themselves. What are they for? – Anne Robinson

There are still parts of Wales where the only concession to gaiety is a striped shroud. – Gwyn Thomas

The Welsh are the only nation in the world that has produced no graphic or plastic art, no architecture, no drama. They just sing. – Evelyn Waugh, *Decline and Fall*

Wales is the land of song, but no music. – David Wulstan

Canada

What is a Canadian? A Canadian is a fellow wearing English tweeds, a Hong Kong shirt and Spanish shoes, who sips Brazilian coffee sweetened with Philippine sugar from a Bavarian cup while nibbling Swiss cheese, sitting at a Danish desk over a Persian rug, after coming home in a German car from an Italian movie . . . and then writes to his Member of Parliament with a Japanese ballpoint pen on French paper, demanding that he do something about foreigners taking away Canadian jobs. – Anon

The beginning of Canadian cultural nationalism was not "Am I really that oppressed?" but "Am I really that boring?" – Margaret Atwood

Americans are benevolently ignorant about Canada, while Canadians are malevolently well informed about the United States. – J. Bartlet Brebner

A country so square that even the female impersonators are women. – Richard Brenner

A country without a soul . . . live, but not like the United States, kicking. – Rupert Brooke

Canadian books may occasionally have had a mild impact outside Canada; Canadian literature has had none. – E. K. Brown

I found their jokes like their roads – very long and not very good, leading to a little tin point of a spire which has been remorselessly obvious for miles without seeming to get any nearer. – Samuel Butler

The beaver is a good national symbol for Canada. He's so busy chewing he can't see what's going on. – Howard Cable

I don't even know what street Canada is on. – Al Capone

Canada could have had French culture, American know-how, and English government. Instead it got French government, English know-how, and American culture. – John Colombo

Toronto as a city carries out the idea of Canada as a country. It is a calculated crime both against the aspirations of the soul and the affection of the heart. – Aleister Crowley

Canada has never been a melting pot, more like a tossed salad. – Arnold Edinborough

So this is Winnipeg. I can tell it's not Paris. – Bob Edwards

Canada's climate is nine months winter and three months late in the fall. – Evan Esar

My generation of Canadians grew up believing that, if we were very good or very smart, or both, we would someday graduate from Canada. – Robert Fulford

For some reason, a glaze passes over people's faces when you say "Canada". – Sondra Gottlieb

Canada is the boring second fiddle in the American symphony. – Andrei Gromyko

Canada's history is as dull as ditchwater and her politics is full of it. – Maurice Hutton

The cold narrow minds, the confined ideas, the by-gone prejudices of the society are hardly conceivable; books there are none, nor music, as to pictures, the Lord deliver us from such! The people do not know what a picture is. – Anna Jameson

Winnipeg is like Fargo, North Dakota, without the action. – Billy Jay

Canada reminds me of vichysoisse – it's cold, half French and difficult to stir. – Stuart Keate

How utterly destitute of all light and charm are the intellectual conditions of our people and the institutions of our public life! How barren! How barbarous! – Archibald Lampman

(of her hometown, Napanee) It's just a little town where everybody knows everybody and their business. There's nothing to do except get drunk. – Avil Lavigne

It's going to be a great country when they finish unpacking it. – Andrew H. Malcolm

Canadians have been so busy explaining to the Americans that we aren't British, and to the British that we aren't Americans that we haven't had time to become Canadians. – Helen Gordon McPherson

Quebec does not have opinions, only sentiments. – H. L. Mencken

The purity of the air of Newfoundland is without doubt due to the fact that the people never open their windows. – J. G. Millais

Canada is the perpetual wallflower that stands on the edge of the hall, waiting for someone to come and ask her for a dance. – Kevin Myers

Canadians are cold so much of the time that many of them leave instructions to be cremated. – Cynthia Nelms

Very little is known of the Canadian country since it's rarely visited by anyone but the Queen and illiterate sports fishermen. – P. J. O'Rourke

Canada is useful only to provide me with furs. – Madame de Pompadour

The year is divided into one day and one night. – W. W. Reade

Canada is a country where nothing seems ever to happen. A country always dressed in its Sunday-go-to-meeting clothes. A country you wouldn't ask to dance a second waltz. Clean. Christian. Dull. Quiescent. – Carol Shields

Ottawa: a sub-arctic lumber village converted by Royal Mandate into a political cock-fighting pit. – Goldwin Smith

I wouldn't say it's cold, but every year Winnipeg's athlete of the year is an ice fisherman. – Dale Tallon

I fear that I have not got much to say about Canada, not having seen much; what I got by going to Canada was a cold. – Henry D. Thoreau

Canada is a country whose main exports are hockey players and cold fronts. – Pierre Trudeau

A few acres of snow. – Voltaire

Gentlemen, I give you Upper Canada, because I don't want it myself. – Artemus Ward.

Try finding six new things in Winnipeg in January. – Randall White

I find that Newfoundland is said to be celebrated for its codfish, its dogs, its hogs and its fogs. – Sir William Whiteway

Canada is like a loft apartment over a really great party. – Robin Williams

Montreal's not a city. It's a Disney World for alcoholics. – Mike Wilmot

Canadians do not like heroes, and so they do not have them. – George Woodcock

Why did the Canadian cross the road? To get to the middle.

China

Harbin is now being called the Chicago of the East. This is not a compliment to Chicago. – Maurice Baring

Some people are asking why did Beijing, China, get the 2008 Olympics. The word is, China got the Olympics under the theory that giving a country the international spotlight will help them correct their human rights violations. It worked so well with Hitler in 1936 . . . – Jay Leno

I found the pearl of the Orient slightly less exciting than a rainy Sunday evening in Rochester. – S. J. Perelman

Chinese people and Indian people cannot do business together because Indian people can't get along without a bargain, and Chinese people cannot give you a bargain. Their objective is to get every penny from you. – Russell Peters

There are only two kinds of Chinese – those who give bribes, and those who take them. – Russian saying

Seen one wall, you've seen them all. – John Trewick, English footballer

Cuba

In a speech in Florida, President Bush praised all the contributions Cubans have made to America: catching, hitting, outfielding, shortstop. – Jay Leno

The elderly Fidel Castro is recovering from surgery in Cuba. It was pretty serious. I understand he was rushed to the hospital on Donkey One. – Jay Leno

Denmark

(of Copenhagen) We used to build civilisations. Now we build shopping malls. – Bill Bryson, *Neither Here Nor There*

Beer is the Danish national drink, and the Danish national weakness is another beer. – Clementine Paddleford

Who do Danish people never play hide and seek? Nobody wants to look for them. – Swedish joke

Finland

A nation of drunken Captain Birds Eyes. – A.A. Gill

Climate in Finland is like it were raining rocks. – Veijo Meri

France

The first thing that strikes a visitor to Paris is a taxi. – Fred Allen

Fantasies about French women are far superior to the reality of French women. – Anon

France, famed in all great arts, in none supreme. – Matthew Arnold

If I were God and I were trying to create a nation that would get up the nostrils of Englishmen, I would create the French. – Julian Barnes

Europeans, like some Americans, drive on the right side of the road, except in England, where they drive on both sides of the road; Italy, where they drive on the sidewalk; and France, where if necessary, they will follow you right into the hotel lobby. – Dave Barry

"Escargot" is French for "fat crawling bag of phlegm." – Dave Barry

Have the Frenchman for thy friend, not for thy neighbour. – Belgian saying

For the past three years the western front has been about as likely to move as a Frenchman living next door to a brothel. – *Blackadder*

I hardly think that a nation that eats frogs and would go to bed with a kitchen sink if it put on a tutu is in any position to preach couthness. – *Blackadder*

A bad liver is to a Frenchman what a nervous breakdown is to an American. Everyone has had one and everyone wants to talk about it. – Art Buchwald

A relatively small and quarrelsome country in Western Europe, fountainhead of rationalist political manias, militarily impotent, historically inglorious during the past century, democratically bankrupt, Communist-infiltrated from top to bottom. – William F. Buckley Jr

Why was the tunnel built under the English Channel? So the French government could flee to London.

France was long a despotism tempered by epigrams. – Thomas Carlyle

I ran out of deodorant in Paris and had to go all the way to London to buy a new stick. – Dave Chappelle

The Almighty in His infinite wisdom did not see fit to create Frenchmen in the image of Englishmen. – Winston Churchill

A bunch of onion selling ne'er-do-wells. – Jeremy Clarkson

The French hate anything that is ugly. If they see an animal that is ugly, they immediately eat it. – Jeremy Clarkson

Frenchmen are like gunpowder, each by itself smutty and contemptible, but mass them together and they are terrible indeed! – Samuel Taylor Coleridge

Things you'd never hear a French person say: I'd like a bottle of Burgundy and a Dairylea dunker please. – Hugh Dennis, *Mock the Week*

It took no more effort than casting a Frenchman into Hell. – Dutch saying

A small acquaintance with history shows that all governments are selfish, and the French governments more selfish than most. – Lord Eccles

I have tried to lift France out of the mud. But she will return to her errors and vomitings. I cannot prevent the French from being French. – Charles de Gaulle

The friendship of the French is like their wine: exquisite, but of short duration. – German saying

I have yet to meet a Frenchman who does not consider himself my superior. – Elizabeth Forsythe Hailey

To err is human. To loaf is Parisian. – Victor Hugo

As sluttish and slatternly as an Irishwoman bred in France. – Irish saying

The French don't say what they mean, don't read as they write, and don't sing according to the notes. – Italian saying

The Italians are wise before the deed, the Germans in the deed, the French after the deed. – Italian saying

The best thing I know between France and England is the sea. – Douglas Jerrold

A Frenchman must be always talking, whether he knows anything of the matter or not. – Samuel Johnson

How many Frenchmen does it take to defend Paris? Nobody knows – it's never been tried.

Army personnel in Kuwait unloaded a dozen faulty tanks that only go in reverse. They've been repackaged and sold to France. – Craig Kilborn

I would have loved France – without the French. – D. H. Lawrence

The French probably invented the very notion of discretion. It's not that they feel that what you don't know won't hurt you; they feel that what you don't know won't hurt them. To the French lying is simply talking. – Fran Lebowitz

No matter how politely and distinctly you ask a Parisian a question, he will persist in answering you in French. – Fran Lebowitz

French troops arrived in Afghanistan last week, and not a minute too soon. The French are acting as advisers to the Taliban, to teach them how to surrender properly. – Jay Leno

This is now the twelfth day of rioting in France. They have been rioting for almost two weeks. And France has still not surrendered. That's like a record. – Jay Leno

A lot of folks are still demanding more evidence before they actually consider Iraq a threat. For example, France wants more evidence. And you know I'm thinking, the last time France wanted more evidence they rolled right through Paris with the German flag. – David Letterman

French films follow a basic formula: husband sleeps with Jeanne because Bernadette cuckolded him by sleeping with Christophe, and in the end they all go off to a restaurant. – Sophie Marceau

The French are tremendous snobs, despite that rather showy and ostentatious Revolution. – Arthur Marshall

The French remind me a little bit of an ageing actress of the 1940s who is still trying to dine out on her looks but doesn't have the face for it. – John McCain

The only way the French are going in is if we tell them we found truffles in Iraq. – Dennis Miller

The French have a new flag – a white cross on a white background.

Paris is like a whore. From a distance she seems ravishing, you can't wait until you have her in your arms. Five minutes later you feel empty, disgusted with yourself. – Henry Miller

Frendship in France is as impossible to be attained as orange trees on the mountains of Scotland. – Lady Mary Wortley Montagu

Lunch kills half of Paris, supper the other half. – Montesquieu

To watch a Frenchman pay for something is to watch him die a slow death. – Robert Morley

I don't know why we don't grow a big hedge up the English Channel. Spoil their light. – Al Murray

We shouldn't insult the French of course, because they're not here to defend themselves. And we know how good they are at that! – Al Murray

The French complain of everything and always. – Napoleon I

A nation protected by a cloud of garlic breath. – *National Lampoon*

The French are a nation of collaborators. – Patrick Nicholls

French wine is mostly inferior to that of Australia but in their own rule-twisting way it's probably hard for the French to find that out for themselves. – Patrick Nicholls

Newly released documents show that in the 1950s Britain and France talked about uniting and becoming one country. That didn't work out because France wanted to be in charge of the army and England wanted to be in charge of the food. – Conan O'Brien

Going to war without the French is like, well, World War Two.

The French are sawed-off sissies who eat snails and slugs and cheese that smells like people's feet. Utter cowards who force their own children to drink wine, they gibber like baboons even when you try to speak to them in their own wimpy language. – P. J. O'Rourke

The French are a smallish, monkey-looking bunch and not dressed any better, on average, than the citizens of Baltimore. True, you can sit outside in Paris and drink little cups of coffee, but why this is more stylish than sitting inside and drinking large glasses of whiskey I don't know. – P. J. O'Rourke

I would rather have a German division in front of me than a French one behind me. – General George S. Patton

The only time France wants us to go to war is when the German Army is sitting in Paris sipping coffee. – Regis Philbin

The ignorance of French society gives one a rough sense of the infinite. – Joseph E. Renan

French singing is endless squawking, unbearable to the unbiased ear. – Jean-Jacques Rousseau

Going to war without France is like going duck-hunting without your accordion. – Donald Rumsfeld

The Frenchman's legs are thin, his soul little. He's as fickle as the wind. – Russian saying

If the French were really intelligent, they would speak English. – Wilfred Sheed

A nation of monkeys with the throats of parrots. – Joseph Sieyès

We can stand here like the French, or we can do something about it. – Marge Simpson

A French traveller with a sore throat is a wonderful thing to behold, but it takes more than tonsillitis to prevent a Frenchman from boasting. – Paul Theroux

Pardon me, I only speak common phrases in French like "I surrender." – Triumph, the Insult Comic Dog

In France one must adapt oneself to the fragrance of a urinal. – Gertrude Stein

France has neither winter nor summer nor morals. – Mark Twain

I do not dislike the French from the vulgar antipathy between neighbouring nations, but for their insolent and unfounded airs of superiority. – Horace Walpole

Raise your right hand if you like the French; raise both hands if you are French.

The French got a reputation for bedroom habits little better than a mink's . – Mae West

France is a country where the money falls apart in your hands and you can't tear the toilet paper. – Billy Wilder

Why do the French have the onion and the Arabs have the oil? – Because the French had first pick.

Germany

It should have been written into the armistice treaty that the Germans would be required to lay down their accordions along with their arms. – Bill Bryson

A frightful dialect for the stupid, the pedant and dullard sort. – Thomas Carlyle

I speak Spanish to God, Italian to women, French to men – and German to my horse. – Charles V, Holy Roman Emperor

Better Turkish hatred than German love. – Croatian saying

When a snake gets warm on ice, then a German will wish well to a Czech. – Czech saying

The German mind has a talent for making no mistakes but the very greatest. – Clifton Fadiman

Oh (you're) German! I'm sorry, I thought there was something wrong with you. – *Fawlty Towers*

A German singer! I should as soon expect to get pleasure from the neighing of my horse. – Frederick the Great, King of Prussia

It's like the Beatles coming together again – let's hope they don't go on a world tour. – Matt Frei on German unification

Wherever Germans are, it is unhealthy for Italians. – Italian saying

Three things are in a poor plight: birds in the hands of children, young girls in the hands of old men, and wine in the hands of Germans. – Italian saying

According to a new survey, Germans are the best-behaved tourists in the world. It's only when they march into your country and want to stay forever, that's when it gets testy. – Jay Leno

Germans possess too much pedantic thoroughness and too little intellectual grace; when they know something, immediately a heavy dissertation with a bagful of citations results instead of a light sketch. – Rosa Luxembourg

There's just something about Germans. You can listen to a nice, young, affable German fellow and he'll be saying things like "Vell, ja, dis is a critical time for Germany now, economically ve are good, but ve have been better.

Ve are investing a lot in ze arts, and emerging globally . . ." and you'll be there listening, thinking, "Mmm, yeah, mmm . . . Hitler, mmm, yeah, Hitler, Hitler, Hitler, Hitler, Hitler, Hitler . . ." – Dylan Moran

The German language sounds like typewriters eating tinfoil, being kicked down the stairs. – Dylan Moran

German is a language which was developed solely to afford the speaker the opportunity to spit at strangers under the guise of polite conversation. – *National Lampoon*

Germany's unique contribution to Europe has been to plunge it into two World Wars. – Patrick Nicholls

Their language lacks any semblance of civilized speech. Their usual diet consists almost wholly of old cabbage and sections of animal intestines filled with blood and gore. – P. J. O'Rourke, *Holidays in Hell*

The larger the German body, the smaller the German bathing suit and the louder the German voice issuing German demands and German orders to everybody who doesn't speak German. For this, and several other reasons, Germany is known as "the land where Israelis learned their manners". – P. J. O'Rourke, *Holidays in Hell*

Because of their cuisine, Germans don't consider farting rude. – P. J. O'Rourke, *Holidays in Hell*

Why do Germans build such high-quality products? So they won't have to go around being nice while they fix them.

One German a beer; two Germans an organization; three Germans a war. – Polish saying

Serve the German with all your heart; your reward will be a fart. – Polish saying.

Peace with the German is like a wolf and a sheep living together. – Polish saying

A dead German, a dead dog. The difference is but slight. – Polish saying

You will sooner catch a ray of the sun than reach an agreement with the German. – Polish saying

The German is as sly as the plague. – Polish saying

Just as the winter cannot turn to summer, so the German can't become a brother. – Polish saying

The East German manages to combine a Teutonic capacity for bureaucracy with a Russian capacity for infinite delay. – Goronwy Rees

One thing I will say about the Germans, they are always perfectly willing to give somebody's land to somebody else. – Will Rogers

Marry a German and you'll see that the women have hairy tongues. – Romanian saying

German is a most extravagantly ugly language. It sounds like someone using a sick bag on a 747. – Willie Rushton

The German may be a good fellow, but it is best to hang him just the same. – Russian saying

If anyone is born a German, God has sufficiently punished him already. – Russian saying

You can tell German wine from vinegar by the label. – Mark Twain

Whenever the literary German dives into a sentence, that is the last you are going to see of him till he emerges on the other side of his Atlantic with his verb in his mouth. – Mark Twain

I heard a Californian student in Heidelberg say, in one of his calmest moods, that he would rather decline two drinks than one German adjective. – Mark Twain

The great virtues of the German people have created more evils than idleness ever did vices. – Paul Valery

The German people are an orderly, vain, deeply sentimental and rather insensitive people. They seem to feel at their best when they are singing in chorus, saluting or obeying orders. – H. G. Wells

The Rhine is of course tedious, the vineyards are formal and dull, and as far as I can judge, the inhabitants of Germany are American. – Oscar Wilde

Whatever music sounds like, I am glad to say that it does not sound in the smallest degree like German. – Oscar Wilde, *The Critic As Artist*

Greece

After shaking hands with a Greek count your fingers. – Albanian saying

Few things can be less tempting or dangerous than a Greek woman by the age of thirty. – John Carne

The weird mixture of smells which together compose the anthology of a Greek holiday under the pines – petrol, garlic, wine and goat. – Lawrence Durrell

Beware of Greeks bearing gifts. – English saying

Out of all those centuries the Greeks can count seven sages at the most, and if anyone looks at them more closely I swear he'll not find so much as a half-wise man or even a third of a wise man among them. – Erasmus

The women of Greece count their age from their marriage, not from their birth. – Homer

Whoever trusts a Greek lacks brains. – Italian saying

Every Greek constitutes his own political party of one. – George Mikes

The only other people we know are Greeks, because Greeks marry Greeks to breed more Greeks, to be loud breeding Greek eaters. – *My Big Fat Greek Wedding*

(They) invented democracy and then forgot how to use it while walking around dressed up like girls. – P. J. O'Rourke

Beware of a gypsy who has become a Turk and of a peasant who has become a Greek. – Romanian saying

Greeks tell the truth, but only once a year. – Russian saying

A crab is no fish and a Greek is no man. – Russian saying

In Greece wise men speak and fools decide. – George Santayana

Three Turks and three Greeks make six heathens. – Serbian saying

Haiti

If Haiti goes thirty-six straight hours without having a coup, the United Nations sends an inspection team to find out what's wrong. – Dave Barry

Hungary

Do not trust a Hungarian unless he has a third eye on his forehead. – Czech saying

Where there is a Hungarian there is anger; where there is a Slovak there is a song. – Czech saying

The Poles and Czechs are like two close leaves, but when joined by the Hungarian, they make three fine thieves. – German saying

The devil seduced Eve in Italian. Eve misled Adam in Bohemian. The Lord scolded them both in German. Then the angel drove them from paradise in Hungarian. – Polish saying

India

(of Calcutta) I shall always be glad to have seen it – for the same reason Papa gave for being glad to have seen Lisbon – namely that it will be unnecessary ever to see it again. – Winston Churchill

The Indian wears seven veils, which must be removed if his true face is to be seen. – English saying

Delhi is the capital of the losing streak. It is the metropolis of the crossed wire, the missed appointment, the puncture, the wrong number. – Jan Morris

Indian people live in the hottest climate . . . and we're covered in hair! Who came up with that? Is this supposed to be a joke? – Russell Peters

In India, "cold weather" is merely a conventional phrase and has come into use through the necessity of having some way to distinguish between weather which melt a brass doorknob and weather which will only make it mushy. – Mark Twain

Iraq

The Persian Gulf is the arsehole of the world, and Basra is eighty miles up it. – Peter Forster

Ireland

We don't have anything as urgent as mañana in Ireland. – Stuart Banks

Geographically, Ireland is a medium-sized rural island that is slowly but steadily being consumed by sheep. – Dave Barry

Dublin University contains the cream of Ireland: rich and thick. – Samuel Beckett

The Irish are a very popular race – with themselves. – Brendan Behan

Other people have a nationality. The Irish and the Jews have a psychosis. – Brendan Behan

If it were raining soup, the Irish would go out with forks. – Brendan Behan

Irish weather consists of rain: lots of it. It has been known for the rain to cease, sometimes for as much as two weeks at a time. But when this happens, the Irish complain of drought, pestilence and imminent bankruptcy. – Stan Gebler Davies

Like an Irishman's obligation, all the one side, and always yours. – English saying

This is one race of people for whom psychoanalysis is of no use whatsoever. – Sigmund Freud

Ireland: the *Big Issue* seller of Europe. – A.A. Gill

The Irish people do not gladly suffer common sense. – Oliver St John Gogarty

The Irishman is never at peace except when he is fighting. – Irish saying

The Irish are a fair people; they never speak well of one another. – Samuel Johnson

Why did God invent alcohol? – To prevent the Irish from ruling the world.

Italy, at least, has two things to balance its miserable poverty and mismanagement: a lively intellectual movement and a good climate. Ireland is Italy without these two. – James Joyce

When Irish eyes are smiling, watch your step. – Gerald Kersh

The problem with Ireland is that it's a country full of genius, but with absolutely no talent. – Hugh Leonard

The Irish do not want anyone to wish them well; they want everyone to wish their enemies ill. – Harold Nicolson

Israel has recalled its ambassador to El Salvador after the ambassador was found drunk and naked in the yard of his residence. Today Israel announced that he's their new ambassador to Ireland. – Conan O'Brien

An Irish homosexual is one who prefers women to drink. – Sean O'Faolain

The Irish are not at peace unless they are at war. – George Orwell

You know it is summer in Ireland when the rain gets warmer. – Hal Roach

Did you hear about the Irish kamikaze pilot? – Eighteen successful missions.

I showed my appreciation of my native land in the usual way – by getting out of it as soon as I possibly could. – George Bernard Shaw

An Irishman's heart is nothing but his imagination. – George Bernard Shaw

Put an Irishman on a spit and you can always find another one to turn him. – George Bernard Shaw

If one could teach the English to talk and the Irish to listen, society would be quite civilized. – Oscar Wilde

Why did the Irishman buy a plate with four corners? – So he could have a square meal.

Israel
Hitler's revenge on the world. – Anon

An Israeli man's life was saved when he was given a Palestinian man's heart in a heart transplant operation. The guy is doing fine, but the bad news is he can't stop throwing rocks at himself. – Jay Leno

They want to calm down those Israelis. I don't like the people down the end of my road but I haven't bought a tank. – Al Murray

Italy
There are no pianists in Italy, and if you can only play the scale of C with both hands, you pass for a great artist. – Georges Bizet

The Italians' technological contribution to mankind stopped with the pizza oven. – Bill Bryson, *Neither Here Nor There*

England is a paradise for women, and hell for horses: Italy a paradise for horses, hell for women. – Robert Burton

Sign language is useful to the deaf but vital to the Italians. – Paul Carvel

Genoa has mountains without wood, sea without fish, women without shame, and men without conscience. – English saying

When an Italian tells me it's pasta on the plate, I check under the sauce to make sure. – Alex Ferguson

If there is a Hell, Rome is built on top of it. – German saying

An ass in Germany is a professor in Rome. – German saying

Half an Italian in a house is one too many. – German saying

Venice is excessively ugly in the rain – it looks like King's Cross. – John Gielgud

The best thing about Italy is the border. – Denny Hulme

Rome reminds me of a man who lives by exhibiting to travellers his grandmother's corpse. – James Joyce

(Italians are) so terribly physically all over one another. They pour themselves one over the other like so much melted butter over parsnips. – D. H. Lawrence

Nobody in Rome works and if it rains in Rome and they happen to notice it, they blame it on Milan. – Fran Lebowitz

If you're eating spaghetti the Italian way, do you know what is in your left hand? A fly swatter. – Paul Lynde

Three Italians engaged in a friendly chat can make more noise than the average English mass demonstration in Trafalgar Square. – George Mikes, *Shakespeare and Myself*

It is not impossible to govern Italians. It is merely useless. – Benito Mussolini

Italy is not technically part of the Third World, but no one has told the Italians. – P. J. O'Rourke, *Holidays in Hell*

The Italians have had two thousand years to fix up the Forum and just look at the place! – P. J. O'Rourke, *Holidays in Hell*

The first time I passed through Switzerland I had the impression it was swept down with a broom from one end to the other every morning by housewives who dumped all the dirt in Italy. – Ernesto Sábato

In Italy, the whole country is a theatre and the worst actors are on the stage. – George Bernard Shaw

Cross yourself once before an Andalusian and thrice on spotting an Italian. – Spanish saying

All things atrocious and shameless flock from all parts to Rome. – Publius Cornelius Tacitus

Were the inhabitants of Italy as charming as their country, all other regions would be depopulated, I think. – Hester Lynch Thrale

Since World War Two, Italy has managed, with characteristic artistry, to create a society that combines a number of the least appealing aspects of socialism with practically all the vices of capitalism. – Gore Vidal

Italy is a paradise inhabited by devils. – Henry Wotton

A bomb fell on Italy. It slid off. – Henny Youngman.

I bought my wife a little Italian car. A Mafia. It has a hood under the hood. – Henny Youngman

Japan
The Japanese have almost as big a reputation for cruelty as do young children. – Dennis Bloodworth

The Japanese idea of fun is to lock a naked man in a room for eighteen months and allow him to exist only on food that he wins in competitions. – Emma Colverd

I don't greatly admire Japanese women; they have no figures to speak of, and look as if a bee had stung them in the eye. – Crosbie Garstin

When it comes to Japanese civilization, it's mostly eyewash. Kabuki theatre is only just preferable to root-canal work. The three-stringed guitar is a sad waste of cat. – A. A. Gill

They have 21st-century bogs and 13th-century bog roll. – A. A. Gill

The Japanese . . . travel in packs at a jog trot and get up at 6 a.m. and sing their company song under your hotel window. They are extraordinary shoplifters. They eschew the usual clothes and trinkets, but automobile plants, steel mills and electronics factories seem to be missing from wherever they go. – P.J. O'Rourke

Is there a Japanese smile that does not seem like an expression of pain? – Paul Theroux

The Japanese have perfected good manners and made them indistinguish-able from rudeness. – Paul Theroux

Korea
They eat dogs in Korea. It's true. A few days earlier, Christmas dinner had a Frisbee in its mouth. – Joan Rivers

Lebanon
Last night Israel bombed the runways at Beirut's airport, putting a stop on all flights in and out. So I'm sorry everybody, you're just gonna have to cancel that relaxing weekend getaway to Beirut. – Conan O'Brien

Lithuania
A Lithuanian is not worth a cheap slipper. – German saying

The Lithuanian has fair words for all, but is square with none. – Polish saying

Did hogs feed here or did Lithuanians have a feast here? – Polish saying

The Lithuanian is stupid like a pig but cunning like a serpent. – Polish saying

Luxembourg
On a clear day you can't see Luxembourg at all. This is because a tree is in the way. – Alan Coren

Mexico
What are the first three words in every Mexican cookbook? – "Steal a chicken."

Poor Mexico, so far from God and so near to the United States. – Porfirio Diaz

What's the difference between Batman and a Mexican? – Batman can go anywhere without Robin.

In addition to oil, silver and tequila, Mexico is the number one producer of Americans. – Argus Hamilton

What do you call a Mexican in a suit? – The accused.

A country where men despise sex, and live for it. – D. H. Lawrence

Why are Mexicans so short? – When they're young, their parents say, "When you get bigger you have to get a job."

According to a new geographic literacy study four out of ten American students couldn't find Iraq on a map. However ten out of ten Mexicans could find the U.S. without a map. – Jay Leno

What do you call a Mexican without a lawnmower? – Unemployed.

If we are going to start rewarding no skills and stupid people, let the unskilled jobs, let the kind of jobs that take absolutely no knowledge whatsoever to do – let stupid and unskilled Mexicans do that work. – Rush Limbaugh

Run, like Mexican water through a first-time tourist. – *Married . . . With Children*

The White House looked into a plan that would allow illegal immigrants to stay in the United States. The plan called for a million Mexicans to marry a million of our ugliest citizens. – Dennis Miller

How do you stop a Mexican tank? – Shoot the guy pushing it.

Thousands of Mexicans gathered in Mexico City to protest high food prices. The protest only lasted an hour, because everyone had to leave for their jobs in Los Angeles. – Conan O'Brien

Why did God give Mexicans noses? – So they'll have something to pick in the winter.

Morocco
Diarrhoea City, terrible place. You don't even have to eat anything for that. It's the dust from the camel shit. One of the worst places I've ever been. – Michael Caine

Netherlands

Like the Germans, the Dutch fall into two quite distinct physical types: the small, corpulent, red-faced Edams, and the thinner, paler, larger Goudas. – Alan Coren

A dark German, a fair Italian, and a red Spaniard seldom bode good, as does a Dutchman of any colour. – German saying

Holland is a country where the earth is better than the air; where profit is sought more than honour; where there is more sense than esprit, more goodwill than good humour, more prosperity than pleasure and where a visit is preferable to a stay for life. – German saying

Its inhabitants are a heavy, barge-built, web-footed race. – Sir Francis Bond Head

A donkey is a horse translated into Dutch. – G. C. Lichtenberg

We always like our pop stars to be like Greek gods: bigger, better and uglier than us. We hate the bores, Jesus Christ and the Dutch. Especially the Dutch. – Malcolm McLaren

New Zealand

I believe we were all glad to leave New Zealand. It is not a pleasant place. Amongst the natives there is absent that charming simplicity . . . and the greater part of the English are the very refuse of society. – Charles Darwin

A country of thirty thousand million sheep – three million of whom think they're human. – Barry Humphries

I wasn't misquoted. I just got it slightly wrong. I actually said, "It's a poxy little island in the Pacific." In fact, it's two islands. – Scott Johnson

A country of inveterate, back woods, thick-headed, egotistic philistines. – Vladimir Ilyich Lenin

Terrible tragedy of the South Seas. Three million people trapped alive. – Thomas Jefferson Scott

Altogether too many sheep. – George Bernard Shaw

Norway

The best that can be said for Norwegian television is that it gives you the sensation of a coma without the worry and inconvenience. — Bill Bryson

It is difficult to describe Norwegian charisma precisely but it is somewhere between a Presbyterian minister and a tree. — Johnny Carson

The Norwegian language sounds like German spoken underwater.

How do Norwegians forge ten-crown bills? They scrape one zero off a hundred bill. — Swedish joke

I don't like Norwegians at all. The sun never sets, the bar never opens, and the whole country smells of kippers. — Evelyn Waugh

Pakistan

Pakistan is the sort of place every man should send his mother-in-law to, for a month, all expenses paid. — Ian Botham

Poland

How do you sink a Polish battleship? Put it in water. — American joke

How can you tell a Polish firing squad? It stands in a circle. — American joke

How do you tell which is the groom at a Polish wedding? He's the one with the clean bowling shirt. — American joke

What sign is at the bottom of Polish swimming pools? No Smoking. — American joke

When a Polish admiral wanted to be buried at sea, five sailors died digging his grave. — American joke

Poland has experienced a tremendous amount of history due to the fact that it has no natural defensible borders, which makes it very easy to conquer. Many times the other nations didn't even mean to invade Poland; one night they'd simply forget to set the parking brakes on their tanks, and they'd wake up the next morning to discover that, whoosh, they had conquered Poland. — Dave Barry

There are few virtues which the Poles do not possess and there are few errors they have ever avoided. — Winston Churchill

Love without jealousy is like a Pole without lice. – French saying

The Pole has a large mouth but nothing behind it. – German saying

What an Englishman cares to invent, a Frenchman to design, or a German to patch together, the stupid Pole will buy. – Polish saying

A single Russian hair outweighs half a Pole. – Russian saying

Where the women are stronger than the men. – Russian saying

Have you seen the new Polish jigsaw puzzle? – One piece. – Henny Youngman

Portugal

A bad Spaniard makes a good Portuguese. – Spanish saying

Take from a Spaniard all his good qualities, and there remains a Portuguese. – Spanish saying

A blue eye in a Portuguese woman is a mistake of nature. – Spanish saying

Russia

The Italians have voices like peacocks, German gives me a cold in the head, and Russian is nothing but sneezing. – Edward Bulwer-Lytton

In Russia a man is called reactionary if he objects to having his property stolen and his wife and children murdered. – Winston Churchill

The Russian knows the way, yet he asks for directions. – German saying

If a Russian is in the hills, count your olives. – Greek saying

Moscow is Los Angeles without the sun or grass. – Lillian Hellman

The difference between a Russian wedding and a Russian funeral is that at a funeral there's one person not having vodka.

In Russia they treated me like a Tsar – and you know how they treated the Tsar. – Bob Hope

A nation of sheep. Angry sheep, but nevertheless sheep, and in sheep's clothing. – James Kirkup

Moscow, as I saw it once, is Horrorsville. – James Kirkup

Brutish, dumpy, boorish lardbags in cardboard double-breasted suits . . . They can be sent to Siberia for listening to the wrong radio station. – P. J. O'Rourke

Moscow has changed. I was here in 1982, during the Brezhnev twilight, and things are better now. For instance, they've got litter. In 1982 there was nothing to litter with. – P. J. O'Rourke, *Holidays In Hell,* 1989

Russia's a little bit like a critically ill patient. Every day you have to get up and take the pulse and hope that nothing catastrophic happened the night before. – Condoleezza Rice

Russia is a country that buries its troubles. Your criticism is your epitaph. You simply say your say, and then you're through. – Will Rogers

In Russia we only had two TV channels. Channel One was propaganda. Channel Two consisted of a KGB officer telling you: turn back at once to Channel One. – Yakov Smirnoff

In the United States you have freedom of speech. You can go up to Ronald Reagan and say, "I don't like Ronald Reagan." In the Soviet Union you have the same thing. You can go up to Chernenko and say, "I don't like Ronald Reagan." – Yakov Smirnoff

Russians will consume marinated mushrooms and vodka, salted herring and vodka, smoked salmon and vodka, salami and vodka, caviar on brown bread and vodka, pickled cucumbers and vodka, cold tongue and vodka, red beet salad and vodka, scallions and vodka – anything and everything and vodka. – Hedrick Smith, *The Russians*

The devil you can ban with the cross, but a Russian you can never get rid of. – Ukrainian saying

How can you tell a Russian? Go to sleep and he will rob you. – Ukrainian saying

Better the devil in your house than a Russian. – Ukrainian saying

If a Russian tells you it's dry, put your collar up. – Ukrainian saying

What is A Russian string trio? A Russian string quartet that has returned from the West.

Slovakia

Potatoes are not food, Slovaks are not human beings. – Hungarian saying

If you take a Slovak in to stay, he will turn you out of your house any day. – Hungarian saying

South Africa

I've travelled this old world of ours from Barnsley to Peru,
I've had sunshine in the Arctic and a swim in Timbuktu;
I've seen unicorns in Burma and a yeti in Nepal,
And I've danced with ten-foot pygmies in a Montezuma hall;
I've met the King of China and a working Yorkshire miner,
But I've never met a nice South African.
No, he's never met a nice South African.
– Spitting Image

Spain

The Spaniard is a bad servant, but a worse master. – Thomas Adams

The French are wiser than they seem, and the Spaniards seem wiser than they are. – Francis Bacon

A whale stranded upon the sea shore of Europe. – Edmund Burke

A country that has sold its soul for cement and petrol, and can only be saved by a series of earthquakes. – Cyril Connolly

Forget Spanish. There's nothing in that language worth reading except Don Quixote, and a quick listen to the CD of Man of La Mancha will take care of that. There was a poet named Garcia Lorca, but I'd leave him on the intellectual backburner if I were you. As for everyone's speaking it, what twaddle! Who speaks it that you are really desperate to talk to? The help? Your leaf blower? – Dame Edna Everage

In a Spanish inn, you will find only what you have brought there yourself. – French saying

Spain imports tourists and exports chambermaids. – Carlos Fuentes

Spaniards are like fleas: once they are there, it is difficult to get rid of them. – German saying

A Spaniard and a braggart are the same thing. – German saying

He who would eat in Spain must bring his kitchen along. – German saying

The Spaniard is a Frenchman turned inside out. – German saying

A Spaniard may be trusted, but no further than your nose. – German saying

All Spaniards have sticky fingers. In past centuries, the pots on the stove would have padlocks on them. – German saying

Spain would be a fine country, if there were no Spaniards in it. – German saying

The Spanish wine, my God, it is foul, catpiss is champagne compared, this is the sulphurous urination of some aged horse. – D. H. Lawrence

Nothing ill in Spain but that which speaks. – Portuguese saying

The only good that comes from the east is the sun. – Portuguese saying

Three Spaniards, four opinions. – Spanish saying

Sweden

(in winter) This time of year's a must for depression fans. – Samantha Bee

Sweden is where they commit suicide and the King rides a bicycle. – Alan Bennett

What's the difference between Swedes and mosquitoes? Mosquitoes are only annoying in the summer. – Danish joke

Keep Denmark clean – show a Swede to the ferry. – Danish saying

Why do Swedes always crawl around on the floor when they're in a store? They're hunting for low prices. – Norwegian joke

What is the difference between Swedes and Norwegians? The Swedes have nice neighbours. – Norwegian joke

Tedious, clean-living Boy Scout types, strangers to graffiti and littering but who are possessed of an odd suicidal mania. Speculation is that they're slowly boring themselves to death. This is certainly true if their cars and movies are any indication. – P. J. O'Rourke

Their heads are too square. – P. G. Wodehouse

Switzerland

A country to be in for two hours, to two and a half, if the weather is fine, and no more. Ennui comes in the third hour, and suicide attacks you before the night. – Lord Brougham

It is a curst, selfish, swinish country of brutes placed in the most romantic region of the world. – Lord Byron

Nothing good comes from Switzerland. Cuckoo clocks and Toblerones! Toblerones! It's impossible to eat a Toblerone without hurting yourself! – Billy Connolly

Since its national products – snow and chocolate – both melt, the cuckoo clock was invented solely in order to give tourists something solid to remember it by. – Alan Coren

A country where very few things begin, but many things end. – F. Scott Fitzgerald

Switzerland has produced the numbered bank account, Ovaltine and Valium. – Peter Freedman

You might as well run your head against a wall as talk to a Swiss. – French saying

No more money, no more Swiss. – French saying

The Swiss has two bad nights when he can't sleep – one where he has overloaded his stomach, and the other where he is lying awake thinking about how he can overload it again. – German saying

A nation of money-grabbing clockmakers. – Nick Lowe

Switzerland, which I have always managed to avoid, is the very devil I knew it would be. I mean the people are so ugly; they are simply hideous. They have no shape. All the women have pear shaped derrières, ugly heads, awful feet. – Katherine Mansfield

Pity the Swiss. They've got France to the left, Austria to the right, Germany up above, Italy down below. You'd never sell that flat! – Al Murray

A whole country of phobic handwashers living in a giant Barclays Bank. – Jonathan Raban

I look on Switzerland as an inferior sort of Scotland. – Sydney Smith

The only interesting thing that can happen in a Swiss bedroom is suffocation by feather mattress. – Dalton Trumbo

Switzerland is simply a large, humpy, solid rock, with a thin skin of grass stretched over it. – Mark Twain

It has produced nothing but theologians and waiters. – Oscar Wilde

How butch is an army who has a wine opener on its knife? How tough are they in combat? – "Many of you have never opened Chardonnay under fire." – Robin Williams

Turkey
I never saw a place I liked worse, nor which afforded less pleasure or instruction, nor antiquities which less answered their description. – James Bruce

If you can imagine a man having a vasectomy without anaesthetic to the sound of frantic sitar-playing, you will have some idea what popular Turkish music is like. – Bill Bryson

Where the Turk treads, for a hundred years the soil bears no fruit. – German saying

How will you tell a Turk? By the blood on his hands. – Greek saying

A Turk who hears the word "paradise" asks, "Is there any gold to be looted there?"

Will they ever be civilized? I think not. Such a fine country ought to be in better hands. – John Webster

United States
There is science, logic, reason; there is thought verified by experience. And then there is California. – Edward Abbey

In the course of my life I have tried Boston socially on all sides: I have summered it and wintered it, tried to drunk and tried it sober; and, drunk or sober, there's nothing in it – save Boston. – Charles Francis Adams Jr

I've just returned from Boston. It's the only thing to do if you find yourself up there. – Fred Allen

I'm a little hoarse tonight. I've been living in Chicago for the past two months, and you know how it is, yelling for help on the way home every night. – Fred Allen

The American arrives in Paris with a few French phrases he has culled from a conversational guide or picked up from a friend who owns a beret. – Fred Allen

In America you watch TV and think that's totally unreal, then you step outside and it's just the same. – Joan Armatrading

I went to Dayton, Ohio, recently. Know what's a fun thing to do there? Pack up and get the fuck out, that 's what. – Dave Attell

Boston: a festering mud puddle. – Ellis Arnall

All American writing gives me the impression that Americans don't care for girls at all. What the American male really wants is two things: he wants to be blown by a stranger while reading a newspaper and he wants to be fucked by his buddy when he's drunk. – W. H. Auden

A study shows that California kids are in general overweight and out of shape. Out of shape kids have it tough in California. They have to hear about it from their real dad, their step dad, their mom's trainer, and their life coach. – Jim Barach

In Tulsa, restaurants have signs that say, "Sorry, we're open." – Roseanne Barr

Americans who travel abroad for the first time are often shocked to discover that, despite all the progress that has been made in the last thirty years, many foreign people still speak in foreign languages. – Dave Barry

Americans would rather live next to a pervert heroin addict Communist pornographer than a person with an unkempt lawn. – Dave Barry

Just get on any major highway, and eventually it will dead-end in a Disney parking area large enough to have its own climate, populated by large nomadic families who have been trying to find their cars since the Carter administration. – Dave Barry

Miami does not have a visitor-friendly airport. At Miami International, a cramped and dingy labyrinth, the message is: Just Try To Find Our Baggage Claim Area! – Dave Barry

He was driving at sixty-five miles an hour, which in Miami is the speed limit normally observed inside car washes. – Dave Barry

I don't even bother to honk at motorists who almost kill me. Generally it's a bad idea to honk down here anyway, inasmuch as the South Florida motoring public is as heavily armed as Iraq, but not as peace-loving. – Dave Barry

Florida's number three industry, behind tourism and skin cancer, is voter fraud. – Dave Barry

In New York, tip the taxicab driver forty dollars if he does not mention his haemorrhoids. – Dave Barry

Washington is nicknamed "The Evergreen State" because it sounds better than "The Incessant Nagging Drizzle State". – Dave Barry

A Texan virgin is a girl who can run faster than her brother.

No realistic, sane person goes around Chicago without protection. – Saul Bellow

Someone had said that in Los Angeles all the loose objects in the country were collected, as if America had been tilted and everything that wasn't tightly screwed down had slid into Southern California. – Saul Bellow

America is the only country in the world where a housewife hires a woman to do her cleaning so she can do volunteer work at the day-care centre where the cleaning woman leaves her child. – Milton Berle

The amazing thing is that there are people who have never left this country, who talk about the fact that we are the greatest country on Earth. How dumb is that? If you haven't left here, you don't know! – Lewis Black

(about Boston traffic) The last person to get across that town in under three hours was yelling, "The British are coming! The British are coming!" – Lewis Black

While I was in Miami, they stole my rental car, because apparently, they didn't have enough time to load up a gun and shoot me. – Lewis Black

A pretty good sign that somebody has had it with showbiz or is retiring is when they move to Palm Springs. Its nickname is Death's Waiting Room. – Sonny Bono

First prize: a week in Detroit. Second prize: two weeks.

Miami Beach is where neon goes to die. — Lenny Bruce

To an American the whole purpose of living, the one constant confirmation of continued existence, is to cram as much sensual pleasure as possible into one's mouth more or less continually. Gratification, instant and lavish, is a birthright. — Bill Bryson

Clearly, some time ago makers and consumers of American junk food passed jointly through some kind of sensibility barrier in the endless quest for new taste sensations. Now they are a little like those desperate junkies who have tried every known drug and are finally reduced to mainlining toilet bowl cleanser in an effort to get still higher. — Bill Bryson

(of Los Angeles) I think it's only right that crazy people should have their own city, but I cannot for the life of me see why a sane person would want to go there. — Bill Bryson, *The Lost Continent*

I come from Des Moines. Somebody had to. — Bill Bryson

When you tell an Iowan a joke, you can see a kind of race going on between his brain and his expression. — Bill Bryson

America is like an unfaithful love who promises us more than we get. — Charlotte Bunch

Washington, D.C. is a little too small to be a state, but too large to be an asylum for the mentally deranged. — Anne Burford

God Bless America, but God Help Canada for putting up with it.

America is the best half-educated country in the world. — Nicholas Butler

Isn't it nice that people who prefer Los Angeles to San Francisco live there? — Herb Caen

It is a scientific fact that if you live in California you lose one point of your IQ every year. — Truman Capote

In California everyone goes to a therapist, is a therapist, or is a therapist going to a therapist. — Truman Capote

The reason they call it the American Dream is because you have to be asleep to believe it. — George Carlin

You know the good part about all those executions in Texas? Fewer Texans. — George Carlin

New York is an exciting town where something is happening all the time, most of it unsolved. – Johnny Carson

Whatever starts in California unfortunately has a tendency to spread. – Jimmy Carter

(of California) The sun shone all day, but the people were boring as hell. – Kim Cattrall

One of the first things schoolchildren in Texas learn is how to compose a simple declarative sentence without the word "shit" in it.

I guess God made Boston on a Sunday. – Raymond Chandler

Los Angeles is a city with the personality of a paper cup. – Raymond Chandler

The only grounds for divorce in California are marriage. – Cher

What should you do if you see a New Yorker jogging? Trip him up and give the lady's purse back to her.

Americans always try to do the right thing after they've tried everything else. – Winston Churchill

Most Americans barely have the brains to walk on their back legs. – Jeremy Clarkson

(of Detroit) You wouldn't get thirty yards before someone put a hole in your head so they might steal your toenails. – Jeremy Clarkson, *The World According to Clarkson*

(of Washington, DC) Just three blocks south of Capitol Hill you find yourself in an area where seventy percent of the population are gunmen and the other thirty per cent have been shot. – Jeremy Clarkson, *The World According to Clarkson*

America is the only nation in history which has miraculously gone directly from barbarism to degeneration without the usual interval of civilization. – Georges Clemenceau

There's nothing more American tourists like than stuff they can get at home. – Stephen Colbert

Californians have this thing about open space. They have lots of it – mostly between their ears. – Peter Cook

America is where you can become a blueblood simply by having more greenbacks. – Bill Copeland

American women mostly have their clothes arranged for them. And their faces too, I think. – Noël Coward

Hotels in Vegas didn't used to be so nice. I remember when I first started, I stayed at dumpy hotels. In fact, one hotel was such a dump *they* stole *my* towel. – Rodney Dangerfield

America is dumb, it's like a dumb puppy that has big teeth that can bite and hurt you, aggressive. – Johnny Depp

I do not know the American gentleman. God forgive me for putting two such words together. – Charles Dickens

Their demeanour is invariably morose, sullen, clownish and repulsive. I should think there is not, on the face of the earth, a people so entirely destitute of humour, vivacity, or the capacity for enjoyment. – Charles Dickens

Americans have two brains, one in the usual place, and the other where the heart should be. – Marlene Dietrich

Why am I returning to Brooklyn? Because I love to wake up to garbage trucks and gunshots. – Diane Dixon, athlete

America knows nothing of food, love, or art. – Isadora Duncan

In America the geography is sublime, but the men are not. – Ralph Waldo Emerson

New York is a sucked orange. – Ralph Waldo Emerson

Los Angeles is like one of those machines that treat flour. When the wheat goes in, it's full of interesting ingredients – but it goes through this machine and what you get out at the end is perfect white crap. – Brian Eno

In Los Angeles, by the time you're thirty-five, you're older than most of the buildings. – Delia Ephron

I'm more nervous here in the lovely little tucked-away Forrest Theatre in Philadelphia than I would be on Broadway in New York in front of nicely dressed people. – Dame Edna Everage

It rains so much in Seattle, the state flower is mildew.

There's only one thing for Chicago to do, and that's to move to a better neighbourhood. – Herman Fetzer

Texans are living proof that Indians screwed buffaloes.

Philadelphia is the greatest cemetery in the world . . . I once spent a year there. I think it was on a Sunday. – W. C. Fields

If a woman dropped her glove on the street in Philadelphia, she was liable to be arrested and hauled before a judge on a charge of strip-teasing. – W. C. Fields

North Carolina is the place you fly over on the way to Florida. – John Fleischman

Chicago: a façade of skyscrapers facing a lake and behind the façade, every type of dubiousness. – E. M. Forster

California is like a bowl of granola; full of fruits, nuts, and flakes. – Gallagher

Sometimes I think this country would be better off if we could just saw off the eastern seaboard and let it float out to sea. – Barry Goldwater

People come to Washington believing it is the centre of power. I know I did. It was only much later that I learned that Washington is a steering wheel that's not connected to an engine. – Richard Goodwin

Houston is six suburbs in search of a centre. – Nigel Goslin

Storing your car in New York is safer than entering it in a demolition derby. But not much. – Daniel S. Greenberg

I really love playing and living in New York. There's such a high energy here. Everybody's fighting for that same cab. – Wayne Gretzky

In Montana, a policeman will pull you over because he's lonely. – Rich Hall

There is a growing feeling that perhaps Texas is really another country, a place where the skies, the disasters, the diamonds, the politicians, the women, the fortunes, the football players and the murders are all bigger than anywhere else. – Pete Hamill

There's never any shortage of suckers. Every year in America over eighty billion dollars are bet on games of chance, excluding weddings and elections. – Argus Hamilton

A study said years of research found no link between cell phone use and brain damage. Californians just talk that way naturally. – Argus Hamilton

If it wasn't for mouth-to-mouth resuscitation, there'd be no romance at all in Phoenix, Arizona. – Argus Hamilton

Their pedestrian lights flash "Mosey" and "Don't Mosey". – Argus Hamilton, on the Phoenix pace of life

If there ever was an aviary overstocked with jays it is that Yaptown-on-the-Hudson called New York. – O. Henry

In Washington, the first thing people tell you is what their job is. In Los Angeles you learn their star sign. – Simon Hoggart

In every American there is an air of incorrigible innocence, which seems to conceal a diabolical cunning. – A. E. Housman

American beer is a lot like making love on a canoe – it's fucking close to water. – Eric Idle

Typical Hollywood crowd – all the kids are on drugs, and all the adults are on roller skates. – Eric Idle

(of Los Angeles) The town is like an advertisement for itself; none of its charms are left to the visitor's imagination. – Christopher Isherwood

Downtown Los Angeles is at present one of the most squalid places in the United States. – Christopher Isherwood

I dearly love the state of Texas, but I consider that a harmless perversion on my part, and discuss it only with consenting adults. – Molly Ivins

Man: I'm self-centred and obsessed with my physical appearance.
Woman: Really? I'm from Los Angeles, too. – Richard Jeni

There is an obesity epidemic. One out of every three Americans . . . weighs as much as the other two. – Richard Jeni

I am willing to love all mankind, except an American. – Samuel Johnson

Los Angeles is about as artificial as a major conurbation can be without being a genuine theme park. – Dylan Jones

Every country gets the circus it deserves. Spain gets bullfights. Italy gets the Catholic Church. America gets Hollywood. – Erica Jong

San Francisco is forty-nine square miles surrounded by reality. – Paul Kantner

Washington, DC is a city of Southern efficiency and Northern charm. – John F. Kennedy

People in New York have black teeth and their breath smells of beer. And the men are even worse. – Charlie Kerfeld

Only in American banks can you find the pens chained to the counter and the doors wide open. – Brandon Kerr

People here in Los Angeles are disgusted now about a sex scandal involving Arnold Schwarzenegger. Apparently for seven years, he carried on a sexual relationship with his own wife. – Craig Kilborn

You know what they say about Chicago: if you don't like the weather, wait fifteen minutes. – Ralph Kiner

America is a melting pot; the people at the bottom get burned while all the scum floats to the top. – Charlie King

If you fall down in New York, there is always someone happy to pick you up by your wallet.

Never criticize Americans. They have the best taste that money can buy. – Miles Kington

The American has no language. He has dialect, slang, provincialism, accent and so forth. – Rudyard Kipling

(of Chicago) I urgently desire never to see it again. It is inhabited by savages. – Rudyard Kipling

San Francisco is a mad city – inhabited for the most part by perfectly insane people. – Rudyard Kipling

The trouble with us in America isn't that the poetry of life has turned to prose, but that it has turned to advertising copy. – Louis Kronenberger

Thanks to the Interstate Highway System, it is now possible to travel from coast to coast without seeing anything. – Charles Kuralt

You're not legally dead in California until you lose your tan. – Tommy Lasorda

People in L. A. drive like baboons on crack – they've stolen the keys and sort of figured out how to switch the thing on. – Hugh Laurie

America is neither free nor brave, but a land of tight, iron-clanking little wills, everybody trying to put it over everybody else. – D. H. Lawrence

If you're going to America, bring your own food. – Fran Lebowitz

There are two modes of transport in Los Angeles: car and ambulance. Visitors who wish to remain inconspicuous are advised to choose the latter. – Fran Lebowitz

I doubt very much that Los Angeles has become less awful, it's just that in contrast to New York it *seems* less awful. You never have to have human contact here; there are very few actual humans to have contact with. – Fran Lebowitz

Los Angeles: a circus without a tent.

New York: the only city where people make radio requests like "This is for Tina – I'm sorry I stabbed you." – Carol Leifer

According to a new study, fifty per cent of Americans are not getting enough exercise. We hear this all the time. You want American to exercise more, make the remote heavier. – Jay Leno

This weekend the *Los Angeles Times* hosted the annual "L.A. Festival of Books". Books in L.A.? When did that happen? – Jay Leno

If God doesn't destroy Hollywood Boulevard, he owes Sodom and Gomorrah an apology. – Jay Leno

Welcome to Vegas, the only city in the world where Chinese take-out means an Asian escort service. – Jay Leno

The crime problem in New York is getting really serious. The other day the Statue of Liberty had both hands up. – Jay Leno

Social scientists say San Francisco's population is decreasing faster than any other city in the nation. The people of San Francisco are not reproducing. I wonder why . . . – Jay Leno

New York now leads the world's great cities in the number of people around whom you shouldn't make a sudden move. – David Letterman

New York . . . when civilization falls apart, remember, we were way ahead of you. – David Letterman

The mayor of New York City suspects that the Fulton Fish Market, a long time New York City landmark, is now being controlled by organized crime. There may be something to that. Today I went there for lunch and ordered lobster, and they served it tied-up, face down, in a pool of butter. – David Letterman

New York is great. If you're here and want a one-of-a-kind souvenir, be sure to take home the police sketch of your assailant. – David Letterman

Fall is my favourite season in Los Angeles, watching the birds change colour and fall from the trees. – David Letterman

Chicago – a pompous Milwaukee. – L. L. Levinson

Americans are people who laugh at African witch doctors and spend a hundred million dollars on fake reducing systems. – L. L. Levinson

The trouble with America is that there are far too many wide-open spaces surrounded by teeth. – Charles Luckman

There's nothing wrong with Southern California that a rise in the ocean level wouldn't cure. – Ross MacDonald

I miss New York. I still love how people talk to you on the street – just assault you and tell you what they think of your jacket. – Madonna

Los Angeles is a constellation of plastic. – Norman Mailer

It is not necessary to have relatives in Kansas City to be unhappy. – Groucho Marx

Practically everybody in New York has half a mind to write a book – and does. – Groucho Marx

When a New Yorker looks as if he's got a suntan, it's probably rust.

American women expect to find in their husbands a perfection that English women only hope to find in their butlers. – W. Somerset Maugham

When you become used to never being alone, you may consider yourself Americanized. – Andre Maurois

If, in New York, you arrive late for an appointment, say, "I took a taxi." – Andre Maurois

If a contest had ninety-seven prizes, the ninety-eighth would be a trip to Green Bay. – John McKay

A car is useless in New York, essential everywhere else. The same with good manners. – Mignon McLaughlin

American youth attributes much more importance to arriving at driver's licence age than at voting age. – Marshall McLuhan

Nobody ever went broke underestimating the taste of the American public. – H. L. Mencken

Maine is as dead, intellectually, as Abyssinia. Nothing is ever heard from it. – H. L. Mencken

For all its size and all its wealth and all the progress it babbles of, the Deep South is almost as sterile, artistically, intellectually, culturally, as the Sahara Desert. – H.L. Mencken

Chicago is unique. It is the only completely corrupt city in America. – Charles Merriam, unsuccessful mayoral candidate, 1911

On my first day in New York a guy asked me if I knew where Central Park was. When I told him I didn't, he said, "Do you mind if I mug you here?" – Paul Merton

What should Americans do to become more popular when travelling abroad? Pretend to be Canadian. – Paul Merton

It was decided almost two hundred years ago that English should be the language spoken in the United States. It is not known, however, why this decision has not been carried out. – George Mikes

Americans stick their nose where it doesn't belong more than Cyrano de Bergerac giving head. – Dennis Miller

Washington, DC, is to lying what Wisconsin is to cheese. – Dennis Miller

Americans can eat garbage, provided you sprinkle it liberally with ketchup, mustard, chilli sauce, Tabasco sauce, cayenne pepper, or any other condiment which destroys the original flavour of the dish. – Henry Miller

I have never been able to look upon America as young and vital, but rather as prematurely old, as a fruit which rotted before it had a chance to ripen. – Henry Miller

California is the land of perpetual pubescence, where cultural lag is mistaken for renaissance. – Ashley Montagu

Hell has been described as a pocket edition of Chicago. – Ashley Montagu

Americans suffer from an enforced ignorance. We don't know about anything that's happening outside our country. – Michael Moore

Boston is a town where there are three pastimes: politics, sports, and revenge. – Lawrence C. Moulter

I'd like to thank the Americans for their help in the War Against Terror, because if you hadn't funded the IRA for thirty years, we wouldn't know how to deal with terrorists, would we? – Al Murray

In Los Angeles, it's like they jog for two hours a day and then they think they're morally right. That's when you want to choke people. – Liam Neeson

Due to the transit strike, New Yorkers are not allowed to drive into the city unless there are at least four people in every car. The situation has become so desperate some New Yorkers have been forced to talk to their neighbours. – Conan O'Brien

The American political system is like fast food – mushy, insipid, made out of disgusting parts of things, and everybody wants some. – P. J. O'Rourke, *Parliament of Whores*

Pasadena: a cemetery with lights.

Typical of America, always confusing quantity and quality – to the eternal detriment of the latter. – Michael Palin, *Diaries 1969-1979*

I love the English lifestyle, it's not as capitalistic as America. People don't talk about work and money, they talk about interesting things at dinner. The British are much more intelligent and civilised than the Americans. – Gwyneth Paltrow

Pittsburgh is Hell with the lid taken off. – James Parton

America is a country that doesn't know where it is going but is determined to set a speed record getting there. – Laurence J. Peter

(of San Francisco) Truly it is only those who place all happiness in money who could submit, for the sake of gain, to live in such a place. – Ida Pfeiffer

New York's such a wonderful city. Although I was at the library today. The guys there are very rude. I said, "I'd like a card." He said, "You have to prove you're a citizen of New York." So I stabbed him. – Emo Philips

Los Angeles is so plastic. I would have felt more at home if I'd covered myself in clingfilm. – Gordon Ramsay

I won't say it's remote up here in Washington State, but my last speech was reviewed in *Field and Stream*. – George Raveling, basketball coach

Los Angeles: less a city than a perpetual convention.

The national dish of America is menus. – Robert Robinson

America is a nation that conceives many odd inventions for getting somewhere but can think of nothing to do when it gets there. – Will Rogers

We don't know what we want, but we are ready to bite somebody to get it. – Will Rogers

Asking Europe to disarm is like asking a man in Chicago to give up his life insurance. – Will Rogers

If the world comes to an end, I want to be in Cincinnati. Everything comes there ten years later. – Will Rogers

France may claim the happiest marriages in the world, but the happiest divorces in the world are "made in America". – Helen Rowland

Frustrate a Frenchman, he will drink himself to death; an Irishman, he will die of angry hypertension; a Dane, he will shoot himself; an American, he will get drunk, shoot you, then establish a million dollar aid programme for your relatives. – S.A. Rudin

I'd rather be in jail in Sacramento than be the mayor of Boston. – Bill Russell

I've tried to like L. A., but it's akin to making love to a dormant woman. – Mort Sahl

Here is the difference between Dante, Milton and me. They wrote about Hell and never saw the place. I wrote about Chicago after looking the town over for years and years. – Carl Sandburg

Boston is a moral and intellectual nursery always applying first principles to trifles. – George Santayana

The best thing about playing in Cleveland is that you don't have to make road trips there. – Richie Scheinblum, baseball player

In California, when they pull you over, you have to have an ID with two pictures – before plastic surgery and after. – Arnold Schwarzenegger

They say life's what happens when you're busy making other plans. But sometimes in New York, life is what happens when you're waiting for a table. – *Sex and the City*

Samantha: I'm always surprised when anyone leaves New York. I mean, where do they go?
Miranda: The real world?
Samantha: A homeless man showed me his dick on the way here. It doesn't get any realer than that.
– *Sex and the City*

The one hundred percent American is ninety-nine percent idiot. – George Bernard Shaw

An asylum for the sane would be empty in America. – George Bernard Shaw

The American male does not mature until he has exhausted all other possibilities. – Wilfred Sheed

If I owned Texas and Hell, I would rent out Texas and live in Hell. – Philip H. Sheridan

Adultery – which is the only grounds for divorce in New York – is not grounds for divorce in California. As a matter of fact, adultery in Southern California is grounds for marriage. – Allan Sherman

When it's one hundred degrees in New York, it's seventy-two in Los Angeles. When it's thirty degrees in New York, in Los Angeles it's still seventy-two. However, there are six million interesting people in New York, and seventy-two in Los Angeles. – Neil Simon

While travelling near Tampa, Florida, I passed the Jehovah's Witness Assembly Hall and was struck by the fact that that must be where they make them. – Gene Spafford

(of Oakland, California) When you get there, there isn't any there there. – Gertrude Stein

Anyone (like Ernest Hemingway) who marries three girls from St Louis hasn't learned much. – Gertrude Stein

The new Airbus plane, the A380, is capable of holding eight hundred passengers. Or four hundred Americans. – Jon Stewart

New York is a city so decadent that when I leave it I never dare look back lest I turn into salt and the conductor throw me over his left shoulder for good luck. – Frank Sullivan

All creative people should be required to leave California for three months every year. – Gloria Swanson

Unfortunately, there's a big anti-intellectual strain in the American south, and there always has been. We're not big on thought. – Donna Tartt

The difference between Los Angeles and yoghurt is that yoghurt has real culture. – Tom Taussik

Just a nation of two hundred million used-car salesmen with all the money we need to buy guns and no qualms about killing anybody else in the world who tries to make us uncomfortable. – Hunter S. Thompson

America is a large, friendly dog in a very small room. Every time it wags its tail, it knocks over a chair. – Arnold Toynbee

There is a theory that almost anything that's fun is going to be ruined sooner or later by people from California. They tend to bring seriousness to subjects that don't deserve it, and they tend to get very good at things that weren't very important in the first place. – Calvin Trillin

Speaking of New York, as a traveller I have two faults to find with it. In the first place there is nothing to see; and in the second place there is no mode of getting about to see anything. – Anthony Trollope

You want a friend in Washington? Get a dog. – Harry S. Truman

It was wonderful to find America, but it would have been more wonderful to miss it. – Mark Twain

It is by the goodness of God that in our country we have those three unspeakably precious things: freedom of speech, freedom of conscience, and the prudence never to practise either of them. – Mark Twain

We are the lavishest and showiest and most luxury-loving people on the earth; and at our masthead we fly one true and honest symbol – the gaudiest flag the world has ever seen. – Mark Twain

Satan to newcomer: The trouble with you Chicago people is, you think you are the best people down here; whereas you are merely the most numerous. – Mark Twain, *Pudd'nhead Wilson's New Calendar*

America is a land where a citizen will cross the ocean to fight for democracy – and won't cross the street to vote in a national election. – Bill Vaughan

Half of the American people have never read a newspaper. Half never voted for President. One hopes it is the same half. – Gore Vidal

During the winter Seattle residents don't get frostbite: they grow mould.

In some Chicago neighbourhoods, looking for a parking space is not unlike panning for gold. – Gary Washburn

Daniel Boone would have a tough time finding this place. The population is about two hundred and fifty. That's counting the pregnant people twice. – David Weathers, baseball player, on his home town of Five Point, Tennessee

I moved to New York City for my health. I'm paranoid and New York was the only place where my fears were justified. – Anita Weiss

The Americans, like the English, probably make love worse than any other race. – Walt Whitman

One is impressed in America, but not favourably impressed, by the inordinate size of everything. The country seems to try to bully one into a belief in its power by its impressive bigness. – Oscar Wilde

It is absurd to say that there are neither ruins nor curiosities in America when they have their mothers and their manners. – Oscar Wilde, *A Woman Of No Importance*

Of course, America had often been discovered before Columbus, but it had always been hushed up. – Oscar Wilde

America is one long expectoration. – Oscar Wilde

In America the young are always ready to give to those who are older than themselves the full benefits of their inexperience. – Oscar Wilde

Chicago is a sort of monster-shop, full of bustle and bores. – Oscar Wilde (of Niagara Falls) A vast unnecessary amount of water going the wrong way and then falling over unnecessary rocks. – Oscar Wilde

When good Americans die, they go to Paris; when bad Americans die, they go to America. – Oscar Wilde

When I approached the checkout counter of a Miami store, the clerk said, "Cash, cheque, or stickup?" – Pat Williams

Miami is so tough, they use Mace as a breath-freshener down there. – Pat Williams

Crime is down in Miami. They ran out of victims. – Pat Williams

At a Washington party, it is not enough that the guests feel drunk; they must feel drunk and important. – Thomas Wolfe

The only way to improve Pittsburgh would be to abandon it. – Frank Lloyd Wright

The loss of the physical city of Washington would be a benefit not only to government, but to aesthetics. – Philip Wylie